The State of China's State Capitalism

Juann H. Hung • Yang Chen
Editors

The State of China's State Capitalism

Evidence of Its Successes and Pitfalls

palgrave
macmillan

Editors
Juann H. Hung
Xi'an Jiaotong-Liverpool University
Suzhou, Jiangsu, China

Yang Chen
Xi'an Jiaotong-Liverpool University
Suzhou, Jiangsu, China

ISBN 978-981-13-0982-3 ISBN 978-981-13-0983-0 (eBook)
https://doi.org/10.1007/978-981-13-0983-0

Library of Congress Control Number: 2018957329

This Palgrave Macmillan imprint is published by the registered company Springer Nature Singapore Pte Ltd.
The registered company address is: 152 Beach Road, #21-01/04 Gateway East, Singapore 189721, Singapore

Preface

China's rapid economic growth since the inception of its reform and opening-up policy in late 1978 has been the envy of many developed and developing countries. Its powerful state intervention to keep its economy going after the global financial crisis of 2008 indeed helped the country to serve as a major locomotive of the world economy when most of the advanced economies were stuck in serious and prolonged recession. Ian Bremmer, in an article published in *Foreign Affairs* in 2009 under the title "State Capitalism Comes of Age: The End of the Free Market?", even argued that China's state capitalism was not just an anti-cyclical tool but also a source of its long-run economic boom.

China's success at its experiment with "state capitalism", or "socialism with Chinese characteristics," would seem to suggest that it is an economic model worthy of emulation by other countries. China's state capitalism is a system in which market forces are allowed to operate but subject to powerful and frequent state interventions, and in which the private sector is allowed to expand while state-owned enterprises (SOEs) have remained an important part of the economy to compete with the private sector for resources. To those who are suspicious of a free market system or uncontrolled capitalism such a state capitalism would seem a better model for seeking a good balance of sustained growth and economic stability.

However, after a breath-taking pace of growth over the past three decades, China's growth model is facing increasing challenge on multiple fronts. At home, while its rapid economic growth has lifted the average living standard of its citizens, it is also associated with a substantial increase in income inequality and unaffordable housing prices. Going forward, China's growth prospect is also becoming more constrained by limited resources such as the labour force, land, and energy. The pollution of air, due to the heavy usage of pollution-intensive fossil fuels during China's rapid industrialization and fast urbanization, has increasingly raised the public's concern about environmental sustainability and efficient use of energy. The Chinese government is now under great domestic and international pressures to conduct a series of deeper reforms in industrial upgrading, environmental protection, and social welfare enhancement. Have these issues been particularly acute because of China's state capitalism?

We hope this book, a collection of research papers on some contemporary economic and financial issues in China, based on rigorous research by the collaboration of students and faculties in International Business School Suzhou in Xi'an Jiaotong-Liverpool University, could help readers draw some lessons about China's state-capitalism growth model. We present these papers as chapters in six parts.

Part I (Chaps. 1 and 2) and Part II (Chaps. 3 and 4) present research on issues resulting from the Chinese fiscal system of revenue centralization and spending decentralization. After the 1994 tax-sharing reform, a mismatch between local governments' revenue and spending responsibilities started to emerge. Consequently, local government increasingly resorted to land sale to help finance their expenditures, arguably resulting in a wide range of severe problems. To name just a few. Sales of public land by government officials are a recipe for corruption. The excessive land acquisitions from peasants with inappropriate compensation breed social conflicts. Conversion of agricultural land for non-agricultural purposes undermines food security. Strategies aiming at reaping more land-sale revenues tend to aid and abet property bubbles. Local governments' rising need to rely on issuing bonds to close their budget gaps has been adding to their debt to GDP ratios. Against this backdrop, Chap. 1 examines the effect of China's fiscal system on local governments' land leasing behaviours, controlling for other factors, both theoretically and empirically. Chapter 2 investigates what factors—such as the fiscal gap, governments' investments in housing, other local governments' spending, and financing behaviour—have contributed to the issuance of urban investment bonds (UIB) across 31 provinces in China. Chapter 3 investigates evidence of housing bubbles in different locations of China by examining housing price data at the provincial and city levels from late 1990s to 2016. Chapter 4 investigates whether the entry of a new Wanda Plaza increases the county-level average land prices, aiming at shedding light on the dynamics between local policymakers and real estate developers.

Part III presents research related to energy and environmental issues in China. China's rapid economic development has resulted in a rapid rise of its excess demand for energy, and of a serious pollution of its environment. Its energy shortage still imposes considerable obstacles on urban development even though substantial government budgets have been devoted to energy-infrastructure constructions such as Three Gorges Project and West-East Electricity Transmission Project. Its severely polluted environment has meant the majority of Chinese people are exposed to unhealthy air, water, and soil. To curb carbon emission, the Chinese government tested a pilot carbon emission trading markets in 2013 to pave way for the official establishment of national carbon market in 2017. As it is potentially the largest carbon trading market in the world, finding the key factors that drive the carbon permit price to help forecast its future price is important for both investors and government. Chapter 5 thus explores the prospect of forecasting the carbon permit price in three pilot markets (Beijing, Shanghai, and Shenzhen) using the structural time-series modelling approach. To shed light on appropriate policies for inducing energy-saving consumption behaviour, Chap. 6 investigates whether consumers undervalue future expected electricity costs relative to purchase prices when they choose among different types of refrigerators. The authors found that there is considerable energy efficiency gap in China's refrigerator market, suggesting the need of using government subsidy to encourage consumption of energy-saving electronic appliances.

Part IV presents research related to income inequality. Along with China's remarkable economic growth, income inequality in China has also become more serious. Its Gini coefficient reached 0.491 in 2008, from 0.343 in 1990. Since 2008, China's Gini coefficient has been edging down somewhat, but it was still higher than the worrisome level of 0.4 as of 2015 (at 0.462). Chapter 7 investigates whether China's fiscal system of revenue centralization and spending decentralization has been effective in mitigating the problem of rising inequality. Chapter 8 ascertains whether the rising income inequality has resulted in effective state intervention intended to boost Chinese people's nationalism. Chapter 9 aims to solve the puzzle of the rising gender income inequality in China. The gender income gap started to emerge soon after China's economic reform began in late 1978. After early 1990s, the rise in that gap quickened pace despite the narrowing gap between male and female educational attainment. What happened? Does it reflect a rise in gender discrimination or the change of economic structure?

Part V contains two chapters related to issues in foreign direct investment (FDI). Inward FDI has been instrumental to China's rapid economic growth after the early 1990s. Even though empirical studies of FDI's impact on host countries' economic growth are quite diverse in general, almost all studies focusing on China have found unambiguous evidence that inward FDI made a significant and positive impact on China's economic growth. Clearly, the Chinese government's growth strategy of attracting FDI and their technology transfer by offering various incentives has worked. However, China's outward FDI has been rising faster than its inward FDI in the past decade. Is it partially due to a policy shift in response to the rapid accumulation of China's foreign exchange reserves? Or is it driven by changes in fundamental determinants of FDI flows? Chap. 10 inquires what made FDI inflows more beneficial to China's growth than in most other developing countries. It does so by investigating why in the literature the estimated effect of inward FDI on economic growth is significantly higher in China than in India. Chapter 11 investigates what are the major determinants driving the movement in China's outward FDI.

Part VI presents research intended to shed light on China's corporate tax and the optimal model for forecasting cash flow in various industries in China. Starting from 2000, China's authority has published a series of tax regulations to improve the sophistication of China's tax regime. In 2002, the State Council stopped unauthorized corporate tax rebate from the local government. In 2007, State Council states that the top statutory corporate tax rate becomes 25%, which is lower than the previous tax rate (33%) by 8%. In addition, foreign-invested enterprises (FIEs) and China's domestic enterprises (DEs) share the same corporate tax rate (25%) thereafter (prior to that change, FIEs enjoyed a preferential tax rate of 30%, whereas DEs paid a higher tax rate at 33%). Within the context of 2007 tax reform, Chap. 12 investigates two questions. First, has the 2007 tax reform increased or decreased corporate marginal tax rates of China's listed companies? Second, in what ways are the changes in the marginal tax rate different with respect to companies' characteristics (such as ownership and industry)? Chap. 13 aims to offer an optimal model suitable for forecasting cash flow—the lifeblood of a firm—in various Chinese industries. It does so by investigating the relationship between accruals and cash flow prediction in China's industries, drawing upon existing models explored in studies of US and UK industries.

Suzhou, China

Juann H. Hung
Yang Chen

Acknowledgments

We are very grateful to Jacob Dreyer and Anushangi Weerakoon for their professional comments and help. We also acknowledge the funding support RDF13-03-07 from Xi'an Jiaotong-Liverpool University and project funding provided by International Business School Suzhou (IBSS). Miss. Yu Han is acknowledged as well for her excellent research assistance.

Contents

List of Figures

List of Tables

PART I

Land and Debt

CHAPTER 1

Fiscal Decentralization, Yardstick Competition in Determining Chinese Local Governments' Land Conveyance Behavior

Wenyin Yang and Yang Chen

1.1 Introduction

Over the past ten years, China has witnessed a rapid growth in local governments' state-owned land use right transfer along with the expansion of urban area, land expropriation and development of land for non-agricultural constructions. Notably, the land conveyance fee accounts for 9% of local fiscal revenues in 1999 and increases to more than 60% in 2011 (Ye and Wang 2013). Local governments' land transaction revenues increased more than $193 billion to roughly $629 billion in 2013 according to the Ministry of Finance.

"Land finance", narrowly defined as the local government's dependence on the income from leasing or selling land to fund its fiscal expenditure, has become a prominent phenomenon. In a broad sense, land finance includes land conveyance fee, land-related taxes and mortgages through which local governments acquire via the rights to use lands. Although the land conveyance fee increases fiscal income, stimulates urban

W. Yang • Y. Chen (✉)
International Business School Suzhou, Xi'an Jiaotong-Liverpool University, Suzhou, China
e-mail: yang.chen@xjtlu.edu.cn

J. H. Hung, Y. Chen (eds.), *The State of China's State Capitalism*,
https://doi.org/10.1007/978-981-13-0983-0_1

growth and facilitates industrialization through exploitation of surplus land (Ye and Wang 2013), it has induced a wide range of severe problems. First, corruption related to land and real estate transaction is one of the major concerns. Prior audits have indicated rent-seeking behavior in land sales in 95% of provinces surveyed (CKGSB knowledge 2014). Second, the excessive land acquisitions from peasants with inappropriate compensation reduce peasants' welfare and may result in social conflicts. Moreover, conversion of agricultural land for non-agricultural purposes undermines food security. Land finance pushes up the housing price through increasing land price, which catalyzes bubbles in real estate industry. Furthermore, it results in waste and severely inefficient use of land resource (Li et al. 2013a). As mentioned by Li and Zhang (2014), although land finance boosts the economy to some extent, it leads to an increasingly unsustainable economic structure, reducing the overall efficiency of economic development. Therefore, the identification of the underlying reasons behind land finance is imperative.

A misunderstanding of the underlying reasons is very likely to lead to invalid approaches to address the problems caused by land finance (Ye and Wang 2013). Our research probes into the causes of Chinese local governments' land-leasing behaviors, a major component of "land finance". We propose two questions. The first is related to whether fiscal decentralization has been a significant contributor to land-leasing behavior since 2003. The second concerns whether yardstick competition contributes to local governments' land-leasing behavior.

The existing studies of Chinese local governments' land-leasing behaviors point out one widely recognized institutional cause—the fiscal decentralization system established since the 1994 tax distribution reform. The fiscal pressure amplified by the fiscal decentralization system leads to local governments' aggressive pursuit of extra-budgetary revenues. However, a new trend observed in data after 2003 questions fiscal decentralization's role as a main contributor to land finance (Li et al. 2013a). Another view claims that inter-jurisdictional gross domestic product (GDP)-oriented competition resulting from the cadre evaluation system intensifies the land-leasing behavior. Before 2003, local governments conducted land sales mostly by negotiation featuring low prices to attract foreign direct investment (FDI). However, after the enactment of the 2002 regulations on the conveyance of land use rights by tender, auction and listing and the 2003 regulations which prohibit land sales by negotiation, land-leasing behaviors may not be FDI-oriented. This chapter examines the varied roles fiscal decentralization and yardstick competition play in explaining Chinese local governments' land-leasing behaviors.

In the following section, we provide a comprehensive literature review. In the third section, we construct a theoretical framework based on the principal-agent model to evaluate if fiscal decentralization system and yardstick competition are two important contributors to Chinese local governments' land-leasing behaviors. In Sect. 1.4, we present the empirical strategy followed by the results and findings shown in Sect. 1.5. The last section concludes.

1.2 Literature Review

According to existing studies of governments' land-leasing behaviors, the vertical strategic interaction between central and local governments and the horizontal competition among local governments are two main contributors to the increasing reliance of local governments on land conveyance. Other factors include the land use system and land expropriation policy, which comprise the institutional foundation for "land finance" (Wu et al. 2015). The current land expropriation system allows the transactions of land in the first-degree land market once approved by rural collectives. Furthermore, the local government's monopoly power enables it to earn high profit margins due to the high selling price and low expropriation price which in effect motivates land finance (Mi 2011). This chapter mainly focuses on fiscal decentralization and the horizontal competition.

The mechanism through which Chinese fiscal decentralization system affects land finance can be found in a large strand of literature. Ye and Wang (2013) argued that fiscal decentralization through the delegation of responsibility for providing public goods and services to local government imposes balanced budget requirements limiting government's spending and indebtedness. Payne (2003) pointed out that local officials turn to "off-budget" activities to circumvent the budget constraints. The tax distribution reform in 1994 led to large amounts of fiscal income outflow to central government while assigning more expenditure-related tasks to local governments, hence, widening the fiscal gap and forcing them to transfer land use rights to gain extra-budgetary income (Zhang et al. 2011; Tao et al. 2007; Li et al. 2013a; Ye and Wang 2013). In the 1994 reform, the center started to permit the sub-national governments to keep the entire land conveyance fee as an extra-budgetary revenue base. This further encouraged local governments to seize the lucrative opportunity.

However, Li et al. (2013a) discovered that after year 2003, the fiscal gap tended to be stable while the land finance kept growing.

In terms of the measures of fiscal decentralization, Wu and Li (2010) adopted the proportion of per capita local fiscal spending (or income) with respect to the national figures. Li et al. (2013b) adopted the budgetary fiscal gap. Most of the literature adopted panel data regression to test the effect of fiscal decentralization on land finance. Cao and Luo (2012) employed time-series data to perform the Johansen co-integration test. This method facilitated the identification of the long-run equilibrium relationship between land finance and fiscal decentralization. However, due to the time-series and nationwide aggregated nature of the data Cao and Luo's paper failed to take into account the cross-section heterogeneity.

Liu et al. (2012) pointed out that in recent years the central government has been increasing the transfer payment which does not curb the land finance problem, thus implying that there is a more fundamental issue besides fiscal decentralization that promotes land financing. In the centralized political system, local governments' performance is evaluated by their superior governments based on GDP as a "yardstick", that is, promotion and demotion are based on relative economic performance. One typical way for central government to evaluate local governments is called "target responsibility" system where local governments are assigned tasks whose accomplishments will be judged compared with others. Therefore, local governments compete with each other by pursuing higher GDP and are motivated to grab benefits from land. This kind of competition is commonly referred to as "yardstick competition".

There are several theories accounting for this kind of competition. One is the "GDP-oriented promotion tournament theory" by Zhou (2007) which explained the political incentives to expedite economic development in China. In Zhou's paper, promotion tournament is defined as competition created by superior governments for subordinate governments where the "winner" can be promoted. In this game, superior governments stipulate the rules. In this perspective, political promotion provides an innate and enormous incentive for Chinese officials to enhance economic performance but it results in some problems such as uncooperative relationship and overlapping construction among different jurisdictions. Another theory is "yardstick competition" proposed by Besley and Case (1995) in the context of tax-setting where voters compare taxes set by different jurisdictions and decides whether to reelect the governors. In this situation, the incumbent governors are concerned about what others are doing and engage in yardstick competition when they set taxes. As opposed to the promotion tournament theory, in Besley and Case's framework there is no centralized power to control personnel since officials are elected by voters. To apply "yardstick competition" in the context of China's political system, Caldeira (2012) introduced the top-down "yardstick competition" adapted from the original Besley and Case (1995) model. However, in Caldeira's paper, the competition is oriented at public spending which is not so realistic in China where the central government emphasizes more on GDP in evaluating relative performance. Belleflamme and Hindriks (2005) proposed that in the presence of adverse selection and moral hazard, yardstick competition brings about both disciplining and selecting effects on politicians. We attempt to figure out if this is still the case in the context of "land finance".

Based on Zhou's tournament theory, Li and Zhang (2014) adopted the fixed asset investment because governments tended to increase fixed asset investment to stimulate the economy and win the competition. Wu and Li (2010) and Li et al. (2013a) utilized the per capita FDI to depict the competition due to the fact that attracting foreign investment was a crucial economic development target. Liu et al. (2012) adopted local governments' official turnover rates to calculate the intensity of competition stemming from career uncertainty. Li et al. (2013b)'s paper came up with a compelling idea that the objective local government attempted to maximize might have changed from "economic growth" to "social welfare" partly due to the enactment of regulations on the conveyance of land use rights by tender, auction and listing in 2002 and the 2003 regulations to prohibit land sales by negotiation. In the first phase before 2003, local government competed by lowering land price to attract FDI; in the second phase since 2003 governments tend to increase land price to fund the expenditure for welfare competition.

The literature suggests different econometric methods to study the competitive behavior for local governments. Li et al. (2013a) used a dynamic spatial autocorrelation model to examine the strategic competition among local governments. The spatial lag of the dependent variable captures the horizontal strategic interaction among local governments. Namely, other districts' land-leasing strategies enter the decision-making function of land leasing for a particular district. The justification for a time lag is that local government's reliance on land finance could have an inertia component. A contiguity matrix is employed to measure the competition at city level within provinces. Wu and Li (2010) adopted a fixed-effect regression supported by Hausman test. Instead of using a spatial weight matrix, they employed per capita FDI to indicate the competition intensity among local governments. As claimed by Wu et al. (2015), there is an intrinsic link between fiscal decentralization and yardstick competition with respect to their contribution to local governments' land-leasing activities. On one hand, the vertical imbalances induced by fiscal decentralization reinforce the incentives to engage in yardstick competition to gain more transfer payments. On the other hand, yardstick competition in the face of the budget constraint imposed by fiscal decentralization further prompts local governments to exploit land financing.

We focus on fiscal decentralization and yardstick competition though some other important factors cannot be overlooked. Liu et al. (2012) argued that economic growth propels urbanization and increases demand for land leasing. Li et al. (2013b) suggested that the reliance on land finance varies with different phases of economic development. Another important factor is the property price. A prosperous housing market is often associated with higher demand for land leasing. Wen and Goodman (2013) argued that land is derivative of demand for housing service and that housing price determines land price. Excess demand for housing in China pushes up the housing price and subsequently raises the land price. The rise in land price would lead to the rise in land-leasing revenue. Based on above critical review and analyses, we propose the hypotheses as below.

***Hypothesis 1**: Fiscal decentralization positively affects the local government's land-leasing activities.*

***Hypothesis 2**: Yard stick competition intensifies the local government's land-leasing activities.*

***Hypothesis 3**: Foreign direct investment motivates local government's land-leasing activities.*

***Hypothesis 4**: GDP growth contributes to intensified land-leasing activities.*

***Hypothesis 5**: Land conveyance fees are positively related to housing prices.*

1.3 Theoretical Framework

1.3.1 The Model Setup

Caldeira (2012) modified the yardstick competition model introduced by Besley and Case (1995) to fit in a relatively centralized political system in China and set the yardstick as the amount of public spending. We adapt

Caldeira (2012)'s model to demonstrate the fiscal decentralization and yardstick competition as positive contributors to the land-leasing activities with the "yardstick" being the GDP. Crucially, we assume the land-leasing-related income is an important part which funds local governments' economic activities. In the model, we introduce a concept named "land-exploitation capacity" and define it as the level of sustainable land resources that a local government can transfer the right of usage in the first-degree land market.

In the principal-agent framework, local governments possess more information than the central government regarding income from land leasing and the amount of efforts to improve social welfare. Specifically, local governments are of two different types. Good governments do not waste resources or incur rent-seeking rents, while bad ones do. The model is set within two periods with a discount factor whereby the central government utilizes reappointment as an incentive. The central government cannot directly observe the effort and has only partial information on local land finance. It monitors the observable GDP to evaluate the performance of local officials.

Our theoretical framework is constructed as follows. First, the case of fiscal centralization without land leasing is presented as a benchmark. Second, the case of fiscal decentralization without yardstick competition is examined. We show that both types of local governments are motivated to acquire land income when the center delegates the right of use of land to the local. Third, yardstick competition is introduced as well. Central government attempts to better distinguish the nature of local governments (to avoid adverse selection) and desires to promote effort (to avoid moral hazard), thus it deliberately creates competition with GDP being the yardstick to motivate local officials to behave in a way it desires. The central government creates the competition by reappointing or dismissing local governments on the basis of their relative performance in promoting local aggregate outputs.

In the following model, we assume that there are three discrete levels of "land-exploitation capacity" (C_i) which indicates the sustainable level of land resources that a local government can lease in the first-degree land market: C_l (low), C_m (middle), C_h (high). *Ceteris paribus*, there are three corresponding levels of land income (L_i): low, middle, high denoted as L_l, L_m, L_h, respectively. Land income $L_i = a*C_i$ ($i = l,m,h$; a is a constant). Local governments know C_i and L_i, while the central government does not. The central government only knows the probability p_l, p_m, p_h with which each level of land income level L_l, L_m or L_h occurs. Since local government expenditure is a crucial part of local GDP and land income finances a larger proportion of government expenditure, we assume that local GDP varies positively with the land income in the short run. $G(L_i)$ is an increasing function and $G(L_l)$, $G(L_m)$, $G(L_h)$ are assumed to be evenly spaced with Δ. There are two types of governments: the "good" (g) ones do not waste resources or seek rents, while the "bad" (b) ones do. The latter takes rents $r_i = 0$, Δ or 2Δ from GDP. γ denotes the fraction of good local government and $(1-\gamma)$ is the fraction of the bad local government; it is assumed that $\gamma \geq 1/2$. The local government's strategy is denoted by $G(a^*C_i, \theta_i)$, with $k\in(l,m,h)$ and $\theta_i\in(g,b)$. A governor can at most stay in office for two periods; the discount factor δ satisfies $1/2 < \delta < 1$.

Therefore, in this model, there are five discrete levels of GDP denoted as G_i:

Land income	*High*	*Middle*	*Low*
Good	$G(a^*C_h)=G1$	$G(a^*C_m)=G2$	$G(a^*C_l)=G3$
Bad	$r=0$ $r=\Delta$ $r=2\Delta$	$r=0$ $r=\Delta$ $r=2\Delta$	$r=0$ $r=\Delta$ $r=2\Delta$
	G1 G2 G3	G2 G3 G4	G3 G4 G5

The central government's objective is to maximize GDP, and it aims to distinguish the "bad" governments from the "good". It observes the GDP level and uses it to evaluate the nature of the local government and decides whether to reappoint the local governor or not. The incentive mechanism adopted by the central government is $m(G_i)\in[0,1]$, which corresponds to the probability that it reappoints a local governor who produces a GDP level G_i ($i = 1,2,3,4,5$).

Local government chooses a strategy to maximize expected utility. A "bad" government in the second period has no discipline and will waste 2Δ. The expected utility of a "bad" local government is $EV(G_i, L_i) = r_i + \delta^*m(G_i)^*2\Delta$. The expected utility for the "good" government is the GDP it achieves. Thus, the good government endeavors to achieve optimal GDP level in both period 1 and period 2.

1.3.2 The Centralized Fiscal System

We first consider fiscal centralization as a benchmark case for comparison. Under fiscal centralization, all land incomes received by local governments are collected by the central government and redistributed back to local governments in the form of transfer payment T_i. This is the case of perfect information. The strategies for local governments are $G(T_i,g) = G(T_i)$ and $G(T_i,b) = G(T_i)-r_i$. Strict dominance arguments rule out $G(T_i,b) = G(T_i)$, as long as $\delta < 1$. If the central government observes $G_i = T_i$, it will always believe that the local government is bad, so we have $m(T_i-\Delta) = m(T_i-2\Delta) = 0$. Then, it can be inferred that for a bad government, $EV(T_i-\Delta,T_i) = \Delta + \delta * m(T_i-\Delta)*2\Delta = \Delta < EV(T_i-2\Delta,T_i) = 2\Delta+\delta*m(T_i-2\Delta)*2\Delta = 2\Delta$. Namely, a bad government will always incur the highest level of waste and generate $G_i = G(T_i)-2\Delta$.

Under the centralized fiscal system, both types of governments have no incentives to acquire higher land income beyond their land-exploitation capacity because the central government knows fully about their land income and collects all of it.

1.3.3 The Decentralized Fiscal System Without Yardstick Competition

A "good" government always has $G(L_h,g) = G1$, $EV_h = G1$; $G(L_m,g) = G2$, $EV_m = G2$; $G(L_l,g) = G3$, $EV_l = G3$. Therefore, when central government observes G4 or G5, it will always regard the government as "bad". Hence, $m(G4) = 0$, $m(G5) = 0$. One can also infer that a good government has incentives to go beyond their capacity of land-exploitation for higher GDP and gains higher utility. Now, consider the "bad" government, applying strict dominance rule, strategies $G(L_l,b) = G3$, $G(L_m,b) = G2$, $G(L_h,b) = G1$ are ruled out. For instance, $EV(G1,C_h) = 0 + \delta*m(G1)*2\Delta < EV(G3,C_h) = 2\Delta + \delta*m(G3)*2\Delta$. Hence, local government who sets G1 is good with certainty, thus, central government has $m(G1) = 1$. Having $m(G4) = 0$, $m(G5) = 0$, $m(G1) = 1$, we then have $EV(G4,C_l) = \Delta + \delta*m(G4)*2\Delta = \Delta < EV(G5,C_l) = 2\Delta + \delta*m(G5)*2\Delta = 2\Delta$. Thus, confronted with low land-exploitation capacity C_l, a "bad" government will always choose to waste 2Δ and produce G5 in period one.

Next, consider the case where local government observes G3. The probability of being a good local government is $P(g|G3) = \gamma p_l/[\gamma p_l + (1-\gamma)(p_h + p_m)]$. If $p_l >= p_h + p_m$ $(p_l \geq 1/2)$, $P(g|G3) = \gamma p_l/[\gamma p_l + (1-\gamma)(p_h + p_m)] > \gamma$, which means that the central government is willing to believe governments which produce G3 is good. To locate the equilibrium, here we assume $p_l \geq 1/2$ is the case. Thus, $m(G3) = 1$. For a "bad" government facing C_m, we have $EV(G4,C_m) = 2\Delta + \delta*m(G4)*2\Delta = 2\Delta < EV(G3,C_m) = \Delta + \delta*m(G3)*2\Delta = \Delta + \delta 2\Delta$. Thus, $G(L_m,b) = G3$ is the preferred strategy. For a "bad" government facing C_h, we have

$EV(G2,C_h) = \Delta + m(G2)\delta 2\Delta < EV(G3,C_h) = 2\Delta + \delta 2\Delta$. Thus, $G(L_h,b) = G3$ is its preferred strategy.

After calculating the expected utility from different strategies regarding how much waste to incur, we can derive the best strategies for a "bad" government with different levels of land-exploitation capacities are:

$$G(L_l,b) = G5, \text{where the } EV(G5,C_l) = 2\Delta + \delta * m(G5) * 2\Delta = 2\Delta;$$
$$G(L_m,b) = G3, \text{where the } EV(G3,C_m) = \Delta + \delta * 2\Delta(\text{assuming } p_l >= 1/2);$$
$$G(L_h,b) = G3, \text{where the } EV(G3,C_h) = 2\Delta + \delta 2\Delta.$$

To sum up, we show that decentralization induces the "bad" governments to reduce wastes on resources. $G(L_m,b) = G3$ instead of $G(L_m,b) = G4$. Intuitively, the bad government cuts in waste when their land-exploitation capacity is at the intermediate level in order to get reappointed and grab the maximized rent in period 2. Furthermore, we show that $EV(G3,C_h) > EV(G3,C_m) > EV(G5,C_l)$, so the "bad" local government has incentives to over-exploit the land in terms of converting too much farmland for construction land to gain a higher level of income as the source of excessive rent. The above analysis is summarized as,

Proposition 1 Fiscal decentralization encourages bad-type local governments to pursue a higher level of GDP than in the centralized regime and intensifies their land-leasing activities.

1.3.4 The Decentralized Fiscal System with Yardstick Competition

Consider a case where two jurisdictions have similar levels of economic development and land-exploitation capacities. Central government's reappointment strategy is $m(G_i, G_j) = 0$ or 1. Caldeira (2012) describes a situation where the central government believes two jurisdictions have identical "shocks". In our case, the central government compares two jurisdictions with similar land-exploitation capacities. However, due to asymmetric information, the local government can "cheat" by surpassing its land-exploitation capacity and understating its land income.

When the central government knows that two local governments have the same land-exploitation capacity and similar economic conditions, it will set $m(G_i,G_j) = 0$ if $G_i < G_j$. Therefore, facing the same land-exploitation capacity as the good government, the "bad" government will grab as much rent as possible, knowing that it is less likely to be reappointed even though it grabs the least amount of rent.

Thus, for the moment, the best strategies for "bad" governments are $G(L_l,b) = G5$; $G(L_m,b) = G4$; $G(L_h,b) = G3$. Compared with the "good" government with C_m who produces G2, the best expected utility for a "bad" government with C_m will be $EV(G4,C_m) = 2\Delta$ with strategy $G(L_m,b) = G4$. However, if it deviates from its land-exploitation capacity to a higher level C_h (note that the cost of attaining a higher level of C_k is assumed to be zero in this case because of the monopoly power of the government in the land transaction process), its expected payoffs will be:

$$EV(G3,C_h) = 2\Delta + \delta * m(G3,G2) * 2\Delta = 2\Delta;$$
$$EV(G2,C_h) = \Delta + \delta * m(G2,G2) * 2\Delta = \Delta + \delta * 2\Delta;$$
$$EV(G1,C_h) = 0 + \delta * m(G1,G2) * 2\Delta = \delta * 2\Delta.$$

$EV(G2, C_h)$ is greater than $EV(G3,C_h)$, $EV(G1,C_h)$, and is also greater than the best it can get with $EV(G4,C_m)$. Therefore, the "bad" government has incentives to grab more land income. The positive effect is that the "bad" government now promotes the local economy by 2Δ. However, it reduces the "yardstick" competition's selection effect since the "bad" government via exploiting land finance gets reappointed after period 1 and then faces no discipline and generates a waste of 2Δ in period 2. Compared with the "good" government which produces G3 with low land-exploitation capacity, the best expected utility for a "bad" government with low land-exploitation capacity will be $EV(G5,C_l) = 2\Delta$. If a "bad" government converts more arable land to construction land, it will have

$$EV(G2,C_m) = m(G2,G3)\delta 2\Delta = \delta 2\Delta;$$
$$EV(G3,C_m) = \Delta + m(G3,G3)\delta 2\Delta = \Delta + \delta * 2\Delta;$$
$$EV(G4,C_m) = 2\Delta + m(G4,G3)\delta 2\Delta = 2\Delta.$$

We can see that $EV(G3,C_m)$ is greater than both $EV(G2,C_m)$, $EV(G4,C_m)$, and is also greater than the best it can get with $EV(G5,C_l)$. Hence, the "bad" government has incentives to surpass its land-exploitation capacity and grab more land income. However, note that

G3>G5, so the positive effect is that the "bad" government now promotes their economy by 2Δ. However, it weakens the "yardstick" competition's selection effect since the "bad" government via exploiting land finance, gets reappointed after period 1 and then faces no discipline and generates a waste of 2Δ in period 2. Facing competition from a bad government, a "good" government is motivated to aim for a high land-exploitation capacity level, while a "bad" government will give up the competition because the best expected utility for it now is $E(G3, C_h) = 2\Delta$ which is not different from the best utility if it remains at its original level of land exploitation.

Proposition 2 Under yardstick competition, both types of local governments strive to gain more land income. Although the availability of land financing motivates the "bad" government to promote GDP in the current period (disciplining effect), it weakens the selection effect of the yardstick competition.

In summary, both fiscal decentralization and yardstick competition lead to intensified land-leasing activities. Although land leasing results in short-term economic growth, it violates the sustainability principle because too much arable land is converted into construction land, which brings about a waste of land resources. Yardstick competition's disciplining effect is still at work, while easy accessibility to exploit the land for local governments dampens yardstick competition's selection effect. The theoretical analysis provides a general framework for the following empirical analysis.

1.4 The Empirical Framework

1.4.1 The Econometric Specification

The above theoretical framework suggests that both fiscal decentralization and yardstick competition exert positive influence on land leasing. We formally test their impacts using a sample of 31 Chinese provinces during the period of 2003–2011.

Spatial econometrics is a rigorous technique since it studies the spatial dependence among variables of different entities, while traditional econometrics often assumes independence across entities. Intuitively, due to the yardstick competition and strategic interactions among local governments, land conveyance fees are correlated across entities. Chen (2014) suggested that one should examine if there is spatial dependence before applying spatial econometrics. Moran (1950) devised Moran's I to detect this spatial autocorrelation. Moran's I measures the linear correlation between regional value and the weighted average value of its neighbors. If Moran's I is different from zero, there exists spatial autocorrelation; a positive value implies spatial dependence, while a negative one implies spatial heterogeneity; a larger Moran's I suggests greater spatial clustering (Ward and Gleditsch 2007). We compute the Moran's I and find that there is significant spatial autocorrelation. To address the "spatial dependence", we adopt a spatial autoregression (SAR) where the spatial lag captures the land-leasing behaviors of geographically close neighbors, that is, the neighbor provinces' weighted average land conveyance fees. If the spatial correlation is ignored, we tend to underestimate the variance and obtain upward biased t-values (Ward and Gleditsch 2007). We also include fiscal decentralization and official turnover rate as two main explanatory variables, and control for the impact of per capita GDP and property price. The benchmark econometric specification is:

$$Y_{it} = \rho WY_{it} + \alpha FIS_{it} + \beta TUR_{it} + \gamma GDPPC_{it} + \delta PRO_{it} \\ + \mu_i + u_{it}\, i = 1,\ldots,N; t = 1,\ldots T.$$

This is a spatial autoregression model with fixed effect where Y_{it} represents the size of land conveyance fee; W is a $N \times N$ spatial-weighting matrix (W is a matrix form of $\sum w_{ij}$, where $w_{ij} = 0$ when $i = j$); WY_{it} is a spatially lagged dependent variable which measures the weighted average of other neighboring provinces' land conveyance fee; FIS_{it} indicates the extent of fiscal decentralization; TUR_{it} represents competition intensity due to perceived career uncertainty; $GDPPC_{it}$ represents per capita GDP; PRO_{it} represents the housing price; μ_i represents the fixed effect and u_{it} is the error term. The selection of spatial weight matrix is of great importance. For the contiguity matrix or the inverse-distance matrix, W is assumed to be time-invariant. However, if the correlation between areas is measured by economic conditions (e.g., $w_{ijt} = 1/\left|GDP_{it} - GDP_{jt}\right|$), the weight matrix is time-variant. In this study, we adopt a contiguity matrix. If two provinces share the same border, $w_{ij} = 1$; if they do not have common border, $w_{ij} = 0$. The defect of constructing the spatial weight matrix using distances between capital cities is that two geographically close provinces might seem distant from each other because of the size of the province or the location of the capital city. However, we also adopt the railway distance to compute the spatial weight matrix for robustness check. We do not use the economic distance as weights because it is likely to render endogeneity problem (Qu and Lee 2015). Kelejian and Piras (2014) pointed out that typical spatial models and corresponding estimation procedures will be invalid in the case of endogenous spatial weight matrix. In our spatial weight matrix, the row standardization is applied so that $W\Upsilon_{it}$ and Υ_{it} will have the same dimension and the spatial autoregressive coefficient can be clearly defined in terms of magnitude and direction.

Most researchers use FDI to measure the intensity of competition since local governments typically transfer land via negotiation to attract foreign investment and boost local economic development. However, due to the enactment of the regulation enforcing the provisions of the state-owned land use right via competitive bidding, auction and listing-for-sale, reliance on contract sales of land use right to compete for FDI might not be as strong as before. In other words, the magnitude of FDI might not be a key factor explaining the variance of land conveyance fee after 2003. We are thus also interested to test if FDI still plays a role in affecting the land-leasing activities for local governments. The empirical model is formulated as follows:

$$Y_{it} = \theta FDI_{it} + \alpha FIS_{it} + \gamma GDPPC_{it} + \delta PRO_{it} + \mu_i + u_{it}\ i = 1,\ldots,N; t = 1,\ldots,T.$$

In this baseline model, instead of employing the spatial lag to represent the yardstick competition, we directly use FDI as the proxy for competition intensity.

1.4.2 *The Empirical Strategy*

We attempt to obtain unbiased estimators of ρ, α, β, γ, δ for spatial autoregressive model using generalized method of moments (GMM). If the spatial autoregressive coefficient ρ is positively significant, there is yardstick competition among the entities. In other words, there is "spillover" effect in terms of the local governments' land-leasing decisions. We are also expecting positive signs for competition intensity, decentralization and economic growth rate.

It is very likely that neighboring local governments affect one another's land-leasing behavior, so the spatial lag of the dependent variable is usually endogenous. Therefore, the standard Ordinary Least Square (OLS) estimation demanding exogeneity of explanatory variables cannot apply to this circumstance. Elhorst (2003) pointed out that the response coefficients are both biased and inconsistent when a spatially lagged dependent variable is included. After conducting the Hausman specification test for endogeneity, it is verified that the inclusion of spatial lag induces endogeneity problem. To counter this endogeneity issue, we need to employ other estimation methods.

The two-stage least squares (2SLS), GMM and maximum likelihood (ML) estimation methods have been employed in past literature to overcome the endogeneity issue and we adopt GMM estimation in our research for several reasons. The instruments utilized may be the weighted average of other provinces' control variables (Caldeira 2012) or the first- and second-order spatial lag of Y_{it} (Li et al. 2013a). Notably, the 2SLS estimator is no longer efficient among Instrumental Variable (IV) estimators if errors are not identically and independently distributed, that is, if there exists heteroskedasticity or autocorrelation in error terms. Under this circumstance, GMM serves as an efficient solution. Moreover, GMM is more efficient than 2SLS when the number of instrumental variables exceeds the number of endogenous variables (Chen 2014). ML estimation can also be implemented. However, Elhorst (2012) suggested that GMM estimators outperform ML estimators when there are endogenous explanatory variables. He also suggested that when the dimension of a spatial weight matrix exceeds 400, GMM estimator is more reliable or some adjustments have to be made for the ML procedure. Lee and Yu (2014) summarized the merits of GMM estimation over the ML estimation: GMM estimation avoids some computational inconvenience regarding the likelihood function; certain GMM estimation works for short spatial dynamic panel data, while ML does not; GMM performs more efficiently under the case of non-normal distributed error terms; GMM remains valid for model with time effects and non-row-normalized spatial weight matrices.

We perform prerequisite tests to identify the appropriate estimation techniques and to check whether the important assumptions of the estimation method have been met. First, we check for the panel stationarity of each variable using the panel unit root test proposed by Im et al. (2003). It turns out that for each variable the null hypothesis of the panel unit root is rejected. Therefore, it is not necessary to take the first difference of variables to make the estimation valid or to conduct the co-integration test.

Next, we conduct two tests to examine if the error terms satisfy the "identically and independently distributed" assumption. The test for the null hypothesis "the variances of error terms are equal across entities" results in a p-value = 0.0000. It suggests that there is heteroskedasticity in error terms. Therefore, we will adopt "heteroskedasticity-robust standard error" in the estimation process. Meanwhile, the test for the null hypothesis "there is no autocorrelation among error terms in the same entities" shows that p-value = 0.0456. It implies that the assumption of independence over time has been violated. Thus, we should rationally adopt heteroskedasticity- and autocorrelation-consistent standard errors. However, the clustered standard error commonly used in panel date regression seems problematic because the spatially lagged variable is not independently distributed across entities. The existence of heteroskedasticity and autocorrelation in error terms also suggests that GMM estimator is more justified than 2SLS estimators.

Next, we test for potential multi-collinearity among the explanatory and control variables on the right-hand side of the regression specification. The result of Variation Inflation Factor (VIF) for each variable being less than 10 implies that there is no significant multi-collinearity among the chosen variables. In addition, we provide statistical evidence for choosing a fixed effect model. Intuitively, the fixed effect model is preferred due to some time-invariant factors that are different from province to province, such as cultural, historical or institutional factors which are hard to measure. In order to verify whether a fixed effect or random effect model is more appropriate, Hausman test is employed. The p-value = 0.0000 strongly rejects the null hypothesis that "differences in coefficients are not systematic", hence the fixed effect model outperforms the random effect model.

We adopt Kelejian and Prucha (1998)'s approach of treating weighted averages of other provinces' control variables as instruments for the spatial lag. After conducting the two-stage GMM estimation, we have to do diagnostic tests to test for the validity of the instrumental variables to ensure the GMM estimator is not biased or inconsistent. Three related tests for IVs are conducted in this research. The first is the under-identification test testing if "there exists under-identification problems". The test statistic is given by Kleibergen-Paap rk LM statistic instead of Anderson LM statistic because error terms are not *i.i.d.* To some extent, the under-identification test delivers information about the instrumental relevance. We further conduct weak identification test to see if there is weak instrument which will jeopardize the asymptotic normality of the estimators' distribution even in large sample. The weak identification test tests if for the null hypothesis "there exists weak instrument". A thumb of rule for rejection of such a null hypothesis is for the test statistic to exceed 10. With the absence of *i.i.d.* assumption of the error terms, we refer to Kleibergen-Paap rk Wald F statistic. Next, we test the instrumental exogeneity by conducting the overidentification test. The null hypothesis is that all the instrumental variables are exogenous (uncorrelated with the error terms) and we employ the Hansen J statistics to test it.

There are 14 sets of instrumental variables. We aim to choose the optimal set via comparing the three test statistics discussed above. However, overidentification test is only applicable under overidentification condition. Thus, the tests for instrumental exogeneity using overidentification test are paradoxical for one instrumental variable. After comparing the test statistics, we eliminate some invalid sets of instrumental variables and select the set with the best performance (with the best test statistics and fit of the regression). The instruments we select in this chapter are the weighted average of logarithmic official turnover, logarithmic fiscal gap and logarithmic per capita GDP. Another set of instruments (the weighted average of logarithmic fiscal gap and logarithmic per capita GDP) also perform quite well.

As for regression specification, we apply fixed effect to conduct the estimation after the standard Hausman specification test which confirms that fixed effect model is preferred to the random effect model. We use the heteroskedasticity- and autocorrelation-robust standard errors for this case.

1.5 Data Description

In our study, there are three proxies to measure competition intensity: the spatial lag of the land transaction price, FDI and the official turnover rate. The starting period of this study is year 2003 since it is then that the land leasing and sale policy and the statistical coverage for the land conveyance fees are changed.

We make several adjustments to the data for consistency. First, all the terms in monetary values such as land transaction price, fiscal expenditure, fiscal revenue and FDI are deflated using the consumer price index (1978 as base year). Second, we use market exchange rates to convert US dollar-based FDI into renminbi-based. We also take logs of every variable before running the regression to study the effect of percentage change of independent variable on the percentage change of the dependent variable. Fiscal gap is measured as the difference of budgetary expenditure and revenue over the budgetary income. $COMPETITION_{it} = (\sum T_{it} - T_{it})/2N$, where $\sum T_{it}$ is the sum of turnover rates of mayors and party secretaries in China in year t, T_{it} is its own provincial-level turnover rate in year t; the denominator 2N is the total number of mayors and party secretaries and N denotes the number of provinces in China at t. Since the number of Chinese provinces remain fixed, N is a fixed number. The competition intensity is an increasing function of $\sum T_{it}$ and a decreasing function of T_{it}. Intuitively, when an incumbent official perceives higher turnover in the whole nation, the perceived uncertainty of his or her career path increases, then he or she will work harder. However, when he or she has already known his or her career path, less effort will be made due to the decreased uncertainty, hence less competition.

Our sample consists of 279 observations (31 provinces from 2003 to 2011). We collect data on fiscal-related variables, FDI, GDP and population from CEIC Database and China Statistical Yearbook (various years). We compute the turnover rate using the information on Chinese governors and provincial secretaries collected from assorted sources documenting their biographies. The data for inter-province railway distances is from Wang et al. (2014).

1.6 Main Results

We plot Moran's I index from 2003 to 2011. Figure 1.1 shows that the Moran's I is positive and greater than 0.58 which suggests positive spatial autocorrelation. In general, Moran's I exhibits an ascending trend over the time span, suggesting the strategic competition has been intensified.

Comparing the adjusted R-square, the magnitude and significance of coefficients, we can see from Table 1.1 that the choice of GMM estimation (model 1) is more reasonable than 2SLS (model 2) and OLS estimation (model 3). The fit of regression to data is better using GMM estimation than 2SLS and OLS since the adjusted R-square is 0.7366 greater than 0.3909 and 0.6718. Moreover, many independent variables tend to be insignificant and implausibly small using 2SLS or OLS estimation. Furthermore, as shown in Table 1.1, only our benchmark specification which takes all proposed factors into account fits into the data. Other specifications fail to produce significant and reasonable coefficients except for the coefficient of the spatial lag which is always significant and positive.

We employ GMM along with the instrumental variables (the weighted average of the logarithmic fiscal gap, turnover and GDP per capita); the regression results of benchmark specification are shown in Table 1.2. The coefficient for spatial lag is positive and significant at 5% level. Specifically, a 1 percentage increase in the neighbors' weighted average land conveyance fees leads to a 0.4 percentage rise in the local province's land conveyance fees. This result provides evidence of the spillover effect of land-leasing activities. One jurisdiction will incorporate its neighbors' land-leasing decisions into its decision-making in order to outperform others. This is aligned with *Hypothesis 2*. The coefficient of fiscal gap is also positive and significant. This supports *Hypothesis 1* that fiscal decentralization is a positive contributor to land-leasing behavior. However, compared with competition in land sale, a 1% rise in the fiscal gap contributes to 0.23% increase in the land-leasing fee. This result is in line with the observation in Li et al. (2013a)'s paper that after year 2013 the relationship between decentralization and land-leasing intensity is not pronounced. Compared with the spillover effect, the effect of fiscal gap is weaker, suggesting that the internal factor—promotion incentive—plays a larger role than the external force—budget constraint. Notably, the impact of per capita GDP on land leasing is substantial: a 1% change in GDP per capita results in a 0.87% rise of land conveyance fee. This suggests that richer jurisdictions rely more on land-related income to finance spending on public goods and services, which sheds light on *Hypothesis 4*. The positive impact of competition intensity on local government's land conveyance fee implies that the perceived career uncertainty may contribute to the land-leasing behavior as well, but with a weaker impact and less significance than yardstick competition. The property price is only significant at a level slightly higher than 15%. However, the relationship between housing price and land-leasing fee is positive. *Hypothesis 5* is weakly supported.

The Kleibergen-Paap rk LM statistics is 29.406 with p-value 0.0000 which suggests the absence of under-identification. Both Cragg-Donald Wald F statistic (21.652) and Kleibergen-Paap rk Wald F statistic (17.902) are greater than the 5% Stock-Yogo weak identification critical value and greater than the rule of thumb value 10, which indicates that the instrumental variables are not weakly related to the spatial lag. The Hansen J statistics fails to reject the null hypothesis of exogeneity of all instrumental variables even at 15% level, which is satisfactory. The validity of these instrumental variables ensures that the GMM estimators are efficient. Similar results using another set of valid instrumental variables (the weighted average of logarithmic fiscal gap and per capita GDP) are shown in Table 1.3, model (2). The comparison of estimators of these two regressions using different sets of IVs is displayed in Table 1.3. The adjusted R-squared for the benchmark specification of over 0.7 demonstrates good fitness to the data.

In addition to the benchmark specification, we further examine the dynamic spatial autoregression model. In particular, we augment the benchmark specification with the first-order time lag of the land conveyance fee and the first-order time lag of the weighted average of neighbors' land-leasing fees. The results for the dynamic specifications are presented in Table 1.4. As illustrated by models (2) and (4), the first-order time lag of the land conveyance fee is highly significant at 1% level, implying that there is "inertia" in local governments' reliance on land leasing. Once they rely heavily on land leasing for funding their expenditure, it tends to be more difficult for them to alleviate this dependence immediately. In fact, this inertia effect is so strong that after it is taken into consideration, other factors seem to lose their significance. In contrast, as illustrated by model (3) and model (4), the time lag of the weighted average of neighboring governments' behaviors is extremely insignificant, implying that when local governments compete with each other, they are inclined to consider others' contemporaneous land-leasing behaviors for comparisons.

The regression results for the alternative specification are shown in Table 1.5, model (2). It is clear that the impact of FDI is insignificant. This result is consistent with the evidence provided by Li et al. (2013b), showing that after 2003 FDI has begun to lose its momentum as a positive contributor to the land-leasing intensity. This sheds light on *Hypothesis 3*. Note that in model 3 of Table 1.5, we also provide the regression result using the official turnover rate as the proxy for competition in absence of the spatial lag. The result shows that this proxy is highly significant at 1%. However, a 1 percentage change in turnover only accounts for a 0.21 percentage change in land-leasing fee. Compared with 0.4, the coefficient of the spatial lag, the effect of turnover is much weaker. To sum up, the strategic interaction best explains the competitive behaviors of local governments in terms of land leasing.

We also utilize the spatial weighting matrix based on railway distance to do the robustness check and the results are exhibited in Table 1.6. Model (1) employs the weighted average of logarithmic fiscal gap, turnover and GDP per capita as instrumental variables, while model (2) employs the weighted average of logarithmic fiscal gap and GDP per capita. As we can see, the coefficients of the spatial lags are still significant at 10% significance level. A 10 percentage rise in neighbors' land income results in a 4.9% increase in the local government's land-leasing income which is slightly greater than the impact identified using the contiguity matrix.

1.7 Conclusion

The substantial rise in land-leasing income of Chinese local governments is associated with a wide range of social problems such as peasants' welfare loss, surging housing prices and unsustainability of arable lands. To facilitate the identification of solutions for policy makers, we investigate the underlying institutional and political reasons of the rapidly growing land-leasing volume. After a critical review of the existing literature, we propose five hypotheses with a focus on the impact of fiscal decentralization and yardstick competition on land-leasing activities. Our theoretical model illustrates how fiscal decentralization and yardstick competition incentivize local governments to "grab" the land-related income in an unsustainable way. We also prove that the availability of land finance dampens the "selection effect" of yardstick competition. In the empirical study, using a provincial-level panel data of 31 Chinese provinces from 2003 to 2011, we adopt the spatial autoregression (SAR) model to study the yardstick competition among the local governments. To estimate the SAR model, GMM estimation is employed with validated instrumental variables. Besides the benchmark SAR model, we further include time lags and test for competition induced by attracting FDI and perceived career uncertainty. The results from our empirical study can be summarized as follows.

First, since 2003, fiscal decentralization has been a less significant contributor to land-leasing behaviors as compared to earlier years. Second, while yardstick competition greatly contributes to the land-leasing behaviors, attracting FDI plays an insignificant role. Third, local governments appear to have "inertia" reliance on land-leasing income. Fourth, regional economic development is still at a phase where its reliance on land finance is indispensable. Fifth, housing price exhibits a positive relationship with land conveyance fee.

Our research offers valuable implications for policy makers to mitigate the reliance on land financing. Faced with a range of issues that "land financing" has caused, governments should think of a less myopic way to finance deficit and to develop the local economy. However, the temptation for using land leasing as an alternative source of income is somewhat irresistible. Thus, institutional reforms are imperative to limit governments' monopoly power in the expropriation and sale of land.

As explicated in our theoretical framework, assigning local governments the right to transfer the usage of land motivates local governments to boost local economic development while weakening the "selection effect" of a typical yardstick competition. The ease for local governments to tap into the windfall land revenues explains for the failure of the "selection effect". Limitations on governments' discretion to expropriate lands from rural collective and governments' monopoly power to sell land use right in the first-degree land market should be imposed. As suggested by Wu et al. (2015), the rural collective economic organizations should be given the rights to transfer the land use right to land users and thus help form the integrated rural-urban land market system. Furthermore, the market mechanism should be set into motion to improve efficiency of land allocation. In fact, the 2002 regulation which restricts the land sales by negotiation is one step forward toward the liberalization of the land market. As our empirical result points out, the land conveyance fee is not significantly correlated with FDI, while the relationship between housing price and land-leasing fee is positive. One possible explanation is that local governments tend to push up the housing price to attract real estate developers to bid for land for higher revenues. Another possible explanation is that local governments, by pushing up the housing price, acquire more land-related incomes to finance the local public goods and services provision.

The second set of policy implications is that the tax distribution system between central and local government can be adjusted to reduce the need to finance fiscal expenditure via land leasing. The fiscal decentralization system as demonstrated by both our theoretical model and empirical analysis also intensifies the land-leasing behaviors. Fiscal decentralization aggravates the local governments' fiscal burden, inducing them to seek extra-budgetary income. Current fiscal decentralization implicitly delegates local governments the liberty to preserve the land sales revenues instead of reporting and handing them over to the central government, and local governments are ready to use the income from land sales to fund their public spending. At the same time, land-leasing activities should be strictly monitored and land-leasing income should be managed in a more transparent and proper manner.

Last but not least, yardstick competition should be alleviated to a moderate level. Our empirical result shows that competitive strategic interactions among local governments tend to intensify land-leasing behavior either through an increase in land price or a rise in volume. This not only leads to an unhealthy spiral rise in housing prices but also results in redundant constructions at the expenses of arable lands—a terrible waste of land resources. Local governments, instead of competing fiercely to outperform others, should think of a more cooperative way both in terms of constructions and sustainable economic relationship. The GDP-directed performance evaluation system is mainly responsible for this yardstick competition in land leasing. Central government should incorporate other indicators for cadre evaluation and promotion.

This research is valuable in that our theoretical model provides insights into the motivations for local governments to exploit land financing, while our empirical part incorporates more up-to-date data and exploits an advanced technique—spatial econometrics. In future research, city-level data can be exploited to see the effects of fiscal decentralization and yardstick competition on municipal governments' land-leasing behaviors; spatial econometric specifications and estimators can be explored to deal with the endogenous spatial weight matrix; the theoretical model can be further modified into a continuous version; and the contribution of welfare-oriented yardstick competition in land financing can be examined.

Appendix

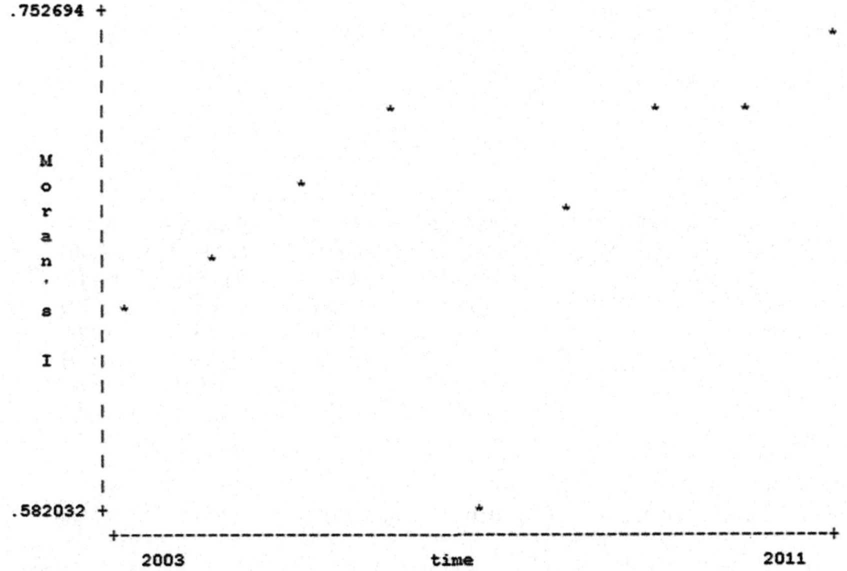

Fig. 1.1 Moran's I for spatial autocorrelation in land conveyance fee (2003–2011)

Table 1.1 Benchmark models with GMM, 2SLS and OLS estimations

	Dependent variable y		
	(1)	*(2)*	*(3)*
W_y	0.395**	0.407*	0.500***
	(2.00)	(1.92)	(3.39)
Turnover	0.113	0.0929	0.0655
	(1.49)	(1.15)	(1.30)
Fiscal gap	0.232*	0.206	0.170
	(1.69)	(1.43)	(0.89)
GDP pc	0.876**	0.887***	0.776*
	(2.40)	(2.80)	(1.95)
Property price	0.337	0.308	0.259
	(1.39)	(1.39)	(0.76)
Constant		−2.245****	−2.228**
		(−3.95)	(−2.23)
N	279	279	279
Ad R-squared	0.7366	0.3909	0.6718

Notes: The dependent variable y denotes the logarithm of the deflated land-leasing fees, and W_y denotes the logarithm of the deflated weighed average of neighboring provinces' land-leasing fees. *t* statistics in parentheses

*$p < 0.1$, **$p < 0.05$, ***$p < 0.01$, ****$p < 0.001$

Table 1.2 GMM estimations with IVs

	Dependent variable y				
	(1)	*(2)*	*(3)*	*(4)*	*(5)*
W_y	1.064****	1.088****	1.087****	0.481***	0.395**
	(26.16)	(25.05)	(25.02)	(2.59)	(2.00)
Turnover		−0.0940*	−0.0946*	0.0890	0.113
		(−1.69)	(−1.68)	(1.20)	(1.49)
Fiscal gap			−0.0388	0.175	0.232*
			(−0.32)	(1.31)	(1.69)
GDP pc				1.045***	0.876**
				(3.16)	(2.40)
Property price					0.337
					(1.39)
N	279	279	279	279	279
Ad.R-squared	0.7016	0.7019	0.7009	0.7362	0.7366

Notes: The dependent variable y denotes the logarithm of the deflated land-leasing fees, and W_y denotes the logarithm of the deflated weighed average of neighboring provinces' land-leasing fees. *t* statistics in parentheses

*$p < 0.1$, **$p < 0.05$, ***$p < 0.01$, ****$p < 0.001$

Table 1.3 GMM estimations using different IVs

	Dependent variable	
	(1)	*(2)*
W_y	0.395**	0.405**
	(2.00)	(2.04)
Turnover	0.113	0.109
	(1.49)	(1.43)
Fiscal gap	0.232*	0.230
	(1.69)	(1.67)
GDP pc	0.876**	0.856**
	(2.40)	(2.33)
Property price	0.337	0.337
	(1.39)	(1.38)
N	279	279
Ad.R-squared	0.7366	0.7368
LM statistic	29.406	29.289
rk Wald F-statistic	17.902	26.976
Hansen J-statistic	2.337	2.103

Notes: Dependent variable is the logarithm of the deflated land-leasing fees, and W_y denotes the logarithm of the deflated weighed average of neighboring provinces' land-leasing fees. *t* statistics in parentheses

$^{*}p < 0.1$, $^{**}p < 0.05$, $^{***}p < 0.01$, $^{****}p < 0.001$

Table 1.4 Introducing first-order time lag of the dependent variable and the first-order time lag of spatial lag

	Dependent variable			
	(1)	*(2)*	*(3)*	*(4)*
W_y	0.405**	0.424*	0.510	0.666*
	(2.04)	(1.81)	(1.38)	(1.87)
Turnover	0.109	0.104	0.0608	0.0160
	(1.43)	(1.14)	(0.45)	(0.12)
Fiscal gap	0.230	0.177	0.169	0.0665
	(1.67)*	(1.14)	(0.83)	(0.34)
GDP pc	0.856**	0.298	0.660*	0.284
	(2.33)	(0.86)	(1.67)	(0.86)
Property price	0.337	0.352	0.292	0.206
	(1.38)	(1.22)	(0.85)	(0.60)
Lag y		0.284***		0.317***
		(2.96)		(3.11)
Lag W_y			0.0515	−0.180
			(0.33)	(−1.02)
N	279	248	248	248

Notes: The dependent variable is the logarithm of the deflated land-leasing fees, and W_y denotes the logarithm of the deflated weighed average of neighboring provinces' land-leasing fees. Lag y denotes first-order time lag of logarithmic transaction price value; Lag W_y denotes first-order time lag of logarithmic weighted average of neighbors' transaction price values. *t* statistics in parentheses

$^{*}p < 0.1$, $^{**}p < 0.05$, $^{***}p < 0.01$, $^{****}p < 0.001$

Table 1.5 Models using different measures of competition

	Dependent variable		
	(1)	*(2)*	*(3)*
W_y	0.395**		
	(2.00)		
Turnover	0.113		0.213****
	(1.49)		(5.20)
Fiscal gap	0.232*	0.274	0.361*
	(1.69)	(1.48)	(1.95)
GDP pc	0.876**	1.481***	1.372****
	(2.40)	(3.44)	(4.35)
Property price	0.337	0.506	0.521*
	(1.39)	(1.46)	(1.66)
FDI		−0.0733	
		(−0.75)	
Constant		−2.493**	−2.320**
		(−2.56)	(−2.34)
N	279	274	279

Notes: The dependent variable is the logarithm of the deflated land-leasing fees, and W_y denotes the logarithm of the deflated weighed average of neighboring provinces' land-leasing fees. *t* statistics in parentheses

$^{*}p < 0.1$, $^{**}p < 0.05$, $^{***}p < 0.01$, $^{****}p < 0.001$

Table 1.6 Robustness check using railway distance-based spatial weight matrix

	Dependent variable	
	(1)	*(2)*
W_yl	0.492*	0.491*
	(1.69)	(1.69)
Turnover	0.0671*	0.0674*
	(1.71)	(1.72)
Fiscal gap	0.104*	0.105*
	(1.65)	(1.66)
GDP pc	0.986***	0.987***
	(2.67)	(2.67)
Property price	0.179	0.179
	(1.55)	(1.45)
N	261	261

Notes: The dependent variable denotes the logarithm of the deflated land-leasing fees; W_yl is the weighted average of neighboring province's land conveyance fees using railway distance-based matrix. *t* statistics in parentheses

$^{*}p < 0.1$, $^{**}p < 0.05$, $^{***}p < 0.01$, $^{****}p < 0.001$

References

Belleflamme, P. and Hindriks, J. (2005), "Yardstick competition and political agency problems", *Social Choice and Welfare*: 24(1), 155–169.

Besley, T. and Case, A. (1995), "Incumbent behavior: vote-seeking, tax-setting and yardstick competition", *America Economic Review*: 85(1), 25–45.

Caldeira, E. (2012), "Yardstick competition in a federation: theory and evidence in China", *China Economic Review*: 23(4), 878–897.

Cao, Y. P. and Luo, J. (2012), "Empirical analysis and countermeasures research on the relationship between local government land finance and taxation system", *Journal of Hunan Finance and Economics University*: Vol. 28 (in Chinese).

CKGSB Knowledge. (2014), "The role of land sales in local government financing in China".

Chen, Q. (2014), Advanced econometrics and applications in Stata. 2nd ed. Beijing: Higher Education Press.

Elhorst, J. (2003), "Specification and estimation of spatial panel data models", *International Regional Science Review*: 26(3), 244–268.

Elhorst, J. (2012), "Dynamic spatial panels: models, methods, and inferences", *Journal of Geographic Systems*: 1(14), 5–28.

Im, K. S., Pesaran, M. H., and Shin, Y. (2003), "Testing for unit roots in heterogeneous panels", *Journal of Econometrics*: 115(1), 53–74.

Kelejian, H. H. and Prucha, I. R. (1998), "A generalized spatial two-stage least squares procedure for estimating a spatial autoregressive model with autoregressive disturbances", *The Journal of Real Estate Finance and Economics*: 17(1), 99–121.

Kelejian, H. H. and Piras, G. (2014), "Estimation of spatial models with endogenous weighting matrices, and an application to a demand model for cigarette", *Regional Science and Urban Economic:* Vol. 4, 140–149.

Lee, L. F. and Yu, J. H. (2014), "Efficient GMM estimation of spatial dynamic panel data with fixed effect", *Journal of Econometrics*: Vol. 180, 174–197.

Li, X., Hong, G. Z. and Huang, L. X. (2013a), "The mystery of land finance growth in China: tax-sharing reform, strategic interaction of land finance", *China Economic Quarterly*: 12(4), 1141–1160 (in Chinese).

Li, Y. G., Gao, B. and Xu, C. Z. (2013b), "Promotion incentives, land finance and economic development's regional difference—An estimation based on the panel data simultaneous equation model", *Industrial Economic Survey*: Vol. 1, 100–109 (in Chinese).

Li, Y. G. and Zhang, S. J. (2014), "Performance of officials and promotion tournament-evidence from Chinese cities", *Economic Survey*: 31(4), 116–150.

Liu, J., Wu, J. N. and Ma, L. (2012), "Local official's promotion and land finance in china: an empirical analysis of panel data from municipal-level cities", *Journal of Public Management*: 9(2), 11–23 (in Chinese).

Mi, T. (2011), "Analysis on causes and threats of land finance", *Anhui Agriculture Journal*: 17(3), 37–39 (in Chinese).
Moran, P. A. (1950), "A test for the serial independence of residuals", *Biometrika*: 37(1/2), 178–181.
Payne, J. E. (2003), "A survey of the international empirical evidence on the tax-spend debate", *Public Finance Review*: 31(3), 302–324.
Qu, X. and Lee, L. F. (2015), "Estimating a spatial autoregressive model with an endogenous spatial weight matrix", *Journal of Econometrics*: Vol. 184, 209–232.
Tao, R., Yuan, F. and Cao, G. Z. (2007), "Regional competition, land leasing and local fiscal effect", *World Economics*: Vol. 10, 15–27.
Ward, D. M. and Gleditsch, S. K. (2007), "An introduction to spatial regression models in social sciences", unpublished paper.
Wen, H. and Goodman, A. (2013), "Relationship between urban land price and housing price: Evidence from 21 provincial capitals in China", *Habitat International*: Vol. 40, 9–17.
Wu, Q. and Li, Y. L. (2010), "Fiscal decentralization, government competition and land finance", *Trade and Economy*: Vol. 7, 51–59 (in Chinese).
Wu, Q., Li, Y. L. and Y, S. Q. (2015), "The incentives of China's urban land finance", *Land Use Policy*: Vol. 42, 432–442.
Wang, Q. X., Jiang, Y. and Chen, Z. Y. (2014), Regional economics study methods: based on applications of ArcGIS, GeoDa and R. Beijing: Economic Science Press.
Ye, F. Z. and Wang, W. (2013), "Determinants of land finance in china: a study based on provincial-level panel data", *Australian Journal of Public Administration*: 72(3), 293–303.
Zhang, L., Wang, X. B. and Xu, X. X. (2011), "Fiscal incentive, political incentive and local officials' land supply", *China Industrial Economics*: Vol. 4, 35–43.
Zhou, L. A. (2007), "Study into Chinese officials' promotion tournament", *Economic Research*: Vol. 7, 36–50 (in Chinese).

CHAPTER 2

Determinants of the Urban Investment Bonds in China

Daike Li and Yang Chen

2.1 Introduction

During the last decade, there is a dramatic increase of the so-called quasi municipal bond, namely, the urban investment bond (UIB) issued by four levels of local governments.[1] The UIB[2] is defined as the bond issued by financing vehicle companies[3] and established by local governments, which includes enterprise bond and notes with various maturities (short term, medium term, and long term). The main function of UIB is to finance the infrastructure construction and welfare spending of local governments (Cao 2011; Feng 2013).

Xu and Wang (2013) claimed that the monthly issuance volume of the UIB in 2012 has become comparable to the medium- and long-term loan that enterprises borrowed from the bank. Wang and Li (2013) states that the UIBs significantly affect the prospective of Chinese economy as most of the fixed asset investment is funded by that. Therefore, an in-depth study of the factors shaping the volume of UIB issuance has become

D. Li • Y. Chen (✉)
International Business School Suzhou, Xi'an Jiaotong-Liverpool University, Suzhou, China
e-mail: yang.chen@xjtlu.edu.cn

J. H. Hung, Y. Chen (eds.), *The State of China's State Capitalism*,
https://doi.org/10.1007/978-981-13-0983-0_2

imperative. We are interested to answer what are the determinants of the issuance of UIBs and in particular whether there is any strategic interaction among local governments in bond issuance.

2.2 Background

The Chinese central government implemented the tax sharing reform in 1994, which significantly cut the taxes the local government could collect but kept the expenditure responsibility unchanged (Li et al. 2013). Figure 2.1 shows that the ratio of the local government revenue to the central government revenue plummeted to 1 in 1994 and remained unchanged afterward, nearly half of the pre-1994 level. The ratio of the local government expenditure to the central government expenditure increased dramatically from 2000 to 2013, almost tripling the pre-2000 level.

Facing large gaps between the revenue and expenditure, local governments began to issue debt, get loan from banks, and even delay maturity repayments to meet their increasing level of expenditure, resulting in the rapid increase in the debt balance. Figure 2.2 indicates that the local government debt balance has increased from 3.37 Billion RMB in 1996 to 10,716 Billion RMB in 2010, which is 26% of the national gross domestic

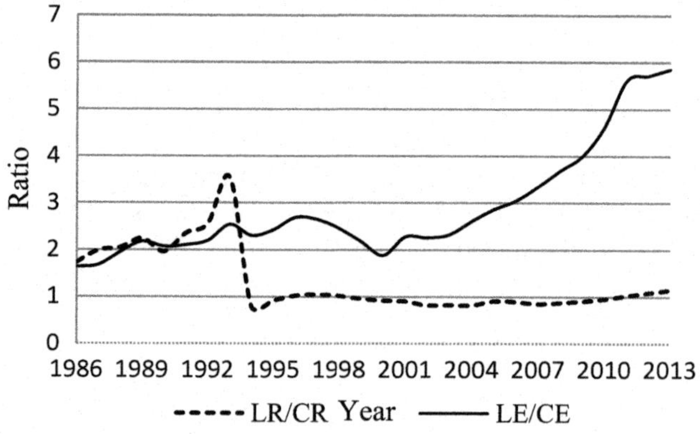

Fig. 2.1 Revenue and expenditure ratios. (Notes: LR/CR = (local government revenue)/(central government revenue), LE/CE = (local government expenditure)/(central government expenditure); Data of government revenues and expenditures are sourced from WIND, calculated by authors)

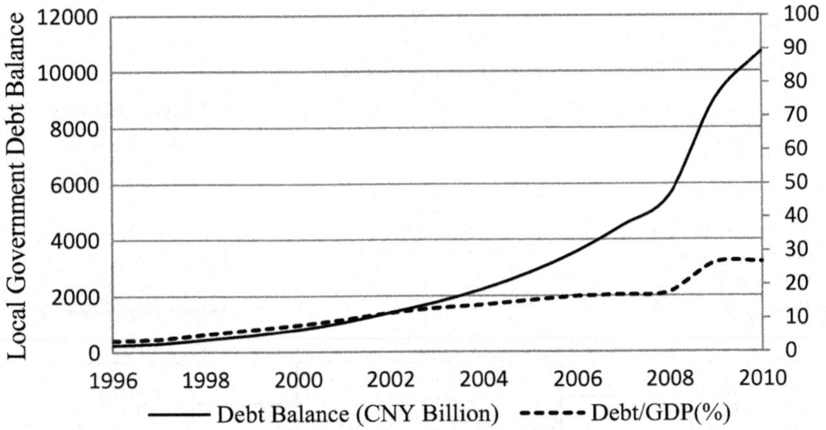

Fig. 2.2 Debt balance and debt to GDP ratio of local governments. (Notes: Estimated from the data released by National Audit Office of the P.R.C. (2011) and WIND)

product (GDP) in that year. Although by "The Budget Law of The People's Republic of China", local governments are not allowed to issue local government bonds unless the law or the State Council permits, the local governments managed to issue bonds by setting up local government financing vehicle companies (Tu 2010). Figure 2.3 shows the operating mechanism of local government financing vehicles. The majority of the local government debts are funds provided by banks and securities market in the forms of loans and UIBs. According to the China Audit Office (2011), bank loans and bonds issued by the local government financing vehicles make up 50% of the local government debt,[4] which is far beyond the other forms of local government debts.

Xu and Wang (2013) stated that the first UIB was issued by the Shanghai government in 1993. Up to 2004 (see Fig. 2.4), the issuance of UIBs was almost stagnant. The following period of 2005–2008 witnessed a steady but slow increase in the issuance volume and types of bonds. Furthermore, during this period, the main issuers of UIBs were the relatively developed provinces and cities in China such as prefecture-level cities in Zhejiang province, Jiangsu province, and Guangdong province. The year 2009 saw a dramatic increase of UIB, which nearly sextupled that in 2008. Tu (2010), Shao (2013), Cao (2011), and Feng (2013) all accredited this

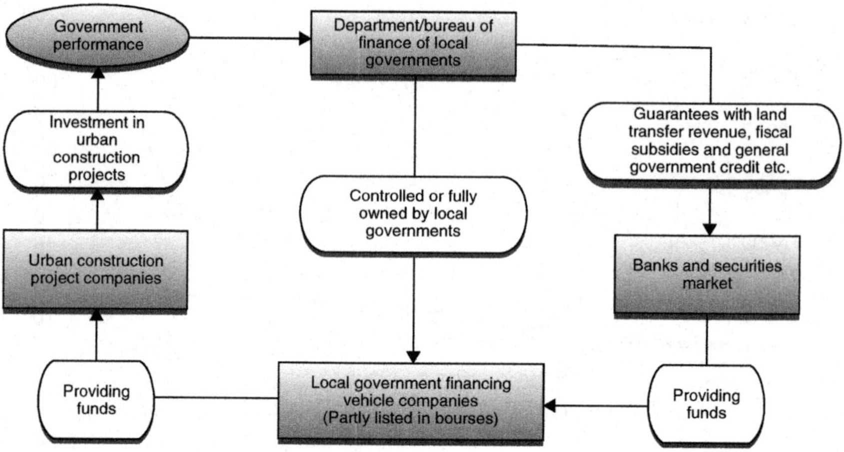

Fig. 2.3 Operating model of local government financing vehicles companies. (Source: Feng 2013)

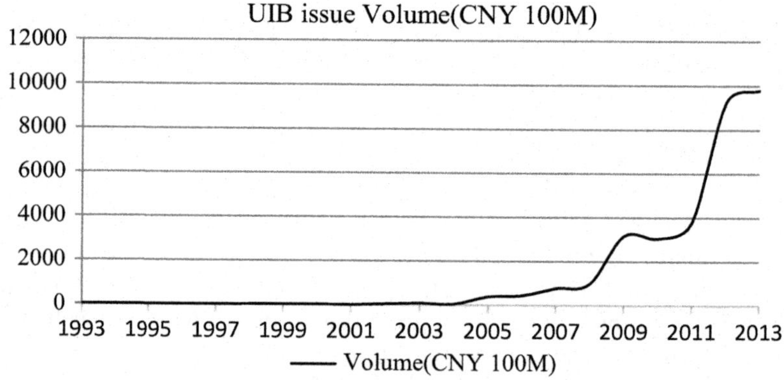

Fig. 2.4 The volume of urban investment bonds (1993–2013). (Source: WIND, calculated by authors)

increase to the central government's explicit support for local governments to develop local government financing vehicle companies. In 2008, the economy of China was negatively influenced by the global finance crisis. To maintain the economic growth, the central government carried out the "Four Trillion Investment Program", and local governments were required to provide matching funding amounting to 20 trillion. However, the revenues of local governments were far below the capital demand, they therefore turned to debts. In 2009, the central government explicitly showed acquiesces in the debt-issuing behavior of local government, leading to the sharp increase of the UIBs. However, in the following year, the central government was afraid of potential risks and implemented a series of regulations to restrict the development of local financing vehicle companies, leading to a slight decrease in the size of UIBs in 2010. Nevertheless, because of the newly implemented restrictions on housing price and land selling in 2012, the revenue of local government was sharply reduced, spurring them to rely more on debt issuing. Since 2012, the amount of issued urban investment debt has been soaring again (Shao 2013; Xu and Wang 2013; Tu 2010).

2.3 Literature Review

One strand of studies focused on the potential risks of UIBs. Ba (2009) and Yang and Huang (2010) claimed that the risks of UIBs mainly came from three areas: the opacity and the soft budget constraint of the debt-issuing behavior of the local government financing vehicle company, the moral hazard of these vehicles, and the possibility to squeeze the room of using monetary policy. Overall, most scholars think the risks of UIB issuance is currently under control (Gu and Li 2013; Liu et al. 2013; Lei 2011a, b). Other studies described the development of UIBs. For example, Lei (2011a, b) analyzed this issue from the institutional perspective and claimed that the rapid development of UIBs was due to unreasonable fiscal relationship among different levels of government, the soft budget constraint of local government, and the disordered government governance system. Other researchers (Gu and Li 2013; Tang 2011; Gong et al. 2011; Zhu and Gao 2010) also assessed this problem from the angle of the fiscal decentralization and claimed that the prompt increase of UIBs was inevitable because of the scarcity of fiscal resource for local government after the tax sharing reform in 1994. However, all these arguments were supported merely by descriptive analysis without solid theoretical foundation and statistical evidences, which make their conclusions far from convincing.

Empirical studies on UIBs are still rare. Using the Cobb-Douglas model, Mou and Fu (2013) concluded that the borrowing behavior of local government had path dependency, which meant that the bond issue strategy had inertia. Miao et al. (2013) used the Granger Causality test and the Johansen–Juselius method on the fiscal gap data since 1994 and concluded that the volume of local government debt did not have any connection with the budgetary revenue. This result coincided with the fact that the central government's regulations that stipulate that local governments cannot have fiscal deficit when they set the budget, spurring the local governments to seek extra-budgetary funding such as land conveyance fees, bank loans, and UIBs. He and Man (2012) addressed this problem from the perspective of land finance. They used the Two Stage Least Square (2SLS) model to test on the UIB data during the period of 2002–2010 and concluded that sales of land had a significantly positive correlation with the bond volume.

Three major shortages exist among the current empirical studies of UIBs. First, the datasets applied by above research are all before 2010 while the UIB issuance volume has dramatically increased after 2010. Therefore, the results of these studies are not necessarily applicable to explain the current situation. Second, most studies are concerned with one specific element, which is not sufficient to explain the variation of UIBs among different regions. Third, no studies have paid attention to the strategic interactions among local governments in the bond issuance behavior even though the competition and imitation with neighbor governments might significantly affect the amount of debts issued by local governments. We fill in the gap in this chapter by using the most recent data to address the strategic behavior in bonds issuance controlling for fiscal gap, expenditure on public welfare, real estate investment, and economic development. We also use two-year dummies to measure the policy shocks in year 2009 and 2012.

2.4 Empirical Strategy

We adopt the generalized spatial autoregression model proposed by Anselin (1988) as below:

$$y_{it} = \rho W_{ij} y_{it} + \tau y_{it-1} + \beta X_{it} + u_{it}, u_{it} \sim i.i.d\left(0,\sigma_u^2\right) \tag{2.1}$$

where y_{it} stands for the issuance volume of UIBs in province i in year t. W_{ij} is the spatial weight matrix with an order of $N \times N$, which can be set based on the spatial distance or economic distance of different regions. In the literature, common spatial distances include the linear contiguity, rook contiguity, and bishop contiguity (Sheng et al. 2010). Economic distances usually consider trade flows, total border length of shared frontier, the degree of convenience of transportation, K-nearest neighbor node, distance decay function, or the product of the above matrixes (Sheng et al. 2010).

We adopt four different spatial weight matrixes using the inverse of railway distance, trade flows between any two provinces, rook contiguity of provinces, and GDP ranks (see Appendix for detailed calculation). The matrixes calculated on the basis of the rook contiguity and railway distance are static as these two elements are kept unchanged during the period from 2005 to 2013. In contrast, economic matrixes based on trade flows and GDP ranks are dynamic ones as these two factors changed from year to year. Normally, the static weighting matrix built on geographic information tends to be exogenous while the economic dynamic matrixes may suffer from endogenous problems. Thus, regression models using static matrixes are more convincing than those using dynamic ones (Harry and Gianfranco 2014; Qu and Lee 2015). The term $W_{ij}y_{it}$ (spatial lag term) is the weighted average of the random variable y, and ρ is the spatial autoregression coefficient. When ρ is significantly positive, we can conclude that there is imitation or competition behavior among provincial governments in issuing UIB. The term X_{it} denotes other explanatory variables listed in data section. To investigate whether the bond issuance has inertial dependence, the model includes the first-order time lagged term. u_{it} is the error term, which is assumed to follow an identical and independent normal distribution with constant variance. We conduct the Ljung-Box test to check whether the u_{it} has such attributes.

The parameters in Eq. (2.1) can be estimated by the maximum likelihood estimation. We carry out four regression analyses using different spatial weight matrices. In each model, we check three aspects to make sure that the specification is right. First, we resort to the "bsktest" proposed by Baltagi et al. (2003) to check against fixed versus random effect in spatial regression. In this test, the null hypothesis is that the model does not need to consider the random effect while the alternative hypothesis is that the model should consider random effects and spatial autocorrelation. Second, we use the Ljung–Box test to check whether the residuals of each model are randomly distributed. If we cannot reject the null hypothesis which states that there is no autocorrelation among residuals, we can conclude that the residuals are randomly distributed. Furthermore, we use the Kappa value to check whether the variables in a specific model are perfectly linearly correlated. If the Kappa value is less than 100, there is minimal collinearity among the elements; if the Kappa value is between 100 and 1000, it indicates imperfect collinearity; and if the Kappa value is larger than 1000, it suggests perfect collinearity.

2.5 Data Description

We use a panel dataset covering 31 provincial-level administrative units[5] in mainland China from 2005 to 2013. We do not consider including data before 2005 as provinces seldom issued UIBs before that year. All the data are adjusted by the consumer price index collected from WIND and the base year is 2005. The descriptive analyses and definitions of main variables are summarized in Table 2.1.

Table 2.1 Summary statistics of main variables of interests

Variable	*Mean*	*SD*	*Max.*	*Min.*
y_{it}(100 million)	97.60	152.8284	1180.20	0.78
D_{ij}(km)	1313.11	693.46	3469	113
GR_{ijt}(10,000 tons)	437.05	1297.88	37,761	0
TR_{ijt}(10,000 tons)	7807.49	20687.58	393834.4	0
$Rail_{it}$(km)	2022.36	1175.188	6313	137
fis_gap_{it}(100 million)	862.91	652.4867	5341.32	17.52
fdi_{it}(100 million)	308.65	377.167	1802.69	0.80
GDP_{it}(100 million)	11,030	9569.547	48,494	251
$Wy_{it}\_railway$(100 million)	106.61	100.346	403.01	9.81
$Wy_{it}\_GDPrank$(100 million)	118.15	169.87	1180.20	0.80
Wy_{it}_trade(100 million)	125.68	131.63	565.22	0
$Inv\_housing_{it}$(100 million)	1611.02	1458.65	7150.27	10.21
$Inv\_welfare_{it}$(100 million)	688.92	532.47	2594.50	17.58
$Debt\_interest_t$(%)	6.541	0.402	7.280	5.850
Inv_edu_{it}(100 million)	95.65	64.60	353.28	4.64
Inv_envir_{it}(100 million)	524.57	417.22	2005.94	8.45
Inv_cul_{it}(100 million)	68.70	77.08	560.31	1.02
R_{it}(100 million)	1264.7	1205.2	7081.5	33.8
E_{it}(100 million)	2468.0	1777.3	12415.2	151.2

Variable definitions

y_{it}—the volume of urban investment bonds in province i in year t; sourced from WIND

D_{ij}—the spherical distance between capital cities in province i and j ($i \neq j$); sourced from Google Map

GR_{ijt}—the transaction of goods between province i and j through railway in year t; sourced from China Transportation Yearbooks (2005–2013)

(*continued*)

Table 2.1 (continued)

TR_{ijt}—total transaction of goods between province i and j through railway, waterway, and road in year t (2005–2013); sourced from China Transportation Yearbooks and China Statistical Yearbooks (2005–2013)
$Rail_{it}$—railway distance between capital cities of province i and j; sourced from Xu and Wang (2013)
fis_gap_{it}—the difference of province i's government expenditure and revenue in year t; sourced from WIND and calculated by authors
fdi_{it}—foreign direct investment of province i in year t; sourced from WIND
GDP_{it}—GDP of province i in year t, sourced from WIND and calculated using expenditure approach
$Wy_{it}\_railway$—the spatial lag of y_{it} with weight matrix constructed using the railway distance
$Wy_{it}\_GDPrank$—the spatial lag of y_{it} with weight matrix constructed using GDP rank
Wy_{it}_trade—the spatial lag of y_{it} with weight matrix constructed using total goods transaction between province i and j through railway, waterway and road in year
$Inv\_housing_{it}$—fixed investment in real estate sector of province i in year t; sourced from WIND
$Inv\_welfare_{it}$—aggregate government spending in public education and health care of province i in year t; sourced from WIND
$Debt\_interest_t$—medium and long-term loan interest rates (3–5 years) in year t; sourced from WIND
Inv_edu_{it}—fixed investment in education of province i in year t; sourced from WIND
Inv_envir_{it}—fixed investment in environment of province i in year t; sourced from WIND
Inv_cul_{it}—fixed investment in culture industry of province i in year t; sourced from WIND
R_{it}—Fiscal revenue of province i in year t; sourced from WIND
E_{it}—Fiscal expenditure of province i in year t; sourced from WIND

2.6 Main Results

2.6.1 *Moran's I Statistics*

We use the Moran's I statistics to show that adjacent provinces may have similar behaviors on bond issuing. The index is shown as:

$$I = \frac{\sum_{i=1}^{n}\sum_{j\neq i}^{n} w_{ij}\left(x_i - \bar{x}\right)\left(x_j - \bar{x}\right)}{s^2\sum_{i=1}^{n}\sum_{j=1}^{n} w_{ij}}, s^2 = \frac{1}{n}\sum_{i}\left(x_i - \bar{x}\right)^2$$

where n is the number of regions of interest, and w_{ij} is the spatial weight (when region i and region j are adjacent to each other, $w_{ij} = 1$; otherwise, $w_{ij} = 0$). We generalize the weights to include economic indicator weighted matrixes considering inter-region trade flow, railway mileage, and GDP rankings. The value of I is between −1 and 1. When I is greater than 0, it indicates that regions with similar values are close to each other. Therefore, we can use the Moran's I statistic to have a preliminary test on whether the issuance of bonds among 30 provinces in China has spatial spillover effect. A large value indicates that adjacent provinces are competing with (or imitating) each other on issuing UIBs. Furthermore, we can use the bootstrap method to conduct a hypothesis test where the null hypothesis is the Moran's I statistic is equal to zero. The results are presented in Fig. 2.5.

Figure 2.5 shows the Moran's I statistics of issuance volume of the UIB from 2005 to 2013 for all provinces. All figures are positive at 5% significance level, which strongly indicates that neighboring provinces have issued similar size of bonds every year. However, this does not necessarily suggest that a province competes with its neighbors in issuing UIB as it is also possible that neighboring provinces have similar factors determining the UIB issuance. To exclude the second possibility, we estimate the generalized spatial autoregression model and check the multi-collinearity of explanatory variables. Specifically, a significant positive coefficient of the spatial lag term and low multi-collinearity of the modeled variables can prove that these significant positive Moran's I statistics are caused by the underlying fact that provinces are competing with or imitating each other in issuing UIB.

2.6.2 Main Results Based on the Rook Contiguity Weight Matrix

In this subsection, we construct the weight matrix W_{ij} based on the rook contiguity rule, namely, w_{ij} equals to 1 when province i and province j are contiguous; otherwise, w_{ij} equals to 0. Then the matrix is standardized to ensure the sum of every row is 1 (see Appendix).

Table 2.2 shows the regression results based on the rook contiguity weighting matrix. As the bsktest suggests, all six models apply random effect specifications, which means that the spatial correlation cannot be ignored in each of the six models. This conclusion coincides with the Moran's I statistics. Second, all the kappa values are smaller than 100, which implies very limited collinearity. The Ljung-Box test results, however, illustrate that only models (4), (5), and (6) have normally and independently distributed residuals, which satisfy the assumption of the generalized spatial autoregression model regression. In other words, these three models fit the data more adequately than the other three models. As these models show, the coefficient of the spatial lag term is significantly

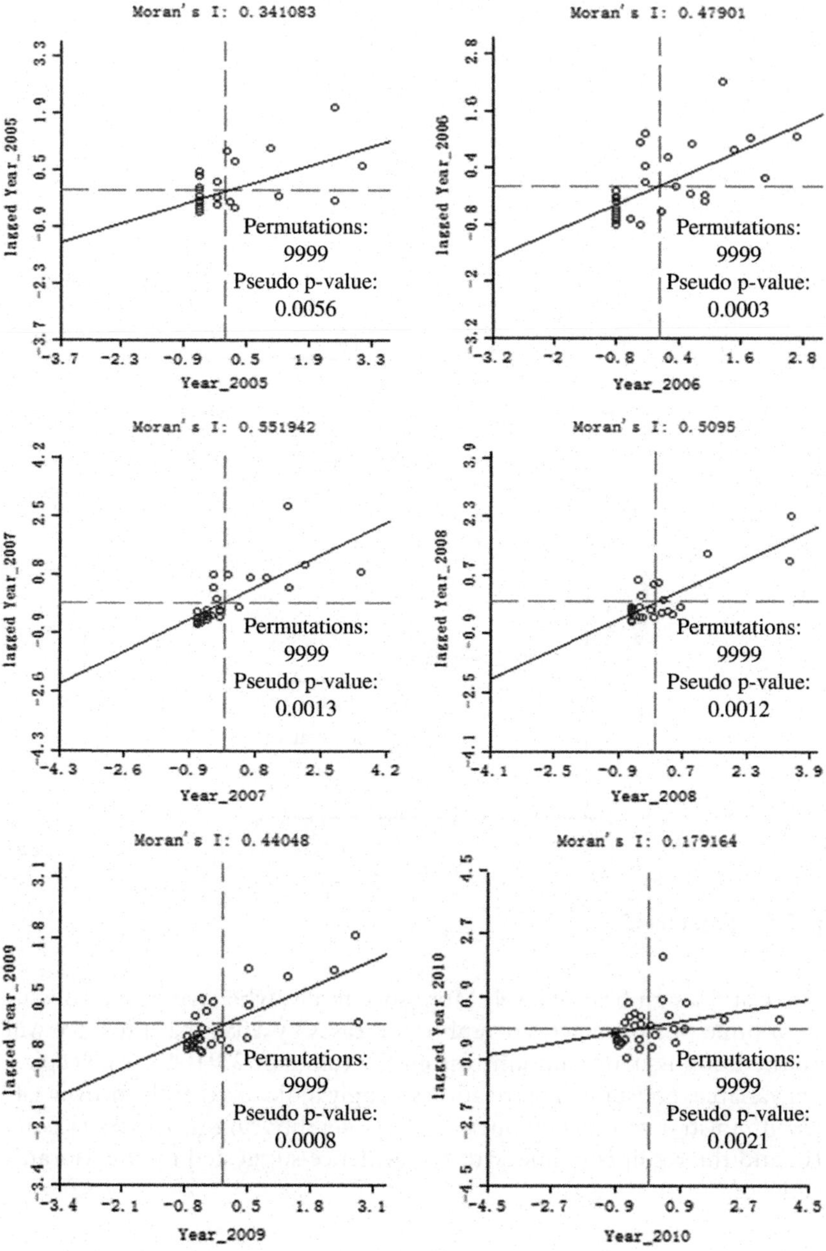

Fig. 2.5 Moran's I statistics (2005–2013)

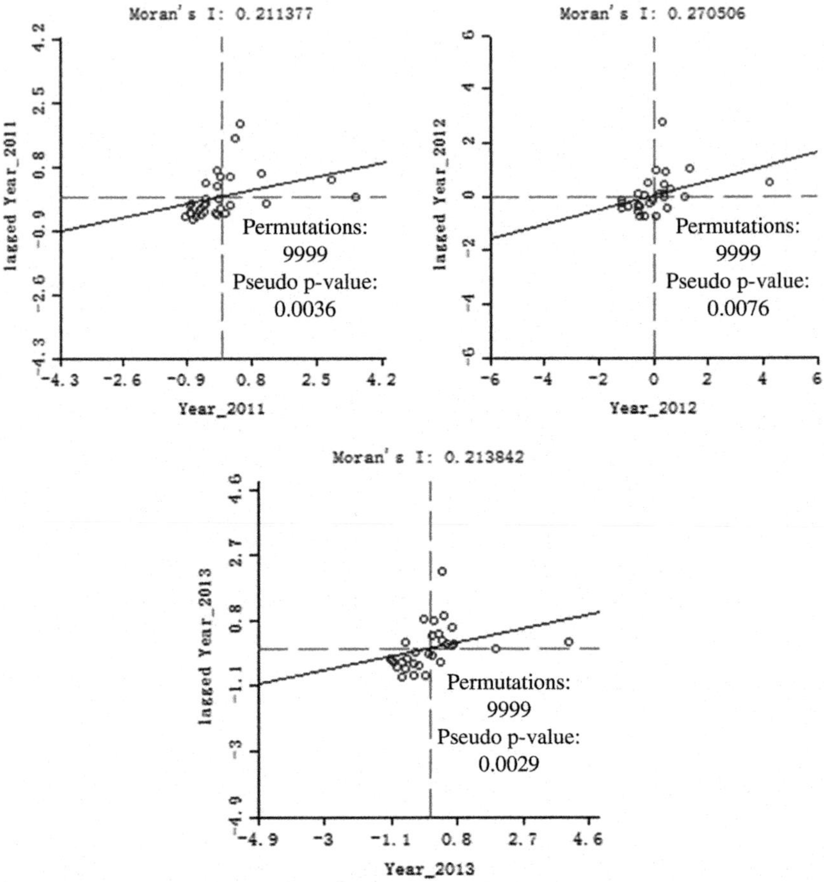

Fig. 2.5 (continued)

positive at 5% significance level. More specifically, whenever the UIB issuance volume of a province's neighbor increases by 10%, that province will raise the bond issuance amount within the range of 2.91–4.76%, keeping other variables constant. This relation strongly indicates that the provincial-level administrative units compete with its neighboring provinces to issue UIB, and the result is in line with the evidence suggested by the Moran's I statistics.

Table 2.2 Estimations based on rook contiguity weight matrix

Variable	*(1)*	*(2)*	*(3)*	*(4)*	*(5)*	*(6)*
Intercept	−6.829***	−6.225***	−5.503***	−3.935***	−3.676***	−2.499*
	(0.417)[a]	(0.425)	(0.677)	(0.809)	(0.842)	(0.057)
$W_{ij}y_{it}$	0.476***	0.512***	0.471***	0.291**	0.172(0.142)	0.133
	(0.057)	(0.059)	(0.066)	(0.101)		(0.122)
log(*Inv_housing*)	0.583**	0.575**	0.488***	0.552**	0.546**	0.738**
	(0.179)	(0.176)	(0.193)	(0.197)	(0.201)	(0.003)
log(*Inv_welfare*)	0.734***	0.802***	0.783***	0.607**	0.614**	0.731**
	(0.209)	(0.2145)	(0.219)	(0.228)	(0.231)	(0.255)
log(fis_gap)		0.165	0.183	0.317**	0.319**	0.331**
		(0.107)	(0.107)	(0.118)	(0.121)	(0.123)
log(UIB_1)			0.086*	0.143**	0.117*	0.118*
			(0.042)	(0.045)	(0.047)	(0.047)
year09[b]				0.617***	0.793***	0.798***
				(0.145)	(0.149)	(0.160)
year12[c]					0.438**	0.460**
					(0.139)	(0.144)
Log(GDP_1)						−0.346
						(0.285)
Bsktest	0	0	0.003	0.002	0.0001	0.0002
(*p* value)	Random	Random	Random	Random	Random	Random
Kappa value	22.1	34.9	43.7	49.9	56.8	79.0
Ljung-box	0	0	0	0.230	0.230	0.693
(*p* value)						
N	279	279	279	279	279	279

***, **, and * represent for 1%, 5% and 10% signifance levels, respectively

[a]Numbers in brackets are the standard errors of the coefficients

[b]Dummy variable which equals 0 before 2009 and 1 from 2009 to 2013

[c]Dummy variable which equals 0 before 2012 and 1 from 2012 to 2013

Note that the coefficients of the term log(*Inv_housing*) are all significant under 1% significant level. This suggests that when a province's investment in real estate sector rises by 10%, its UIB amount grows within the range of 5.83–7.38%. Similarly, coefficients of the term log(*Inv_welfare*) are also significantly positive under 1% significance level. As the statistics shows, the UIB volume of a province would increase within the range of 6.0–8.02% should its investment in public welfare including education, culture, and environment rise by 1%. We also find that widening fiscal gap is a major element inducing the provincial government to increase its debt level. Specifically, a 10% increase in a province's fiscal gap (government expenditure minus revenue) leads to a rise of its UIB amount within the range from 3.17% to 3.31%. The issuance of UIB is also path dependent.

Furthermore, both policy dummies are significantly positive. The *year09* coefficent is positive at 1% significance level and indicates that the central government's implicit support to issue UIB leads to a rise of UIB by 0.617–0.798%, keeping other variables constant. In comparison, the policy in 2012 is less influential as it increases a province's UIB amount by 0.428–0.46%. Contrary to the hypothesis that provinces with higher GDP level in a certain year tend to issue more bonds in the following year, regression results imply that the coefficient of log(GDP_1) is insignificant.

2.6.3 Robustness Check

In this subsection, we conduct similar estimations using the other three weighting matrices, railway mileage, GDP rank, and trade flows, keeping other variables unchanged. We first calculate the Moran's I statistics and present them in Fig. 2.6 and Table 2.3, respectively. We present the estimations results using each of the three weighting matrices in Table 2.4.

Figure 2.6 provides information about the trend of Moran's I statistics using different weighting matrices. In Table 2.3, we provide values and significance levels for Moran's I statistics under four weight matrixes. Apart from the Moran's I statistics based on trade flows among provinces, which are insignificant at 10% significance level, other statistics are all significantly positive at least at 5% significance level. This indicates that the UIB amount of a province is positively related to the UIB issuance volume of its neighbors, who are close to it in railway distance or in economic performance. Among these three significant link channels, a province's UIB amount is mostly affected by its neighbors with higher GDP. Before 2009, the rook contiguity was the dominant

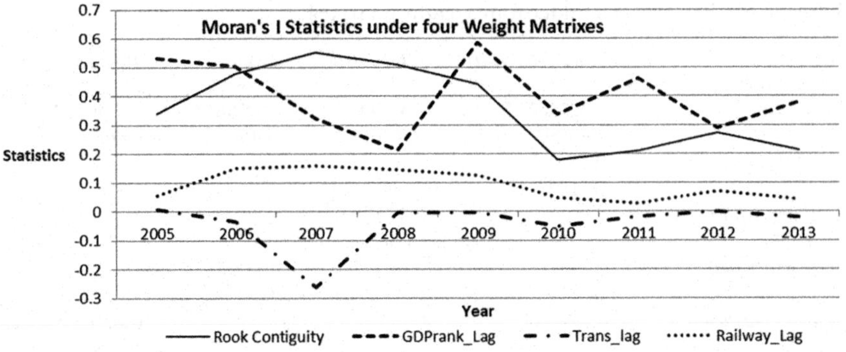

Fig. 2.6 Moran's I statistics under four weight matrixes

Table 2.3 Moran's I statistics under four weight matrixes

Year	*Rook contiguity*	*GDP rank*	*Trade*	*Railway*
2005	0.341**	0.532**	0.006	0.054*
2006	0.479***	0.503**	−0.036	0.150***
2007	0.552***	0.324*	−0.262	0.160***
2008	0.510***	0.212**	−0.004	0.145***
2009	0.440***	0.586***	−0.040	0.125***
2010	0.180**	0.338**	−0.051	0.048*
2011	0.211**	0.460***	−0.017	0.028*
2012	0.271**	0.288**	−0.001	0.068**
2013	0.213**	0.378***	−0.021	0.042*

***, **, and * represent for 1%, 5% and 10% signifance levels, respectively

linking channel. Provincial-level governments tried to keep its UIB issuance in line with those of its neighbors. The GDP ranking effect was at the second place, suggesting a province also tried to keep its UIB amount at comparable levels with those of the two provinces, which were just in front of it in GDP in the previous year. Therefore, it reveals that local governments treat UIB as an effective tool in the GDP-oriented yardstick competition. From 2009 onward, however, this trend has reversed as the GDP rank effect has become more significant than the rook contiguity effect throughout this period.

At the same time, the Moran's I statistics using the railway distance-based weighting matrix has been fluctuating around 0.1, suggesting provincial governments also paid marginal attention to the bond issuance of

Table 2.4 Estimations under four weight matrixes

Variable	*Rook contiguity*	*GDP rank*	*Trade*	*Railway*
Intercept	−3.935***	−3.394***	−8.488***	−7.306***
	(0.809)	(0.888)	(1.050)	(0.683)
Log(*Wy_rook*)	0.291**			
	(0.101)			
log(*Wy_GDPrank*)		0.411***		
		(0.068)		
log(*Wy_trade*)			−0.095	
			(0.113)	
log(*Wy_railway*)				0.659***
				(0.084)
log(*Inv_housing*)	0.552**		0.688*	0.590**
	(0.197)		(0.272)	(0.215)
log(*Inv_welfare*)	0.607**		0.715**	0.596*
	(0.228)		(0.245)	(0.242)
log(UIB_1)	0.143**	0.238***		
	(0.045)	(0.054)		
year09	0.617***			
	(0.145)			
log(Fis_gap)	0.317**	0.687***		
	(0.118)	(0.159)		
Random/fixed effect	Random	Fixed	Fixed	Random
Kappa value	49.9	4.26	38.3	37.4
Adjust R^2	0.743	0.693	0.689	0.6804
N	279	279	279	279

***, **, and * represent for 1%, 5% and 10% signifance levels, respectively

provinces, which are close to them in terms of railway mileages although the majority of these provinces did not share borders with them. In contrast, the trade flow effect was ignorable during this period as the corresponding Moran's I statistics were just below 0 and were all insignificant at 10% significance level, suggesting that one province's influence on another province of UIB issuance is not related to its trade connection with that province.

Table 2.4 reports estimations using four different weighting matrices. Coefficients that are insignificant at 5% significance level are omitted. It can be seen that the UIB issuance connection based on trade flows is weak as the coefficient of the spatial lag term log(*Wy_trade*) is very small (−0.095), and it is not significant at 10% significance level. This is in line with the corresponding Moran's I statistics. Other three coefficients of the spatial lag terms are highly significant. Model (1) has the highest adjust R^2 using the contiguity weight matrix. Further, coefficients of log(*Inv_housing*) and log(*Inv_welfare*) are positive, confirming that investments in the real estate sector, healthcare, culture, education, and environmental areas play important roles in shaping the volumes of UIBs. Results also show that the coefficients of year12 and log(*GDP_1*) are insignificant at all specifications and not reported. This indicates that the central government's policy in 2012 to encourage local government to expand expenditure had little effect to increase the UIB level.

2.7 Conclusion

This chapter analyzes the determinants of UIBs among provincial-level governments in China, with a focus on the spatial spillover effect. Panel data covering 31 provinces are used during the period of 2005 to 2013. Results indicate a high degree of inter-provincial interaction in UIB issuance, which is supported by the Moran's I statistics and the significantly positive coefficients of the spatial lag terms in the empirical analyses. First, a province competes with its close neighbors sharing the same border to issue UIB. For example, a province raises the UIB amount by 1.72–4.76% when neighbors' bond issuance rises by 10%. Second, a province's UIB issuance is also affected by those provinces with higher GDP in the previous year. A province may raise its UIB amount by 4.11% when its GDP competitors increase bond issuance by 10%. Third, a province also tries to keep its UIB issuance volume in line with provinces, which are geographically close to it in terms of railway distance. This effect, however, is only marginal compared with the contiguity and GDP rank effect.

We also find that the fiscal gap, government investment in construction and public welfare, UIB issuance volume in the previous year, and the central government's supporting policy in 2009 significantly contributed to the increase of bonds issuance. In particular, coefficients of the government investment in housing and welfare are significantly positive under three weighting matrices. However, the central government's policy in 2012 that encourages the local government to increase spending has little effect on boosting the UIB level. Furthermore, a province's UIB level does not significantly relate to its outputs, implying economic growth are not constraints to the issuance of UIBs.

This chapter sheds light on explaining the competitive behavior in bond issuance for provincial-level governments, though it has a few limitations. For example, dynamic weighting matrixes based on annual GDP rank and trade flows among provinces can suffer from endogenous problems. We address the problem by controlling the kappa value under 100 and excluding variables, which may be economically endogenous. Future research may consider using more sophisticated estimation methods, such as GMM to tackle endogeneity. It is also worthwhile to explore alternative strategic factors, which influence bonds issuance.

Appendix

Weight Matrix Using GDP Ranking

To get the weighting matrix based on GDP ranking of a certain year, we first sort the 31 provinces by their GDP scales. Then we assign the two provinces, which are immediately above a certain province in GDP ranking with value 1, otherwise 0.[6] Specifically, each one of the four municipalities (Beijing, Tianjin, Shanghai, and Chongqing) is compared with their three counterparts separately, and the same principle applies to other

	Beijing	Tianjin	Hebei	Shanxi	Innermongolia	Liaoning	Jilin	Heilongjiang	Shanghai	Jiangsu	......	Xinjiang
Beijing	0	0	0	0	0	0	0	0	1	0	......	0
Tianjin	1	0	0	0	0	0	0	0	1	0	......	0
Hebei	0	0	0	0	0	0	0	0	0	0	......	0
Shanxi	0	0	0	0	0	0	0	1	0	0	......	0
InnerMongolia	0	0	0	0	0	0	0	0	0	0	......	0
Liaoning	0	0	1	0	0	0	0	0	0	0	......	0
Jilin	0	0	0	0	1	0	0	0	0	0	......	0
Heilongjiang	0	0	0	0	0	0	0	0	0	0	......	0
Shanghai	1	0	0	0	0	0	0	0	0	0	......	0
Jiangsu	0	0	0	0	0	0	0	0	0	0	......	0
⋮	⋮	⋮	⋮	⋮	⋮	⋮	⋮	⋮	⋮	⋮	⋱	⋮
Xinjiang	0	0	0	0	1	0	1	0	0	0	......	0

Matrix 1 Rank matrix in 2004

27 provincial administrative units. In this way, we get the first matrix. Matrix 1 is an example, which shows the initial GDP ranking matrix in 2004. For example, in 2004, the two provinces that were immediately beyond Tianjin in terms of GDP were Beijing and Shanghai. Therefore, the first element of the second row and the ninth element in the same row are assigned 1, with others being 0.

After obtaining the initial matrixes, we can standardize them to weight matrixes whose sum of row elements is equal to 1. To do this, we first calculate the sum of elements in each row, and then divide each element with the corresponding row sum.

Weight Matrix Using Trade Flow

The *Wy_trade* is the weighted average of UIB amount based on the annual inter-provincial trade flows in every year. As data on trade flows is not

	Beijing	Tianjin	Hebei	Shanxi	InnerMongolia	Liaoning	Jilin	Heilongjiang	Shanghai	Jiangsu	......	Xinjiang
Beijing	0	0	0	0	0	0	0	0	0.5	0	......	0
Tianjin	0.5	0	0	0	0	0	0	0	0.5	0	......	0
Hebei	0	0	0	0	0	0	0	0	0	0	......	0
Shanxi	0	0	0	0	0	0	0	0.5	0	0	......	0
InnerMongolia	0	0	0	0	0	0	0	0	0	0	......	0
Liaoning	0	0	0.5	0	0	0	0	0	0	0	......	0
Jilin	0	0	0	0	0.5	0	0	0	0	0	......	0
Heilongjiang	0	0	0	0	0	0	0	0	0	0	......	0
Shanghai	0.5	0	0	0	0	0	0	0	0	0	......	0
Jiangsu	0	0	0	0	0	0	0	0	0	0	......	0
⋮	⋮	⋮	⋮	⋮	⋮	⋮	⋮	⋮	⋮	⋮	⋱	⋮
Xinjiang	0	0	0	0	1	0	1	0	0	0	......	0

Matrix 2 Weight matrix based on GDP rank in 2004 with row standardization

available from official records and the only data on the goods transportation through waterway, roadway, and railway is available, we calculate the trade flows through the following steps. We firstly define that:

$Trade\_flow_{ijt}$ = The trade flow between Province i and Province j in year t
= Goods transportation through railway, waterway and road between Province i and Province j in year t;
$Trans\_rail_{it}$ = The goods transportation through railway of province i in year t;
$Trans\_water_{it}$ = The goods transportation through waterway of province i in year t;
$Trans\_road_{it}$ = The goods transportation through road of province i in year t.

With assumption as:

$$\frac{Trade\_rail_{ijt}}{Trans\_rail_{it}} = \frac{Trade\_flow_{ijt}}{Trans\_rail_{it} + Trans\_water_{it} + Trans\_road_{it}}.$$

Therefore, we get:

$$Trade\_flow_{ijt} = \frac{Trade\_rail_{ijt} \times \begin{pmatrix} Trans\_rail_{it} + Trans\_water_{it} \\ + Trans\_road_{it} \end{pmatrix}}{Trans\_rail_{it}}$$

Therefore, we can get the trade flow matrix of every year. Then we standardize the trade flow based weight matrix of every year. By multiplying the weight matrix with the corresponding UIB amount in that year, we can finally get the weighted average of UIB amount.

Weight Matrix Using Railway Mileage

The calculation of weighted average of UIB amount is basically the same as the above two except a significant difference is that the weight matrix is static. We adopt the railway distance between capital cities in province i and province j to construct the weight.

Notes

1. The Chinese government comprises the central government and local governments. Local governments govern at four levels: provinces, prefecture-cities, counties, towns, and villages.

2. For simplicity, in this chapter, we use UIB to denote the Urban Investment Bond.
3. Financing vehicle companies are always known as the "Urban Construction Investment Companies" (*chengtou gongsi*) in China (Feng 2013).
4. It is nearly impossible to get to know the exact volume of the bank loans received by the financing vehicle company due to the opacity of the borrowing behavior of local government.
5. These 31 provincial-level administrative units include: the 22 (I counted only 20, is it supposed to be 20?) provinces (Hebei, Shanxi, Liaoning, Jilin, Heilongjiang, Jiangsu, Zhejiang, Anhui, Fujian, Jiangxi, Shandong, Henan, Hubei, Hunan, Guangdong, Hainan, Sichuan, Yunnan, Shaanxi, Gansu), the five autonomous rejoins or zizhiqu (Guangxi, Inner Mongolia, Ningxia, Tibet, Xinjiang Uyghur) and the four municipalities or zhixiashi (Beijing, Tianjin, Shanghai, Chongqing). For simplicity reasons, we call provincial-level administrative units as "provinces" in this chapter.
6. For the province which has the largest GDP among the 31 units, we assign 1 to the province, which is just below it in terms of ranking. Additionally, for the province which is ranked the second place in the GDP scale, we assign 1 only to the province holding the greatest GDP.

References

Anselin, L., (1988), "Lagrange multiplier test diagnostics for spatial dependence and spatial heterogeneity", *Geographical Analysis*: 20(1), 1–17.

Ba, S. S., (2009), "The assessment of risk of the local government financing vehicles", *The Southwest Finance*: 9 (in Chinese).

Baltagi, B. H., Song, S. H. and Koh, W., (2003), "Testing panel data regression models with spatial error correlation", *Journal of Econometrics*: 117, 123–150.

Cao, D. W., (2011), "Analysis and consideration on local government financing platform for corporate financing", *Commercial Research*: 408, 100–104 (in Chinese).

Feng, X. Y., (2013), "Local government debt and municipal bonds in China: Problems and a framework of rules", *The Copenhagen Journal of Asian Studies*: 31(2), 23–53.

Gong, Q., Wang, J. and Jia, K., (2011), "Local government debts from the perspective of fiscal decentralization", *Economy Research*: 7 (in Chinese).

Gu, X. J. and Li, W. Q., (2013), "Development of the local government financing vehicles with urbanization", *Academic Journal of Zhongzhou*: 10, 39–42 (in Chinese).

Harry H. K., Gianfranco P., (2014), "Estimation of spatial models with endogenous weighting matrices, and an application to a demand model for cigarettes", *Regional Science and Urban Economics*: 46, 140–149.

He, Y. and Man, Y. Y., (2012), "Risk control of local debt financing–An analysis from the land public finance perspective", *Finance & Trade Economics*: 5, 45–50 (in Chinese).

Lei, C. Y., (2011a), "Agency cost, externality and the over-borrowing of the local government financing vehicle companies in China", *The Macroeconomics Study*: 10, 15–39 (in Chinese).

Lei, C. Y., (2011b), "The causes of the increase of the Chinese local government debt: Institutional explanation framework", *Economy Research and Review*: 38, 23–32 (in Chinese).

Li, X., Hong, G. Z. and Huang, L. X., (2013), "The mystery of land finance growth in China: tax-sharing reform, strategic interaction of land finance", *China Economic Quarterly*: 12 (4), 1141–1160 (in Chinese).

Liu, H., Zhang, Y. Y. and Liu, H. W., (2013), "Analysis of debt characteristics and risks of local government financing platforms: A case study of a province in East China". *Journal of Finance and Economics*: 39 (5), 123–133.

Miao, X. L., Yang, Y. Q. and Shi, Y. P., (2013), "The motivation of local government debt increase: From budget expenditure to economic growth expectation", *Journal of the Yunnan University of Finance and Economics*: 1, 84–91 (in Chinese).

Mou, L. T. and Fu, C., (2013), "The path dependency of the development of the local government debt risk–based on the Cobb-Douglas model", *The Finance and Accounting Monthly*: 2, 11–14 (in Chinese).

National Audit Office of the People's Republic of China, (2011), "The audit result of the local government debt", available at http://www.audit.gov.cn/n1992130/n1992150/n1992500/2752208.html

Performance Report of National Audit Office of the People's Republic of China, (2011), National Audit Office of China. http://www.audit.gov.cn/en/n746/n752/n768/c66722/content.html

Qu, X, and Lee, L., (2015), "Estimating a spatial autoregressive model with an endogenous spatial weight matrix", *Journal of Econometrics*: 184, 209–232.

Shao, Y. J., (2013), "Analysis and study on the situation of Chinese Urban Investment Bond", *West Financial*: 12, 11–16 (in Chinese).

Sheng, T. Y., Feng, D. T. and Sun, T. S., (2010), Spatial Econometrics. Beijing: Peking University Press (in Chinese).

Tang, Y. J., (2011), "Fiscal decentralization and the development of local government financing vehicles: Foreign pattern and Chinese model", *Shanghai Finance*: 3 (in Chinese).

Tu, Y. Y., (2010), "The history and risk control of the Urban Investment Bond", *Chinese Finance*: 7, 45–47 (in Chinese).

Wang, S. C. and Li, Y. J., (2013), "Cause analysis and recommendations on local government debts based on the audit results", *Audit Study*: 5, 40–45 (in Chinese).

Xu, G. and Wang, Y. W., (2013), "Although tough, the road should go on–An in-depth study on Urban Investment Bond", *Finance Development Review*: 3, 70–97 (in Chinese).

Yang, W. and Huang, T. T., (2010), "The risk analysis of the Chinese local government financing vehicles", *Chinese Finance*: 6 (in Chinese).

Zhu, Z. Y. and Gao, Y. Z., (2010), "The fiscal pressure and the official performance: A through study on the local government debt", *Reform*: 12 (in Chinese).

PART II

Real Estate Sector

CHAPTER 3

China's Housing Price: Where Are the Bubbles?

Xiaocong Zhang and Juann H. Hung

3.1 Introduction

China's housing price has been rising in a seemingly explosive fashion in its major cities since the late 1990s. The aggregate housing price/disposable income ratio in China has stayed at or above an elevated level of 7 since 2004 (Fig. 3.1).[1] In coastal cities like Wenzhou, Sanya, Beijing, and Shenzhen, that ratio rose above 10 after 2009 (Wang et al. 2013). In comparison, that ratio did not go beyond 6 in the UK, the US, Australia, Canada, and Ireland at the peak of their housing prices during 2007–2008, before the housing bubbles burst in those countries and ushered in a serious recession.

Many observers have argued that China's housing prices in many of its major cities are bubbles. By default, all bubbles will burst sooner or later. If China has housing bubbles, it would be reasonable to expect that they would burst at some point down the road as well, with likely grave economic and political consequences. If housing prices in those Chinese cities are indeed bubbles, how long are they likely to last before they burst?

X. Zhang • J. H. Hung (✉)
International Business School Suzhou, Xi'an Jiaotong-Liverpool University, Suzhou, China
e-mail: Juann.Hung@xjtlu.edu.cn

J. H. Hung, Y. Chen (eds.), *The State of China's State Capitalism*,
https://doi.org/10.1007/978-981-13-0983-0_3

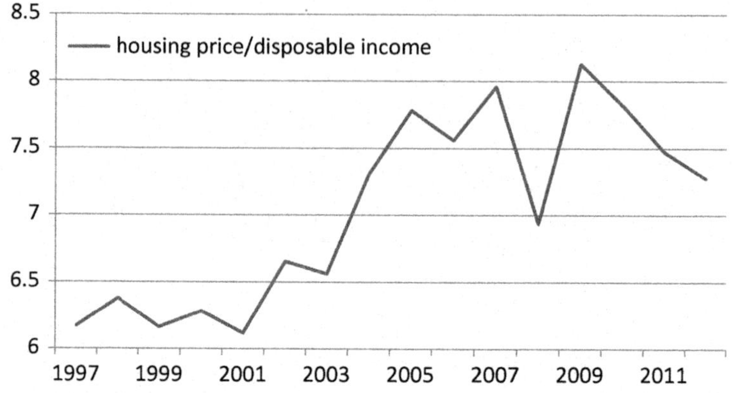

Fig. 3.1 Housing price/disposable income. Data from CEIC and processed by authors

Will they burst in a similar fashion as previous housing bubbles in other countries? Or can they be sustained at their current level, waiting for economic fundamental variables to catch up, due to unique Chinese characteristics?

To be sure, the most convincing evidence of a financial bubble is the burst of that bubble. The problem with such an *ex post* "method" of detecting a bubble is that it is useless in terms of warning the government into action to avoid/minimize the potentially hefty cost of the burst of a bubble. It would be much more helpful to detect a bubble *ex ante*, so policymakers may be able to implement policies to avoid the catastrophe of an economic "hard landing" associated with the burst of a bubble.

The purpose of this chapter is thus twofold. First, it aims to date the timeline of housing bubbles in China's provinces and major cities by the Generalized Sup-ADF Test (GSADF) test and price-to-rent analysis methods. Second, it aims to assess whether it is likely that these housing bubbles will not burst in a catastrophic pattern because of special Chinese factors. To the extent of our knowledge, no other papers have adopted the GSADF method to study China's housing prices at the provincial level.

3.2 Methods of Detecting Housing Price Bubbles in the Literature

There are various methods of detecting housing bubbles in the literature. For example, Malpezzi (1999) maintained that a sustained excess of a housing price/income ratio over its long-run equilibrium level would signal a housing price bubble. Poterba et al. (1991) pointed out that a sustained excess of the return on housing assets over the cost of holding them would signal a housing price bubble, since in the long-run no-arbitrage equilibrium, the return on housing investments (including rent and capital gain) should equal the total cost of holding those assets. In equilibrium, the house price is equal to the present value of future house price and rent incomes, expressed as follows:

$$P_t = \frac{E(P_{t+1}|I_t) + R_t}{1+r} \tag{3.1}$$

Rearranging the above expression, we obtain,

$$\frac{R_t}{P_t} = r - \frac{E(p_{t+1}|I_t) - p_t}{p_t}$$
$$= \text{Required rate of return} - \text{Expected rate of capital gain}$$

Or,

$$\frac{R_t}{P_t} + \text{Expected rate of capital gain} = \text{Required rate of return} \tag{3.2}$$
$$= \text{Rate of user cost}$$

Where P_t is housing price at time t, r is the required return rate, and R_t is rent income in period t. From the above expression, it is clear that that an excessively high price-to-rent ratio over a sustained period signals the existence of a housing bubble.

In addition to the above methods based on measuring the degree of deviation from the long-run equilibrium, many economists have also used the right-tail unit root test to detect asset price bubbles.[2] This latter approach is an extension of the rational bubble theory, which decomposes asset prices into the fundamental component (which follows a random walk process) and the bubble component (which is explosive). This concept can be illustrated as follows[3]:

The log of expected return in the next period (r_{t+1}) is the difference between the log of next period's price and the current dividend [$\ln(P_{t+1} + D_t)$] and the log of current price [$\ln(P_t)$], as follows:

$$r_{t+1} = \ln\left(P_{t+1} + D_t\right) - \ln\left(P_t\right) \tag{3.3}$$

By the first-order Taylor expansion, the first term is expressed as the weighted average of $\ln(P_{t+1})$ and $\ln(D_t)$:

$$\begin{aligned} r_{t+1} &= \mu + \theta \ln\left(P_{t+1}\right) + \left(1-\theta\right)\ln\left(D_t\right) - \ln\left(P_t\right) \\ &= \mu + \theta p_{t+1} + \left(1-\theta\right)d_t - p_t \end{aligned}$$

where

$$p_t = \ln\left(P_t\right) \text{ and } d_t = \ln\left(D_t\right)$$

$\theta = \dfrac{1}{1+e^{\ln\left(\overline{d/p}\right)}}$, with $\overline{(d/p)}$ being the long-term dividend-to-price ratio, which normally should be close to 1;

$$\mu = \left[-\ln(\theta) - (1-\theta)\ln\left(\frac{1}{\theta} - 1\right)\right]. \tag{3.4}$$

After rearrangement and continuing substitutions, we can obtain the following:

$$p_t - d_t = \lim_{i\to\infty}\left[\left(p_{t+i} - d_{t+i}\right)\theta^i\right] + \sum_{i=1}^{\infty}\left[\theta^i\left(\theta\Delta d_{t+i} - r_{t+i}\right)\right] + \frac{\mu}{1-\theta}, \tag{3.5}$$

where $\sum_{i=1}^{\infty}\left[\theta^i\left(\theta\Delta d_{t+i} - r_{t+i}\right)\right]$ refers to the accumulated effect of varying dividends and discount rates on the price-dividend rate, and $\dfrac{\mu}{1-\theta}$ is a constant. Since θ is less than 1, $\lim_{i\to\infty}[(p_{t+i} - d_{t+i})\theta^i]$ is discounted to 0.

It follows that we can express the fundamental components of the price-dividend ratio as:

$$(p_t - d_t)^f = \sum_{i=1}^{\infty}\left[\theta^i\left(\theta\Delta d_{t+i} - r_{t+i}\right)\right] + \frac{\mu}{1-\theta}. \tag{3.6}$$

However, an explosive component could exist in price p_{t+i}. Thus, the price-dividend ratio consists of a fundamental component and a bubble component as follows:

$$p_t - d_t = (p_t - d_t)^f + B^t \tag{3.7}$$

Where B^t is the explosive component at time t.

Evans (1991) pointed out that when testing periodically collapsing bubbles, a right-tail ADF test is prone to making a type II error by not rejecting the null hypothesis of no bubble. Phillips et al. (2011) thus proposed to use the sup ADF (SADF) test to improve upon the typical right-tail ADF test by repeating the ADF test in many rounds on recursive subsamples, arguing that the SADF test is more sensitive in detecting the transformation of a time series from a random walk to a nonlinear explosive process. Soon afterward, Phillips et al. (2012) proposed the GSADF to improve over the SADF test by allowing the flexible choice of subsample durations. That paper demonstrates that the moving-sample GSADF test outperforms the SADF test in detecting multiple bubble episodes and seldom gives false alarms, due to its ability to cover more subsamples of the data.

3.3 Research Method

We use the GSADF test to detect housing price bubbles in China's four municipality cities and 30 provinces (including autonomous regions). We then use the price-to-rent analysis to detect housing bubbles at the city level.

3.3.1 *The GSADF Method*

GSADF is an application of the right-tail ADF test used to test the explosive component in asset prices. A typical regression equation of the right-tail ADF test on a financial bubble is specified as follows:

$$y_t = \alpha * T^{-\sigma} + \beta_1 y_{t-1} + \sum_{i=1}^{k} \beta_i \Delta y_{t-i} + \varepsilon_t, \tag{3.8}$$

where α and σ are constants controlling the size of drift, and T is the entire period of the time series.

The null and alternative hypotheses are set as follows:

$$H_0 : \beta_1 = 1(\text{no bubble})$$
$$H_a : \beta_1 > 1(\text{bubble exists})$$

Based on the above framework, Phillips et al. (2011) proposed SADF to spot speculative bubbles as they emerge.

To detect periodically collapsing bubbles, Phillips and Yu (2011) further suggested using the supremum of recursively determined ADF t-statistics to identify the time when the bubble component becomes dominant in the price process. In other words, they proposed conducting the right-tail ADF test sequentially on rolling subsamples. In the first round, the test is simply the test on the asset price over the initial sample period, defined as the *initial window size* (w_1), where the subscript 1 denotes that it is the first round of the test. In the second round, the same test is applied over two subperiods: w_1 and w_2, where $w_2 = w_1 + 1$ period. In the third round, the test is applied over three subperiods: w_1, w_2, and w_3, where $w_3 = w_2 + 1 = w_1 + 2$. In the final round, the sample period is equal to the full sample size T. The SADF statistics in the i's round of the test is the maximum of the ADF in all the i tests conducted in that round.[4]

In the GSADF test, the GSADF statistic in each round is the highest ADF statistics emerging from all tests conducted in that round, with the last test ending on the date that gives the highest ADF statistics. For example, the GSADF statistic for date $w_1 + 2$ is the largest statistic among the three tests conducted in the third round—that is, the suprema of GSADF on w_1, $w_1 + 1$, and $w_1 + 2$ (see Fig. 3.2 for a graphical illustration).

The date on which the GSADF statistics begin to exceed the critical value is counted as the beginning of a bubble formation. After a bubble begins, the first date on which the GSADF statistics fall below the critical value is counted as the beginning of the bubble collapse. The rule can be formally defined as below:

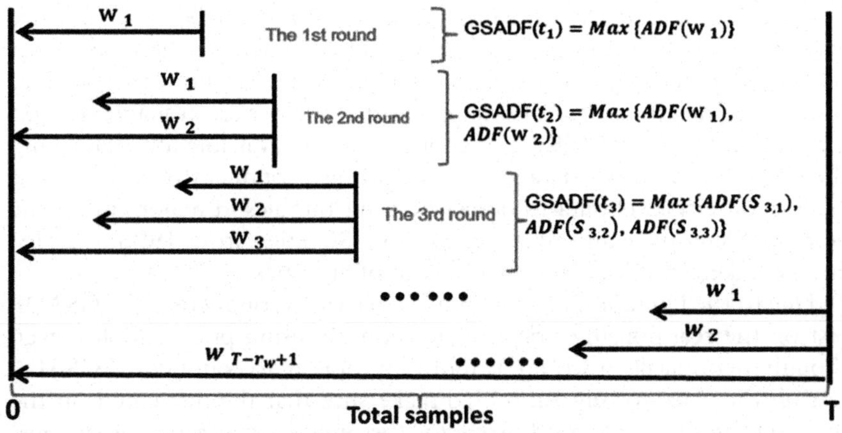

Fig. 3.2 Generalized sup ADF test

$$\hat{r}_{start} = \inf\left\{r : GSADF\left(r\right) > CV_{w_1}^{T}\left(r\right)\right\}$$

$$\hat{r}_{collapse} = \inf\left\{r : GSADF\left(r\right) < CV_{w_1}^{T}\left(r\right)\right\}$$

Where *CV* is critical value, which depends on the total sample size T and the initial window size w_1.

Phillips et al. (2012) reported that the GSADF test outperformed the SADF test in detecting multiple periodically collapsing bubbles with higher discriminative power.

3.3.1.1 *Data*

China is a large country, with vast differences in economic performances and housing prices among its provinces and major cities, making it easy for aggregate national data to mask housing bubbles in some localities. Thus, this chapter focuses on detecting housing price bubbles in some provinces or cities, although we also conduct the test on the national average of housing prices.

We conduct the GSADF test, both on the average national data and on each of China's 30 provinces (including four autonomous districts and four municipalities, which are provincial-level administrative divisions in China), by using monthly housing prices published by the National Bureau of Statistics. Admittedly, provincial data are not ideal because they are averages of different localities in the province, making it hard to detect housing bubbles that may exist only in some cities but not others in that province. Unfortunately, housing price data for cities are available only on a yearly basis and after 1992, not enough data are available for performing the GSADF test on city data. Therefore, we also conduct the price-to-rent analysis on city-level data to detect housing bubbles in major cities. The yearly housing price and rent data in those 30 cities, from 1993 to 2015, are also taken from the National Bureau of Statistics.

Due to the limitation of rent data, we resort to conducting the GSADF test on the real housing price for detecting housing price bubbles, even though theoretically it would be more appropriate to conduct the GSADF test on the price-to-rent ratio.[5] To make sure that the movement in the real housing price is a good proxy for the price-to-rent ratio for the purpose of bubble detection, we examined whether there is an explosive component in the city rent data themselves with the simple right-tail ADF test. Since residential rents have risen more rapidly in cities than at the provincial level, we can infer that there is no bubble in the provincial rent data if these cities' rent data do not have an explosive component. The results of the simple right-tail ADF test on city rent data indicate that no explosive autoregression in rent indices is detected, since all ADF statistics are much lower than critical values at 90% confidence level (Table 3.1).

3.3.1.2 Empirical Implementation Issues

In conducting the GSADF test, the choice of the initial window size faces tradeoffs: when the window size is too short, the subsample lengths will

Table 3.1 Right-tail ADF tests on rent index of major cities in China

City	*ADF-statistic*	*P-value*
Beijing	−1.188307	0.331
Shanghai	−0.803629	0.182
Chongqing	−1.183953	0.319
Tianjin	−2.310246	0.835
Hangzhou	−2.543885	0.889
Nanjing	−4.849967	0.999
Right-tailed test**	H0: Unite root Ha: Explosive process	

**Critical values are based on a Monte Carlo simulation

not be enough for conducting the test, while a window size too long will lose too much information about the beginning and end of a bubble. Following the rule of thumb suggested by Phillips et al. (2013), we set the initial window size (w_1) at 30 months, but we also conduct the test with initial window sizes of 20 and 40 months to check robustness.[6] Furthermore, to make sure outliers are not counted as price bubbles, we need to be sure that a "bubble-like" period (i.e., the period in which the GSADF statistics exceed the critical value) lasts long enough to be qualified as a bubble period. In this chapter, we set six months as the minimal threshold required for a bubble.

When we conduct simulations to find the critical values for GSADF statistics, the constant drift $\alpha^* T^{-\sigma}$ is set to equal T (i.e., both α and σ are set to unity), as recommended by Phillips et al. (2013) and Caspi (2013). Another issue for simulation is how many reiterations are appropriate to obtain an acceptably precise critical value. Phillips et al. (2012) set it to be 5000 times, while their later paper (2013) set it at 10,000 times. In this paper, we also choose 10,000 replications, mainly because our experiments also indicate that the critical values are rather stable after repeating 10,000 times.[7] (see Appendix 1 for more detail.)

Finally, we need to decide the number of lags for the Δy_{t-i} term of the empirical regression. Based on information criterions, both Diesteldorf et al. (2016) and Pavlidis et al. (2013) chose four lags for their studies. However, Phillips et al. (2013) found that adding more lags led to the distortion of statistics and critical values in recursive Dickey-Fuller tests such as GSADF and SADF tests, especially when small samples are used. In our experience, for this chapter, we found that the GSADF statistics became more unstable and demonstrated an upward shift when we added more lags. Thus, we set the number of lags to zero in this chapter.

3.3.1.3 *Empirical Results*

On the average national housing price, the results of the GSADF test indicate that we cannot reject the "no bubble" hypothesis at the 5% significant level at any time during the 1998–2016 period (Table 3.2). (For a graphical presentation of the GSADF results, please see Appendix 2.) This should not come as a surprise, since it is easy for the national average to mask bubbles in some provinces or cities.

Figure 3.3 shows the number of provinces for which a housing price bubble can be detected at the 5% significance levels, under the initial window size of 30 months, in different "dates" from 2000 to 2016.[8] To avoid

Table 3.2 GSADF test on nationwide housing price

Confidence level (%)	*Bubbles detected (window size = 20 months)*	*Bubbles detected (window size = 30 months)*	*Bubbles detected (window size = 40 months)*
90	2	3	4
95	0	0	0
99	0	0	0

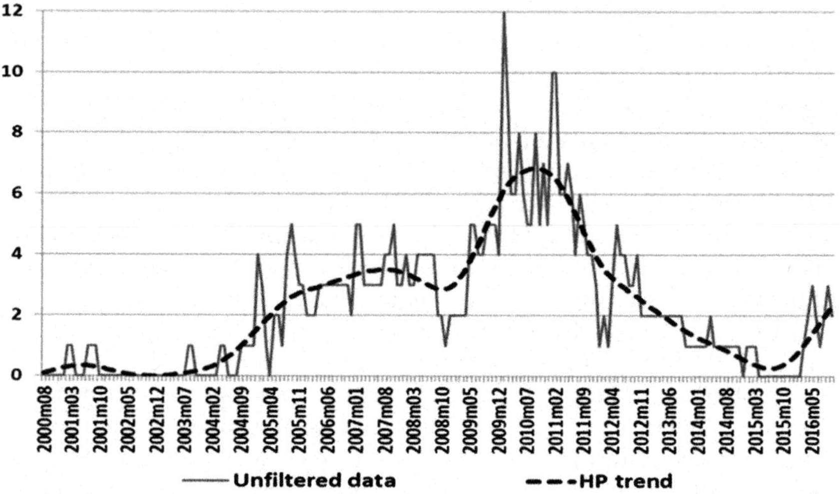

Fig. 3.3 Number of bubble provinces in China. (Detected by GSADF test at 5% significance level)

counting outliers as bubbles, we also show the number smoothed by the Hodrick–Prescott filter (HP). The HP-filtered number of bubble provinces was between 6 and 7 from 2010 M1 to 2011 M4, indicating that more than six provinces on average had housing bubbles in that period, at the 5% significance level.

We can roughly divide the evolution in housing bubbles into five periods:

1. The dormant period of 2000–2004, a period when the number of bubble provinces began at zero in 2000 and stayed below 2 until 2004.

2. The warming up period of 2004–2007, a period when the number of bubble provinces hovered around 4.
3. The retreating period of 2008–2009H1, a period when the number of bubble provinces dropped to below 2 in 2008H2 and 2009H1, following several regulations enacted to dampen the housing market.[9]
4. The bubble-forming period of 2009H2–2010, a period in which the huge stimulus package enacted in 2008 (to counter the contractionary effect of the global financial crisis of 2008–2009) started to have a powerful impact on heating up the housing market. The number of bubble provinces peaked in 2010 and stayed at an elevated level at around 6 until 2012.
5. The moderating period of 2012–2015, a period in which the number of bubble provinces steadily climbed down until 2015 when it began to rise again in 2016.

Where were those housing bubbles most concentrated? Figure 3.4 indicates that the majority of those housing bubbles occurred in the four municipalities (i.e., Beijing, Chongqing, Shanghai, and Tianjin), followed by south-east coastal provinces (i.e., Hebei, Shandong, Jiangsu, Zhejiang, Fujian, Guangdong, Hainan, and Guangxi), but with somewhat different timing profiles.

The most serious overpricing occurred during 2009–2011, when housing bubbles were detected in 3.08 out of four municipalities, and 2.25 out of seven south-east coastal provinces, on average. However, at the peak during 2009–2011, there is hardly any evidence of housing bubbles among either the three north-east provinces or the 15 inland provinces.[10] To gain a perspective on the relative severity of bubbles at the provincial level, we use the Borda method to rank these provinces after removing outliers.[11] The method sets five episodes as the threshold level and assigns points to each province depending on the number of bubble episodes it has experienced during our sample period:

- 1 point is assigned to a province that has not experienced more than five episodes of bubbles,
- 2 points are assigned to a province that has experienced more than five episodes but less than the national average (i.e., the average number of episodes/province),
- 3 points are assigned to a province that has experienced more episodes than the national average.

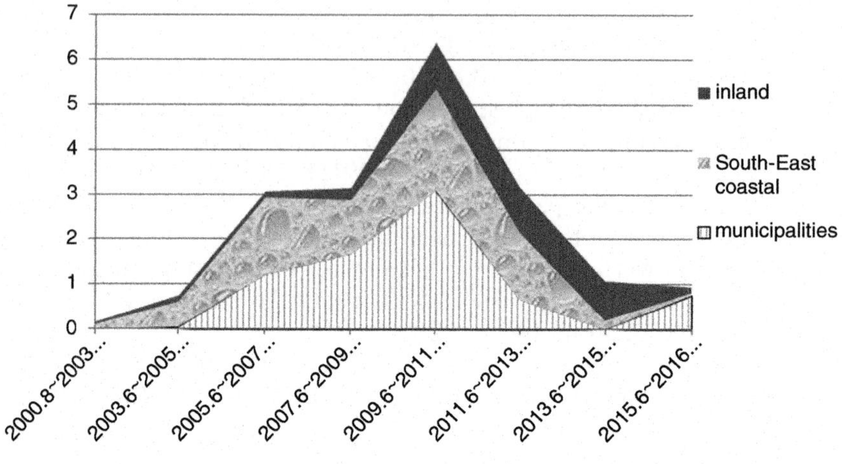

Fig. 3.4 Average number of provinces/municipalities where H0 is rejected at 5% significant level

Moreover, we apply an adjustment factor to those points based on whether an episode is detected at 10%, 5% or 1% significance level. Table 3.3 illustrates this method with the example of Anhui province, showing 10 total points for Anhui when the initial window size = 40.

In case the severity points are sensitive to different initial window sizes, we repeat the same method to find the point for each province at the window size of 30 and 20, respectively. Adding up the points for each province under window sizes of 20, 30, and 40, we arrived at the total points for each province presented in Table 3.3. In Table 3.3, the average total points per province are 25.5, with a standard deviation of 10.5 and minimum points of 18. Thus, we make the following classification: a province with 18 points is a no-bubble province, a province with 36 points (=25.5 + 10.5) and above is a bubble province, and a province with points lower than 36 but higher than 18 is a slight-bubble province. The graphical presentation of the GSADF test results on each of the bubble provinces is presented in Appendix 3, that of each of the slight-bubble provinces in Appendix 4, and that of each of the no-bubble provinces in Appendix 5.

Based on Table 3.4, we produce Fig. 3.5 to indicate the geographical distribution of housing bubbles in China.[12] Figure 3.5 clearly shows that provinces in the north west, north east, and the inland of China, which

Table 3.3 Calculating the severity points of housing price bubbles, the example of Anhui (window size = 40)

(1)	*(2)*	*(3)*	*(4)*	*(5)*	*(6)*	*(7)*
GSADF significance level (%)	*Number of bubble episodes*	*Average number of episodes per province*	*(2)–(3)*	*Points assigned based on number of episodes*	*Adjustment factor for GSADF significance*	*Point = (5)*(6)*
10	34	22.70	>0	3	1	3
5	8	13.37	<=0	2	2	4
1	0	N/A	N/A	1	3	3
				Point (window = 40)		10

Note: The threshold number of episodes is 5. At the 1% significant level, the average number of bubble episodes is only 2, below the threshold number

Table 3.4 The severity of housing price bubbles by province, based on points derived from GSADF tests

No-bubble provinces		*Slight-bubble provinces*		*Bubble provinces*	
Total points = 18		*18< total points <36*		*Total points ≥36*	
Province	*Points*	*Province*	*Points*	*Province*	*Points*
Gansu	18	Shandong	19	Chongqing	36
Guangdong	18	Hebei	20	Beijing	45
Hainan	18	Ningxia	21	Jiangsu	45
Heilongjiang	18	Guizhou	23	Jiangxi	45
Henan	18	Guangxi	25	Shanghai	45
Hubei	18	Anhui	26	Tianjin	45
Hunan	18	Sichuan	28	Zhejiang	45
Inner Mongolia	18	Fujian	30		
Jilin	18	Average point/province = 25.5; S.D. = 10.6			
Liaoning	18				
Qinghai	18				
Shanxi(陕西)	18				
Shanxi(山西)	18				
Xinjiang	18				
Yunnan	18				

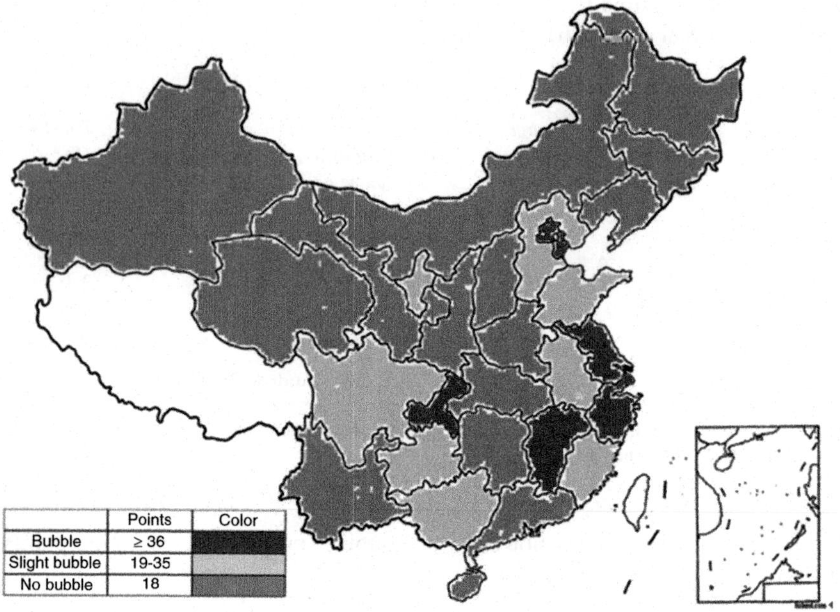

Fig. 3.5 Distribution of China's housing bubbles detected by GSADF test

have lower population density than the coastal provinces, are generally bubble free. All bubble or slight-bubble provinces are mainly huddled around three areas: (1) the Jiangsu, Shanghai, and Zhejiang area, (2) the Beijing and Tianjin area, and (3) the Chongqing and Sichuan area.

Table 3.5 shows the number of bubble months in the bubble provinces at different significant levels, under an initial window size = 30 months, from March 1998 to December 2016.[13] From the distribution of bubble durations across the three significance levels (10%, 5%, and 1%), we can also glean the relative degree of severity versus longevity of bubbles in these bubble provinces. Zhejiang province (126 months at 10% and 62 months at 1% significance level) stands out as the province that has experienced the longest and most severe housing bubbles. Comparing Jiangsu and Jiangxi, we see that, at the 10% significance level, the number of bubble months is higher in Jiangsu (95) than in Jiangxi (66). However, that number decreased more rapidly (along with a decline in the significance level) in Jiangsu (the number of bubble months being 95-51-9, in correspondence to 10%-5%-1% significant level) than in

Table 3.5 The duration of all bubble episodes in bubble provinces (months)

Significant level	*10%*	*5%*	*1%*
Zhejiang	126	106	62
Tianjin	85	62	10
Beijing	65	53	32
Jiangsu	95	51	9
Jiangxi	66	51	23
Shanghai	46	31	18
Chongqing	57	27	4

Note: The timing of bubbles is detected by GSADF under window size = 30 months

Jiangxi (66-51-23), suggesting that housing bubbles in Jiangsu are longer lasting but less severe than those in Jiangxi. Similarly, the number of bubble months in the descending order of the significance level in Beijing (65-53-32) and in Tianjin (85-62-10) also suggests that housing bubbles in Beijing are more severe, but shorter-lasting, than in Tianjin.

Among the seven bubble provinces listed in Table 3.5, Jiangxi is quite special. Even though it is neither a south-east coastal province nor one of the four municipalities, its housing bubble episodes (the number of bubble months being 66-51-23 in correspondence to 10%-5%-1% significant level) are more severe and longer-lasting than those in Shanghai (46-31-18). As it is close to Zhejiang, which has experienced the most severe housing bubbles and is well known for housing speculation, we suspect the spillover-effect may have contributed to the price explosion in Jiangxi.

Surprisingly, Guangdong, a coastal and prosperous province, is not one of the bubble provinces detected by our method, since many analysts, for example, Wang et al. (2013), have raised concerns about the housing price in Guangzhou and Shenzhen, the two biggest cities in Guangdong. This result very likely has stemmed from the huge gap between income per capita between the rich and poorer cities in Guangdong. In 2016, the disposable income per capita in 11 cities among Guangdong's 21 cities was below 20,000 RMB/year, while that in Guangzhou and Shenzhen—the two richest cities in the province—was higher than 40,000 RMB/year. (In comparison, none of Zhejiang's 11 cities and only one of Jiangsu's 13 cities had disposable income per capita below 20,000 RMB.)[14] Therefore, it is most likely that the average housing price in Guangdong has masked bubbles that have existed in the richer cities such as Guangzhou and Shenzhen.

3.3.2 The Price-Rent Ratio Method

The above discussion suggests that it is important to investigate housing prices at the city level. However, since we do not have monthly housing price data at the city level, we resort to using the price-to-rent ratio analysis on yearly city data. According to Poterba et al. (1991), the no-arbitrage condition dictates that the rent-to-price ratio be equal to the user cost minus the expected house price appreciation:

$$\left(\frac{R}{P_t}\right)^e = \left[(1-\theta)(i+\tau_p)+\alpha+\delta+m\right]-\pi^e \tag{3.9}$$

Where

$1-\theta$ is the tax deduction factor,
i is the risk-free interest rate,
τ_p is the property tax on the proportion of house value,
δ is the depreciation rate,
α is the risk premium on housing assets,
m is the maintenance cost,
π^e is the expected house price appreciation.

Based on the concept of the no-arbitrage condition, consulting with both the Chinese and the international standards of the thresholds of the price-to-monthly rent (P/R) ratio, we choose the range of 200–270 as the benchmark for indicating the underpricing and overpricing of a property. A P/R ratio below 200 indicates that the housing properties are underpriced, while a P/R ratio above 270 signals bubbles in the housing market.[15] This threshold seems reasonable in light of the fact that, in the years before the housing crisis of 2007–2008, as the housing market heated up in the US, the US national P/R ratio rose from 273 (in 2005) to 294 (in 2007).[16] As we have shown above, the average national price tends to mask the severity of bubbles in the most bubble-infected cities. So, it is not unreasonable to regard that a city's P/R ratio greater than 270 signals housing bubbles in that city.

3.3.2.1 Empirical Results

Table 3.6 presents the P/R ratios of capital cities of each province and major cities of special interest, including Wenzhou, a city famous for

Table 3.6 The price/rent ratio in different Chinese cities (annual average)

City	*1999–2002*	*2003–2005*	*2006–2008*	*2009–2011*	*2012–2014*
Beijing	138.462	133.899	252.385	**344.208**	**332.203**
Changchun	159.775	134.769	165.346	251.306	219.239
Changsha	103.018	108.441	157.767	231.438	**275.973**
Chengdu	84.42	117.114	200.568	240.814	
Chongqing	72.853	100.772	137.773	193.051	
Dalian	129.885	140.152	192.38	201.257	215.226
Fuzhou	86.971	118.21	208.787	**299.124**	
Guangzhou	130.452	141.87	231.795	**296.388**	
Guiyang	95.321	116.138	162.604	207.184	218.688
Harbin	88.608	98.42	122.308	176.069	174.289
Haikou	85.461	117.231	179.958	**298.271**	248.23
Hangzhou	112.209	145.935	225.359	**363.191**	384.698
Hefei	116.896	166.355	220.101	**325.889**	
Huhehaote	76.713	85.642	125.462	116.458	
Jinan	104.54	143.661	190.077	**272.356**	
Kunming	169.861	157.693	172.873	177.863	216.08
Lanzhou	107.279	145.806	203.694	252.801	
Nanchang	105.777	157.268	212.611	248.445	
Nanjing	119.637	130.892	180.602	**296.94**	**367.636**
Nanning	95.133	112.066	145.239	200.608	
Ningbo	86.674	134.373	213.794	**340.319**	
Qingdao	100.585	161.762	215.583	257.862	**297.992**
Shanghai	95.064	150.175	171.632	266.154	262.513
Shenyang	130.284	145.15	170.049	216.244	
Shenzhen	141.848	173.663	**294.772**	**430.123**	**459.111**
Shijiazhuang	141.195	124.54	177.414	265.421	**306.178**
Taiyuan	128.155	164.883	199.945	247.474	247.899
Tianjin	94.59	115.025	191.749	262.514	**271.253**
Wenzhou		187.596	258.319	**448.837**	**448.455**
Wuhan	98.233	125.212	211.505	**282.464**	**309.798**
Wulumuqi	144.968	154.582	203.962	**285.289**	
Xiamen	106.679	160.408	**308.908**	**387.092**	**440.053**
Xian	92.62	133.032	178.324	221.504	**271.548**
Xining	130.299	144.177	212.067	224.98	**270.476**
Yinchuan	185.417	179.972	190.591	263.852	246.394
Zhengzhou	119.745	134.452	200.506	264.312	

Note: By the international standard, a price/monthly rent ratio greater than 300 indicates that the property is overpriced, while a ratio lower than 200 indicates that it is underpriced housing speculators.[17] Before 2006, the P/R ratios of all cities were all below 200, indicating housing prices during this period were undervalued nationwide. During 2009–2011, housing bubbles suddenly caught on rapidly in many cities.

Several interesting observations emerging from Table 3.5 are as follows:

- Housing bubbles did not begin in most cities until 2009, with Xiamen and Shenzhen being the only two cities with housing bubbles during 2006–2008.
- Shenzhen, the richest city in Guangdong, has signs of severe housing bubbles with a P/R ratio exceeding 400 during 2009–2011 and 2012–2014. The province's second largest city, Guangzhou, also has a P/R ratio close to 300 during 2009–2011. This confirms our view that the average housing price of Guangdong has marked the bubble phenomena of these two cities.
- All three major cities in Zhejiang—Wenzhou, Hangzhou, and Ningbo—showed signs of a housing bubble. Moreover, the P/R ratio in Wenzhou, famous for housing speculation, has always been higher than those in Hangzhou.
- Cities from the north east (namely, Harbin, Shenyang, Dalian, and Changchun) and most of those from inland provinces (i.e., Taiyuan, Huhehaote, Nanning, Chengdu, Guiyang, Kunming, and Yinchuan) have been either undervalued or near the lower end of a normal range (200–270), even after 2009.
- A few inland cities have shown signs of slight bubbles, in contrast with the results from provincial data. The P/R ratios in Wuhan (of Hubei), Lanzhou (of Gansu), and Wulumuqi (of Xinjiang) have all exceeded the threshold of 270.

3.4 What Are the Causes of China's Housing Bubbles?

The empirical evidence presented in the preceding two sections makes a strong case that housing bubbles have infected many major cities and coastal provinces since 2009. Will these bubbles burst and seriously inflict harm on the real economy, in the same way as most previous housing bubbles in other countries? Or, could these housing "bubbles" in China be sustained due to special characteristics of the Chinese system and institutions? As a way to gain insight to this question, this section considers some factors that may have lent support to the seemingly unsustainable level of China's housing prices in those "crisis" cities/provinces.

3.4.1 Baby Boom and Culture?

Mankiw and Weil (1989) found that the US housing boom in the 1970s and subsequent bust in the 1990s were closely related to the baby boom in the 1950s and the subsequent baby bust in the 1970s. Could it be true too that China's housing boom began to emerge 20 years after its baby boom? To ascertain whether that may be true, we use the GSADF test to detect whether there was a baby boom in China about 20 years before its housing boom began in 2005. To make sure it is appropriate to apply GSADF to detect the baby boom and bust, we first conducted the GSADF test on the log of the US population. The results shown in Fig. 3.6 agree exactly with Mankiw and Weil's (1989) judgment about the timing of the baby boom-bust cycle in the US, suggesting the GSADF statistics can identify these events successfully.

We then apply GSADF to China's population. The results are presented in Figs. 3.7 and 3.8: the Chinese population is most explosive during 1985–1995, which can be regarded as a baby boom. The period 20 years after 1985–1995 is 2005–2015 while the median is exactly around 2009–2011, the most explosive time of housing prices detected in this chapter. This demographic pattern may help explain the fierce rise of housing price: if the elasticity of housing demand to price is roughly constant in China: an explosive rise in demand for housing, implied by growing into adulthood of babies born over 1985–1995 during 2005–2015, will lead to an explosion in housing price. In other words, the demographic profile appears to be consistent with driving a strong rise in housing demand since 2005.

Shiller (2000) pointed out that the culture and people's psychology are crucial for understanding investment and consumption behavior. In that light, we consider whether, given the timing of China's baby boom from 1985 to 1995, the combination of China's cultural factors and its one-child policy further pushed up housing demand and housing price?[18]

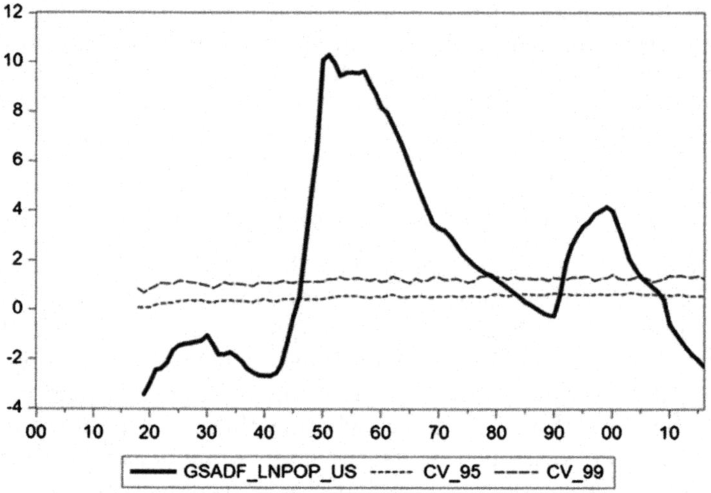

Fig. 3.6 GSADF test on log of US population (window = 20)

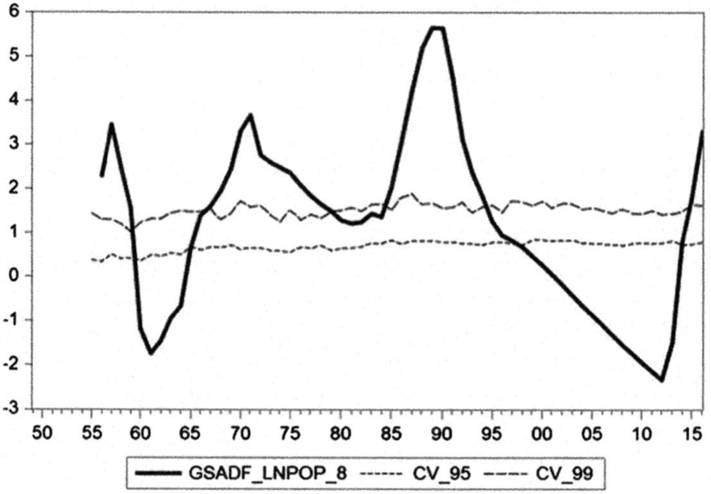

Fig. 3.7 GSADF test on log of US population (window = 8)

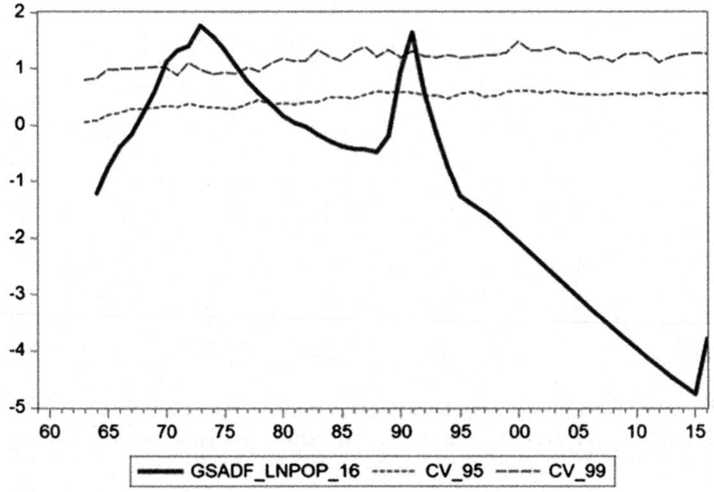

Fig. 3.8 GSADF test on log of US population (window = 16)

Chinese traditionally have tended to value ownership of houses as a symbol of status and preserver of family wealth; therefore, they are much more willing to work hard for the purpose of owning a house than most people of other cultures. For instance, Figure 3.9 shows that, compared with most other countries, China has a much higher home-ownership rate, about 90% in 2013 in the urban areas.[19] Furthermore, the high male/female ratio in China, caused by the one-child policy, has intensified the demand for housing.[20] As the gender ratio becomes further imbalanced, the competition among young males in the marriage market becomes more intense. Consequently, given the Chinese culture of valuing house ownership and unceasing parental caring for their grownup offspring, housing demand is further pushed up by parents who would try every means to purchase houses for their sons to increase their competitiveness in the marriage market. This view is supported by Fig. 3.10, which indicates that 22.5% of families with adult children have ownership of multiple houses in 2014, while only 14.9% of families without adult children have multi-house ownership in the same year.

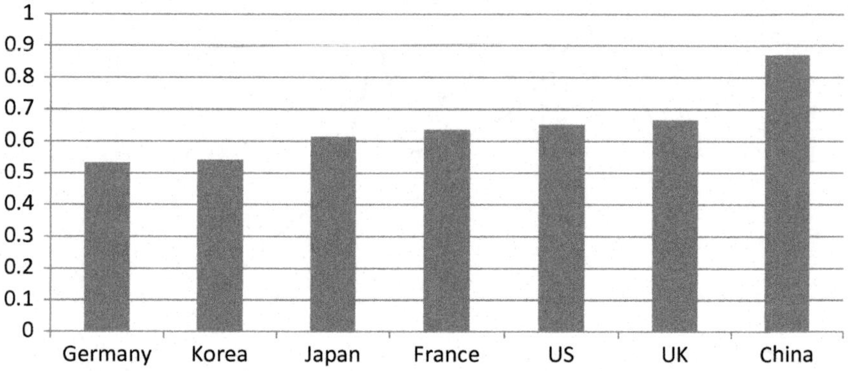

Fig. 3.9 Urban home-ownership rate in China vs some other countries. (Sources: Eurostat 2012; Statistics Bureau of Japan 2008; Statistics Korea 2005; CHFS 2013)

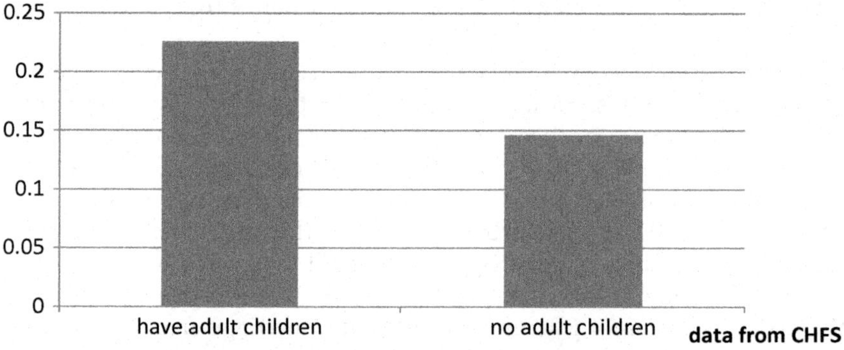

Fig. 3.10 Multi-house ownership rates in two groups of families in China

Indeed, Rosenzweig and Zhang (2014) confirmed that the one-child policy, in combination with the Chinese tradition of life-long parental caring for their offspring, has contributed to the high-saving motive of parents for providing for their offspring.

3.4.2 Policy-Induced Speculation?

In China, policies intended to "stabilize" the housing market can be very nimble. It can be enacted and then be reversed rapidly. For example,

Table 3.7 Summary of key changes in housing policies, 2007–2014

Issued time	*Down-payment*			*Mortgage rate*
	First house, area <90 m²	*First house, area >90 m²*	*Second house*	
27-Sep-2007	20%	30%	40%	>1.1*basic rate
5-Dec-2007				
22-Oct-2008	20%		(N/A)	>0.7*basic rate
17-Apr-2010	(N/A)	30%	50%	>1.1*basic rate
26-Jan-2011	(N/A)	(N/A)	60%	>1.1*basic rate
30-Sep-2014	30%		Release restriction on reapplication of mortgage loan	>0.7*basic rate

Table 3.7 provides a summary of key policy changes from 2007 to 2014, which are chronicled as follows:

- In September of 2007, the government introduced policies to deter purchases of second houses by requiring a 40% down-payment for second-house mortgages, with the effect of paralyzing the housing market.[21] However, two months later in December of 2007, the restriction on what counted as a second house was relaxed to "improve households' living standard."[22]
- Because of the weak performance of the housing market in 2008, the down-payment for a house purchase was dropped from 30% to 20% at the end of 2008, and the central bank decreased the lower bound of the mortgage rate to 0.7 times that of the basic loan rate.[23] Meanwhile, the constraint on owning a second house appeared to be relaxed as well.
- In another government edict issued in 2010 to cool down the real estate market, the down-payment for a second house was set at 50%, and the mortgage-rate floor was set to be 1.1 times that of the basic loan rate.[24]

Table 3.8 Loan-rate and reserve-rate cuts in 2015

Date	*Change in the loan rate (%)*	*Change in required reserve rate (%)*
4-Feb		−0.5
1-Mar	−0.25	
20-Apr		−1
11-May	−0.25	
28-Jun	−0.25	−0.5
26-Aug	−0.25	−0.25
24-Oct	−0.25	−0.5
Total change	−1.25	−2.75

- An even more strict restriction came in 2011, when a policy applied to more than 50 cities required a 60% down-payment for second-house purchases and a mortgage rate higher than 1.1 times that of the basic loan rate.[25]
- Starting in 2014, the restrictions on house purchases began to be reversed. In 2014, China's Banking Regulatory Commission announced a policy to allow the second house be regarded as the first one after the first house's mortgage is paid off.[26]
- In 2015, several rounds of cuts in the loan rate, the reserve rate, or both were announced (Table 3.8).

To assess the effect of these policy changes on housing price movements, we show the GSADF statistics of housing prices in Beijing, Jiangsu, and Zhejiang following these policy changes in Figs. 3.11, 3.12, and 3.13. From these figures, it is apparent that the above government interventions achieved the intended effect on the movement of housing prices in those cities. Furthermore, we present Fig. 3.14, which is the number of bubble provinces detected at the 5% significant level, to show the effect of these policies nationwide. Figure 3.14 confirms that those government policy changes indeed were quite effective in moving the housing price in the intended direction. Usually Beijing, the capital of China, is the place that first introduces corresponding measures after the new policies are issued; therefore, the figure of Beijing shows that those policies took effect on housing prices almost immediately without lags.

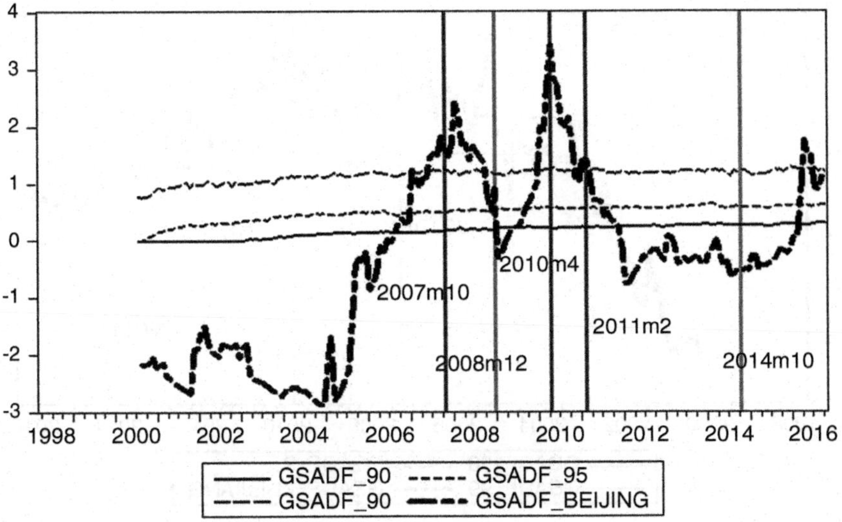

Fig. 3.11 Response of housing price to policy changes (Beijing)

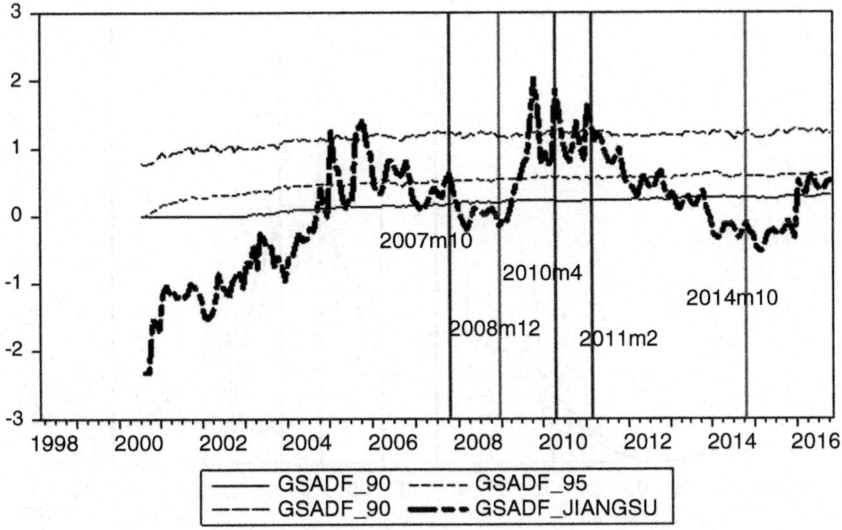

Fig. 3.12 Response of housing price to policy changes (Jiangsu)

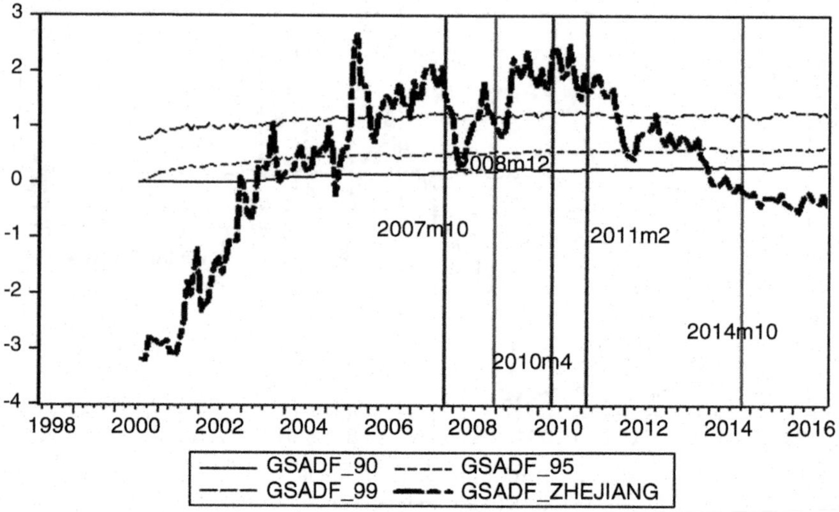

Fig. 3.13 Response of housing price to policy changes (Zhejiang)

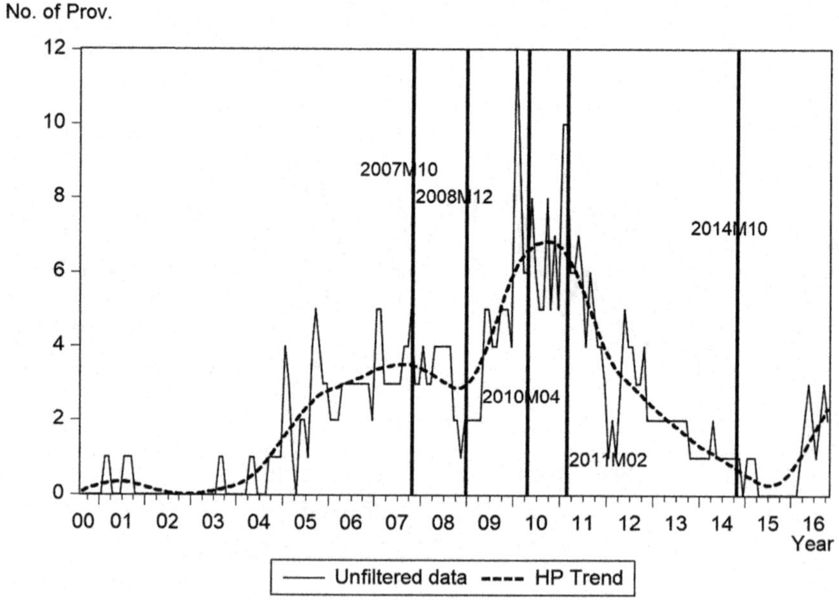

Fig. 3.14 Response of housing price to policy changes (nationwide). (Detected by GSADF test at 5% significance level)

These findings suggest that the Chinese government wields enormous power over the housing price. It is well known that the Chinese government is the landlord of all land in China, and that the price of the land it offers to developers (which is a significant part of the housing price) is really a multi-year rental on the land, and a major source of finance for local governments. Given this unique system, plus the fact that real estate properties are the main component of most Chinese people's wealth, the government has a particularly strong motivation to prevent a housing "bubble" from collapsing. Allowing a housing bubble to burst not only could cause a severe economic recession and social (and even political) instability, but also it may simultaneously weaken the government's ability to conduct stimulus macroeconomic policy to revive the economy.

In short, the government seems to be happy to reap financial benefits from rapidly rising housing prices, even to a degree that would be regarded as bubble by the standards used in this chapter. At the same time, the government also monitors the housing market closely and intervenes forcefully to dampen the market any time the situation appears to be getting out of control. However, those interventions apparently are aimed at slowing housing price growth rather than popping the bubble. With this knowledge, both household and speculators would seem rational to keep the housing market going strong even when housing prices are apparently overvalued. Indeed, according to a report by People's Bank of China (PBoC),[27] a massive amount of private loans were created in Wenzhou for housing speculation, which reached approximately 22 billion RMB in 2011 (Wu 2011). Zhang (2005) also argued that activities/policies of policymakers and real estate developers are mainly responsible for the soaring housing price.

3.5 Conclusion

This chapter uses the GSADF test and price-to-rent analysis to detect housing bubbles in China's provinces and in major cities. The results of the GSADF test indicate that house prices skyrocketed in several provinces from 2009 to 2011, a period during which housing bubbles were detected in the four municipalities and the south-east coastal provinces, especially in Beijing, Tianjin, Shanghai, Chongqing, Zhejiang, Jiangsu, and Sichuan. Fewer bubbles were detected inland, and none were seen in north-east and north-west areas.

Results of the price-to-rent analysis, which is applied to major cities (as opposed to provinces in the GSADF tests) by using annual data, are generally consistent with those in the GSADF test. In addition, the price-to-rent analysis detected the following not found by the GSADF test. First, there are bubbles detected in Shenzhen and Guangzhou, the two largest cities of Guangdong, despite Guangdong itself not having a housing bubble. Second, only two cities—namely, Xiamen and Shenzhen—showed some traces of a bubble before 2009, but that number increased to 13 during 2009–2011.

Even though we have detected housing bubbles in China, we hold the view that these Chinese "housing bubbles" will not likely burst in the same fashion and with similar consequences as previous bubbles in other countries in the near future. Instead, it is more likely that these bubbly high prices will either have some moderate downward adjustments or stay relatively flat for two reasons. Frist, demand for houses is strongly supported by the Chinese tradition of valuing house ownership and parents' life-long provision for their children, including buying houses to help their male offspring secure a marriage in the tight marriage market following the one-child policy. Second, the Chinese government is very powerful in controlling the housing market, and it has several incentives for not allowing the housing "bubbles" to burst in a damaging and out-of-control fashion. Of course, these reasons do not necessarily guarantee that these housing bubbles will never burst in the long run.

Appendix

Appendix 1: GSADF Critical Values Under Different Replications

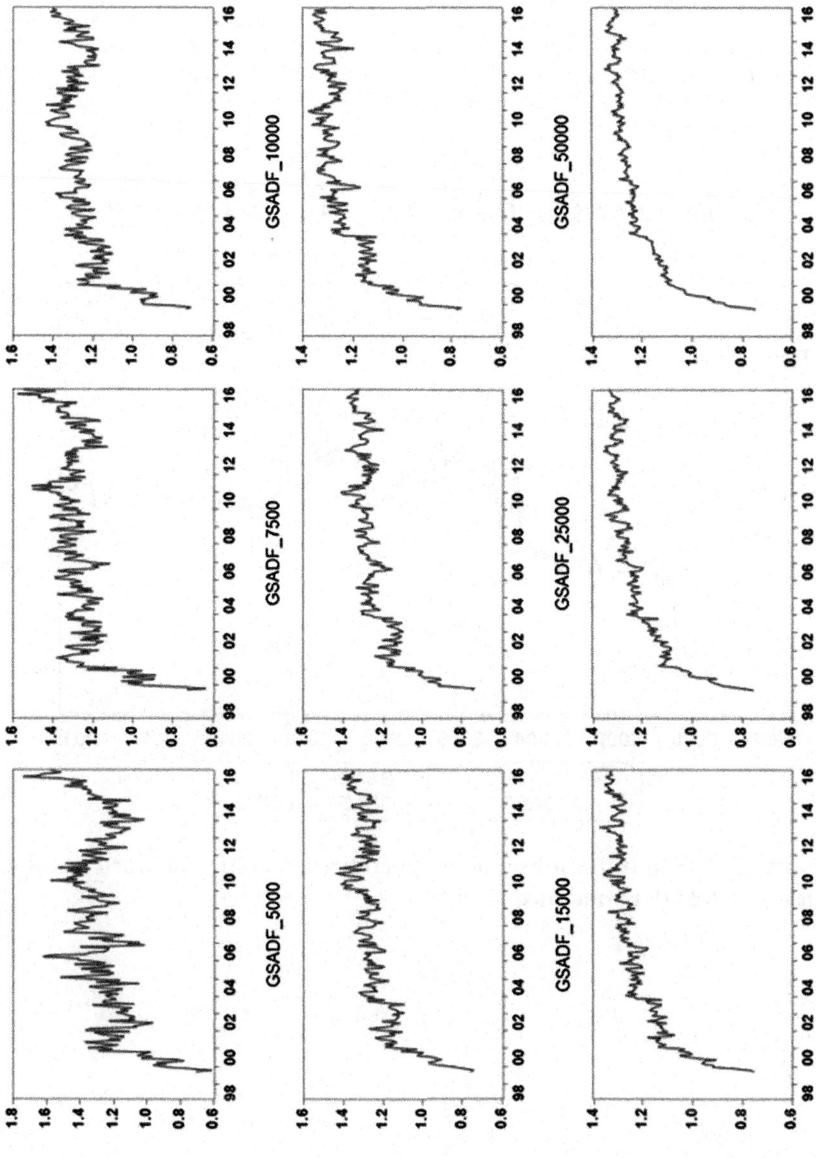

Repeating times	1000	3000	5000	7500	10,000	15,000	25,000	50,000
Mean	1.259	1.248	1.244	1.241	1.24	1.232	1.231	1.229
Median	1.262	1.272	1.269	1.273	1.272	1.266	1.264	1.266
Maximum	1.738	1.435	1.435	1.411	1.377	1.373	1.355	1.35
Minimum	0.614	0.711	0.748	0.74	0.763	0.755	0.756	0.75
Std. dev.	0.167	0.12	0.117	0.113	0.108	0.109	0.111	0.108
Skewness	−0.608	−1.807	−1.747	−1.855	−1.882	−1.83	−1.815	−1.939
Kurtosis	4.56	7.436	6.959	7.138	7.083	6.882	6.472	7.054

Appendix 2: GSADF Test on China's Average Housing Prices

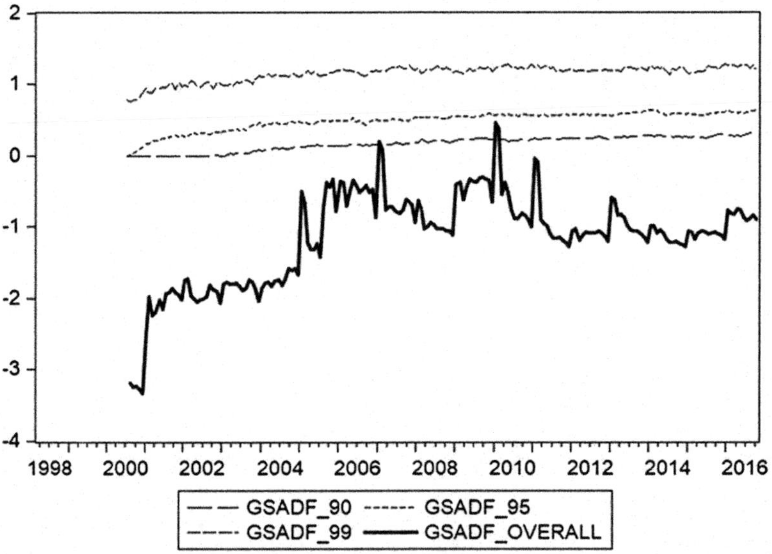

Note: In this and the subsequent appendices, naming rule for critical values is "GSADF confidence level."

Appendix 3: GSADF Test on Real Housing Price of Bubble Provinces

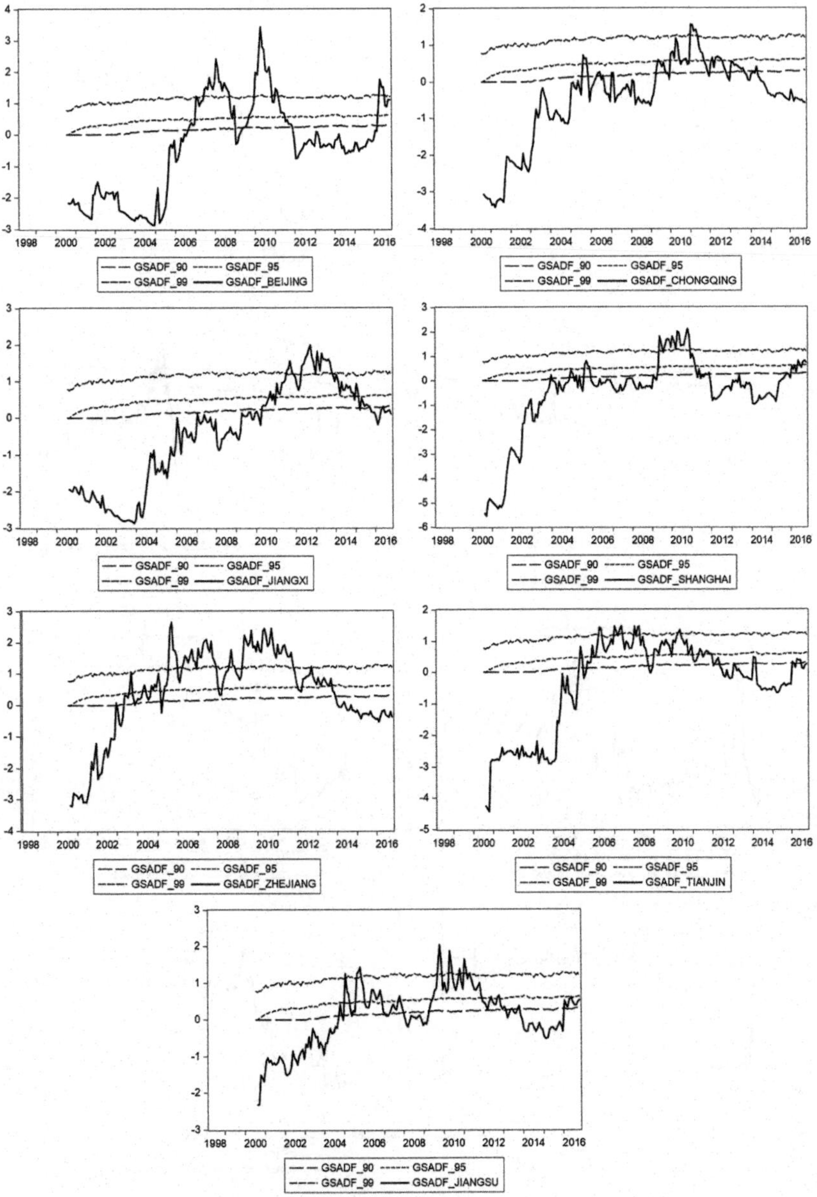

Appendix 4: GSADF Test on Real Housing Price of Slight-Bubble Provinces

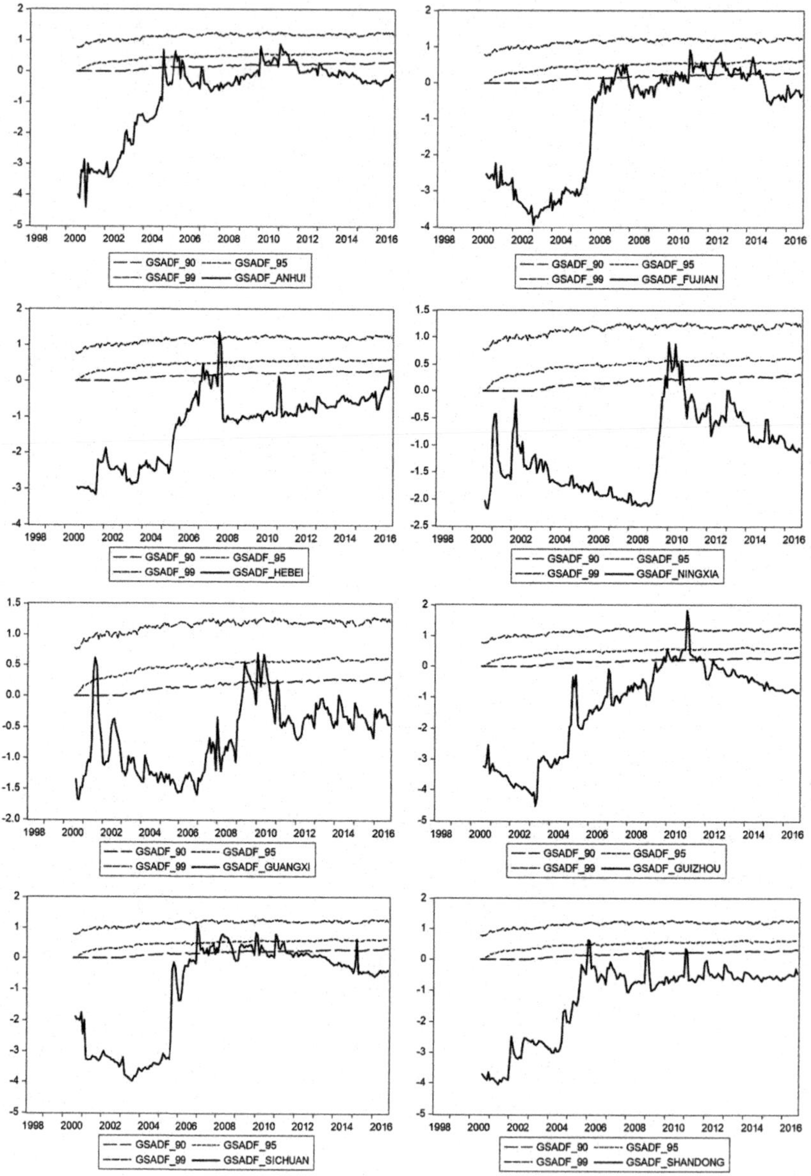

Appendix 5: GSADF Test on Real Housing Price of No-Bubble Provinces

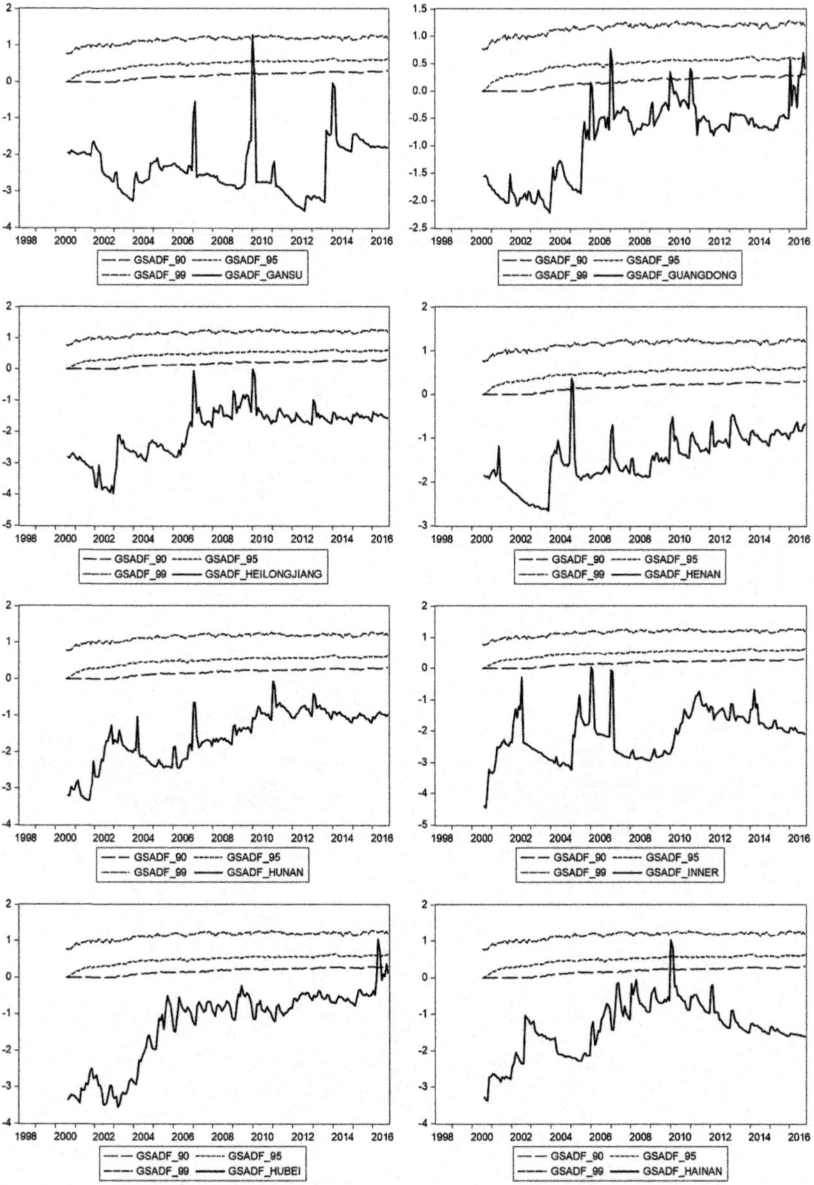

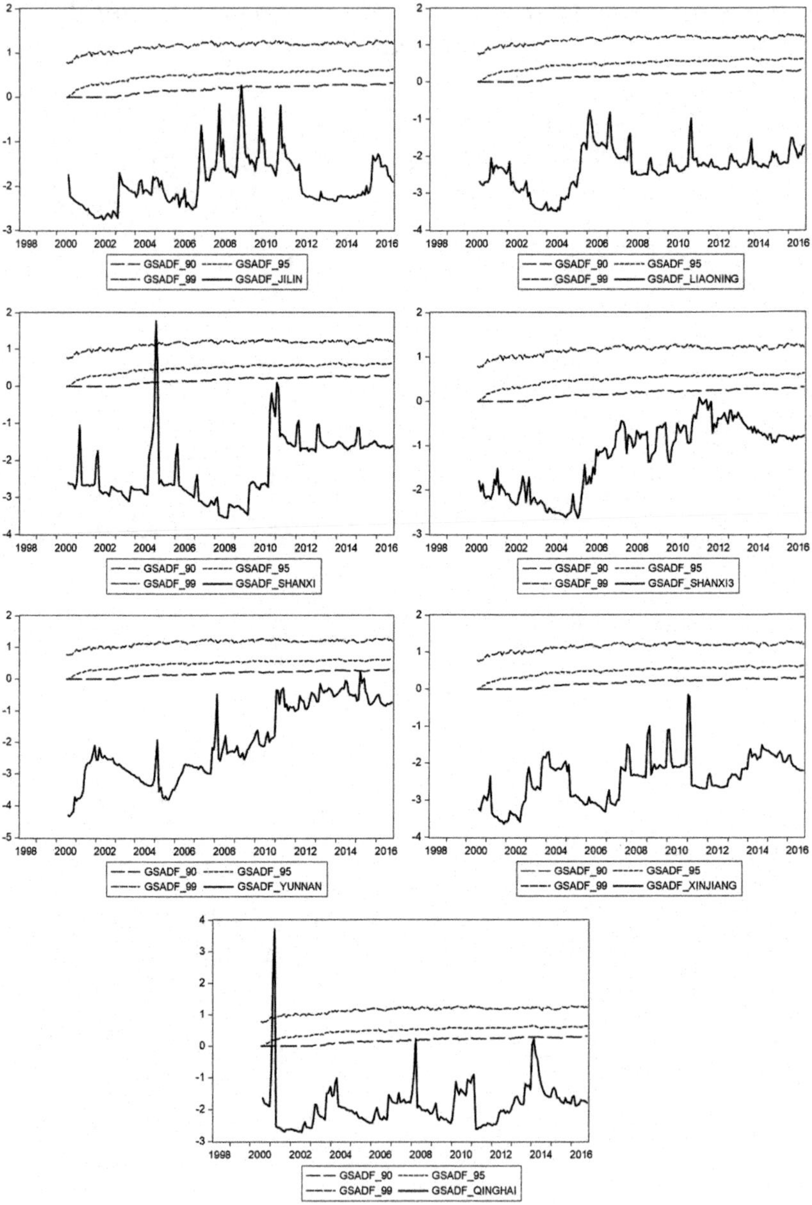
GSADF_90
GSADF_95
GSADF_99
GSADF_JILIN
GSADF_LIAONING
GSADF_SHANXI
GSADF_SHANXI3
GSADF_YUNNAN
GSADF_XINJIANG
GSADF_QINGHAI

Notes

1. The housing price/income ratio is set to equal (housing price per m^2 * area per person)/average disposable income .
2. The right-tail unit root test is a test of the null hypothesis of a unit root against the alternative of a root that is greater than unity. In comparison, a typical unit root test of a time series is a left-tail test of the null hypothesis of a unit root against the alternative of a root that is lower than unity.
3. For example, see Campbell and Shiller (1988).
4. In the SADF method, the beginning of the bubble is stamped on the first date on which the ADF t-statistic is greater than the corresponding critical value of the right-tail unit root test. The end of the speculative bubble is stamped on the first day when the ADF t-statistic is below the aforementioned critical value. In such a way, the SADF can detect the formation and collapse of bubbles. The authors argue that their tests have a greater power of test because they are sensitive to changes that occur when a process transits from a unit root to a mildly explosive root and vice versa.
5. Rent data at the provincial level are unavailable on a monthly or quarterly basis. Even though quarterly rent indexes are available for 30 capital cities, they are available only for 52 quarters (from Q1 1998 to Q4 2010), not enough for conducting credible GSADF tests.
6. The authors suggest 1% of total number of observations (T) as an ideal choice of the initial window size when the sample size is large enough, while $T^*(0.01 + 1.8/\sqrt{T})$ is a better alternative rule for setting window size when the sample size is limited. Since our sample size is modest (224 months), we follow the alternative rule of thumb.
7. We conducted simulations with reiterations of 1000, 2000, 3000, 5000, 7500, 10,000, 15,000, 25,000, and 50,000 times.
8. To make the picture clearer and avoid the disturbance of outliers, we used HP filter to signal the trend. To prevent losing too much information due to the HP filter, we choose a low λ (=500) instead of what is typically used for monthly data (λ = 14,400).
9. For example, "Notice on Enhancing Credit Regulation on Commercial Real Estate" (关于加强商业性房地产信贷管理的通知) was issued by People's Bank of China, in 2007 (No. 359). This act was aimed to control the ownership of second houses and set the down-payment for them as 40% of the property value.
10. The three north-east provinces are Heilongjiang, Jilin, and Liaoning. The 15 inland provinces are Anhui, Gansu, Guizhou, Henan, Hubei, Hunan, Inner Mongolia, Jiangxi, Ningxia, Qinghai, Shanxi(山西), Shanxi(陕西), Sichuan, Xinjiang and Yunnan.

11. We remove outliers by not counting "bubbles" that lasted longer than 20 months or shorter than 6 months. For example, there are six periods in which Guangxi's GSADF statistics exceeded the critical values; however, when we check the data, we found all six periods scatter in different years. So we did not count those six periods as bubble periods for Guangxi.
12. Those with 18 points are colored blue, those points ≥36 are red (because the average total points for all provinces are about 25.5 and standard deviation is 10.5), and the rest with points 19–35 are yellow.
13. After experimenting with different window sizes, we found that bubble episodes identified by three different window sizes (20, 30, and 40) have little differences. Consequently, we only present the results obtained from setting the window size to 30 months.
14. The disposable income data are from the National Bureau of Statistics.
15. See Kuang (2016)—and Ma and Sun (2008) for more discussion on the Chinese and international standards of the P/R ratio.
16. See https://smartasset.com/mortgage/price-to-rent-ratio-in-us-cities
17. They refer to Wenzhou housing speculators (温州炒房团), words often referred to in newspapers.
18. The one-child policy was introduced in 1979 as part of China's population planning. The policy began to be phased out since 2015. The policy allowed exceptions for many special groups, including ethnic minorities.
19. Of course, this extremely high homeownership rate (the share of households that are owners) is partly attributable to the fact that many young and elderly adults live with their parents in China. When young adults live with their parents, or elder people live with their grown children, or people live with their housemates, they count as part of someone else's household. Moreover, poor people in China tend to share a small room in cities to save rent. Both factors will reduce the number of households counting as renters in the data, thereby raising the Homeownership rate.
20. See Wei and Zhang (2011).
21. See "Notice about enhancing credit regulation on commercial real estate" 《关于加强商业性房地产信贷管理的通知》, issued by People's Bank of China, Year 2007 No. 359.
22. See "Additional notice about credit regulation on commercial real estate" 《关于加强商业性房地产信贷管理补充通知》, issued by People's Bank of China, Year 2007 No. 452.
23. See "Notice about further decrease of commercial private mortgage rate" 《关于扩大商业性个人住房贷款利率下浮幅度等有关问题的通知》, issued by People's Bank of China, Year 2008 No. 302.
24. See "Notice about curbing rapid rise of housing prices in some cities" 《关于坚决遏制部分城市房价过快上涨的通知》, issued by the State Council (国务院), Year 2010 No. 10.

25. See "Notice about further enhancing macro regulation on real estate market", issued by the State Council, Year 2011 No. 1.
26. See "Notice about further improvement in housing financial service", issued by People's Bank of China, Year 2014 No. 287.
27. The writer, Guolian Wu, is the chairperson of PBoC's Wenzhou branch.

References

Campbell, J. and Shiller, J. (1988), "The Dividend-Price Ratio and Expectations of Future Dividends and Discount Factors", *The Review of Financial Studies*: 1(3), 195–228.

Caspi, I. (2013), "Rtadf: testing for bubbles with Eviews", *MPRA Paper*, No.58791.

Diesteldorf, J., Meyer, S., and Voelzke, J. (2016), "New evidence for explosive behavior of commodity prices", *CQE Working Papers*: 2016, (50).

Evans, G. (1991), "Pitfalls in Testing for Explosive Bubbles in Asset Prices", *The American Economic Review*: 81(4), 922–930.

Ma, D. and Sun, X. (2008), "A research on the real rent-to-price ration in Chinese real estate market", *Study & Exploration*: 2008(2), 149–153.

Malpezzi, S. (1999), "A Simple Error Correction Model of House Prices", *Journal of Housing Economics*: 1999(8), 27–62.

Mankiw, N. G., and Weil, D. N. (1989), "The baby boom, the baby bust, and the housing market a reply to our critics", *Regional Science and Urban Economics*: 1989(19), 235–258.

Pavlidis, E. G. et al. (2013), "Episodes of Exuberance in Housing Markets: In Search of the Smoking Gun", Working Paper of Globalization and Monetary Policy Institute of Federal Reserve Bank of Dallas, No.165.

Phillips, P. C., Shi, S. and Yu, J. (2012), "Testing for Multiple Bubbles", Cowless foundation Discussion Papers, No. 1843.

Phillips, P. C., Shi, S. and Yu, J. (2013), "Testing for multiple bubbles: Historical episodes of exuberance and collapse in the S&P 500", *International Economic Review*: 56(4), 1043–1078.

Phillips, P. C., Wu, Y., and Yu, J. (2011), "Explosive behavior in the 1990s NASDAQ: When did exuberance escalate asset values?", *International Economic Review*: 52(1), 201–226.

Phillips, P. C. and Yu, J. (2011), "Dating the Timeline of Financial Bubbles during the Subprime Crisis", *Quantitative Economics*: 2(3), 455–491.

Poterba, J., Weil, D., and Shiller, R. (1991), "House Price Dynamics: The Role of Tax Policy and Demography", *Brookings Papers on Economic Activity*: 1991(2), 143–203.

Rosenzweig, M. and Zhang, J. (2014), "Co-residence, life-cycle savings and intergenerational support in urban China", Center Discussion Paper of Economic Growth Center, Yale University, No. 1039.

Shiller, R. (2000), Irrational Exuberance. Princeton, New Jersey: Princeton University Press.

Wang, Y., Wang, D., and Wei, Y. (2013), "Spatial differentiation patterns of housing price and housing price-to-income ratio in China's cities", unpublished paper presented at '2013 21th International Conference on Geoinformatics', Kaifeng, China, 20–22 June 2013.

Wei, S. and Zhang, X. (2011), "The Competitive Saving Motive: Evidence from Rising Sex Ratios and Savings Rates in China", *Journal of Political Economy*: 119(3), 511–564.

Wu, G. (2011), "An Investigation on the market of Wenzhou Private Lending", *Zhejiang Finance*, 2011(8), 25–27.

Zhang, Y. (2005), "The "Wenzhou Factor" in Rapid Growth of Housing Price in Hangzhou", *Commercial Times*: 2005(11), 69–70.

CHAPTER 4

When Wanda Plaza Comes to the Yangtze River Delta: Will the Land Prices Increase?

Ziwei Zhang and Yang Chen

4.1 Introduction

The "urban complex" that combines hotel, retail, leisure and residential functions as an independent commercial zone is developing fast in China. There have been many urban complexes emerging in Chinese cities especially in the developed regions. Wanda Plaza that is successfully operated by the large property company, Dalian Wanda Commercial Properties Co., Ltd. (Wanda for short hereafter), serves as one example. The Wanda Plaza comprises a shopping mall, a movie theater, a restaurant, a supermarket and a hotel with integrated facilities for the convenience of consumers. As of 2016 Wanda has already opened 168 Wanda Plazas in China. When such an urban complex starts operation in a city, it may have certain impact on the local economic development. For example, a Wanda Plaza attracts a large number of consumers to purchase goods and services; a wide range of other businesses may flock into and agglomerate in this area as well for profit. With easy access to food, clothing, amusement and other business services, residents are more willing to purchase nearby housing. Firms would also like to purchase the land lot and build factories beside

Z. Zhang • Y. Chen (✉)
International Business School Suzhou, Xi'an Jiaotong-Liverpool University, Suzhou, China
e-mail: yang.chen@xjtlu.edu.cn

J. H. Hung, Y. Chen (eds.), *The State of China's State Capitalism*,
https://doi.org/10.1007/978-981-13-0983-0_4

Wanda Plaza to tap into the potential consumer market. In this case, the entry of a new Wanda Plaza is likely to have positive effects on local land prices. However, when more people live and or work near a Wanda Plaza, the level of crime, noise, traffic congestion and pollution might as well increase. If so, the development of a new Wanda Plaza and other businesses may impose a negative impact on local land prices. We are thus interested to study whether the benefit of the entry of a Wanda Plaza to land prices outweighs its cost.

We focus on the Yangtze River Delta to explore the impact of the entry of Wanda Plazas on local land prices using three unique datasets. The first dataset includes information on the entry of 26 Wanda Plazas in places in the Yangtze River Delta. The second includes county-level land transaction information in 109 counties from 2008 to 2016. The third dataset incorporates social-economic variables such as population, gross product, fixed asset investment, fiscal revenue, fiscal expenditure, aggregate outputs in construction industry and real estate sector investment in 109 Chinese counties from 2008 to 2016. Based on hedonic price modeling, we apply difference-in-difference (DID) method to estimate the effect of a Wanda Plaza on land prices. The results suggest that a new Wanda Plaza opening increases the price of industrial land by about 10–15% and that of residential land by about 22–25%. The results also suggest that gross regional products have positive impacts on residential and commercial land prices, real estate investments significantly link with industrial and commercial land prices and local fiscal revenues only associate with residential land prices.

4.2 Literature Review

Dalian Wanda Commercial Properties Co., Ltd., a subsidiary of Dalian Wanda Group, is the largest real estate developer in China and has been listed in Hong Kong since 2014 (Financial Times 2014). It owns properties like Wanda Plazas, superstar karaoke bars, department stores and Wanda Cinema movie theaters. Among these properties, Wanda Plaza is the focal point of Wanda Commercial Properties and it is a functional complex with hotels, office spaces, movie theaters, shopping malls and apartments, all of which forms an independent commercial zone.

The literature suggested two channels through which the openings of Wanda Plazas affect the land prices, namely, accessibility and externalities. Sirpal (1994) argued that when a shopping center was introduced to a community, it brought consumers the accessibility of necessities, convenience of shopping and diversity in the form of entertainment. The same paper analyzed the effect of different sizes of shopping centers on surrounding dwelling prices and found that the size of shopping centers is positively correlated with housing prices. Des Rosiers et al. (1996) had similar findings. Using the micro-level housing data, Pope and Pope (2015) found a positive impact of 159 Walmart shopping centers in the United States on the values of houses that are nearby. With similar arguments, we expect that the entry of a new Wanda Plaza would boost local land prices.

However, there are also negative externalities incurred when Wanda Plaza enters a region. For example, the crime rate, garbage accumulation, noise, traffic jam and pollution are likely to increase when a new "business district" is formed. A few studies provided evidence showing that these disamenities brought harmful effects on the real estate market. For instance, Lim and Missios (2007) considered the damaging effects of a landfill site on values of houses situated nearby. Comparing the impacts of a larger landfill site and that of a smaller site on surrounding housing prices, they concluded that landfills had adverse impacts on the prices of surrounding houses. In addition, both Pope (2007) and Linden and Rockoff (2008) investigated if cases of sex crimes reduced the housing prices of neighboring districts and drew the same conclusion that the risk of crime decreased the value of nearby housing. This strand of literature suggested that the negative external costs imposed by the opening of a Wanda Plaza might drive down the land prices.

As opposed to Pope and Pope (2015), our study focuses on the land market in China, which has been paid less attention compared with studies of the Chinese housing market. Bao et al. (2014) studied the land prices in Beijing and concluded that location is crucial. Kau and Sirmans (1979) argued that the prices of land were associated with the distance the land was to town. Few studies looked at the neighborhood effects on the values of land. There were studies that explored the relationship between location and prices of different lands including Kowalski and Paraskevopoulos (1990) and Peiser (1987). Kowalski and Paraskevopoulos (1990) focused on industrial land while Peiser (1987) paid attention to the non-residential land. Peiser also showed that office land values benefitted significantly from the employment agglomeration. These studies indicated that neighborhood characteristics had varied impacts on different types of lands.

When real estate developers purchase land, they do not consider it in isolation. The location and the locational attributes such as being close to schools or central business districts are also taken into account. Rosen (1974) came up with the concept "hedonic price", which refers to the implicit prices of characteristics. Early studies used the traditional cross-sectional hedonic analysis. For example, Ridker and Henning (1967) implemented the least squares regression with cross-sectional data to analyze the effect of air quality on surrounding housing prices. However, the estimates of traditional cross-sectional model suffered from omitted variable bias (Calabrese et al. 2006; Bayer and Timmins 2007). To mitigate the omitted variable bias problem, economists turned to use quasi-experiments. Black (1999), Figlio and Lucas (2004) and Chay and Greenstone (2005) gave examples of quasi-experiment in their studies. Kuminoff and Pope (2012) pointed out that quasi-experiments introduced exogenous sources of temporal shocks in the attribute of interests and adding a temporal variation can help difference away the time-invariant variables. Thus, we can compare the implicit prices of the attributes before and after the shock to obtain consistent estimates. In addition, Parmeter and Pope (2012) provided detailed process about how to apply the quasi-experiment identification strategy—difference-in difference model to the hedonic price model. Therefore, we follow their DID strategy to identify the effects of entry of a new Wanda Plaza on regional land prices.

4.3 Data

We utilize three main datasets to conduct the following empirical analyses. The first includes information of entry of Wanda Plazas in the Yangtze River Delta. The second includes land transaction prices and the third includes social-economic variables in 109 Chinese counties. The Wanda Plaza dataset contains the specific addresses and the opening time of each Wanda Plaza in the Yangtze River Delta, and this information is manually collected from the Dalian Wanda official website. The address information can be found from each individual plaza's homepage and the opening time usually appears in the most recent news regarding Wanda Commercial Properties Co. Ltd. (2017) website shows that there are 37 Wanda Plazas in total in the Yangtze River Delta. However, due to the limited data on land transaction, we did not use all entry information.[1] Since the land transaction data is available from 2008 to 2016, Wanda Plazas that opened before or after this time period are not included in our sample. Table 4.7

provides the summary statistics of the year and city, when the Wanda Plazas started operation. Panel B illustrates the distribution of months of opening in our sample. December is the month that the majority of Wanda Plazas start to operate. Panel B demonstrates the distribution of Wanda Plazas in Yangtze River Delta comprising of Shanghai, Jiangsu, and Zhejiang provinces.

The land transaction data includes land prices and transaction dates in 109 administrative districts and counties[2] compiled from Wind Financial. The land transaction data is sorted out based on different types of land: residential, commercial and industrial. We aggregate the micro-level transaction data into county level and aim to study how the annual average land prices change with openings of new Wanda Plazas in the Yangtze River Delta.

We also collect data on population,[3] gross product, fixed asset investment, fiscal revenue, fiscal expenditure, output in construction sector and real estate investment. The majority of this data was found in the province-level or city-level statistical yearbooks which are accessible in the China Statistical Yearbook Database. We also search for CEIC China+Global Package (CEIC) and the statistical bulletins to complete this dataset. The statistical bulletins are provided by the county-level Bureau of Statistics. Table 4.8 demonstrates the mean, standard deviation and number of observations of sale prices for three types of land and the seven regional-level socio-economic related variables. The land prices vary greatly among different types of land, of which the values of the land used for residence are the highest. The standard deviations of the regional characteristics are large as well, indicating regional-level heterogeneity.

4.4 Methodology

We first introduce the conventional hedonic strategy to examine whether the entry of a new Wanda Plaza has any impact on land price. The benchmark model is as follows:

$$\log(P_{it}) = \alpha + \beta_1 \log(X_{it}) + \beta_2 D_{iq} + \varepsilon_{it}, \tag{4.1}$$

where $\log(P_{it})$ is the log-linearized form of land price[4] in region i; $\log(X_{it})$ is the log-linearized form of macroeconomic variables in region i; D_i is the binary indicator variable that indicates a Wanda Plaza q is operated in region i while the control group is the region that does not have Wanda

Plazas nearby. The coefficient of the variable $D_i(\beta_2)$ is of main interest, the estimate of β_2 represents the effect which a Wanda Plaza has on the average land prices of counties. However, results derived from such analysis may suffer from omitted variable bias. We instead use the difference-in-different identification strategy in the panel data set shown as

$$\log(P_{it}) = \alpha + \beta_1 \log(X_{it}) + \beta_2 D_{iq} + \beta_3 D_{iq} * \text{Post}_{iq} + \varepsilon. \tag{4.2}$$

We add an interaction term $D_{iq} * \text{Post}_{iq}$ in the regression function. Post_{iq} is a time indicator, which means whether the land is traded in region i after the opening of Wanda Plaza q. Thus, we introduce the time element of the opening of Wanda Plazas. The coefficient on $D_{iq} * \text{Post}_{iq}$ (β_3) is of primary interest in our research. According to Stock and Watson (2012),

$$\hat{\beta}_3^{dd} = \left(\overline{\log(p_{it})}^{\text{open,after}} - \overline{\log(p_{it})}^{\text{open,before}}\right) - \left(\overline{\log(p_{it})}^{\text{not,after}} - \overline{\log(p_{it})}^{\text{not,before}}\right). \tag{4.3}$$

Therefore, the estimate of β_3 is the difference between $\log(p_{it})$ in the treatment group and $\log(p_{it})$ in the control group. The treatment group is administrative districts or counties where Wanda Plazas come into operation and the control group is the region without any establishment of Wanda Plazas. The temporal window chosen in our research is one year after the Wanda Plaza starts to operate. It seems that the time window is small which may attenuate the effect of a new Wanda Plaza, and this is especially so as from the time that Dalian Wanda Company announced the establishment of a Wanda Plaza and the start of the presale, the land value nearby has already begun to fluctuate. The average time between the date of granting Wanda Company the permits for presale and the opening date is more than 1.5 years. Thus, it seems better to set the temporal window as one year and a half after the Wanda Plaza starts business. However, if we increase the time span, seven cases of entry information have to be dropped from our sample, resulting in a smaller sample. We eventually choose one year as the comparison time window considering the trade-off. By looking at the land prices before and after the opening of Wanda Plazas, the time-invariant variables that might bias our estimates can be differenced away. However, we must assume that the trends of the land prices in the treatment and control regions are similar before and after the opening of Wanda Plaza.

4.5 Results

4.5.1 Benchmark Model Estimation Results

First, we present the results of the traditional cross-sectional identification following Eq. (4.1). The cross-sectional analysis only includes one dummy variable "open" that indicates whether there is a Wanda Plaza in this region or not. The coefficient of this dummy variable is of interest, which implies the marginal willingness to purchase land near a Wanda Plaza. We then analyze the impacts on the aforementioned three different types of land.

Table 4.1 demonstrates the coefficients and the test-statistics in seven regressions. The estimates of the coefficients on the variable "open" are not significant in all seven regressions implying that the opening of a Wanda Plaza has no impact on residential land prices. However, the local fiscal revenue "Fiscal_R" and gross regional product "GDP" have significant positive influence on average prices of residential land. It shows that when local fiscal revenue increases by 1%, the residential land price will increase by 0.370%, 0.816% and 0.565%, respectively, in models (5), (6) and (7). When the gross regional product increases by 1%, the residential land price will rise by 0.567% shown in model (7). Real estate investments "real_estate_I" are only significant in the first three specifications.

Table 4.2 illustrates estimations of the impacts on commercial land. The coefficients on the indicator variable "open" are significant in the first four regressions. The opening of a Wanda Plaza raises the price of commercial land between the range of 0.2 and 0.6. The regional output also contributes to the rise of land price. Models (13) and (14) illustrate that when "GDP" grows 1%, the commercial land price will see a rise by 1.061% and 1.126% at 1% significance level. The coefficient on fiscal expenditure is significant in model (11) and the coefficient on fiscal revenue is significant in model (12). When adding other control variables, they lose significance.

Table 4.3 shows that the entry of Wanda Plaza entering a region has positive impact on the price of industrial land as well. From model (15) to model (20), they demonstrate that an opening of a Wanda Plaza relative to having no Wanda Plazas in the region can drive the industrial land price up by 40–60%. The real estate investment is positively linked with the price of industrial land. It shows that when local governments and enterprises increase investment in the real estate market by 10%, the industrial

Table 4.1 Benchmark estimations for residential land

	(1)	*(2)*	*(3)*	*(4)*	*(5)*	*(6)*	*(7)*
Variables	*Land_re*	*Land_re*	*Land_re*	*Land_re*	*Land_re*	*Land_re*	*Land_re*
Open	0.137	0.147	0.142	−0.0452	−0.140	−0.321	−0.259
	(0.71)	(0.75)	(0.78)	(−0.18)	(−0.62)	(−1.48)	(−1.20)
Real_estate_I	0.294***	0.278***	0.277***	0.0248	0.114	−0.0608	−0.0177
	(7.22)	(6.09)	(3.85)	(0.23)	(0.94)	(−0.49)	(−0.14)
Popu		0.00395	−0.0341	0.0162	−0.193	−0.434**	−0.540***
		(0.03)	(−0.26)	(0.09)	(−1.12)	(−2.16)	(−2.65)
Fx_asset_I			0.0353	0.222	−0.0261	−0.274*	−0.367**
			(0.40)	(1.60)	(−0.17)	(−1.67)	(−2.20)
Con_product				0.212**	0.138	0.0899	0.00202
				(2.04)	(1.34)	(0.89)	(0.02)
Fiscal_R					0.370***	0.816***	0.565**
					(2.79)	(4.00)	(2.44)
Fiscal_expense						0.179	0.0866
						(0.86)	(0.42)
GDP							0.567**
							(2.23)
Cons	−4.663***	−4.487***	−4.832***	−7.197***	−7.635***	−7.988***	−9.808***
	(−8.64)	(−6.94)	(−5.81)	(−6.60)	(−6.62)	(−7.08)	(−7.07)
N	422	403	399	245	220	207	207
R-sq	0.2532	0.2508	0.2467	0.1574	0.2396	0.2891	0.3037

Notes: $^{*}p < 0.1$, $^{**}p < 0.05$, $^{***}p < 0.01$; t statistics in parentheses

Table 4.2 Benchmark estimations for commercial land

	(8)	(9)	(10)	(11)	(12)	(13)	(14)
Variables	*Land_com*	*Land_com*	*Land_com*	*Land_com*	*Land_com*	*Land_com*	*Land_com*
Open	0.501***	0.497**	0.565**	0.481*	0.192	0.287	0.288
	(2.65)	(2.56)	(2.11)	(1.79)	(0.76)	(1.25)	(1.29)
Fx_asset_I	0.347***	0.351***	0.0734	−0.204	−0.348**	−0.497***	−0.665***
	(7.15)	(6.69)	(0.64)	(−1.18)	(−2.09)	(−3.11)	(−3.70)
Popu		0.00604	0.0915	−0.223	−0.100	−0.289	−0.377*
		(0.05)	(0.48)	(−0.90)	(−0.43)	(−1.30)	(−1.72)
Con_product			0.161	0.0978	0.00668	−0.110	−0.111
			(1.49)	(0.83)	(0.06)	(−0.99)	(−0.99)
Fiscal_expense				0.492**	−0.0526	−0.244	−0.144
				(2.40)	(−0.21)	(−1.03)	(−0.62)
Fiscal_R					0.819***	0.389	0.230
					(3.39)	(1.53)	(0.88)
GDP						1.061***	1.126***
						(3.81)	(4.08)
Real_estate_I							0.211
							(1.57)
Cons	−6.279***	−6.362***	−4.972***	−5.039***	−5.589***	−9.242***	−9.493***
	(−8.99)	(−8.39)	(−4.35)	(−3.96)	(−4.53)	(−6.06)	(−6.24)
N	652	615	263	217	217	217	205
R-sq	0.1309	0.1321	0.2556	0.2181	0.3048	0.3746	0.4272

Notes: $^{*}p < 0.1$, $^{**}p < 0.05$, $^{***}p < 0.01$; t statistics in parentheses

Table 4.3 Benchmark estimations for industrial land

	(15)	*(16)*	*(17)*	*(18)*	*(19)*	*(20)*	*(21)*
Variables	*Land_ind*	*Land_ind*	*Land_ind*	*Land_ind*	*Land_ind*	*Land_ind*	*Land_ind*
Open	0.411**	0.597***	0.523***	0.423***	0.409**	0.367**	0.220
	(2.40)	(4.56)	(3.02)	(2.61)	(2.53)	(2.19)	(1.37)
Popu	0.287***	−0.0528	0.175	0.123	0.0946	0.0667	0.120
	(3.58)	(−0.68)	(1.50)	(1.15)	(0.74)	(0.51)	(0.95)
Fx_asset_I		0.134***	0.199***	−0.0717	−0.102	−0.240**	−0.266**
		(5.83)	(2.91)	(−0.88)	(−1.04)	(−2.08)	(−2.52)
Con_product			−0.0154	−0.100	−0.112	−0.122	−0.00834
			(−0.23)	(−1.53)	(−1.51)	(−1.61)	(−0.12)
Real_estate_I				0.337***	0.342***	0.401***	0.302***
				(5.39)	(5.24)	(5.64)	(4.41)
GDP					0.0640	0.197	−0.00601
					(0.45)	(1.21)	(−0.04)
Fiscal_R						−0.0519	0.179
						(−0.53)	(1.12)
Fiscal_expense							0.0165
							(0.12)
Cons	−4.441***	−5.205***	−6.812***	−5.935***	−6.244***	−6.087***	−6.238***
	(−13.43)	(−13.68)	(−10.26)	(−9.19)	(−6.99)	(−6.59)	(−7.32)
N	635	572	247	232	226	208	196
R-sq	0.0771	0.2282	0.3208	0.4389	0.422	0.3924	0.4472

Notes: *$p < 0.1$, **$p < 0.05$, ***$p < 0.01$; t statistics in parentheses land price will go up within the range of 3–4%. The coefficient of population is only significant in model (15), however, the R-square seems very low (0.0771) when using population as the only explanatory variable. Thus, the change of regional population may not explain the fluctuation in industrial land value.

Overall, the statistical results show when a new Wanda Plaza is established, there is a marginal increase in the willingness to purchase the commercial land and industrial land nearby. However, the building of a Wanda Plaza has no statistical impact on the price of residential land. It also provides evidence that the land used for different purposes is affected by various economic factors. For example, the price of the residential land is positively affected by the gross regional product and the local fiscal revenue; the price of commercial land is affected by the gross regional product; and the price of industrial land is affected by real estate investment. However, the estimate of the impacts of entry or openness of a new Wanda Plaza on land prices may not provide a causal explanation due to omitted variables bias and reverse causality. Instead, it may be that the high land prices resulted in Wanda Company choosing the place for real estate development in the expectation of higher capital returns. The interpretation of the coefficient of "open" as causal possibly suffers from omitted variable bias. We thus turn to the DID identification strategy.

4.5.2 Difference-in-Differences Estimation Results

To deal with endogeneity, the DID identification strategy is implemented for Eq. (4.2). Besides the binary indicator variable, an interaction term $D_{iq} * \text{Post}_{iq}$ is included. The Post_{iq} is another binary indicator variable for land that is traded one year after the opening of a Wanda Plaza. Likewise, we study the effects of entry of Wanda Plaza on three different types of land. Now, the coefficients of the interaction terms are of primary interest.

Table 4.4 shows the estimation results using the DID method. The coefficients on interaction "open*post" are significant in the first three models, which indicate that the price of residential land one year after a Wanda Plaza opens increases by 0.2% compared with one year before. However, upon adding more controls into regression equation, the coefficient of the interaction term is not significant anymore but remains positive. The degrees of fitting, R-squares, are smaller in the first three models (0.253, 0.2472 and 0.2686) than in the last two models (0.3074

Table 4.4 DID estimations for residential land

	(22)	(23)	(24)	(25)	(26)	(27)	(28)
Variables	*land_re*	*Land_re*	*Land_re*	*Land_re*	*Land_re*	*Land_re*	*Land_re*
Open	0.0637	0.0755	0.0585	−0.0749	−0.162	−0.355	−0.292
	(0.32)	(0.38)	(0.31)	(−0.29)	(−0.72)	(−1.63)	(−1.35)
Open*post	0.243***	0.243***	0.227**	0.143	0.111	0.129	0.118
	(2.68)	(2.63)	(2.31)	(1.31)	(0.97)	(1.15)	(1.06)
Real_estate_I	0.258***	0.239***	0.278***	0.0286	0.119	−0.0500	−0.00868
	(6.09)	(5.05)	(3.88)	(0.26)	(0.98)	(−0.41)	(−0.07)
Popu		0.0148	−0.0178	0.0419	−0.161	−0.383*	−0.492**
		(0.11)	(−0.14)	(0.24)	(−0.92)	(−1.87)	(−2.36)
Fx_asset_I			−0.0209	0.177	−0.0602	−0.316*	−0.404**
			(−0.23)	(1.23)	(−0.37)	(−1.89)	(−2.38)
Con_product				0.196*	0.130	0.0785	−0.00580
				(1.87)	(1.25)	(0.78)	(−0.05)
Fiscal_R					0.353***	0.819***	0.575**
					(2.64)	(4.02)	(2.48)
Fiscal_expense						0.148	0.0608
						(0.71)	(0.29)
GDP							0.553**
							(2.18)
Cons	−4.197***	−4.023***	−4.089***	−6.483***	−7.010***	−7.229***	−9.068***
	(−7.49)	(−6.04)	(−4.60)	(−5.30)	(−5.28)	(−5.57)	(−5.88)
N	422	403	399	245	220	207	207
R-sq	0.253	0.2472	0.2686	0.1737	0.2545	0.3074	0.3215

DID, difference-in-difference

Notes: $^{*}p < 0.1$, $^{**}p < 0.05$, $^{***}p < 0.01$; t statistics in parentheses

and 0.3215), which implies the first three models are less fitted than the last two models. However, the 12.9% and 11.8% increase in residential land price in the last two models is economically significant or practically significant (the estimates of the coefficients are comparatively large). Thus, our results suggest that the introduction of a Wanda Plaza has a positive impact on surrounding residential land prices after one year. The impacts of real estate investment are also positive in the first three models at 1% significance level. If investment in real estate increases by 1%, the residential land price rises by 0.258%, 0.239% and 0.278%, respectively. Similar to the results in the benchmark estimation, local fiscal revenue and gross regional product contribute to the rise of local residential land price. Essentially, when local fiscal revenue increases by 1%, the residential land price increases by 0.353%, 0.819% and 0.575% separately as shown in models (26), (27) and (28); when the gross regional product increases 1%, the land price goes up by 0.553% as shown in model (28).

Table 4.5 shows the results for commercial land when using the DID approach. The coefficients on the indicator variable "open" are significantly positive in the first three regressions while the coefficients on the interaction are not significant in all regressions. Gross regional product still makes positive contribution to the rise of price in commercial land while the real estate investment plays a less significant role.

Table 4.6 tests the impacts on the price of industrial land when using the DID approach. The opening of a Wanda Plaza in the Yangtze River Delta has significantly positive impact on the price of industrial land after one year. Results in model 42 indicate that the price of industrial land one year after a Wanda Plaza opened increased by 11.2% compared with one year before it opened. This illustrates that the real estate investment is an essential determinant in the transaction of industrial land. When local governments and corporations increased investment in real estate market by 1%, the industrial land price went up by around 0.3–0.4%. Again, variation in regional population may not explain the fluctuation of industrial land value.

Overall, the opening of Wanda Plaza has a significant impact on the price of the industrial and residential land while it plays a less significant role in shaping the value of commercial land. Among the seven control variables, only three have significantly positive impacts on land transactions, namely, the gross regional product, the real estate investment and local fiscal revenue.

Table 4.5 DID estimations for commercial land

	(29)	(30)	(31)	(32)	(33)	(34)	(35)
Variables	*Land_com*	*Land_com*	*Land_com*	*Land_com*	*Land_com*	*Land_com*	*Land_com*
Open	0.514***	0.515***	0.550**	0.479*	0.176	0.277	0.275
	(2.69)	(2.62)	(2.05)	(1.77)	(0.70)	(1.22)	(1.25)
Open*post	−0.0342	−0.0500	0.0600	0.00836	0.0467	0.0325	0.0374
	(−0.31)	(−0.43)	(0.53)	(0.07)	(0.38)	(0.27)	(0.31)
Fx_asset_I	0.350***	0.357***	0.0563	−0.206	−0.365**	−0.515***	−0.692***
	(6.92)	(6.53)	(0.47)	(−1.18)	(−2.19)	(−3.23)	(−3.86)
Popu		0.00466	0.102	−0.219	−0.0753	−0.274	−0.357
		(0.04)	(0.53)	(−0.87)	(−0.32)	(−1.20)	(−1.60)
Con_product			0.154	0.0976	0.00663	−0.105	−0.106
			(1.41)	(0.82)	(0.06)	(−0.96)	(−0.96)
Fiscal_expense				0.489**	−0.0735	−0.256	−0.158
				(2.36)	(−0.29)	(−1.08)	(−0.68)
Fiscal_R					0.831***	0.399	0.235
					(3.46)	(1.57)	(0.91)
GDP						1.058***	1.122***
						(3.82)	(4.11)
Real_estate_I							0.221*
							(1.65)
Cons	−6.333***	−6.444***	−4.674***	−4.992***	−5.334***	−9.022***	−9.215***
	(−8.69)	(−8.21)	(−3.66)	(−3.43)	(−3.83)	(−5.44)	(−5.59)
N	652	615	263	217	217	217	205
R-sq	0.1292	0.1296	0.2642	0.2192	0.3134	0.3821	0.4378

DID, difference-in-difference

Notes: *$p < 0.1$, **$p < 0.05$, ***$p < 0.01$; *t* statistics in parentheses

Table 4.6 DID estimations for industrial land

	(36)	*(37)*	*(38)*	*(39)*	*(40)*	*(41)*	*(42)*
Variables	*Land_ind*	*Land_ind*	*Land_ind*	*Land_ind*	*Land_ind*	*Land_ind*	*Land_ind*
Open	0.360**	0.571***	0.498***	0.394***	0.388**	0.337**	0.188
	(2.11)	(4.49)	(3.17)	(2.60)	(2.57)	(2.15)	(1.21)
Open*post	0.137***	0.0767	0.0801	0.109*	0.108*	0.141**	0.112*
	(2.71)	(1.48)	(1.21)	(1.77)	(1.69)	(2.15)	(1.88)
Popu	0.263***	−0.0566	0.172	0.133	0.121	0.104	0.163
	(3.28)	(−0.74)	(1.56)	(1.30)	(0.97)	(0.81)	(1.29)
Fx_asset_I		0.124***	0.167**	−0.120	−0.135	−0.288**	−0.296***
		(5.15)	(2.43)	(−1.44)	(−1.36)	(−2.50)	(−2.81)
Con_product			−0.0111	−0.102	−0.102	−0.116	−0.0181
			(−0.17)	(−1.59)	(−1.44)	(−1.60)	(−0.27)
Real_estate_I				0.345***	0.350***	0.414***	0.314***
				(5.54)	(5.37)	(5.86)	(4.60)
GDP					0.0224	0.156	−0.0236
					(0.16)	(0.97)	(−0.15)
Fiscal_R						−0.0591	0.191
						(−0.62)	(1.22)
Fiscal_expense							−0.012
							(−0.12)
Cons	−4.345***	−5.045***	−6.400***	−5.380***	−5.506***	−5.088***	−5.468***
	(−13.18)	(−12.93)	(−8.90)	(−7.64)	(−5.69)	(−5.07)	(−5.91)
N	635	572	247	232	226	208	196
R-sq	0.0868	0.2336	0.3345	0.4558	0.4432	0.4176	0.4642

DID, difference-in-difference

Notes: *$p < 0.1$, **$p < 0.05$, ***$p < 0.01$; *t* statistics in parentheses

4.6 Conclusion

Few studies systematically test whether or not the entry of a leading real estate developer such as Wanda increases local land prices. We make the first attempt to answer this empirical question. Specifically, we explore how different types of land price may vary with the entry of Wanda Plazas and compare the price one year before the opening of the Wanda Plaza and that one year after.

We use three unique datasets including specific addresses and the information on the opening dates of 26 Wanda Plazas in the Yangtze River Delta, the county-level land transaction data, and a dataset including social-economic variables of 109 administrative districts or counties from 2008 to 2016. Based on the hedonic price model that describes how product prices can be explained by their attributes, we apply DID specification to estimate the effect of Wanda Plaza on land prices by comparing the land price one year before Wanda Plazas opened and that one year after they opened. The results from our analysis suggest that the entry or a new Wanda Plaza increases surrounding land prices. The primary analysis suggests that the value of industrial land prices in the districts or counties in the Yangtze River Delta where there is a Wanda Plaza significantly appreciate. The increase of price for residential land is the highest compared with industrial and commercial land when making a comparison of one year before the entry of Wanda Plaza and one year after their entry. The gross regional product contributes positively to the rise of residential land prices and commercial land prices; the real estate investment is positively linked with commercial land price and industrial land price while the local fiscal revenue only has marginal effect on residential land price.

Our empirical evidences reveal preference of the real estate developers to purchase residential and industrial lands near the leading commercial community. In general, the accessibility of necessities, convenience in shopping, and possibility of entertainment within proximity to a Wanda Plaza seem to matter more than the increased costs imposed by potential crime, garbage accumulation, noise, traffic jam and pollution. To some extent, this result contributes to the understanding of the economic value of introducing a leading real estate developer into a community to push up the land value. Future research can be refined, exploring in more detail the impacts of entry of Wanda Plaza on nearby land plots within certain distances with the facilitation of micro-level land transaction data in monthly frequency.

Appendix

Table 4.7 Tabulations of when and where Wanda Plazas opened

Panel A			*Panel B*		
Year Wanda Plaza opened			*City Wanda Plaza opened*		
Year	*Freq.*	*Percent*	*City*	*Freq.*	*Percent*
2008	0	0.00	Shanghai	5	20.83
2009	3	12.50	Nanjing	2	8.33
2010	3	12.50	Wuxi	2	8.33
2011	5	20.83	Suzhou	2	8.33
2012	2	8.33	Changzhou	2	8.33
2013	3	12.50	Xuzhou	1	4.17
2014	4	16.67	Nantong	1	4.17
2015	4	16.67	Huaian	1	4.17
2016	0	0.00	Zhenjiang	1	4.17
			Taizhou	1	4.17
Total	24	100	Hangzhou	1	4.17
			Ningbo	1	4.17
			Wenzhou	1	4.17
			Shaoxin	1	4.17
			Jiaxin	1	4.17
			Jinhua	1	4.17
			Total	24	100

Table 4.8 Summary statistics of land data

	Mean	*s.d.*	*Observations*
Sale price of residential land	1.12	1.97	869
Sale price of commercial land	1.02	2.09	879
Sale price of industrial land	0.05	0.09	784
Regional population	66.28	54.80	794
Gross regional product	22,900,000.00	68,000,000.00	771
Fixed asset investment	2,451,793.00	2,156,409.00	719
Fiscal revenue	533,868.10	608,076.00	766
Fiscal expenditure	677,623.70	854,798.80	433
Gross construction industry product	2,621,841.00	3,131,203.00	392
Real estate investment	936,437.50	1,126,495.00	454

Notes

1. The five Wanda Plazas including Yuyao Wanda Plaza, Wenzhou Pingyang Wanda Plaza, Jiangyin Wanda Plaza, Taicang Wanda Plaza, Yixing Wanda Plaza were all built in county-level cities or counties where there is no corresponding land transaction data available.
2. There are 206 administrative districts and counties in Yangtze River Delta in total. However, there are only 109 districts and counties with land transaction data available in Wind Database.
3. The standard statistics of population refers to the year-end registered population; however, some cities only have data on permanent resident population. We use either of these two depending on availability and term them uniformly as total population.
4. The unit of land price is 10,000 RMB/m^2; the unit of regional population is 10,000; the unit of the other six control variables (gross regional product, fixed asset investment, fiscal revenue, fiscal expenditure, gross construction industry product, and real estate investment) is 10,000 RMB.

References

Bao, H. X. H., Glascock, J. L., Zhou, S. Z. and Feng, L. (2014), "Land value determination in an emerging market: empirical evidence from China", *University of Cambridge working paper.*

Bayer, P. and Timmins, C. (2007), "Estimating equilibrium models of sorting across locations", *The Economic Journal:* 117(518), 353–374.

Black, S. E. (1999), "Do Better Schools Matter? Parental valuation of elementary education", *Quarterly Journal of Economics:* 114(2), 577–599.

Calabrese, S., Epple, D., Romer, T. and Sieg, H. (2006), "Local public good provision: voting, peer effects, and mobility", *Journal of Public Economics:* 90(6–7), 959–981.

Chay, K. Y. and Greenstone, M. (2005), "Does air quality matter? Evidence from the housing market", *Journal of Political Economy:* 113(2), 376–424.

Des Rosiers, F., Lagana, A., Thériault, M. and Beaudoin, M. (1996), "Shopping centres and house values: an empirical investigation", *Journal of Property Valuation and Investment January:* 14(4), 41–62.

Figlio, D. N. and Lucas, M. E. (2004), "What's in a grade? School report cards and the housing market", *American Economic Review:* 94(3), 591–604.

Financial Times. (2014), *Dalian Wanda: Big fish.* Available at: https://search.proquest.com/docview/1648108626?accountid=153081

Kau, J. B. and Sirmans, C. F. (1979), "Urban land value functions and the price elasticity of demand for housing", *Journal of Urban Economics:* 6(1), 112–121.

Kowalski, J. G. and Paraskevopoulos, C. C. (1990), "The impact of location on urban industrial land prices", *Journal of Urban Economics:* 27(1), 16–24.

Kuminoff, N. and Pope, J. (2012), "'Rosen Bias' in the Willingness to Pay for Nonmarket Goods", *mimeo.*

Lim, J. S. and Missios, P. (2007), "Does size really matter? Landfill scale impacts on property values", *Applied Economic Letters:* 14(10), 719–723.

Linden, L. and Rockoff, J. E. (2008), "Estimates of the impact of crime risk on property values from Megan's Laws", *The American Economic Review:* 98(3), 1103–1127.

Parmeter, C. and Pope, J. (2012), "Quasi-experiments and hedonic property value methods", *IDEAS Working Paper Series from RePEc.*

Peiser, R. B. (1987), "The determinants of nonresidential urban land values", *Journal of Urban Economic:* 22(3), 340–360.

Pope, J. (2007), "Fear of crime and housing prices: household reactions to sex offender registries", *Journal of Urban Economics:* 64(3), 601–614.

Pope, D. G. and Pope, J. C. (2015), "When Walmart comes to town: Always low housing prices? Always?", *Journal of Urban Economics*: 87, 1–13.

Ridker, R. G. and Henning, J. A. (1967), "The determinants of residential property values with special reference to air pollution", *Review of Economics and Statistics:* 49(2), 246–257.

Rosen, S. (1974), "Hedonic prices and implicit markets: product differentiation in pure competition", *Journal of Political Economy:* 82(1), 34–55.

Sirpal, R. (1994), "Empirical modeling of the relative impacts of various sizes of shopping centers on the values of surrounding residential properties", *Journal of Real Estate Research:* 9(4), 487–505.

Stock, J. H. and Watson, M. M. (2012), *Introduction to Econometrics* (3rd edition), Edinburgh: Pearson Education Limited.

PART III

Energy and Environment

CHAPTER 5

Forecasting the Carbon Price in China Pilot Emission Trading Scheme: A Structural Time Series Approach

Zhao Mengdi and Soo Keong Yong

5.1 Introduction

Global warming caused by greenhouse gas (GHG) is the most severe environmental problem over the century, and carbon dioxide (CO_2) accounted for 60% of GHG (Xia et al. 2013). China is the largest carbon emitter in the world. As depicted in Fig. 5.1, China accounted for around 30% of worldwide CO_2 emission in 2014, followed by the United States (15%) and India (7%). As a fast-growing economy, its energy usage intensity is high and the coal dominates the energy supply. Historically, China's CO_2 emissions increased at a rate of 3.3% per year between 1990 and 1999, accounting for 13% of global emissions, and these emissions doubled over the next decade, growing at 8.9% per year between 2000 and 2007 (Michieka et al. 2013; Peters et al. 2007).

In view of this situation, the State Council announced on November 26, 2009, at the Copenhagen Climate Conference that China aims to reduce the intensity of carbon dioxide emissions per unit of GDP by

Z. Mengdi • S. K. Yong (✉)
International Business School Suzhou, Xi'an Jiaotong-Liverpool University, Suzhou, China
e-mail: SK.Yong@xjtlu.edu.cn

J. H. Hung, Y. Chen (eds.), *The State of China's State Capitalism*,
https://doi.org/10.1007/978-981-13-0983-0_5

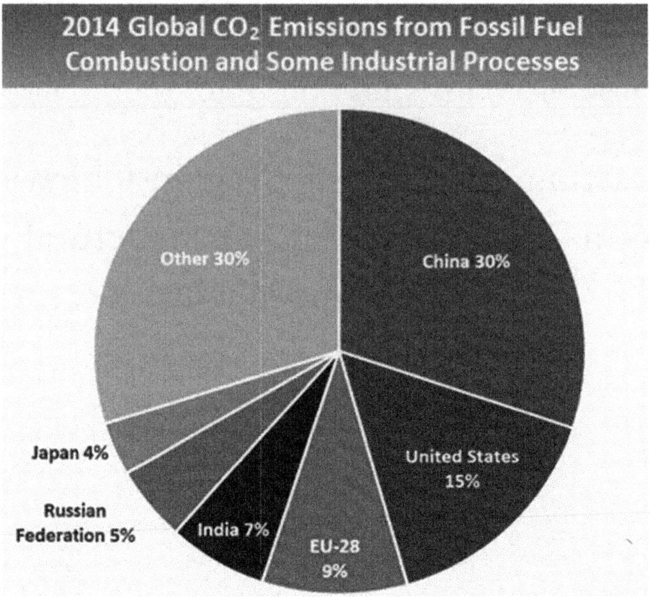

Fig. 5.1 2014 global CO_2 emissions. (Source: Boden, T.A., Marland, G., and Andres, R.J. (2017). National CO_2 Emissions from Fossil-Fuel Burning, Cement Manufacture, and Gas Flaring: 1751–2014, Carbon Dioxide Information Analysis Center, Oak Ridge National Laboratory, U.S. Department of Energy, doi 10.3334/CDIAC/00001_V2017)

40–45% by the year 2020 relative to 2005 levels (Wang et al. 2011). To achieve the target, the Chinese government planned for several major policy options that include market-based environmental policies such as the carbon emission trading scheme (ETS) (Han et al. 2012). As a major step in this direction, the National Development and Reform Commission (NDRC), the body responsible for economic development and pollution emissions under the China State Council, selected seven locations that include four provincial-level municipalities (Beijing, Tianjin, Shanghai, and Chongqing) (Zhao et al. 2014), one special economic zone (Shenzhen) and two provinces (Hubei and Guangdong) (Wang et al. 2015) to establish the pilot emission trading systems during the Twelfth Five-Year Plan. The ultimate objective for these pilot markets was to lay down the framework in order to nationalize the carbon markets at the end of 2017. Figure 5.2 presents the location of seven pilots.

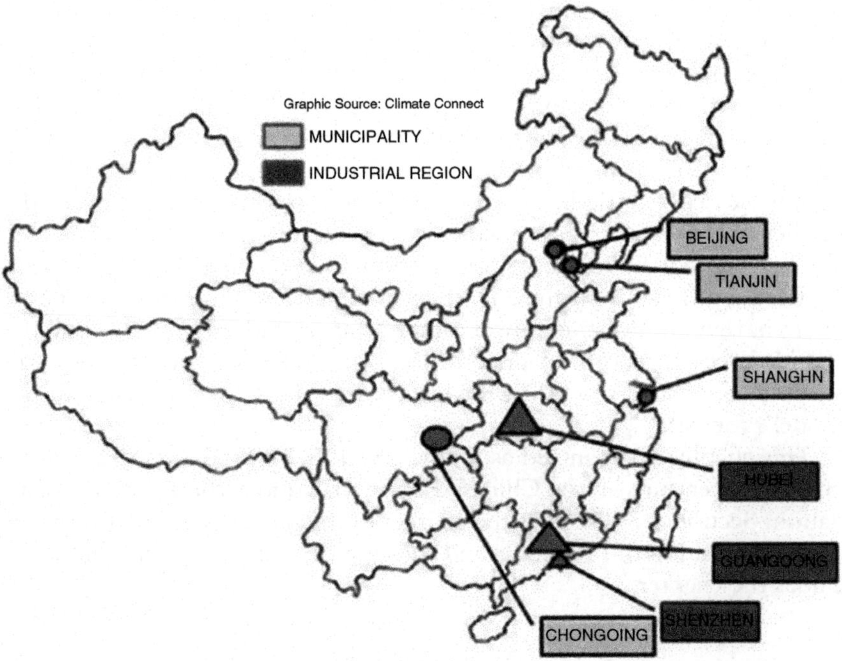

Fig. 5.2 Location of pilot carbon trade schemes in China. (Source: SEI 2012)

Given the importance of the China Carbon Emission Trading Scheme (CCETS), the prediction of the price of carbon emission permit in the Chinese market will facilitate worldwide investors in formulating the appropriate trading strategies. Policy makers can fine-tune the appropriate emission reduction policies based on forecasting, and private companies can formulate reasonable price expectation to make the investment decisions (Koop and Tole 2013). Hence, the focus of this chapter is to provide an exploratory study on the movement of carbon prices from the China pilot ETS using data from Beijing, Shanghai, and Shenzhen, which are the first three pilot markets that started trading in 2013.[1]

Conventional forecasting models such as the autoregressive (AR) model are used for forecasting and predicting in economic and financial analysis. However, one of the major drawbacks for these models requires that the data are stationary with the means remaining fairly constant over time. To circumvent this issue, the structural time series model (STSM) is adopted for analyzing the carbon prices. STSM has the flexibility to allow the parameters in the model to change over time while essential properties in economic data such as the trend and cycle are added in the model as unobserved components to improve predictive power (Broadstock and Collins 2010; Jackman and Greenidge 2010; Kourentzes et al. 2014). In the analysis, we use one-year carbon spot prices from three pilot markets as analysis and use two-month data for out-of-sample forecast to assess the STSM's predictive power of carbon prices. In addition to the unobserved components, we also include energy prices, specifically the oil and coal prices, as explanatory variables in the STSM specification. We find that the energy prices have no forecasting power on the Chinese carbon price. Overall the STSM forecasts of carbon price in the three ETS pilots have low mean squared forecast error (MSFE), which indicates the low variability of the model's forecast.[2]

This chapter is organized as follows: Sect. 5.2 provides an overview of empirical literature on the Chinese ETS market and carbon price determination. Section 5.3 discusses the sources of the data. Section 5.4 provides a brief exposition of the model and the empirical results. Section 5.5 concludes the chapter.

5.2 Relevant Literature

The ETS is one of the most popular environmental policy instrument given its potential to reduce pollution emissions and achieve minimum cost of compliance. After 37 countries and the European Community committed themselves to reducing the carbon dioxide emission in the Kyoto Protocol in 1997 (Aichele and Felbermayr 2013), a multiplicity of regional, national, and even subnational markets have emerged (Newell et al. 2013). This leads to a wealth of literature that discusses and analyzes the development of carbon emission trading markets all over the world.[3] In particular, numerous researches have been conducted on studying the European Union emission trading Scheme (EU ETS) (Declercq et al. 2011) because it is currently the largest carbon market (before China launched its national ETS). Since it started operation in 2005, the EU ETS has progressed through three phases of development with each different phase introducing new policy changes that increase the stringency of the rules and regulations. Given this history, there are numerous studies on analyzing the scheme's effectiveness and its degree of success in achieving various objectives such as curbing greenhouse gas emissions (GHG) and inducing directed technological change (see, e.g., Myklebust et al. 2010; Anderson and Di Maria 2011; Constantini and Mazzanti 2012; Calel and Dechezlepretre 2013; Martin et al. 2014, etc.).[4] This provides the largest source of reference for policymakers around the world including China for designing an ETS framework.

5.2.1 *The Chinese Carbon Market*

China has been the world's largest emitter of carbon dioxide since 2006 (Peters et al. 2007) and with its fast-developing economy, the energy intensity is high and its energy supply is mainly from coal (Jotzo and Löschel 2014). Hence, it is expected that China can contribute to the largest reductions in emission reductions compared to any other country in the world. Given that the first ETS started only in July 2013 in Shenzhen followed by Beijing and Shanghai within the same year, most scholarly studies on the impact of China ETS are still at their infancy stage. Most of the papers focus on reviewing the recent experiences with the Chinese ETS and lessons that can be drawn from international experience. The emphasis is mainly on assessing the possible outcome arising from the different rules and regulations across the different pilot locations (Qi et al. 2014; Zhang et al. 2014). Bo and Freeman (2013) have highlighted the core problems of the Chinese pilot carbon markets, such as latent parochialism and the challenges of initiating the national markets (Rudolph and Schneider 2013).

Due to the geographic differences and regional development diversity, each pilot ETS location faces different challenges. The Shenzhen ETS is the first urban-level "cap-and-trade" carbon ETS to operate in China. Jiang (2014) depicted the further developments for challenges and their policy choices of Shenzhen ETS. Wu et al. (2014) conducted an evaluation of potential uncertainties such as those factors associated with changes in the patterns of economic development; trading activities related to the bankable allowances; carbon leakage risks; and insufficient monitoring, reporting, and verification (MRV) capabilities. Liu et al. (2013) analyzed the economic impact of linking the pilot market of Guangdong and Hubei provinces. It turned out to be a win-win strategy because the linkages would reduce the carbon abatement costs. Cui et al. (2014) analyzed the potential outcome of a nationalized ETS system and found that the cost-saving effect in eastern and western provinces was more pronounced than central provinces.

Some studies focus on analyzing the impact of the ETS system on the electricity market. For example, Teng et al. (2014) assessed the institutional barriers to an effective ETS in China within the current China's electricity market mode land and found that there were major challenges from the "equal share" dispatching model for power stations and from regulated electricity pricing. Therefore, they proposed that the emissions pricing could be a "supply side" model with an "energy saving" model of electricity dispatch from generators before the price liberalization. In addition, Li et al. (2014) found that the existing rigid electricity pricing implied that the carbon pricing such as through the ETS system would be less effective than it would otherwise be. Hence an optimal policy could only be achieved through a deregulated electricity market in order to allow the carbon cost to be passed from the generators to the electricity consumers.

Hübler et al. (2014) analyzed the effects of a future national ETS in China on energy-intensive industries and trade-exposed industries since they were likely to relocate to other countries with less stringent environmental regulations, leading to the potential "carbon leakage" phenomenon. Using simulations, the authors found that industries such as aluminum and electricity were expected to experience non-negligible production losses. An unusual feature in all the Chinese pilot ETS is that they cover both the direct emissions from fossil fuel and those from electricity usage within each location plus the electricity usage from electricity generated outside the scheme (Wu et al. 2014; Jiang et al. 2014; Zhang et al. 2014). This implied that large electricity users such as manufacturers and large buildings would experience higher effective electricity price than without the ETS in place. Therefore, whether this price signal would eventually lead to changes in business operations and investment decisions remain an important question.

5.2.2 *Key Determinants of Carbon Price*

There are many factors that can influence the emission unit allowance price. By analyzing the fundamentals of demand and supply, Christiansen et al. (2005) identified the following factors as being the primary determinants of carbon emission price in EU ETS: policy and regulatory issues, market fundamentals, the emission-to-cap ratio, the role of fuel-switching, weather, and production levels. Mansanet-Bataller et al. (2007) were among the first to uncover the economic relationship between the energy markets and the carbon prices. The research was based on the phase I spot and future data of the EU ETS and this was linked to the fossil fuel (e.g., oil, natural gas, and coal). The authors suggested that energy sources were the principal factors in affecting the carbon price levels. Hintermann (2010) constructed a structural model of allowance price to assess the high level of volatility in the first phase of EU ETS. The result showed that fuel prices and summer temperature played an important role in explaining the carbon price movement. Other subsequent research studies provided further evidence on the relationship between energy price and carbon price (Kim and Koo 2010; Chevallier 2011; Aatola et al. 2013; Boersen and Scholtens 2014; Liu et al. 2014). In addition to the energy prices, there are other factors that can affect the carbon allowance prices. For example, Carraro and Favero (2009) analyzed the economic and financial determinants of carbon market in Europe. The analysis showed that the crucial determinants were expectations about the future international climate policy and the availability of carbon-free technologies, which might be innovated in future.

5.3 Preliminary Data Analysis

The dependent variable in this study is the carbon permit price and there are three explanatory variables—oil, coal, and natural gas price. In particular, these variables are chosen because they are identified in the literature as the top three variables that potentially influenced the demand for permits (Myklebust et al. 2010; Kim and Koo 2010; Chevallier 2011; Aatola et al. 2013; Boersen and Scholtens 2014; Liu et al. 2014). Note that the prices are the daily transaction prices or sales prices.

The daily spot price of carbon emission allowance price is obtained from the Chinese carbon emission trading exchange website. The daily average transaction price represents the carbon price level in this preliminary study. The pilot market was first launched in Shenzhen on June 18, 2013, followed by Shanghai on November 26, 2013, and Beijing on November 28, 2013. However, we do not select the data starting from the first day of market opening due to missing data. In this case, the time span for Shenzhen is from August 08, 2013, to August 08, 2014; the time span for Beijing is from November 29, 2013, to November 29, 2014; and the time span for Shanghai is from December 03, 2013, to December 03, 2014. The two-month prices for each market after the end of time series data for analysis are used for assessing the out-of-sample forecasting capability of the STSM. The unit price is in RMB per ton of carbon dioxide. The analysis in this chapter is only conducted on three out of the seven pilot markets due to the lack of sufficient data to conduct the analysis at the time when this study was conducted.

The daily crude oil price of Daqing Oilfield is used in our analysis and is obtained from the Wind database. As China does not have an oil future market, we cannot use the futures price such as futures Brent oil price in euros per barrel from the Intercontinental Commodities Exchange.[5] Moreover, the production volume of Daqing oilfield comprises about 40% proportion in China's total crude oil production so the oil price of Daqing oilfield can be used as the representative oil price level of China. As mentioned in earlier, the oil price is one of the key determinants of carbon price (e.g., Mansanet-Bataller et al. 2007; Kim and Koo 2010; Chevallier 2011). This is because the oil price tends to move in tandem with other energy prices so that the increase in the oil price level will increase the aggregate price level in the economy. The stated prices are in dollar per barrel and they are converted into RMB per barrel using the daily exchange rate from the Chinese Central Bank.

Coal price is measured by the average transaction price of coal on Chinese harbors such as the ports of Qinhuangdao, Tianjin, and Ningbo. Almost all the coal in China is transported from these major ports and hence the average price can represent the coal price level in China. Liu et al. (2014) showed that there was a correlation between prices of coal and carbon prices. The average daily gas price of the country is also provided by the Wind database. Gas prices have been included as a driver of carbon price because it will affect the fuel-switching behavior of the power installations. For instance, many factories in China are prepared to install gas energy equipment due to its affordability and environmental friendly characteristics in recent years. The carbon emission price is therefore expected to be correlated with the movement of gas price.

Figure 5.3 depicts the graphs of the natural logarithm of the daily average traction price in the three markets in their first year of operation. From the graphs, it is obvious that there is no cyclical and seasonal effect in the series as the available time length of the data is for one single year. As seen from Table 5.1, Shenzhen pilot market has the highest carbon trading price while Shanghai has the lowest. Among the three of them, carbon price of Shanghai pilot market is more volatile while that of Shenzhen is quite stable.

Fig. 5.3 Logarithms of average transaction price for three pilot carbon emission trading markets

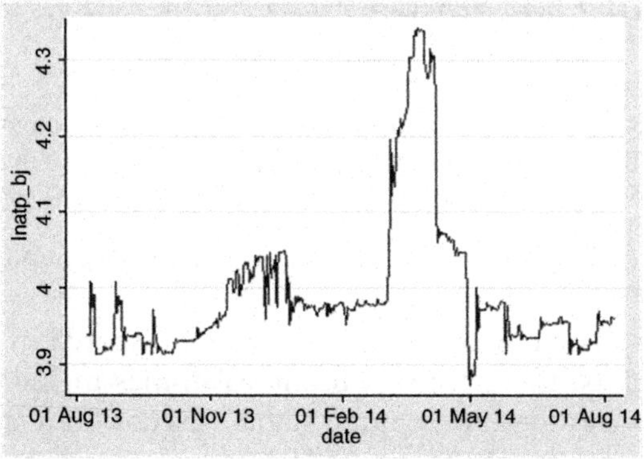

Beijing

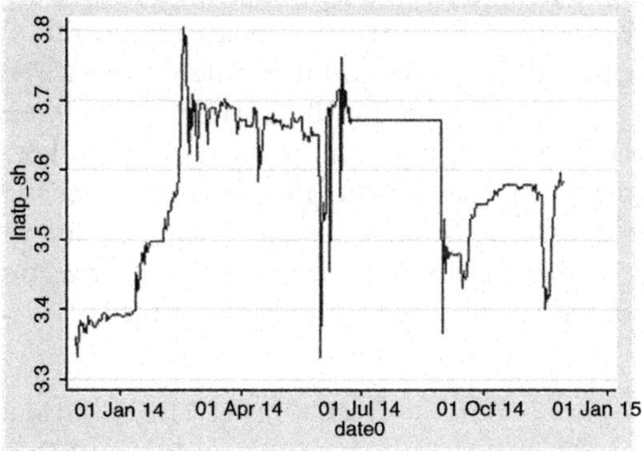

Shanghai

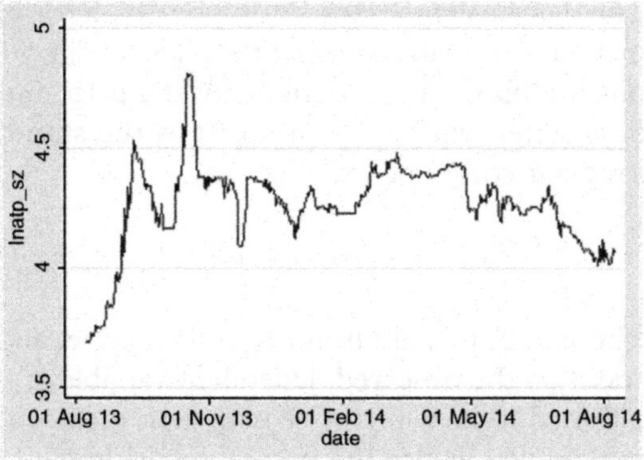

Shenzhen

Table 5.1 Summary statistics for the variables of interests

	Obs	*Mean*	*Std. dev*	*Min*	*Max*
SZ_P	366	4.64	0.029	4.58	4.73
BJ_P	366	3.99	0.096	3.87	4.34
SH_P	366	3.59	0.109	3.33	3.8

Note: SZ, BJ, SH refer to Shenzhen, Beijing, and Shanghai. All the prices are in natural logarithm form

The raw prices of energy are presented in Fig. 5.4. From the graphical plots, there are significant volatilities in the coal and oil prices while gas prices tend to be quite stable. Except for a sharp decrease in the gas price in around February of 2014, the logarithm of price remains around 9.12 ever since. Table 5.2 summarizes the statistics for variables within the one-year period. For the price of energy sources, natural gas price has the least standard deviation and it is much more stable than oil and coal price.

Next, we examine the correlation between the carbon prices with the prices of energy sources in each pilot market. Table 5.3 shows the table of correlation coefficients for the three cities in the different panels. The correlation coefficients are all significant at the 5% significance level. This provides preliminary evidence that the movement of carbon prices is related to the prices of energy sources.

5.4 Modeling the Carbon Permit Prices in the Pilot Markets

The daily average transaction price data for pilot Chinese carbon emission markets are analyzed using the STSM. The STSM is set up in terms of various unobserved components of the price time series. Conventionally, the time series will be decomposed as the sum of trend, seasonal, cycle, and irregular components. That is,

$$Y_t = T_t + S_t + C_t + I_t, \mathrm{t} = 1, 2, \ldots, \mathrm{T}, \tag{5.1}$$

where T, S, C, I are trend, seasonal, cycle, and irregular effects respectively and Y_t is the observed dependent variable at time t. The irregular term I_t is assumed to be white noise with zero mean and variance of σ_τ^2. In Fig. 5.4, the graphs depicts the natural logarithms of the daily average transaction price in the three pilot markets during their first year of operation. From visual inspection of the graphs, there is no evidence of cyclical and seasonal

Fig. 5.4 Logarithm of energy prices

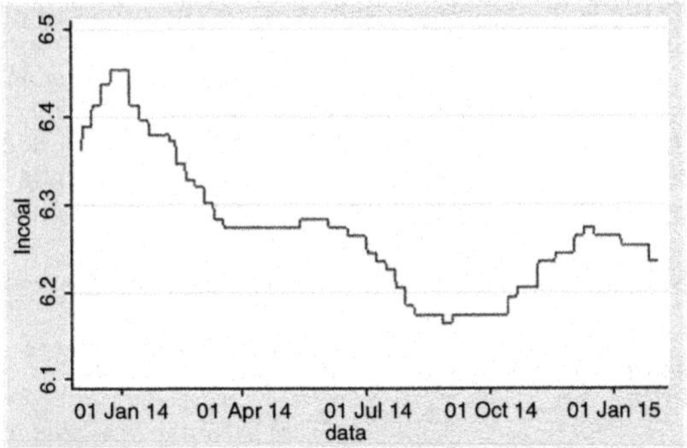

Coal

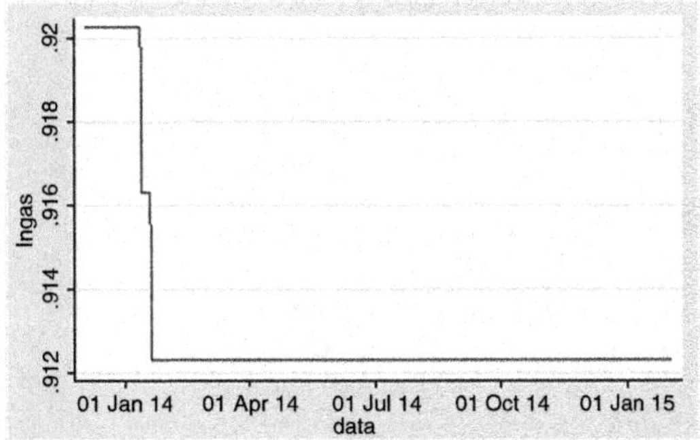

Gas

Oil

effects in the series especially since the time span of the data lasted for only one year. When the right-hand side of the expression contains a trend component T_t and a random disturbance term I_t only, it is the simplest form of the STSM and is known as a *local-level model*. If additional explanatory

Table 5.2 Summary statistics for the prices of energy sources

	Obs	*Mean*	*Std. dev*	*Min*	*Max*
Oil	366	6.46	0.032	6.40	6.54
Coal	366	6.31	0.061	6.17	6.45
Gas	366	0.92	0.004	0.91	0.92

Note: The time length for oil, coal, and gas prices are as same as the Shenzhen trading price in this table

Table 5.3 The correlation coefficients

	Average transaction price	*Gas price*	*Oil price*	*Coal price*
Panel A: Beijing market				
Average transaction price	1.0000			
Gas price	−0.2120*	1.0000		
	(0.0000)			
Oil price	0.1621*	0.1931*	1.0000	
	(0.0008)	(0.0001)		
Coal price	−0.2643*	0.7032*	0.2409*	1.0000
	(0.0000)	(0.0000)	(0.0000)	
Panel B: Shanghai market				
Average transaction price	1.0000			
Gas price	−0.5372*	1.0000		
	(0.0000)			
Oil price	0.4544*	0.1942*	1.0000	
	(0.0008)	(0.0001)		
Coal price	−0.3844*	0.7104*	0.2789*	1.0000
	(0.0000)	(0.0000)	(0.0000)	
Panel C: Shenzhen market				
Average transaction price	1.0000			
Gas price	0.1203*	1.0000		
	(0.0128)			
Oil price	0.6240*	0.1782*	1.0000	
	(0.0000)	(0.0002)		
Coal price	0.3970*	0.5116*	0.3843*	1.0000
	(0.0000)	(0.0000)	(0.0000)	

Note: The *p*-values are in parentheses

variables are believed to be relevant to explaining the dependent variable, they can also be added to the model. Thus, the model formulation can be written as

$$Y_t = T_t + \lambda_t + \gamma_t + \varepsilon_t, \varepsilon_t \sim N\left(0, \sigma_\varepsilon^2\right), \tag{5.2}$$

where the trend T_t is a stochastic trend in form of $T_t = T_{t-1} + \omega_t$, where ω_t is the white noise of trend subject to normal and independent distribution and λ_t and γ_t are the two unobserved components.

Compared to other time series models such as AR model under the Box–Jenkins approach, the STSM has various advantages. It can not only depict the underlying characteristics of a series but also allows the parameters of explanatory variables to vary with time to achieve a more precise prediction. The key to handling the STSM is the state space form where various unobserved components such as trend and cycle are presented by the state of the system (Harvey 1989; Harvey and Shephard 1993). The state space model consists of state equations and observation equations. In this case, the equation for Y_t is the observation equation and the equation for T_t is the state equation. Once the model is written in state space form, the Kalman filter can be used to recursively compute the current estimates and one-step ahead predictions of the state variables. The state space form is used to derive the log likelihood of the observed endogenous variables conditional on their own past and any exogenous variables and the parameters of the functions are estimated by maximum likelihood (ML). For stationary model, the Kalman filter algorithm is used to obtain the prediction error form of the log-likelihood function. On the other hand, if the model is non-stationary, then a so-called diffused Kalman filter is used. This is the major advantage of using the state space model because whether a time series is stationary or non-stationary is not critical for modeling when using the Kalman filter. The full details of the STSM methods and its underlying methodology can be found in Harvey (1989), Harvey and Shephard (1993), and Hamilton (1994). In this study, the STSM in state space form was implemented using the STATA software. The moving average data imputation method was used to impute the holiday period which resulted in missing data in the series, and the possible explanatory variables in this study were confined to energy prices (e.g., oil, natural gas, and coal).

The prices of energy sources are included as explanatory variables in the STSM models and the results are presented in Table 5.4.[6] In the models, the coefficients for unobservable component (trend) are restricted to 1. The coefficients for the logarithms of oil, gas, and coal prices are not statistically significant. The hypothesis that the coefficients for three explanatory variables equal to zero cannot be rejected, which implies that energy prices do not have explanatory power on the carbon emission permits prices in pilot markets. This is contrary to the findings in the EU ETS

Table 5.4 STSM estimation of the pilot carbon markets in Beijing, Shanghai, and Shenzhen

Variables	*Beijing*	*Shanghai*	*Shenzhen*
Ln_oil price	0.026	0.076	0.310
	(0.072)	(0.1181)	(0.281)
Ln_gas price	0.600	−2.662	2.345
	(3.920)	(6.7862)	(9.327)
Ln_coal price	0.080	−0.274	−0.071
	(0.215)	(0.3731)	(0.494)

Note: Standard errors in parentheses. The trend variable is constrained to unity

studies by Mansanet-Bataller et al. (2007) and also Maydybura and Andrew (2011). In these studies, it was shown that in the EU ETS, the price of natural gas was not only closely related with the price of carbon but was also the largest driver of carbon price among all the independent variables they considered in their analysis.

After eliminating the independent variables from the models, the prediction is generated by new STSM with only the unobservable component in the model. Figures 5.5, 5.6, and 5.7 plot the graphs for actual figures and predicted figures. The blue line in each graph is the actual realized carbon price values and the red line is the predicted values. The prediction is conducted on the basis of the past 12-month data and extended to the next two months. We use the one-step method which generates the prediction by estimating the state values at each time period using previous information with the Kalman filter algorithm. In each pilot ETS market, the upper graph depicts the actual price movements over the 14 months period and the predicted line in the last two months is separated by the vertical line; the lower graph shows the actual values and forecasted values in the last two months. From the graphs, it can be seen that the predicted data fitted well with the actual data movements.

To formally evaluate the forecasting performance in addition to the visual inspection, we compute the root mean squared forecast errors (RMSFE). We also use the AR model in which the lagged dependent variable is included as the explanatory variables to conduct to generate forecast in order to compare with the STSM on forecasting capability. The lags are chosen on the basis of the BIC and AIC criteria. The results suggest that it should include four, three, and two lags for Shenzhen, Beijing, and Shanghai pilot markets, respectively. Table 5.5 depicts the RMSFE for

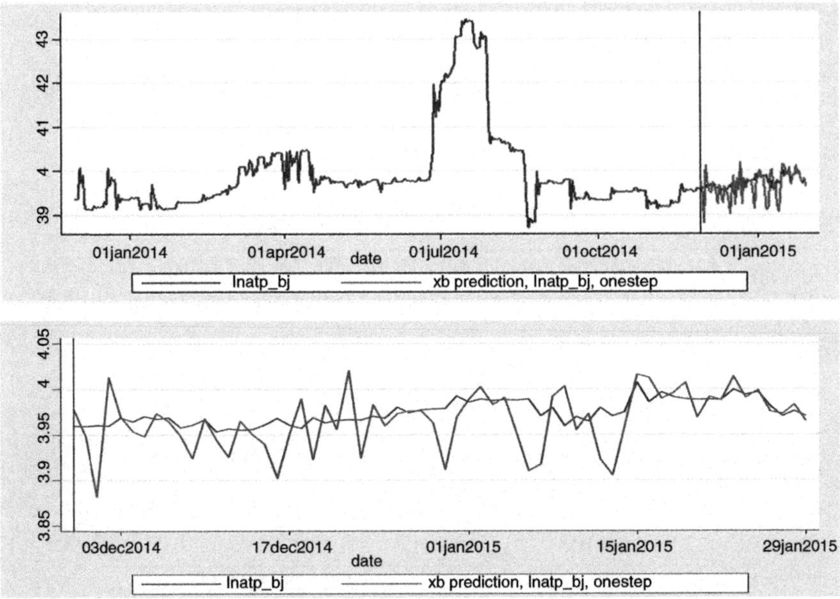

Fig. 5.5 Prediction of movements of carbon allowance prices for Beijing

STSM and AR models. As shown in Table 5.5, the forecasting for Beijing has the highest accuracy with RMSFE of 0.030. All the RMSFE in the STSM are lower than the AR models. This implies that even with basic STSM without explanatory variables, the prediction based on the unobservable components of the carbon price series is quite precise compared with the conventional AR model.

5.5 Concluding Remarks

This study reveals some preliminary findings based on forecasting the carbon price in three of the seven Chinese pilot carbon markets, namely, Beijing, Shanghai, and Shenzhen. The key result shows that the STSM method employed in this study is more effective in forecasting the carbon permit prices than the conventional regression model or the AR model. This finding is useful to both policymakers and private sector analysts. According to the World Resources Institute (WRI) data, China has surpassed the United States and became the world's largest carbon emitter in

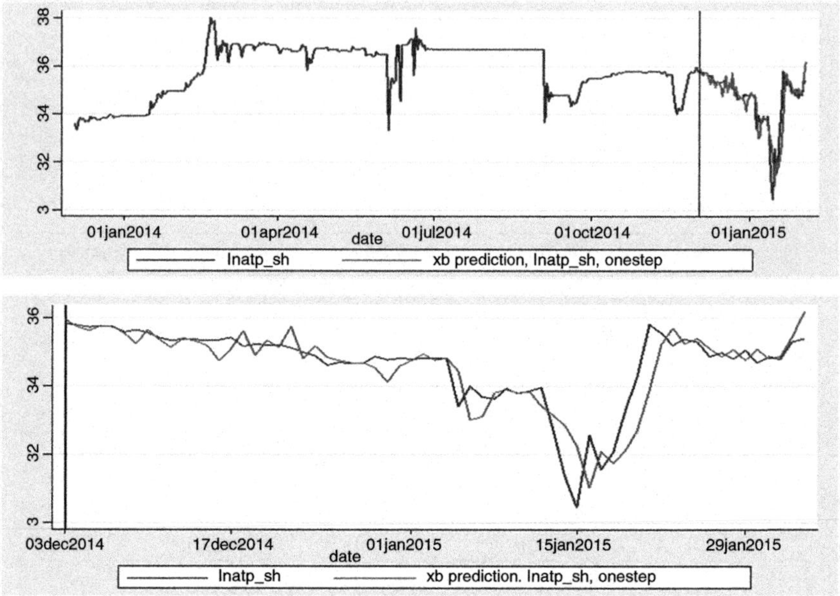

Fig. 5.6 Prediction of movements of carbon allowance prices for Shanghai

2009 (Xu et al. 2014). Hence the national carbon trading market that started in December 19, 2017, will become the biggest carbon market in the world. Therefore, being able to obtain accurate forecast of the Chinese carbon prices will be useful for making policy decisions and business strategies. The expected future carbon price changes will guide and inform the buying and selling behavior for the carbon emission allowance. Specifically, for the ETS regulators, they depend on the forecasting of price to design appropriate emission reduction and policies related to the emission permit allocation. If the carbon price stays low in one pilot market for long period, it may imply that the carbon emission allowance in that region is in a surplus status. The government should consider reallocating the surplus permits and ensure the permit allowance is not excessive so as to curb carbon emission in order to achieve the national carbon emission reduction target.

There are many studies that have applied various prediction models in forecasting the carbon price in the EU ETS such as the combination of traditional autoregressive integrated moving average (ARIMA) and the

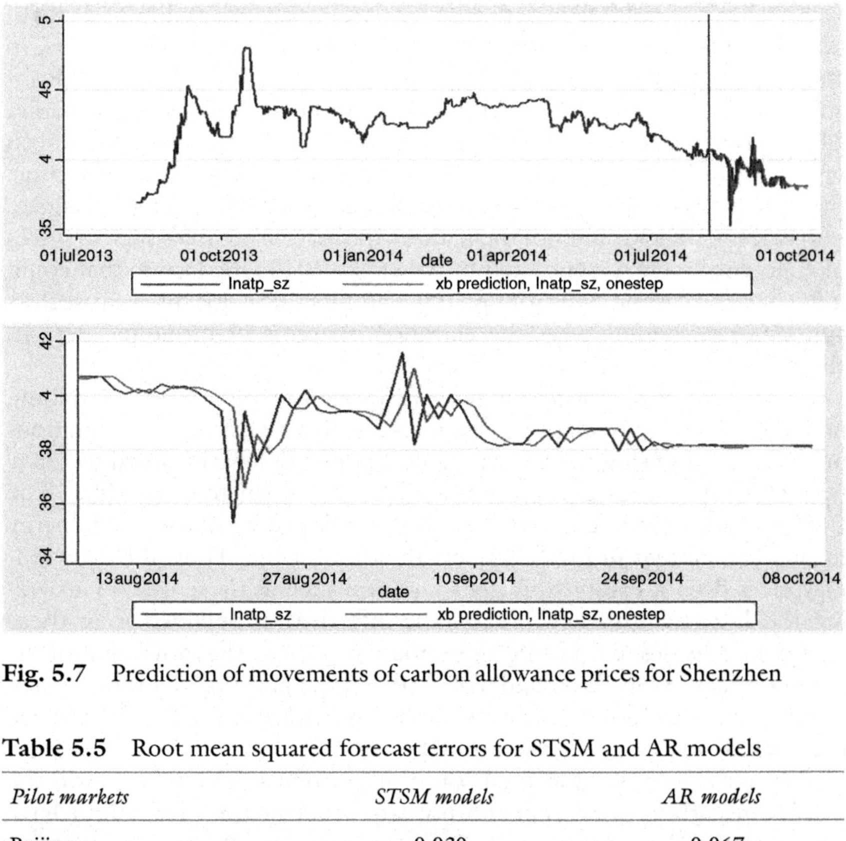

Fig. 5.7 Prediction of movements of carbon allowance prices for Shenzhen

Table 5.5 Root mean squared forecast errors for STSM and AR models

Pilot markets	*STSM models*	*AR models*
Beijing	0.030	0.067
Shanghai	0.060	0.082
Shenzhen	0.092	0.113

least squares support vector machine (LSSVM) by Zhu and Wei (2013), dynamic model averaging (DMA) by Koop and Tole (2013), and the dynamic factor calibration and switching regime calibration by Frunza et al. (2010). The STSM have shown its potential in forecasting the Gram production in India (Singh et al. 2014), OECD-Europe natural gas demand (Dilaver 2010), and traffic-related nitrogen concentrations (Lawson et al. 2011). This study presents an additional option for forecasting the carbon prices using the STSM method.

Another key result from this study is that energy prices do not contribute to forecasting the carbon price in the Chinese pilot ETS markets, in contrast to the findings from other studies on the EU ETS. This is probably due to the short time span of operation in the Chinese pilot market when this study is conducted while the European Union market has been operating for a much longer period comparatively. At this point in time, the factors that may have more influence are those such as the local allocation rules or policies and not the nationwide macro-variables such as prices of energy sources. As suggested by Xu et al. (2014) the factors that could influence the carbon emission in China and its prices for different sectors and different region could be classified in terms of economic output, energy intensity, and industrial structure.

Given that this is a preliminary investigation on the initial trading period of the Chinese pilot carbon markets, there exist various limitations in this study. In using the STSM methodology, we have included the daily transaction prices of energy commodities as explanatory variables. The Chinese future trading market is not as developed as Europe and energy futures such as gas futures contract are not available. Thus, the daily selling prices do not exhibit sufficient variation such as those used in analyzing the European market. Hence, the information obtained from those energy price series may not be appropriate to explain the movement of the carbon prices. As in Koop and Tole (2013), the authors found that when the future energy price indexes are stable in mature and efficient markets, the price drivers do have forecasting power.

Further research could focus on more in-depth investigation on the drivers of carbon price. There are many other factors that might have impact on carbon permit prices, for example, electricity prices, temperature, stock prices, and commodity prices. Those factors have also been proven to be useful in forecasting the EU ETS carbon price in previous studies (see, for instance, Koop and Tole 2013; Mansanet-Bataller et al. 2007). In addition, if the focus is on Chinese pilot market, it will be reasonable to consider regional effects in the model. Factors such as local economic situations and local government policies might not impact on a nationwide carbon market but will likely affect the regional pilot market. Since the energy prices do not have forecasting power on carbon price, future research could analyze whether regional-specific factors have forecasting power to help improve the modeling of carbon prices.

Notes

1. The first pilot market started in Shenzhen in June 2013 followed by Shanghai and Beijing in November of the same year. When this preliminary analysis of the carbon markets was conducted in 2014–15, these three cities recorded the most complete time series dataset. Guangdong started its pilot market in December 2013 but since it is a provincial state, we do not include it in this study.
2. Note that due to the complexity of the Chinese ETS design, the lack of micro-data, and the infancy stage of development of the ETS market at the time when this study was conducted, the analysis is simply exploratory and does not attempt to demonstrate any forms of causality.
3. Besides carbon dioxide, the ETS system has also been implemented to reduce other greenhouse gas emission such as sulfur dioxide (SO_2) under the Clean Air Act Amendments of 1990 in the US and nitrogen oxides (NO_2) in eastern US. Schmalensee and Stavins (2017) provided a recent survey on other ETS markets including the EU ETS.
4. For a survey, see for instance Martin et al. (2016) which focuses on how regulated firms have reacted to the EU ETS.
5. The Brent oil price was used by Koop and Tole (2013) in forecasting the carbon price in European carbon market.
6. The Augmented Dickey-Fuller tests show that the logarithm of carbon price for Shenzhen and Shanghai is significant at 5% and 1% level, respectively, implying that the data are stationary while the price of carbon permit in Beijing has a unit root. Within the price energy sources, only the logarithm of oil price is significant at 10% level (evidence of stationarity) while the logarithm of coal and gas prices is non-stationary time series.

References

Aatola, P., Ollikainen, M., and Toppinen, A. (2013), "Price determination in the EU ETS market: Theory and econometric analysis with market fundamentals", *Energy Economics*: 36, 380–395.

Aichele, R., and Felbermayr, G. (2013), "The Effect of the Kyoto Protocol on Carbon Emissions", *Journal of Policy Analysis & Management*: 32, 731–757.

Anderson, B., and Di Maria, C. (2011), "Abatement and allocation in the pilot phase of the EU ETS", *Environmental and Resource Economics*: 48, 83–103.

Bo, K., and Freeman, C. (2013), "Making Sense of Carbon Market Development in China", *Carbon & Climate Law Review*: 7, 194–212.

Boersen, A., and Scholtens, B. (2014), "The relationship between European electricity markets and emission allowance futures prices in phase II of the EU (European Union) emission trading scheme", *Energy*; 74, 585–594.

BP. (2013), BP Statistical Review of World Energy 2013, BP.
Broadstock, D. C., and Collins, A. (2010), "Measuring unobserved prices using the structural time-series model: The case of cycling", *Transportation Research Part A*: 44, 195–200.
Calel, R., and Dechezlepretre, A. (2013), "Environmental Policy and Directed Technological Change: Evidence from the European carbon market", *Review of Economics and Statistics*: 98, 173–191
Carraro, C., and Alice, F. (2009), "The Economic and Financial Determinants of Carbon Prices", *Finance a Uver: Czech Journal of Economics & Finance*: 59, 396–409.
Chevallier, J. (2011), "A model of carbon price interactions with macroeconomic and energy dynamics", *Energy Economics*, 33, 1295–1312.
Christiansen, A. C., Arvanitakis, A., Tangen, K., and Hasselknippe, H. (2005), "Price determinants in the EU emissions trading scheme". *Climate Policy*, 5, 15–30.
Constantini, V., and Mazzanti. M. (2012), "On the green and innovative side of trade competitiveness? The impact of environmental policies and innovation on EU exports", *Research Policy*: 41, 132–53.
Cui, L. B., Fan, Y., Zhu, L., and Bi, Q. H. (2014), "How will the emissions trading scheme save cost for achieving China's 2020 carbon intensity reduction target?" *Applied Energy*, 1043–1052.
Declercq, B., Delarue, E., and D'haeseleer, W. (2011), "Impact of the economic recession on the European power sector's CO_2 emissions". *Energy Policy*, 39, 1677–1686. Available at: doi:10.1016/j.enpol.2010.12.043
Dilaver, Z. (2010), "OECD-Europe natural gas demand: An outlook to 2020. In: SEEC (Surrey Energy Economics Centre)", 8th BIEE Academic Conference. Oxford, U.K, 22–23 September 2010.
Frunza, M.-C., Guégan, D., and Lassoudiere, A. (2010), "Forecasting Strategies for Carbon Allowances Prices: From Classic Arbitrage Pricing Theory to Switching Regimes". *International Review of Applied Financial Issues & Economics*, 2, 576–596.
Hamilton, J. D. (1994), Time Series Analysis. Princeton: Princeton University Press.
Han, G., Olsson, M., Hallding, K., and Lunsford, D. (2012), "China's Carbon Emission Trading: An Overview of Current Development". FORES (Forum for Reforms, Entrepreneurship and Sustainability).
Harvey, A. C. (1989), Forecasting, Structural Time Series Models and the Kalman Filter. Cambridge: Cambridge University Press.
Harvey, A. C., and Shephard, N. (1993), "Structural time series models", in *Handbook of Statistics* (Eds) G. S. Maddala, C. R. Rao, and H. D. Vinod, Elsevier Science Publishers B V, Amsterdam, 261–302.

Hintermann, B. (2010), "Allowance price drivers in the first phase of the EU ETS". *Journal of Environmental Economics and Management*, 59, 43–56.

Hübler, M., Voigt, S., Löschel, A. (2014), "Designing an emissions trading scheme for China—an up-to-date climate policy assessment". *Energy Policy*, 75, 57–72.

Jackman, M., and Greenidge, K. (2010), "Modelling and forecasting tourist flows to Barbados using structural time series models". *Tourism & Hospitality Research*, 10, 1–13.

Jiang, J. J., Ye, B., and Ma, X. M. (2014), The construction of Shenzhen's carbon emission trading scheme. Energy Policy, 75, 17–21.

Jotzo, F. and Löschel, A. (2014), "Emissions trading in China: Emerging experiences and international lessons". *Energy Policy*, 75, 3–8.

Kim, H. S., and Koo, W. W. (2010), "Factors affecting the carbon allowance market in the US". *Energy Policy*, 38, 1879–1884.

Koop, G., and Tole, L. (2013), "Forecasting the European carbon market". *Journal of the Royal Statistical Society: Series A (Statistics in Society)*, 176, 723–741.

Kourentzes, N., Petropoulos, F., and Trapero, J. R. (2014), "Improving forecasting by estimating time series structural components across multiple frequencies". *International Journal of Forecasting*, 30, 291–302.

Lawson, A. R., Ghosh, B., and Broderick, B. (2011), "Prediction of traffic-related nitrogen oxides concentrations using Structural Time-Series models". *Atmospheric Environment*, 45, 4719–4727.

Li, J., Wang, X., Zhang, Y., Kou, Q., Cai, S., (2014), "The economic impact of carbon pricing with regulated electricity prices in China—an application of a Computable General Equilibrium approach". *Energy Policy*, 75, 46–56.

Liu, L. W., Zong, H. J., Zhao, E. D., Chen, C. X., and Wang, J. Z. (2014), "Can China realize its carbon emission reduction goal in 2020: From the perspective of thermal power development". *Applied Energy*, 124, 199–212.

Liu, Z., Guan, D., Crawford-Brown, D., Zhang, Q., He, K., and Liu, J. (2013), "Energy policy: A low-carbon road map for China". *Nature*, 500, 143–145.

Mansanet-Bataller, M., Pardo, A., and Valor, E. (2007), "CO_2 Prices, Energy and Weather". *Energy Journal*, 28, 73–92.

Martin, R., Muuls, M., and Wagner, U. (2011), Climate change, investment and carbon markets and prices-evidence from manager interviews. Climate Strategies, Carbon Pricing for Low-Carbon Investment Project. Available at: http://climatestrategies.org/publication/climate-change-investment-and-carbon-markets-and-prices-evidence-from-manager-interviews/

Martin, R., Muuls, M., and Wagner, U. (2016), "The Impact of the European Union Emissions Trading Scheme on Regulated Firms: What Is the Evidence after Ten Years?", *Review of Environmental Economics and Policy*, 10, 129–148.

Martin, Ralf, de Preux, Laure B. and Wagner, Ulrich J. (2014), "Industry compensation under relocation risk: A firm-level analysis of the EU Emissions Trading Scheme". *American Economic Review*, 104, 2482–508.

Maydybura, A., and Andrew, B. (2011), "A Study of the Determinants of Emissions Unit Allowance Price in the European Union Emissions Trading Scheme". *Australasian Accounting Business & Finance Journal*, 5, 123–142.

Michieka, N. M., Fletcher, J., and Burnett, W. (2013), "An empirical analysis of the role of China's exports on CO_2 emissions". *Applied Energy*, 104, 258–267

Myklebust, J., Tomasgard, A., and Westgaard, S. (2010), "Forecasting gas component prices with multivariate structural time series models". *OPEC Energy Review*, 34, 82–106.

Newell, R. G., Pizer, W. A., and Raimi, D. (2013), "Carbon Markets 15 Years after Kyoto: Lessons Learned", *New Challenges. Journal of Economic Perspectives*, 27, 123–146.

Peters, G. P., Weber, C. L., Guan, D., and Hubacek, K. (2007), "China's growing CO_2 emissions–a race between increasing consumption and efficiency gains". *Environmental Science & Technology*. 41, 1895–1901.

Qi, S., Wang, B., Zhang, J. (2014), "Policy design of the Hubei ETS Pilot in China". *Energy Policy*, 75, 31–38.

Rudolph, S., and Schneider, F. (2013), "Political barriers of implementing carbon markets in Japan: A Public Choice analysis and the empirical evidence before and after the Fukushima nuclear disaster". *Environmental Economics & Policy Studies*, 15, 211–235.

SEI. (2012), China's Carbon Emission Trading: An Experiment to Watch Closely'. Available at: http://www.sei-international.org/mediamanager/documents/Publications/china-cluster/SEI-PB-2012-China-carbon-markets.pdf

Schmalensee, R., and Stavins, R. (2017), "Lessons Learned from Three Decades of Experience with Cap and Trade", *Review of Environmental Economics and Policy*, 11, 59–79.

Singh, D. P., Thakur A. K. and Ram D. S. (2014), "Application of Structural Time Series model for forecasting Gram production in India". *American International Journal of Research in Science, Technology, Engineering and Mathematics*, 60–62.

Teng, F., Wang, X., Zhiqiang, L. V. (2014), "Introducing the emissions trading system to China's electricity sector: challenges and opportunities". *Energy Policy*, 75, 39–45.

Wang, P., Dai, H. C., Ren, S. Y., Zhao, D. Q., and Masui, T. (2015), "Achieving Copenhagen target through carbon emission trading: Economic impacts assessment in Guangdong Province of China". *Energy*, 212.

Wang, R., Liu, W., Xiao, L., Liu, J., and Kao, W. (2011), "Viewpoint: Path towards achieving of China's 2020 carbon emission reduction target—A discussion of low-carbon energy policies at province level". *Energy Policy*, 39, 2740–2747.

Wu, L., Quian, H., Li, J., (2014), "Advancing the experiment to reality: perspectives on Shanghai pilot carbon emissions trading scheme". *Energy Policy*, 75, 22–30.

Xia, Y. A. N., Fan, Y., and Wu, J. I. E. (2013), "Analysis of low-carbon production chains towards China's emission reduction targets for 2020". *Singapore Economic Review*, 58, 1–18.

Xu, S. C., He, Z. X., and Long, R. Y. (2014), "Factors that influence carbon emissions due to energy consumption in China: Decomposition analysis using LMDI". *Applied Energy*, 127, 182–193.

Zhang, Y. J., Wang, A. D. and Da, Y. B. (2014), "Regional allocation of carbon emission quotas in China: Evidence from the Shapley value method". *Energy Policy*, 74, 454–464.

Zhao, J., Yang, Y., and Suo, C. (2014), "Beijing energy consumption carbon emission characteristics and cause analysis". *Journal of Chemical & Pharmaceutical Research*, 6, 473–477.

Zhu, B., and Wei, Y. (2013), "Carbon price forecasting with a novel hybrid ARIMA and least squares support vector machines methodology". *Omega*, 41, 517–524.

CHAPTER 6

The Energy Paradox: Evidence from Refrigerator Market in China

Yuxiang Ren, Fushu Luan, and Hui Zhou

6.1 Introduction

The economic literature since the early 1980s put forward the concept of energy paradox, which recognizes the energy efficiency gap[1] as an important aspect of energy consumption in a particular market (Blumstein et al. 1980; Shama 1983; Stern and Aronson 1984). This leads to energy efficiency gap being an increasingly popular research topic among economists (Jaffe and Stavins 1994; Koomey and Sanstad 1994; Helfand and Wolverton 2011; Allcott and Greenstone 2012; Busse et al. 2013; Allcott and Wozny 2014; Sallee et al. 2016). Nevertheless, previous studies overwhelmingly focused on the effects of energy efficiency gap quantification in western countries with relative high level of urbanization rate and economic development, while new emerging countries that are worth studying, especially China which is a large country with regional heterogeneity, are neglected by many researchers.

Y. Ren • F. Luan (✉)
International Business School Suzhou, Xi'an Jiaotong-Liverpool University, Suzhou, China
e-mail: Fushu.luan@xjtlu.edu.cn

H. Zhou
Cornell University, Ithaca, NY, USA
e-mail: hz423@cornell.edu

J. H. Hung, Y. Chen (eds.), *The State of China's State Capitalism*,
https://doi.org/10.1007/978-981-13-0983-0_6

A central problem in China is that the energy shortage still brings about considerable obstacles to urban development even though substantial government budgets have been devoted to energy-infrastructure constructions such as Three Gorges Project and West-East Electricity Transmission Project. This may be due to the accelerated process of urbanization in China in the past two decades, which causes demand for residential electricity demand to increase rapidly. Whatsoever, the fact is that electricity shortage has become a barrier to urban sustainable development. A number of cities limit industrial electricity consumption to guarantee potential residential electricity consumption, especially in summer seasons when demand for electricity reaches the peak. For example, the electricity consumption in Hebei province reached 33 million kilowatts in the summer of 2015. Factories with high electricity consumption ratings in Hebei were restricted to producing for six hours per day in order to prioritize residential electricity consumption (Hebei Daily 2015). However, the average residential energy consumption per capita in China still stands at a low level and is only 1/4 of that in OECD countries (Gu and Han 2010). If residential electricity demand continues to rise, it is expected that China's electricity shortage will be increasingly severe if electricity conservation measures remain limited.

Challenged by the existing electricity shortage, the central government has taken energy conversation measures in residential electricity. The National Development and Reform Commission (NDRC) (2011a, b) has also highlighted this, that is, energy-saving appliances and housings must be vigorously promoted and popularized. However, household appliances with energy-conserving technologies cannot spread quickly in China without any policy interventions. Some Chinese researchers investigate this issue using the framework of sociology and behavioral economics while a few of them have made contributions to explaining the formation of the energy efficiency gap in different markets. For instance, Zhao (2009) used the air-conditioner market as an example, illustrating the annual sales share of air-conditioners with a second or higher level of energy-saving rating was merely 5% before the implementation of the "Energy-saving Appliance Purchase Subsidy" policy in 2009. Therefore, it is interesting to concentrate on quantifying the energy efficiency gap in a particular household appliance market in China. Constrained with data availability, this research focuses on China's refrigerator market.

To this end, this chapter examines whether there exists an energy efficiency gap in China's refrigerator market and whether the gap can be quantified using an index if it exists. The research also provides the value of aggregate population-weighted residential electricity price. We prudently record and calculate the charging standards of electricity in every province in mainland China. This electricity charging standard list is of considerable value for researchers interested in studying the electricity consumption and energy efficiency gap in China.

The reminder of this chapter is organized as follows. The next section presents literature review on the energy efficiency gap. This is followed by research design in Sect. 6.3 and data description in Sec. 6.4. Section 6.5 presents main results. Finally, the chapter concludes with a brief discussion of policy implications.

6.2 Literature Review

There is a large strand of literature that attempts to understand the "energy efficiency gap", which refers to the discrepancy between optimal and actual level of adoption of energy efficiency technology (Jaffe and Stavins 1994). In recent years, many empirical studies tried to investigate whether this gap is real and the magnitude of the gap if it exists. They argue that if the gap is real, the private markets will not behave in a standard way. Koomey and Sanstad (1994) present a series of examples for evaluating engineering economic evidence on the spreading of energy efficiency improvements, confirming the existence of market imperfections correlated with energy efficiency. Helfand and Wolverton (2011), for instance, explored why the gap existed between the amount consumers are willing to purchase for energy-saving fuel and the amount that automakers provided. Gillingham and Palmer (2014) proposed the existence of hidden costs, taking imperfect information, lack of salience of energy consumption, or excessive consumer discounting into consideration.

Most of these studies focused on a particular country or a specific industry sector but the findings varied. Taking the auto market as an example, the evidence is mixed. Busse et al. (2013) examined whether car buyers were myopic about future fuel costs by estimating the impact of gasoline prices on short-run equilibrium prices of cars and comparing the possible changes in willingness-to-pay to the corresponding changes in expected future gasoline costs in various fuel economies. They find that vehicle buyers' willingness to pay for fuel economy approximately matched their future fuel expenditures. Sallee et al. (2016) provided similar evidence using a novel identification strategy and high-quality microdata from wholesale used car auctions.

Allcott and Wozny (2014) for the first time quantified the energy efficiency gap using an indicator calculated via the purchase prices and discounted forecasted future costs in the automobile market in the United States. Random utility theory and logit model for panel data were used. They found that American consumers undervalued future gasoline cost relative to purchase prices when they make purchase decisions on automobiles. Specifically, vehicle price moved as if consumers were indifferent between 1 dollar in discounted future gasoline costs and only 76 cents in automobile purchase price. Besides, Greene (2010) estimated the value consumers place on fuel economy using direct or indirect empirical evidence from 28 econometric studies. He found a wide variation in estimates of consumer's willingness to pay for fuel economy. As Allcott and Greenstone (2012) pointed out, quantifying the energy efficiency gap in a particular market is a valuable research field. They believed that different industries and markets were likely to provide distinct results on the magnitude of the energy efficiency gap since the structure of the market and industry varied. Steg (2008) discussed factors influencing household energy conservation behavior, implying potential entry points for government policy intervention. These factors such as education level, knowledge on efficiency rating can be added into random utility model as control variables when necessary.

6.3 Research Design

We first derive how energy efficiency gap is related to consumer's purchase decision in the refrigerator market and how it can be estimated on the basis of the data on price and market share dataset using the random utility theory and standard logit model. After that, we show how we choose the key variables such as market discount rate, provincial average electricity price, and the length of expected lifespan to estimate the present value of expected future electricity cost, which is an indispensable variable in following estimation. Concrete information about how we dispose and collect data will be presented in the section of data description.

6.3.1 *Econometric Model*

Assume that consumer n plans to purchase a refrigerator. The refrigerator market has a total of K types available for the consumer to choose. Using the random utility theory, the utility that consumer n purchase refrigerator type i ($i = 1, 2, \ldots, k$) is:

$$U_{ni} = \beta_0 + \beta_1 price_i + \beta_2 cost_i + \beta' X_i + \zeta_{ni}, \tag{6.1}$$

where $price_i$ is the price of the refrigerator, $cost_i$ is the present value of the expected future electricity cost of the refrigerator during its expected lifespan discounted by inflation-adjusted market discount rate. X_i is a vector that captures other features of refrigerator, for instance, brand, color, efficiency rating, storage volume, defrosting and so on. ζ_{ni} contains all other factors that affect consumers' utility but are not observable. Consumer n can choose to purchase one or not. If consumer n decides not to purchase, then $i = 0$, $U_{n0} = \beta_0$.

Here, ζ_{ni} needs to be highlighted. Intuitively, it can be seen that U_{ni} depends not only on $price_i$, $cost_i$, and X_i, but also depends on ζ_{ni}. This means that consumer's utility can significantly deviate from the value $\beta_0 + \beta_1 price_i + \beta_2 cost_i + \beta' X_i$, which reflects consumer's individual preference on other features of refrigerators. Since this deviation is unobserved, we then assume that ζ_{ni} takes type I extreme value distribution just as Allcott and Wozny (2014) did. As ζ_{ni} takes type I extreme value distribution, it is equivalent to take ζ_{ni} as a variable that has finite positive or negative extremums (Gao 2014). In other words, this assumption means that a consumer's utility gained from purchasing a particular type of refrigerator can theoretically have any finite value due to individual preference differentiation. Although this assumption cannot be tested, it is quite a fundamental assumption in the random utility theory and discrete choice model. Since each consumer's special preference cannot be observed one by one, we just treat it as it can take any finite value. In Allcott and Wozny's (2014) paper, they also defined ε_{ijat} as an unobserved deviation from average usage utility and assume ε_{ijat} takes type I extreme value distribution. The probability that consumer n chooses product i is:

$$P_{ni} = \frac{exp(\beta_0 + \beta_1 price_i + \beta_2 cost_i + \beta' X_i)}{\sum_{i=1}^{K} exp(\beta_0 + \beta_1 price_j + \beta_2 cost_j + \beta' X_j)}. \tag{6.2}$$

If we assume that consumers are homogeneous, the market share of refrigerator type i then satisfies the following relation: $S_i = P_{ni}$ (Kidokoro 2008). Taking natural logarithm of (6.2) we get:

$$InP_{ni} = InS_i = \beta_0 + \beta_1 price_i + \beta_2 cost_i + \beta' X_i$$
$$- \sum_{j=1}^{K} \left[\beta_0 + \beta_1 price_j + \beta_2 cost_j + \beta' X_j \right]. \quad (6.3)$$

When consumer *i* decides not to purchase any type of refrigerator, $i = 0$; the market share that the consumer does not purchase is:

$$InS_0 = \beta_0 - \sum_{j=1}^{K} \left[\beta_0 + \beta_1 price_j + \beta_2 cost_j + \beta' X_j \right]. \quad (6.4)$$

Taking subtraction of Eqs. (6.3) and (6.4)

$$InS_i - InS_0 = \beta_0 + \beta_1 price_i + \beta_2 cost_i + \beta' X_i, \quad (6.5)$$

After rearranging Eq. (6.5) we get:

$$InS_i = InS_0 + \beta_1 price_i + \beta_2 cost_i + \beta' X_i. \quad (6.6)$$

Then, we get the econometric model, where $\alpha = InS_0$:

$$InS_i = \alpha + \beta_1 price_i + \beta_2 cost_i + \beta' X_i. \quad (6.7)$$

We will use Eq. (6.7) to estimate parameters β_1 and β_2 in order to quantify the energy efficiency gap index $L = \widehat{\beta_2} / \widehat{\beta_1}$. L shows how much a consumer is willing to pay for reducing expected future electricity cost that has a present value of 1 unit. If $L = 1$, there is no energy efficiency gap since the consumer is indifferent between spending one more unit on purchase cost and future electricity cost. If $L < 1$, consumer undervalues future electricity cost, which implies the existence of energy efficiency gap in China's refrigerator market. The smaller L is, the larger the efficiency gap. We need to bear in mind that L can be negative, which indicates that the efficiency gap is extremely high in the refrigerator market.

6.3.2 *Choice of Variables*

Having explained the modeling, we now turn to define the key variables $price_i$, $cost_i$, and X_i that will be used in the econometric model. Note that some assumptions are made in the construction of key variables. Summary statistics will be presented in next section.

The variable $price_i$ is measured as the average purchase price of refrigerator type i. We need to bear in mind that in the real world, the price discrimination strategy is frequently adopted by shops and bargaining usually happens. In this circumstance, we do not use suggested retail price provided by manufacturers. Instead, we use the average sales price provided by the 2015 data set from China Market Research Center.

The variable $cost_i$ is measured by the present value of aggregate expected future electricity cost of the refrigerator type i discounted by market discount rate. We need several steps to calculate and estimate it. Consider the following two formulas for calculating $cost_i$.

$$cost_i = \sum_{t=1}^{T} \frac{V_{i,t}}{\left(1+\delta_t\right)^t}, \tag{6.8}$$

where T refers to consumer's expected refrigerator lifespan; $V_{i,t}$ is electricity cost of refrigerator i in year t; δ_t is inflation-adjusted market discount rate in year t.

$$V_{i,t} = P_t \times E_i \times 365, \tag{6.9}$$

where $V_{i,t}$ means electricity cost of refrigerator type i in year t; P_t is national population-weighted average electricity price in year t; and E_i is daily power consumption (DPC) of refrigerator type i.

The variable P_t is the present national population-weighted average electricity price in year t. There is no simple national electricity price that can be directly used. China's electricity power system is very complex. Structurally, it is monopolized by a few state-owned power grids corporations such as State Grid Corporation of China, China Southern Power Grid, and China Huaneng Power Corporation. Each is responsible for supplying electricity within a particular area; thus, this brings about significant regional difference. Apart from electricity supplied by the regional electricity supply division, provinces that have a surplus of electricity are also required to transmit part of the electricity surplus to other provinces that are in shortage which makes electricity price more complicated since electricity power companies need to consider transmission cost. In addition, electricity cost is also largely affected by seasonal and weather factors since inland provinces are highly dependent on hydroelectric power generation.

Herein, we make a simplification that consumers have static electricity expectations on future electricity prices and that expectation is in line with P_{2013}. In other words, we have $P_t = P_t^{\varepsilon} = P_{2013}$. This assumption is reasonable for two reasons. First, electricity pricing policy in each province is relatively stable in recent years after year 2013 when the NDRC issued documents to promote tied pricing and peak and valley pricing across the country. The NDRC also confirmed that in the 12th and 13th Five-Year Plans, electricity pricing policy that aims to conserve energy consumption will not be reversed in short run. With the above assumption, the general formula of P_t is:

$$P_t = P_t^e = P_{2013} = \sum_{i=1}^{31} p_{i,t} \times \alpha_{i,t} = \sum_{i=1}^{31} p_{i,2013} \times \alpha_{i,2013}, \tag{6.10}$$

where $P_{i,t}$ is electricity price in province i in year t and $\alpha_{i,t}$ is a weight of population in province i in year t. The second reason that we use provincial population weight is it reflects the distribution of electricity consumption in using refrigerator across provinces. According to 2014–2015 China Refrigerator Market Report, 99% of urban and 70% of rural families have been able to use refrigerators. Since almost every family needs at least one refrigerator, we can make the inference that the province with a larger size of population must tend to have a higher aggregate refrigerator electricity cost. For simplicity, if we assume that the population weight does not change over years, we have $\alpha_{i,t} \equiv \alpha_{i,2013}$. We have to rely on this assumption since we are unable to accurately estimate future provincial population in China because of high population mobility and change of childbearing policy. We consider 31 provincial-level administrative regions in total including 22 provinces, five autonomous regions, and four municipalities. We now use the Jiangsu province as an example of calculating $P_{i,t}$. The reason for choosing Jiangsu as the example is that it is a typical province that simultaneously adopts tired pricing and peak and valley pricing on residential electricity consumption (State GRID 2013). The electricity price list of Jiangsu in 2013 is presented in Table 6.1:

According to the price list and corresponding documents issued by the Jiangsu Bureau of Commodity Price, the peak period is from 21:00 pm to 08:00 am and the valley time is from 08:00 am to 21:00 pm, with 11 and

Table 6.1 Electricity price of Jiangsu Province in 2013

Price level (RMB/KWH)		*Less than 1000 Volt*	*More than 1000 Volt*
First tier:	0≤e≤2760	0.5283	0.5183
Second tier:	2760<e≤4800	0.5783	0.5683
Third tier:	4800<e	0.8283	0.8183

13 hours' time span respectively. To calculate the average daily electricity cost per kilowatt, we assume that the residential electricity consumption of refrigerators per year goes to the first tier. A calculation can verify this simplification: the standard refrigerator electricity consumption per day is around 0.5 kW·h. Thus, the annual electricity consumption is around $0.5 \times 365 = 182.5$ kW·h. It is far less than the upper limit of first-tier consumption. When the residential electricity consumption is within the first tier, the actual peak and valley price is:

$$price_{peak} = 0.5283 + 0.03 = 0.5583\,\text{CNY};\ price_{valley} = 0.5583 - 0.2 = 0.3583\,\text{CNY},$$

where 0.03 and 0.2 are the peak and valley mark-up and discount for consumption within the first tier. Now, we can calculate the average electricity price of Jiangsu in year 2013 denoted by $P_{Jiangsu,2013}$,

$$p_{Jiangsu,2013} = p_{peak,2013} \times \frac{t_{peak}}{24} + p_{valley,2013} \times \frac{t_{valley}}{24} = 0.5583 \times \frac{13}{24} + 0.3583 \times \frac{11}{24} \approx 0.4666, \tag{6.11}$$

Following the same method, we calculate $P_{i,t}$ for the other provincial regions based on their own pricing mechanisms and finally derive P_t. We will be back to this later in the section of data description, introducing more details about provincial-level facts.

We now turn to the measure of E_i before calculating $V_{i,t}$. As stated in Eq. (6.9), E_i is DPC of refrigerator type i in kilowatt-hour. This amount is usually shown in the guide of how to use the refrigerator. This variable is also included in the dataset provided by CRMC for each type of refrigerator. Herein we rely on the CRMC dataset to calculate the costs of refrigerator usage.

After calculating the cost of refrigerator usage $V_{i,t}$, we need to define T and δ_t to calculate the present value of future expected electricity cost, discounted by the market discount rate. T denotes consumer's expectation of the refrigerator lifespan. Theoretically, if consumers have perfect information about the refrigerator and are fully aware of the lifespan distribution, following the ordinary rule of estimating electricity appliance, consumers will be aware that the lifespan is subject to exponential distribution (Zhao and Xia 2006). The distribution function is $f(T) = \alpha e^{-\alpha T}$, where T = run time and α = the frequency of faults (refrigerator break down) per unit time, also called rate parameter. As the rate parameter α is available (perfect information), consumers can find out the expected lifespan of each type of refrigerator is equal to $1/\alpha$ by taking expectation of the distribution function. However, this is problematic to some extent. First, the assumption of perfect information is likely to fail. The rate parameter α is known by producers but not available for consumers. Second, the assumption of good knowledge of consumers is also not practical. On account of the above factors, we suppose that consumers simply form their expectation based on the national standards of refrigerator GB-T8059-2 (SAC 1995), which requires that the lifespan of refrigerator by design should be no less than 12 years. This simplification implies that when consumers purchase refrigerators, they usually do not take unexpected breakdown into consideration until the refrigerator reaches its retirement life.

δ_t is the inflation-adjusted market discount rate in year t, which is used to calculate the present value of aggregate future expected electricity cost. We define δ_t following Allcott and Wozny (2014). In their view, the calculating market discount rate is equivalent to calculating the inter-temporal opportunity cost of money. The complexity lies in that different means of payment imply different opportunity costs. Allcott and Wozny (2014) summarized the means of payment for automobile purchase into two ways: loans and savings. If the consumer borrows money to finance their consumption, the opportunity cost of paying more to purchase an automobile is the annual loan interest rate; if the consumer uses savings, the opportunity cost is the return that could be realized on savings. They emphasized that when calculating the market discount rate, it must be weighted according to the proportion of consumers with these two means of payment, and at the same time, be adjusted based on inflation expectations.

Practically, Allcott and Wozny (2014) used data from Surveys of Consumer Finances (SCF) in years 2001, 2004, and 2007 to estimate the fraction of two means of payment. They found out that about 37% of automobiles were financed by loans while 63% were paid by cash. They then transformed the nominal interest rate reported by SCF into real interest rate deflated by inflation expectations implied by Treasury Inflation-Protected Securities. For automobiles purchased with cash, they defined the opportunity cost of funds equal to the average rate of return on the equity market, specifically the average real rate of return from the S&P 500 between 1945 and 2008. Using the method above, they came up with the market discount rate by taking a weighted average of the two, which was equal to $r_1 \times w_1 + r_2 \times w_2 = 37\ \% \times 6.9\ \% + 63\ \% \times 5.8\ \% =$ 6.207%. Following this method, we now define our own δ_t. It is still equivalent to the inter-temporal opportunity cost of money adjusted by inflation expectation. However, when we consider the practical situation of the refrigerator market in China, we come up with intricate problems. First, we need to be aware that the absolute price of refrigerators is much lower than automobiles. Few consumers borrow when they purchase refrigerators. This feature determines that we are unable to directly figure out an accurate interest rate that perfectly represents opportunity cost of using loans. Second, constrained with poor statistics on retail sales, we even fail to get accurate statistics regarding the share of purchasing using cash and share of purchasing financed by loan. In other words, neither the weight nor the corresponding real interest rate is available for calculating δ_t. As a result, we have to make some adjustments to the method. However, bear in mind that δ_t is the inter-temporal opportunity cost of money adjusted by inflation expectation. Suppose that the consumer wants to buy a refrigerator with disposable income $Y_d \equiv C + S$, where C is consumption and S is saving. Assume that all the disposable income that he does not consume in the current period eventually goes to savings, we can make an inference that the nominal inter-temporal opportunity cost of money equals to the gross rate of return on investment in China. The real interest rate will be that the nominal rate of return on investment less of inflation expectation. We make two additional assumptions. We first assume that consumers have static expectations about the future inflation rate, $\pi_t^e \equiv \pi_t$. This assumption is reasonable and consistent with empirical evidence as we look at the consumer price index (CPI) provided by Federal Reserve Economic Data (FRED 2015), where the inflation rate measured using CPI was stabilized at 2.6% since year 2012. Second, we assume that consumers have static expectations about the nominal gross rate of return on investment i_t, where $i_t^e = i_t$. This assumption is also rational when we use nominal interest rate of Chinese treasury bonds as the gross rate of return on investment. As we take risk and consumer behavior (risk averse) in to account, the interest rate of Chinese treasury bonds is the best benchmark interest rate since these bonds are risk free and the interest rate is stable. The interest rate of five-year Chinese treasury bonds is 4.42% and hence we can get $\delta_t = \delta_t^{\varepsilon} = 4.42\%–2.6\% = 1.82\%$.

The vector X_i captures other factors that are considered influential on affecting consumers' purchase decision on refrigerator type *i*. The research originally planned to import these factors into X_i, namely, total storage volume, cold-closet volume, freezer volume, color, function of intelligence adjustment, and function of moisturization. However, we met difficulties when collecting some of the variables. For instance, the variable color is ambiguous to be categorized. Decorative designs of refrigerators are far from a simple combination of pure colors. Consider a refrigerator that has a light white chrysanthemum decorated cold-closet door and a fine-grained freezer door with overall amethyst gray as background color. We are unable to attribute this refrigerator into a particular main color. We then try to refine color into more specific variables such as decoration color, background color, stripe color, door color and so on, then the model becomes much more complicated than we had expected. In addition, the percentage of missing observations of detailed factors is significantly high, nearly 30% in the full sample, especially for those refrigerators with prices lower than 1500 CNY. It is difficult as well to find information about a type of refrigerator that has stopped production over five years. Sparing no efforts in searching in ZOL online, Jingdong, and Taobao that are the three largest refrigerator online databases, ultimately, we control three factors—total storage volume, cold-closet volume, and freezer volume. These three variables have clear definitions and low proportion of missing values. Note that the total storage volume is not equal to the sum of cold-closet and freezer volume. Thus, there is no issue of multicollinearity.

6.4 Data Description

The dataset includes statistics from China's refrigerator market in year 2013. Though we use cross-sectional data rather than panel data, concentrating on year 2013 brings some benefits. First, in previous years before 2013, the prices of refrigerators were lower than they should be because the government provided subsidies for energy-saving appliances including refrigerators. Focusing on year 2013 potentially avoids structural break due to policy shock. Second, in 2013 the NDRC systematically general-

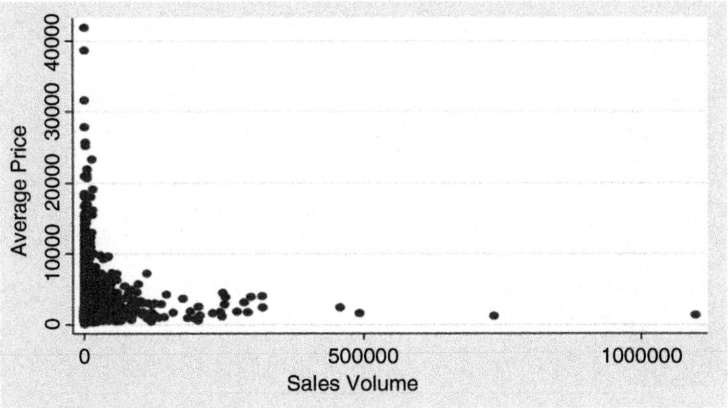

Fig. 6.1 Sales volume and average price

ized tiered pricing and peak and valley pricing on electricity to most of the provinces across the country. Though complexity remains in calculating weighted average nationwide electricity price, it is relatively easy compared with the situation including years before 2013 with consistent pricing framework. And as declared by NDRC, tiered pricing and peak valley pricing serves as the major electricity pricing method in the long run. When we estimate the present value of expected future electricity cost, we take the price system as a stable one, which is a crucial assumption for our research. Third, the dataset of year 2013 has the least amount of missing values compared with data we get for year 2010, 2011, and 2012. Figures 6.1 and 6.2 present two scatter diagrams. Figure 6.1 plots average price against sales volume; Fig. 6.2 plots DPC against sales volume. From them, we can get a preliminary understanding of the distribution of refrigerator sales volume, price, and daily power consumption. We also present a sample of refrigerator market dataset in 2013 China in the appendix. The dataset is rearranged by brand therefore the first 20 observations have the same brand of LG.

6.5 Main Results

We present main results in Table 6.2.

In Table 6.2, all variables are statistically significant at 1% significance level. Based on estimations of $\hat{\beta}_1$ and $\hat{\beta}_2$, which is equal to 0.0001088

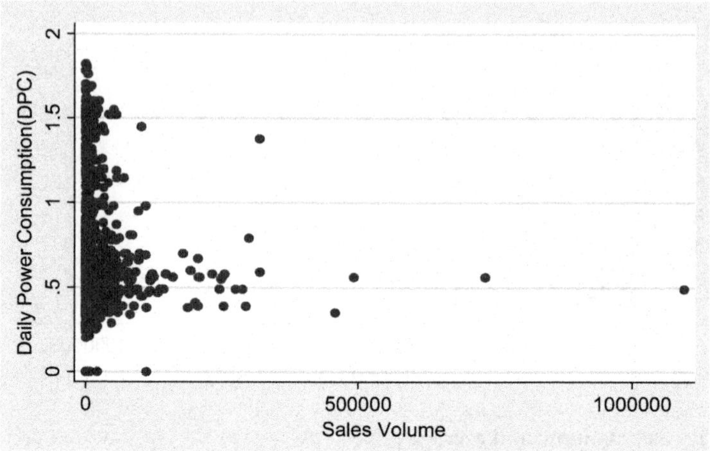

Fig. 6.2 Sales volume and daily power consumption

Table 6.2 Estimation results

Variables	*Coef.*	*Robust std. err.*	*t*	*p>|t|*
Average price	0.0001088***	0.0000349	3.12	0.002
Electricity cost	−0.0004866***	0.0001412	−3.42	0.001
Total volume	0.017561***	0.0024666	7.12	0.000
Cold-closet	−0.0081581***	0.0027738	−2.94	0.003
Freezer	−0.0183034***	0.0024086	−7.60	0.000
_cons	−11.21535***	0.1097893	−102.15	0.000

Notes: *(**, ***): significant at the 10% (5%, 1%) level

and −0.0004866 respectively, we can calculate the energy efficiency gap index $\hat{L} = \frac{\hat{\beta}_2}{\hat{\beta}_1} = -4.472426471 \approx -4.47$. This result is partially consistent $\hat{L}$ with our prior forecast that $\hat{L}$ should be smaller than one, but we did not expect that would have a negative value. Does this value of $\hat{L}$ make sense in quantifying energy efficiency gap? We interpret −4.47 as consumers are indifferent between saving 4.47 CNY more on purchase price of refrigerators and saving 1 CNY in discounted future electricity cost. Interpreted in this way, the result implies that Chinese consumers in refrigerator market are extremely reluctant to pay higher price for energy-saving refrigerators.

The negative sign of $\hat{L}$ indicates that if we want to make up the energy efficiency gap in refrigerator market, there must be a third party paying subsidies directly to consumers or on refrigerators to eliminate consumers' negative willingness to pay. If no third party intervenes the refrigerator market, consumers will be less willing to purchase energy-saving refrigerators with higher prices.

To support our conclusion, we look back to some stylized facts mentioned in former sections. As discussed in data section, we mentioned that the dataset we use comes from year 2013, from when the national subsidies on energy-saving household appliance were canceled. Market prices of refrigerators went back to the price they should be as producers no longer received subsidies from government. Hence, from year 2013, it is more likely for consumers to reveal their truthful preferences when purchasing refrigerators. In this circumstance, it is not strange to see a negative $\hat{L}$. It suggests that providing subsidies to encouraging production of energy-saving appliances is not only necessary but actually consequential when such a huge energy efficiency gap is prevalent in China.

After making interpretations on $\hat{L}$, a discussion about whether $\hat{L}$ is computed by mistake, or it is the true reflection of Chinese refrigerator market has to be made. Since all other variables such as $price_i$, P_t, T, E_i and X_i are either collected from publicly available second-hand statistics publicized by government agencies or generated according to pertinent policies and regulations. It is only δ_t that we might have some discretion to play with for robustness check, which requires that the market discount rate should be equal to inter-temporal opportunity cost of money. Therefore, we may question whether the choice of δ_t significantly affects the final result. To begin with, just think of $\delta_t = 1.82\%$ as a benchmark. Regardless of how δ_t is derived according to alternative theories, there are only two cases, namely, the alternative δ_t is either higher or lower than 1.82%. If δ_t is higher than 1.82%, the result is apparent. Higher δ_t means that consumers weigh the present value more than the future value, which indicates that they tend to undervalue future electricity cost to a higher extent. In this case, $\hat{L}$ remains negative with larger absolute value. Running similar regression generates $\hat{L} \approx -5.40$ when $\delta_t = 5\%$ and $\hat{L} \approx -12.83$ when $\delta_t = 10\%$. Therefore, we conclude that when δ_t is larger than 1.82%, results remain unchanged showing large energy efficiency gap in Chinese refrigerator market. If δ_t is smaller than 1.82%, we should be aware that there is a critical value of δ_t to make $\hat{L}$ positive, but this critical value is theoretically far from logical. How can a country's inter-temporal opportunity cost of money, which we regard as gross return on capital and investment be negative? Henceforth, within a reasonable range of δ_t, $\hat{L}$ remains negative and our interpretations will not be reversed. The difference only lies in the degree of unwillingness to pay which is reflected by the absolute value of $\hat{L}$.

6.6 Conclusion

This chapter makes the first attempt to search for evidences of an energy efficiency gap using the 2013 data on the refrigerator market in China. We find that there exists a considerable energy efficiency gap in the Chinese refrigerator market. Specifically, consumers are indifferent between purchasing more expensive energy-efficient refrigerator with extra 4.47 yuan subsidy and saving 1 yuan in discounted future electricity cost.

The future research might focus on addressing the potential endogeneity issue of prices, for example, using functions of characteristics of other products as instruments for prices of refrigerators. Similar studies can be extended to cars market when such data is available. Such explorations are useful for policy makers in identifying the reasonable range of fiscal subsidies to encourage usage of energy-saving electronic appliances and vehicles.

Appendix

Appendix 1: Refrigerator Market Dataset Sample

Brand	*Code*	*Average price*	*Sales volume*	*Value of sales*	*Total*	*Cold-closet*	*Freezer*	*DPC*	*Market share*
LG	GR M267QGL	18163.00	4585.00	83277355.00	722.00	465.00	257.00	1.28	0.0010845136
LG	GR P247JHM	15475.00	13847.00	214282325.00	637.00	412.00	255.00	1.48	0.0027905798
LG	GR M287QGN	14010.00	497.00	6962970.00	755.00	495.00	260.00	1.15	0.0000906781
LG	GR C2376AZT	12345.00	10750.00	132708750.00	626.00	406.00	220.00	1.25	0.0017282543
LG	GR P247CSP	11914.00	9194.00	109537316.00	617.00	412.00	205.00	1.44	0.0014264948
LG	GR C267FSN	11167.00	1448.00	16169816.00	722.00	465.00	257.00	1.28	0.0002105781
LG	GR P2275NRL	11048.00	4756.00	52544288.00	516.00	348.00	168.00	1.17	0.0006842796
LG	GR B2376AZT	10154.00	14859.00	150878286.00	626.00	406.00	220.00	1.25	0.0019648746
LG	GR C247JYL	9961.00	13779.00	137252619.00	643.00	413.00	212.00	1.40	0.0017874287
LG	GR B267FSN	9651.00	3313.00	31973763.00	722.00	465.00	257.00	1.28	0.0004163915
LG	GR P2274NFB	9305.00	286.00	2661230.00	516.00	348.00	163.00	1.60	0.0000346570
LG	GR P2274NRB	9219.00	50.00	460950.00	516.00	348.00	168.00	1.60	0.0000060029
LG	GR P2275NFL	8354.00	66.00	551364.00	516.00	348.00	168.00	1.17	0.0000071804
LG	GR C2376ATT	8134.00	12422.00	101040548.00	626.00	406.00	220.00	1.25	0.0013158421
LG	GR C2276NCE	7709.00	4799.00	36995491.00	511.00	348.00	163.00	1.15	0.0004817890
LG	GR C227SSD	7705.00	11231.00	86534855.00	554.00	365.00	189.00	1.30	0.0011269358
LG	GR C2275NFK	7579.00	3603.00	27307137.00	511.00	348.00	163.00	1.15	0.0003556184
LG	GR K40DFML	7546.00	14605.00	110209330.00	396.00	248.00	110.00	1.10	0.0014352464
LG	GR P2075TTN	7446.00	7569.00	56358774.00	506.00	348.00	158.00	1.17	0.0007339553

Remarks:

1. Average price is measured in CNY. It is the average of actual transaction price
2. Sales volume is the quantity of sales of refrigerators in China throughout the year 2013

3. Three volume values: total volume (total), cold-closet volume (cold-closet) and freezer volume (freezer) are measured in liters. Total volume is not equal to the sum of cold-closet volume and freezer volume
4. Daily power consumption (DPC) is measured in kilowatt-hour, also called "DU" in Chinese
5. Market share is computed as: $\text{Market share of refrigerator} = \frac{\text{Value of sales}}{\text{Total market sales}}$,
6. The data of brand, code, average price, sales volume and value of sales is provided by CRMC
7. The data of three volume values and power consumption are gathered manually from producers, online shops and database websites. Part of the data also come from researchers in Nanjing University of Information Science and Technology (NUIST)

Stylized facts of refrigerator market dataset:

1. Total observation: 2757 refrigerator types
2. Average price of the refrigerator: 2464.97 CNY
3. Total sales volume: 31151637 refrigerators
4. Total value of sales: 76787744440.00 CNY
5. Average daily power consumption: 0.59 kilowatt-hour per day

Appendix 2: Residential Electricity Charging Standards

Province	*Tariff pricing*	*Peak and Valley pricing*	*Peak price*	*Valley price*	*Flat price*	*1st class limit*	*Peak hour*	*Valley hour*	*Flat hour*	*Time weighted average price*	*Population weight*	*Population weighted price*
Anhui	Yes	Yes	0.5953	0.3153	N/A	180	14	10	N/A	0.4786	0.044848142	0.021465816
Beijing	Yes	No (1)	0.4883	0.4883	N/A	240	N/A	N/A	N/A	0.4883	0.015730319	0.007681115
Chongqing	Yes	No (2)	0.5200	0.5200	N/A	200	N/A	N/A	N/A	0.5200	0.024978258	0.012988694
Gansu	Yes	Yes (triple)	0.7590	0.2610	0.5100	160	8	8	8	0.5100	0.019203632	0.009793853
Guangdong	Yes	Yes (triple)	1.0500	0.3500	0.7000	260	9	8	7	0.7146	0.07916478	0.056569833
Guangxi	Yes	Yes (triple)	0.8457	0.2113	0.5283	190	6	8	10	0.5020	0.035097576	0.017618457
Guizhou	Yes	No	0.4556	0.4556	0.4556	183	N/A	N/A	N/A	0.4556	0.026046135	0.011866619
Fujian	Yes	Yes	0.5283	0.2983	N/A	200	12	12	N/A	0.4133	0.028069136	0.011600974
Hainan	Yes	No	0.6083	0.6083	0.6083	195	N/A	N/A	N/A	0.6083	0.006656565	0.004049189
Hubei	Yes	Yes (triple)	1.0426	0.2780	0.5700	180	6	10	8	0.5665	0.043130079	0.024432471
Hunan	Yes	No (3)	0.5345	0.5345	0.5345	180	N/A	N/A	N/A	0.5345	0.049764332	0.026599035
Hebei	Yes	Yes	0.5500	0.3200	N/A	180	12	10	N/A	0.4083	0.054539208	0.022270177
Henan	Yes	Yes	0.5539	0.4039	N/A	180	12	10	N/A	0.4452	0.070009214	0.031168452
Heilongjiang	Yes	No	0.5100	0.5100	0.5100	170	N/A	N/A	N/A	0.5100	0.028522823	0.01454664
Jiangsu	Yes	Yes	0.5583	0.3583	N/A	230	13	11	N/A	0.4666	0.059046335	0.027552988
Jilin	Yes	Yes	0.5620	0.3290	N/A	170	11	13	N/A	0.4358	0.02046057	0.008916546
Jiangxi	Yes	Yes	0.6300	0.4800	N/A	180	14	10	N/A	0.5675	0.033632388	0.01908638
Liaoning	Yes	Yes (triple)	0.7500	0.2500	0.5000	180	8	7	9	0.5104	0.032650638	0.01666543
Neimeng	Yes	No	0.4650	0.4650	0.4650	170	N/A	N/A	N/A	0.4650	0.018578882	0.00863918
Ningxia	Yes	Yes (triple)	0.6280	0.2692	0.4486	170	8	8	8	0.4486	0.004864127	0.002182047

Province	*Tariff pricing*	*Peak and Valley pricing*	*Peak price*	*Valley price*	*Flat price*	*1st class limit*	*Peak hour*	*Valley hour*	*Flat hour*	*Time weighted average price*	*Population weight*	*Population weighted price*
Qinghai	Yes	No	0.3771	0.3771	0.3771	150	N/A	N/A	N/A	0.3771	0.004298877	0.001621106
Shandong	Yes	Yes	0.5769	0.3769	N/A	210	14	10	N/A	0.4936	0.072389215	0.035728904
Shanghai	Yes	Yes	0.6170	0.3070	N/A	260	16	8	N/A	0.5137	0.010653033	0.005472108
Shanxi	Yes	Yes	0.5070	0.2862	N/A	170	14	10	N/A	0.4150	0.026998135	0.011204226
Shanxi	Yes	No (4)	0.4983	0.4983	N/A	180	N/A	N/A	N/A	0.4983	0.027994761	0.013949789
Sichuan	Yes	Yes (triple)	0.6974	0.2612	0.5224	180	8	8	8	0.4937	0.060295836	0.029766044
Tianjin	Yes	No	0.4900	0.4900	0.4900	220	N/A	N/A	N/A	0.4900	0.00746703	0.003658845
Xinjiang	No	No (5)	0.5203	0.5203	0.5203	N/A	N/A	N/A	N/A	0.5203	0.016838506	0.008761075
Xizang	No	No (6)	0.6267	0.6267	0.6267	N/A	N/A	N/A	N/A	0.6267	0.002320501	0.001454258
Yunnan	Yes	No	0.4670	0.4670	0.4670	120	N/A	N/A	N/A	0.4670	0.034859576	0.016279422
Zhejiang	Yes	Yes	0.5680	0.2880	0.5380	230	14	10	N/A	0.4513	0.040891391	0.018455648

Remarks:

1. All prices in above table are measured in CNY per kilowatt-hour
2. First class limit is measured in kilowatt-hour per month
3. Population weight is computed using statistics of population at the yearend in 2013, provided by National Bureau of Statistics (NBS)
4. Time weighted average price and population-weighted price are calculated using the method in 3.2.3
5. National population-weighted average residential electricity price ≈ 0.502045319 CNY per kilowatt-hour

Notes

1. Beijing is regarded as not adopting peak and valley pricing. The reason is that only households in the suburb of Beijing who do not use central heating but use electric heating are required to undertake peak and valley pricing. The proportion of this part of households is relatively low. For the time being, Beijing has been drafting unified pricing policies since 2014, but it still takes time to do make adjustments
2. Chongqing, Hunan, and Shanxi are regarded as using tiered pricing only. The electricity supplies of the three regions are dependent on adjacent hydroelectric power stations. The prices of residential electricity in these three regions are therefore highly flexible to change with variation of water flow caused by seasonal weather change. Thus, the discount and penalty adjustments of peak and valley hours are also flexible to change. It is difficult to get a consistent value. Therefore, we use the estimated average price computed by corresponding local Bureau of Commodity Price to approximate the true residential electricity price
3. Xinjiang and Xizang are regarded as neither using tiered pricing nor peak and valley pricing. This situation in the short run will not be changed since the power system in these two provinces is less developed

Note

1. The phenomenon that products with energy-conserving technologies which are apparently cost-effective cannot quickly get enough market share is called energy efficiency gap, or equivalently, energy paradox (Jaffe and Stavins 1994).

References

Allcott, H. and Greenstone, M. (2012), "Is there an energy efficiency gap", *Journal of Economic Perspective*: 26(1), 3–28.

Allcott, H. and Wozny, N. (2014), "Gasoline prices, fuel economy, and the energy paradox", *Review of Economics and Statistics*: 96(5), 779–795.

Blumstein, C., Krieg, B., Schipper, L. and York, C. (1980), "Overcoming social and institutional barriers to energy conservation", *Energy*: 5(4), 355–371.

Busse, M. R., Knittel, C. R. and Zettelmeyer, F. (2013), "Are consumers myopic? Evidence from new and used car purchases", *American Economic Review*: 103(1), 220–56.

Federal Reserve Economic Data [FRED]. (2015), Consumer Price Index for China database online.

Gao, J. (2014), Extreme value theory, Gumbel distribution, the maximum likelihood estimation and portfolio distribution model, North China Electric Power University Press, pp. 5–7 (in Chinese).

Gu, X. and Han, X. (2010), "Discussion on trend of residential average energy consumption", Power Demand Side Management: 12(5), 19–24 (in Chinese).

Greene, D. L. (2010), "How consumers value fuel economy: A literature review", No. EPA-420-R-10-008.

Gillingham, K. and Palmer, K. (2014), "Bridging the energy efficiency gap: policy insights from economic theory and empirical evidence", *Review of Environmental Economics and Policy*: 8(1), 18–38.

Hebei Daily. (2015), Six categories of residential electricity consumption are prioritized, Hebei News Press, Hebei Daily, July, pp. 2 (in Chinese).

Helfand, G. and Wolverton, A. (2011), "Evaluating the consumer response to fuel economy: a review of the literature", *International Review of Environmental and Resource Economics*, 2011, pp. 103–146.

Jaffe, A. B. and Stavins, R. N. (1994), "The energy paradox and the diffusion of conservation technology", *Resource and Energy Economics*: 16(2), 91–122.

Kidokoro, Y. (2008), "A representative consumer framework for discrete choice models with endogenous total demand (No. 07-07)". National Graduate Institute for Policy Studies.

Koomey, J. G. and Sanstad, A. H. (1994), "Technical evidence for assessing the performance of markets affecting energy efficiency", *Energy Policy*: 22(10), 826–832.

National Development and Reform Commission [NDRC]. (2011a), The 12th Five Year Plan [online, in Chinese].
National Development and Reform Commission [NDRC]. (2011b), Notification of Residential Electricity Tiered Pricing Reform, No.2011-2617, pp. 1–5 (in Chinese).
Shama, A. (1983), "Energy conservation in us buildings: solving the high potential/low adoption paradox from a behavioral perspective", *Energy Policy*: 11(2), 148–167.
Standardization Administration of China [SAC]. (1995), National Standard for Refrigerator, GB/T 8059-2, Standardization Administration of China Press, Beijing, pp. 1082–1090 (in Chinese).
State GRID. (2013), Industrial and Residential Electricity Price List in Jiangsu Province [online, in Chinese].
Steg, L. (2008), "Promoting Household Energy Conservation", *Energy Policy*: 36(12), 4449–4453.
Sallee, J. M., West, S. E., and Fan, W. (2016), "Do consumers recognize the value of fuel economy? Evidence from used car prices and gasoline price fluctuations", *Journal of Public Economics*: 135, 61–73.
Stern, P.C. and Aronson, E. (1984), Energy Use: The Human Dimension, Freeman, New York.
Zhao, X. and Xia C. (2006), "Storage of units with exponential distribution", *Journal of Naval Aeronautical Engineering Institute*: 21(4), 1–2 (in Chinese).
Zhao, J. (2009), "Battle of energy conservation and emission reduction", *Macroeconomic Management*: 5, 25–27 (in Chinese).

PART IV

Income Inequality

CHAPTER 7

Income Inequality in China and the Role of Fiscal Policies: An Empirical Study of Chinese Provincial Data

Fan Zhang and Juann H. Hung

7.1 Introduction

China's economy has experienced rapid growth and development after the country's reform and opening up at the end of 1978, raising the Chinese people's average standard of living roughly at a commensurate speed. However, along with that remarkable rate of economic growth, the economic inequality issue in China has also become serious since the 1990s. By 2010, about 45% assets owned by urban citizens belonged to the top 10% richest families. According to data from the National Bureau of Statistics, China's Gini index rose at an alarming rate from 0.343 in 1990 to 0.491 in 2008. Since then, that index has been decreasing gradually. However, as of 2015, the index (0.462) was still considerably higher than the worrisome level of 0.4. As history has made clear, a high degree of income inequality is worrisome in many ways. It could cause people to feel discontent, angry, or even desperate, thereby contributing to, declining

F. Zhang • J. H. Hung (✉)
International Business School Suzhou, Xi'an Jiaotong-Liverpool University, Suzhou, China
e-mail: Juann.Hung@xjtlu.edu.cn

J. H. Hung, Y. Chen (eds.), *The State of China's State Capitalism*,
https://doi.org/10.1007/978-981-13-0983-0_7

civility and work ethics. Worse, it has the potential of increasing crime rates and even social or political unrest.

Given the importance of the issue of income inequality, this chapter focuses on ascertaining the effect of Chinese fiscal policies on income disparity. Some researchers have argued that tax and public spending are the primary tools the government can use to tackle the inequality issue. Arguably, China has undergone a series of fiscal reforms in part to reduce income inequality, but many researchers have questioned the effectiveness of those fiscal policies.

Before the economic reform and open up policy was enacted in late 1978, China tried to enhance its comprehensive national strength by developing heavy industries and the Soviet-style centralized system. At that time, China was a highly centralized country, where the central government possessed all the tax revenue (Mi and Liu 2014). However, in 1978, in order to remove disadvantages of centralization, reform was implemented to promote economic growth. To achieve this target, the central government granted some autonomies to local governments and allowed several provinces to have independent fiscal and financial systems. After 1980, fiscal decentralization began to burgeon. In the 1988 fiscal reform, the central government and local governments signed contracts, allowing local governments to submit only a specific fixed amount or a percentage of their tax revenues to the central government, retaining the residual for their own developments. Admittedly, that fiscal decentralization contributed to promoting local economic growth and local revenues. Nonetheless, some researchers pointed out that owing to the differences in initial economic endowments and revenue bases, and too much authority having been transferred to the local governments, this decentralization further enlarged the income inequality as it became more difficult for resources to be transferred from richer to poorer regions (Song 2013).

One consequence of fiscal decentralization is that the share of central government revenues dramatically decreased. To deal with that, in 1994, the central government implemented the tax-sharing reform to achieve some degree of fiscal recentralization. This reform revised the ratio of local revenue submission, separated national and local tax regulations, and differentiated all taxes into central tax, local tax and shared tax. After 1994, the central government gradually enlarged the extent of shared taxes to further increase the degree of fiscal recentralization on the revenue side. For example, before 2002, local governments could retain all individual and corporate income tax (CIT) revenue except for those from centrally owned corporations. However, the central government received 50% of income taxes in 2002 and 60% starting in 2003 (Song 2013).

Compared with the reforms in revenue sharing, there were fewer reforms implemented on the spending side. Although the 1994 tax-sharing reform recentralized the fiscal system on the revenue side, it did not do so on the spending side. Thus, sub-national governments still needed to face the main responsibilities of public expenditure. According to Jia et al. (2014), local governments have had fewer financial resources to fund public expenditure after the tax-sharing reform allowed the central government to keep a large share of the revenue. Thus, the fiscal system in China has presented a large mismatch between revenue and spending responsibilities, especially after 2002.

Researchers have held different views regarding whether fiscal centralization or decentralization is better for income equality. Some theoretical studies claimed that fiscal decentralization would be conducive to raising government efficiency and give more autonomy to local governments to improve economic growth and income equality. A purely centralized fiscal system would decrease incentives of local governments to develop their own economies owing to the fear of financial shortage, since the central government possesses most resources (Song 2013).

However, some other studies argued that fiscal decentralization would worsen the income inequality problem. In a highly decentralized system, local governments primarily rely on their local tax collections to meet public expenditure responsibilities. Fiscal decentralization would prevent central government from carrying out the equalizing and redistributive work (Dollar 2007, cited by Song 2013). From this perspective, China' tax-sharing reform in 1994 should be a good reform for reducing income inequality. In this more centralized fiscal system, the central government could have more resources to establish redistribution programs, ensuring resources be better transferred from the rich to the poor to reduce the income gap. Nevertheless, that recentralization did not work as well as expected. The tax-sharing reform did not seem to have much effect on reducing income inequality: income disparity continued to widen after the early 1990s until it peaked in 2008. Aiming for a harmonious society, the Chinese government paid great attention to fiscal redistribution policies, with the use of progressive income tax and the spending expansion. Nonetheless, those policies appeared to be feeble on mitigating income inequality (Song 2013).

Against this backdrop, the empirical part of this chapter aims to estimate the effect of tax revenue and government spending on income inequality at the provincial level in recent years. To do that, we use data from 30 Chinese provinces with available data, from 2005 to 2010. Focusing on the effect of fiscal policies on income inequality at the provincial level, we do not address the income disparity between different Chinese regions. Although this method may not be appropriate for ascertaining the main causes of income inequality at the national level in China, it provides a general view about the role of fiscal policies in the evolution of income inequality. We will use the urban Gini index of each province as the dependent variable in a multivariate panel regression model to estimate the effects of several types of taxes and expenditures on the Gini index.

Our empirical results suggest that operation tax is the only tax category included in the regression that has a positive and significant impact on reducing income inequality. Perversely, a rise in individual income tax revenue has a positive and significant effect on increasing income inequality. All other taxes included in the regressions—namely, enterprise income tax and the value-added tax (VAT)—did not have significant effects on income inequality. On the spending side, none of the expenditure categories included in our regression has a statistically significant effect on income inequality. In other words, after the 1994 tax-sharing reform of revenue recentralization and spending decentralization, China's provincial fiscal policies have mostly failed to address the income inequality issue. This result is consistent with most previous studies, which have agreed that China's fiscal policies are not effective at reducing income inequality.

7.2 Literature Review

A great deal of research has arisen to estimate how the revenue and expenditure sides of government budgets affect income distribution. A more limited number of those studies have used multivariate econometric analysis to investigate the impact of different types of tax revenues (such as personal income tax (PTI), CIT or payroll tax) and/or expenditures (such as expenditure on education or medical care) on income inequality, typically measured by the Gini coefficient. For example, de Mello and Tiongson (2006), in a cross-country analysis, the overall effects of government expenditures not to be equalizing. In fact, those countries with high inequality were also less likely to have effective redistributive policies in place. On the revenue side, Weller (2007) using cross-country data from 1981 to 2002 found positive effects of progressive taxation on income distribution.

Using a similar estimation method, Claus et al. (2013) found that PIT has a negative effect on income inequality, especially in Asian economies. When PIT increased by 1 percentage point, the income inequality in Asian countries declines by about 0.573 percentage points, compared with a reduction of 0.041 percentage points in the rest of the world. Claus et al. (2013) also found that the increase in CIT reduced the income inequality in the rest of world, whereas it raised income disparity in Asia. The authors attributed the finding of CIT's positive effect on income inequality in Asia to enormous tax concessions and subsidies for firms. Additionally, they found that social security contributions and payroll taxes led to the increase in income inequality, and by a greater extent in Asia. Finally, general taxes on goods and services (GTGS) have regressive effects on income distribution in both Asia and other continents, but that regressive effect is smaller in Asia because of the lower tax compliance and a larger number of company that did not enforce VATs.

On the government spending side, Claus et al. (2013) found that the expenditures of health and education had negative effects on income inequality in Asia and the rest of world. Moreover, they found that both government expenditure on social protection raised income inequality in Asia but lowered income inequality in the rest of the world. The authors attributed this finding to the observation that, in Asia, the benefit coverage was relatively low and the social protection was restricted to people who worked in the formal sectors like civil service or large enterprises.

Empirical studies on the effect of China's government revenue and expenditure on income distribution are even more scant, and with diverse findings. Wang (2010) claimed that the widening income inequality in China since 1984 was partially due to the failure of its income redistribution policies. With decentralized government spending and an incentive system that rewards government officials mainly for their achievements in promoting rapid economic growth at the local level, the policy objectives of local governments were dominated by economic growth, not the welfare of residents. Hence, local governments were keen to encourage capital-intensive investments by providing various preferential policies, depriving resources from small labor-intensive investments. This directly caused income inequality, since employment in China depended on labor-intensive enterprises to a significant extent. On this point, Mi and Liu

(2014) held a similar view. They held the view that China was politically centralized and economically decentralized. After the 1994 tax-sharing reform, the central government has been taking an increasing share of revenue away from the provincial government. However, with the spending remaining decentralized, local governments have been bearing the responsibility for most public expenditure, reducing their capacity to reduce income inequality. Hu and Liu (2009) found that income tax and social relief funds had a restraining effect on the income inequality in urban areas, but pension expenditure deteriorated the inequality and unemployment-compensation expenditure did not have a significant effect on reducing income inequality.

7.3 Empirical Strategy and Data Description

Following Hu and Liu (2009), and Mi and Liu (2014), among others, this chapter conducts a multivariate panel regression analysis to estimate the effect of fiscal revenue and spending on income inequality in China. More specifically, we use fixed-effect panel regressions to estimate the effect of various tax revenues and various types of government expenditures on income inequality at the provincial level, using data from 30 Chinese provinces from 2005 to 2010.

More specifically, our estimation equation is as follows:

$$\text{Gini}_{\text{it}} = \alpha + \beta_1 \text{Tax}_{\text{it}} + \beta_2 \text{Expend}_{\text{it}} + \beta_3 \text{Control}_{\text{it}} + \varepsilon_{\text{it},} \tag{7.1}$$

where Tax is a vector of tax variables, Expend is a vector of expenditure variables and Control is a vector of control variables. β_1 is a vector of coefficients on tax variables, β_2 is a vector of coefficients on expenditure variables, β_3 is a vector of coefficients on control variables, α is the constant, ε is the error term, i represents different provinces in China and t is the time series (from 2005 to 2010).

The dependent variable is the urban Gini coefficient, which is a measure of income inequality used in most studies. There are several means to calculate the Gini index. At the present stage, due to the lack of completely non-overlapping statistical data, we could not calculate our own Gini index for each province. Thus, we use the provincial urban Gini coefficients from 2005 to 2010 estimated by Lee (2013). Appendix shows those Gini coefficients, the total tax revenue and total expenditure for each of the 30 provinces included in our study.

Compared to previous research, we include more categories of tax and expenditure in the list of independent variables. Moreover, to reduce the problems due to omitted variables, some macroeconomic variables are included as control variables.

For measures of fiscal policies on the revenue side, we select VAT, operation tax, individual income tax and enterprise income tax, all measured as the percentage of provincial gross domestic product (GDP). Appendix provides descriptions of these tax variables. Our expectations regarding the effect of these tax variables on income inequality are as follows:

- Individual income tax is progressive in China, with higher-income taxpayers paying more tax and lower-income taxpayers paying less tax or not paying tax at all. Therefore, individual income tax theoretically should have a marginal effect on reducing income inequality.
- Enterprise income tax, which is paid by all enterprises in China and other income groups (excluding sole individual proprietorship enterprises and partnership enterprises), is also progressive. Therefore, we expect that enterprise income tax should be useful in dealing with income inequality issues since it protects the welfare of some small enterprises or enterprises in financial difficulties.
- Operation tax is subject to the turnover tax, which is taxed on the units and individuals who provide taxable services, transfer intangible assets and sell real estate. (Taxable services include transportation, construction, finance, insurance and another seven items.) Since poor people are unlikely to be subject to the operation tax, we expect it to have an impact on reducing income inequality.
- The VAT is at the core of the turnover tax, generated from selling commodities and services. It related to the transition in tax structure (turnover tax—income tax transition) during the last three decades. Since VAT in China applies to commodities and services, not consumer goods, we expect that it is able to lessen the income inequality problem.
- On the expenditure side, we include the expenditures on general public service, education, science and technology, social security and employment and medical and health care. All of them are measured

as the percentage of provincial GDP. Our expectations of the effect of these expenditure variables on income inequality are as follows:

- General public service, which is the largest share of government spending, is mainly for the protection of the normal operation of public service institutions. We expect it to have the effect of reducing income inequality.
- Technology and science spending is aimed to help cultivate innovative talents and improve local technology levels. An increase in this spending should improve the efficient use of resources, boost local economy and individual income level. Thus, we expect this spending will reduce income inequality.
- Medical and health care spending is aimed to help provide protection to people, especially the poor who do not have the financial ability to pay medical and health care fees. We thus expect this type of expenditure to have the effect of reducing income inequality, easing the burden of the poor.
- Education spending and subsidies are aimed at contributing to provide high-quality education and give poor families an opportunity to have the economic capability to receive an education, promote specific skills and earn a higher income. Thus, we expect this spending to reduce income inequality.
- Social security and employment spending are aimed to protect the welfare of citizens, such as unemployed workers and retirees. This type of spending mainly focuses on people who have financial difficulties, like the poor who need the subsidy to meet basic daily needs. We expect this spending item to reduce income inequality.

Besides the taxation and expenditure variables, we also include two control variables to help reduce the problem caused by omitted variables. These two control variables are (1) the log of GDP per capita and (2) the annual population growth rate.

Admittedly, some limitations remained in our research method. First, the sample period is short mainly because we can only find the urban Gini coefficient for each Chinese province from 2005 to 2010. Second, there are missing data within the vector of spending variables, and this would bias the result on the spending side. Third, the Gini coefficient is not a prefect measure of income inequality. According to previous studies, the Gini coefficient may fail to capture the distribution change, which means it may underestimate the true scale of income inequality. Third, the fixed-effect estimation method itself has some drawbacks. For instance, the fixed-effect model cannot be used to estimate time-variant causes of the dependent variables. Finally, the Gini coefficient in urban areas is likely to be lower than the Gini coefficient at the province level, since the former does not have the inequality stemming from that between rural and city regions, underestimating income inequality level within a province.

All data of tax-related variables (VAT, operation tax, individual income tax and enterprise income tax) and expenditure-related variables (general public service, education, science and technology, social security and employment, and medical and health care) for 29 Chinese provinces, from 2005 to 2010, are from the CEIC China database. Those data are all in the unit of one million RMB.[1] To construct independent variables, we measure these data as percentages of the corresponding provincial annual GDP. As for the data for provincial annual GDP from 2005 to 2010, we found them on one official online database named China Data Online, with the units of 100 million RMB. The other two Control variables - provincial GDP per capita and provincial population growth rates are also found on the online database—China Data Online, respectively, with the units of RMB and %. To put provincial GDP per capita as a control variable into the regression, we use its logarithmic form because this better presents the trend of change in GDP in these six years for each province. For provincial population growth rate, we directly use the original data from the database in our econometric regression model as a control variable in regression.

The summary statistics of all those variables are presented in Tables 7.1, 7.2 and 7.3. Respectively, they show the average of each tax and expenditure percentage of total tax revenue and total government expenditure from 2005 to 2010. From Table 7.1, we see that the average value of the Gini index is 30.7 (timed by 100%), which is not above the worrisome line—0.4. The minimum and maximum of the Gini index are relatively 21.9 and 37.8 (formed in 100%), are therefore reasonable, and even the maximum does not cross the worrisome line. This, however, does not meet the value we introduced in the introduction sector that from 1990 to 2000, the Gini coefficient had raised from 0.343 to 0.417; in 2010, it had reached 0.48, which had far exceeded the worrisome level of 0.4 recognized internationally. This difference may be because these Gini coefficients are those the urban level, ignoring the income inequality between regions of rural and urban areas. Therefore, they underestimate the overall inequality degree.

Table 7.1 The summary of variables (all data of fiscal variables are in millions of RMB)

Variable	*Observations*	*Mean*	*Std. dev.*	*Min*	*Max*
Province	30				
Year	6	2007.5		2005	2010
Gini	180	30.6514	2.7383	21.9839	37.8386
Value-added tax	180	1.3326	0.4384	0.4752	2.6939
Operation tax	180	2.2610	1.1446	0.2285	6.1967
Individual income tax	180	0.5893	1.0089	0.1536	7.0113
Enterprise income tax	180	0.9557	0.7003	0.2909	4.4955
General public service expenses	121	3.1574	2.8090	1.0632	19.4229
Education, science & technology	176	3.0895	1.8832	0.3815	13.8309
expenses	122	0.4249	0.4361	0.1279	2.2589
Social security & employment expenses	121	2.8429	1.7950	0.5758	14.0326
Medical & health care expenses	180	1.1386	0.8562	0	6.3140
Log GDP per capita	180	9.9348	0.5631	8.5931	11.2395
Population growth rate	180	5.5077	2.7914	0.42	11.78

Table 7.2 The percentage share of each tax category in the total local tax revenues[a]

Year	*VAT (%)*	*Operation tax (%)*	*Turnover tax (%)*	*Individual income tax (%)*	*Enterprise income tax (%)*	*Income tax (%)*
2005	26.9872	34.0815	61.0687	20.2390	13.2977	33.5367
2006	27.3409	34.2260	61.5668	20.8766	14.2001	35.0768
2007	26.6490	33.4893	60.1382	22.1100	15.6562	37.7663
2008	26.1604	32.4043	58.5646	23.6693	16.7184	40.3876
2009	24.1421	34.8388	58.9809	24.9475	15.3873	40.3348
2010	23.2931	35.1458	58.4839	27.4829	16.1471	43.6569

[a]Raw data sources from CEIC China database, calculated using $(\text{Tax}_j/\text{Total Tax Revenue}_j)*100\%$, where Tax is a vector of tax variables, and j represents a specific province. The turnover tax here only consists of VAT and operation tax

In all tax variables, on the basis of the mean value, we determine that operation tax accounts for the largest proportion (2.3%) of local annual GDP, where it is almost double the amount of VAT and about three times as much of both individual and enterprise income tax. This implies that turnover tax, which includes operation tax and VAT, is of vital importance

Table 7.3 The percentage share of each expenditure item in total local expenditure[a]

Year	*General public services (%)*	*Education (%)*	*Science & technology (%)*	*Social security & employment (%)*	*Medical & health care (%)*
2005		13.7249			4.1216
2006		13.7211			4.1933
2007	16.8555	16.2567	2.4749	13.5625	5.2942
2008	15.1866	16.1805	2.4100	13.2824	5.5819
2009	13.1203	15.1199	2.3564	13.2671	6.4459
2010	11.1438	14.9683	2.3408	11.9520	6.4254

[a]Raw data sources from CEIC China database, calculated using ($Spending_j$/Total Government $Expenditure_j$)*100%, where Spending is a vector of spending variables, and j represents a specific province

to the Chinese government, here with a value of 3.6% of GDP. Compared to that, the share of income tax, which is the sum of individual and enterprise income tax, is relatively small, only taking up 1.5% of GDP on average. From Table 7.2, we can see that compared to other tax variables, operation tax occupies the largest share of total revenue—over 30%. Turnover tax, with the core of VAT and operation tax, obviously accounts for a larger percentage than income tax. However, the gap between the share of turnover and income tax has been narrowing during these years, with a decrease in VAT and apparent increase in individual income tax, and by 2010, the disparity had reduced from 27.6% (= 61.1%–33.5%) to 14.7% (= 58.4%–43.7%).

These results correspond to findings of previous research. From the reform and opening up in 1978, China has been taking turnover tax as the main category of taxes. During that period, the proportion of turnover tax with the core of VAT almost reached 70% of tax revenue. However, after the peak in 1997, the proportion of turnover tax started to decrease continuously. Owing to the rapid growth of the domestic economy, national income has improved significantly, and so does the revenue from the income tax (individual income tax and enterprise income tax). In many areas, the revenue from individual income tax is only behind that from operation tax; and the individual income tax is thus the second largest tax source for local governments. Here, from Table 7.2, we find that in 2005, VAT share was 27.0% and individual income tax share was 20.2%, which is 6.8% less than VAT. Nevertheless, by 2010, individual income tax was raised to 27.5%, which overtook VAT (23.3%) by 4.2%, becoming the second largest tax only behind operation tax. Therefore, it can be seen that China had formed the "double major category" structure in the tax system (the turnover tax with the core of VAT is the first major tax category, and income tax is the second major tax category) (Zhu and Wang 2008).

In accordance with the literature, this "double major category" tax system not only ensures the fiscal revenue, but also plays the role of adjusting the income gap and restraining the wealth disparity. We will discuss whether this is right or not below.

On the spending side, general public service, education and social security and employment expenditures have a relatively large share of local GDP. Technology and science expenditure is the lowest, with the mean value of only 0.4% of GDP, and even its maximum only occupies 2.3%, which is much lower than the other expenditures. Similarly, together with Table 7.3, we find that technology expenditure slightly decreases during these years with the lowest local expenditure share from 2.5% to 2.3%. Compared with it, general public service, education and social security and employment indeed possess larger shares of total local government expenditures. However, all three types of expenditure had decreasing trends in their shares of total expenditure from 2007 to 2010. In 2007, general public service expenditure was the highest with 16.9%; education, and social security and employment expenditures, respectively, took the second and the third place. Nonetheless, the expenditure of general public services drops more rapidly than the other two. By 2010, it fell to third place with 11.1%, and the education expenditure share became the largest with 15.0%. Additionally, although the value of medical and health care expenditure is not very significant, unlike the other four expenditure types discussed above, it increased steadily during the six years from 4.1% to 6.4%.

7.4 Discussion of Regression Results

Table 7.4 presents our estimation results. On the revenue side, operation tax in our model has a significant negative impact on income inequality.[2] A 1 percentage point increase in the operation tax revenue/GDP ratio reduced the Gini coefficient by about 1.90 percentage points. Other categories of tax, VAT either has a positive or statistically insignificant effect on income inequality.

Table 7.4 Fixed-effect estimation results (the value in brackets represents the t-statistic)

Dependent variable: Gini coefficient	*Model 1*	*Model 2*	*Model 3*	*Model 4*
Value-added tax	0.3703	–	−0.4468	1.5584
	(0.34)		(−0.33)	(1.84)
Operation tax	−1.9393	–	−1.8571	−0.8480
	(−4.07)		(−2.82)	(−2.47)
Individual income tax	0.8764	–	1.6790	1.5725
	(1.08)		(1.29)	(2.41)
Enterprise income tax	0.1734	–	0.5654	0.1329
	(0.28)		(0.64)	(0.26)
General public services	–	0.3939	0.3162	0.3362
		(1.34)	(1.08)	(1.48)
Education	–	−0.6875	−0.1953	0.1564
		(−1.51)	(−0.41)	(1.03)
Science & technology	–	0.2632	−0.5822	0.3666
		(0.14)	(−0.3)	(0.24)
Social security & employment	–	0.1637	0.1070	−0.1441
		(0.73)	(0.49)	(−0.89)
Medical & health care	–	0.0258	0.2223	0.3999
		(−0.04)	(0.37)	(1.65)
Log GDP per capita	1.6821	0.4026	0.9461	–
	(3.08)	(0.37)	(0.84)	
Population growth rate	−0.0354	0.0394	0.1383	–
	(−0.14)	(0.09)	(0.33)	
Constant	17.3444	27.0128	23.1133	
	(2.98)	(2.53)	(1.95)	
Number of objectives	180	120	120	
R^2	0.1534	0.0617	0.1910	

In column 4, individual income tax has a significant and positive effect on Gini index, contrary to our expectation. A 1 percentage point increase in individual income tax revenue/GDP ratio increased the Gini coefficient (i.e., income inequality) by around 1.6 percentage points. This suggests that there may be a serious degree of tax evasion by the rich in China. If "only little people pay tax", it would not be surprising that individual income tax is positively related to income inequality.

In columns 1, 3 and 4, operation tax has a significant impact on reducing income inequality. Operation tax is taxed on the units and individuals who provide taxable services, transfer intangible assets and sell real estate. Taxable services include transportation, construction, finance, insurance and another seven items. The tax payment for operation tax is calculated in terms of the turnover, transfer or sales of taxable services or behaviors. Since these taxes mainly hit people who have the money to engage in active trading, it is no surprise that this tax category reduces income inequality. The finding that VAT does not have an effect on income inequality may be due to its high correlation with the operation tax.

Our finding that the individual income tax worsened, rather than improved, the problem of income inequality in China is quite concerning. It suggests that there has been a large scale of tax evasion via various schemes. Agents who have legal responsibility to pay taxes can transfer the payment to other agents by changing their economic behaviors, like changing product prices, adjusting labor wages or the interest payment on investment. In that case, the ultimate taxpayers may differ from the legally regulated taxpayers.

On the spending side, we find that none of the variables is statistically significant. This implies that all types of fiscal spending had little impact on reducing income inequality. One reason why this is the case is offered by Claus et al. (2013). These authors argued that it is difficult to measure the benefit generated from public expenditure on individuals and households. Since most supplies of public goods and services are rationed or subsidized, the public good and service may not be under direct control, and thereby cannot directly meet the demand of individuals. Another insight is offered by Jia et al. (2014). These authors pointed out that, because local citizens cannot participate in the election of local officials and labor is not completely mobile in China due to the Hukou system, local governments would have less incentive to invest in public goods and services that could benefit local citizens. They would rather put resources in infrastructure to attract capital and boom the local economy to boost their own political prospects, ignoring the real interests and welfare equivalence of the citizens. This partially explains why the share of expenditure on technology and medical-health care is relatively low.

The result on education and social security spending is also inconsistent with our expectation. We expected that education spending would help give poor families opportunities to receive an education and earn a higher income, thereby narrowing down the income disparity, and the expenditure on social security protects the welfare of citizens, meets the basic daily needs and equalizes the welfare level. However, the regression results in Table 7.4 show that these two types of government spending do not have significant impacts on income inequality. This ineffectiveness of education and social security and employment expenditure may be due to the inefficiency of government spending.

Appendix presents the trend in the Gini coefficient, the total government spending/GDP ratio and the total tax revenue/GDP ratio for every province in China except for Hunan from 2005 to 2010. We can see from these graphs that almost all provinces have an upward trend in their government expenditure and tax revenue, but these increases do not appear to have a significant positive effect on reducing income inequality except for the operation tax. Moreover, from the analyses in previous sections, we find that except for the operation tax, neither tax policy nor public expenditure helped to mitigate the problem of income inequality.

7.5 Conclusion

This chapter aims to estimate the effect of various provincial government tax revenues and expenditures on income inequality in China, using data from 2005 to 2010. On the revenue side, we find that only operation tax has a significant negative effect on income inequality, as expected. Individual income tax has a significant and positive effect on Gini index, contrary to our expectation. A 1 percentage point increase in individual income tax revenue/GDP ratio increased the Gini coefficient (i.e., income inequality) by around 1.6 percentage points. This suggests that there has been a serious degree of tax evasion by the rich in China. Both VAT and enterprise income tax do not have a significant effect on reducing income inequality. On the spending side, the results indicate that none of various government expenditures has a significant impact on reducing income inequality. This suggests that, among other possibilities, government spending lacks efficiency or pays insufficient attention to the needy.

Appendix

*Appendix 1: In the Following Graphs, Spending = Government Spending*100/GDP, (2) Tax = Tax Revenue*100/GDP, (3) Gini = Gini coefficient*100*

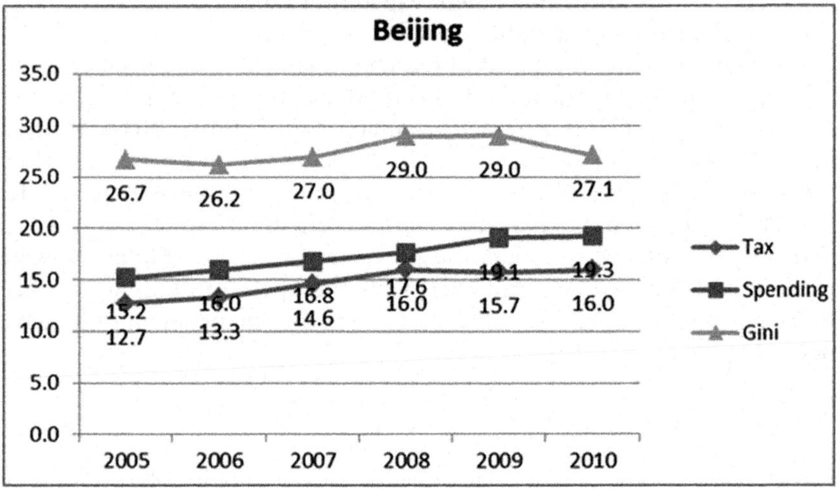

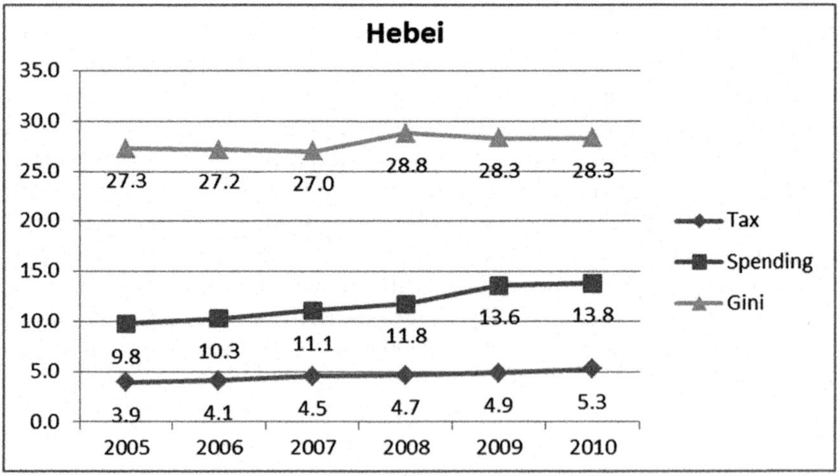

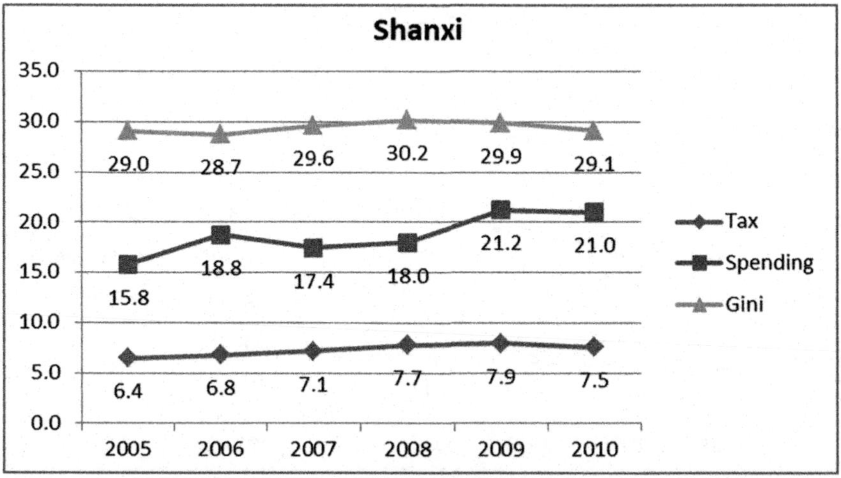
Shanxi
35.0
30.0
25.0
20.0
15.0
10.0
5.0
0.0
29.0
28.7
29.6
30.2
29.9
29.1
15.8
18.8
17.4
18.0
21.2
21.0
6.4
6.8
7.1
7.7
7.9
7.5
2005
2006
2007
2008
2009
2010
Tax
Spending
Gini

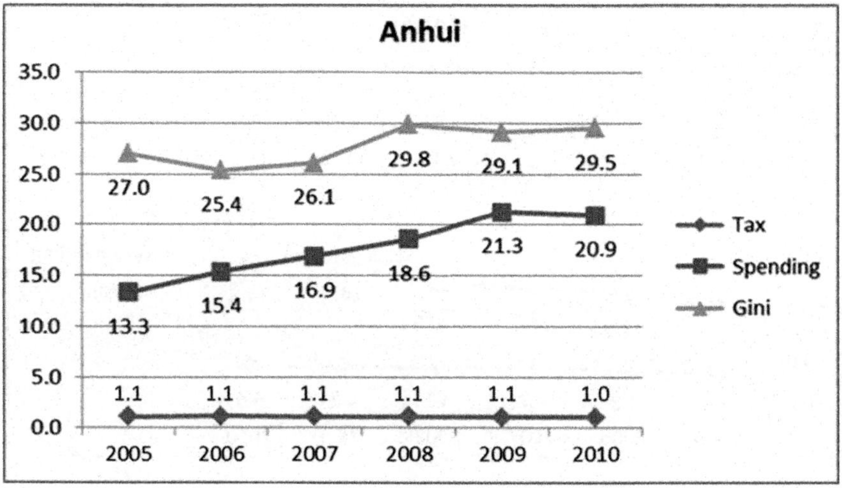
Anhui
35.0
30.0
25.0
20.0
15.0
10.0
5.0
0.0
27.0
25.4
26.1
29.8
29.1
29.5
13.3
15.4
16.9
18.6
21.3
20.9
1.1
1.1
1.1
1.1
1.1
1.0
2005
2006
2007
2008
2009
2010
Tax
Spending
Gini

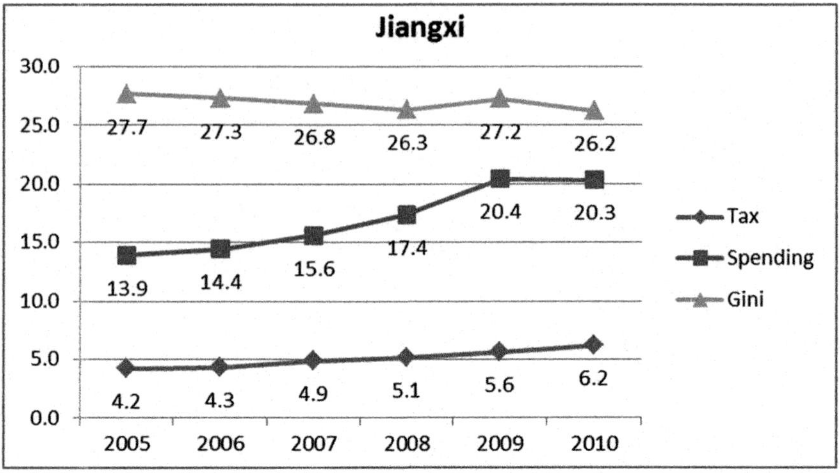
Jiangxi
30.0
25.0
20.0
15.0
10.0
5.0
0.0
27.7
27.3
26.8
26.3
27.2
26.2
20.4
20.3
17.4
15.6
14.4
13.9
4.2
4.3
4.9
5.1
5.6
6.2
2005
2006
2007
2008
2009
2010
Tax
Spending
Gini

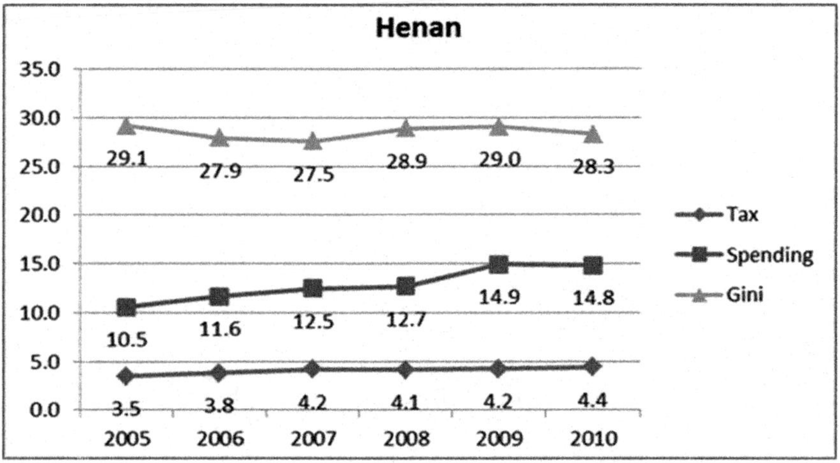
Henan
35.0
30.0
25.0
20.0
15.0
10.0
5.0
0.0
29.1
27.9
27.5
28.9
29.0
28.3
14.9
14.8
12.5
12.7
11.6
10.5
3.5
3.8
4.2
4.1
4.2
4.4
2005
2006
2007
2008
2009
2010
Tax
Spending
Gini

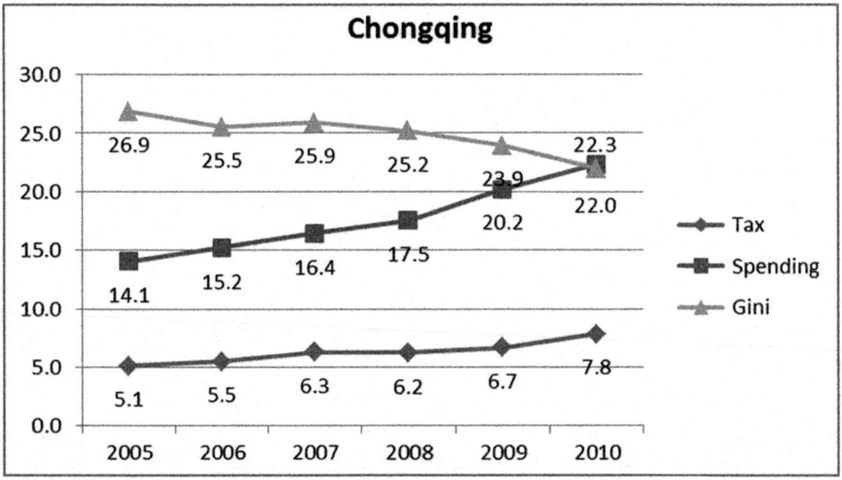
Chongqing
30.0
25.0
20.0
15.0
10.0
5.0
0.0
26.9
25.5
25.9
25.2
23.9
22.3
22.0
20.2
17.5
16.4
15.2
14.1
5.1
5.5
6.3
6.2
6.7
7.8
2005
2006
2007
2008
2009
2010
Tax
Spending
Gini

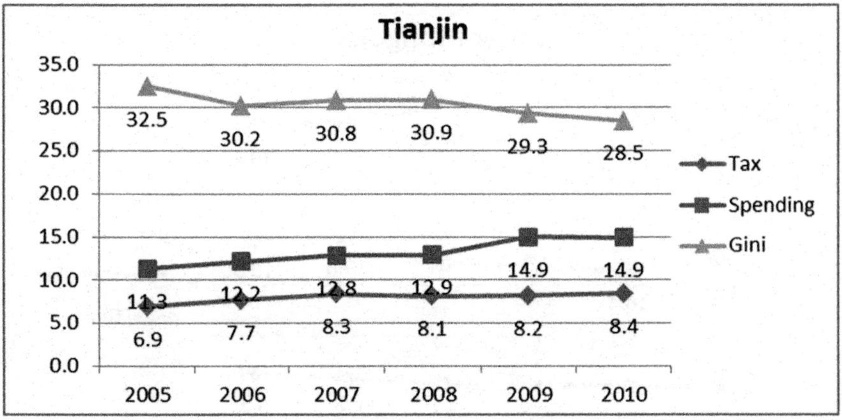
Tianjin
35.0
30.0
25.0
20.0
15.0
10.0
5.0
0.0
32.5
30.2
30.8
30.9
29.3
28.5
11.3
12.2
12.8
12.9
14.9
14.9
6.9
7.7
8.3
8.1
8.2
8.4
2005
2006
2007
2008
2009
2010
Tax
Spending
Gini

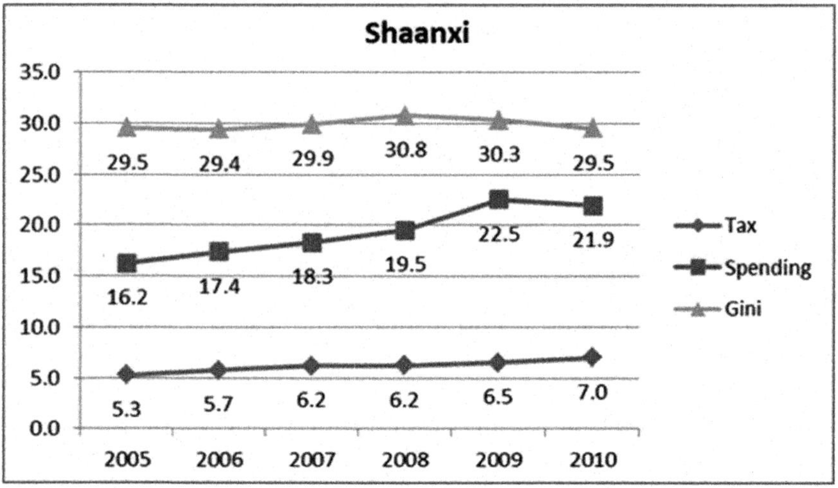
Shaanxi
35.0
30.0
25.0
20.0
15.0
10.0
5.0
0.0
29.5
29.4
29.9
30.8
30.3
29.5
16.2
17.4
18.3
19.5
22.5
21.9
5.3
5.7
6.2
6.2
6.5
7.0
2005
2006
2007
2008
2009
2010
Tax
Spending
Gini

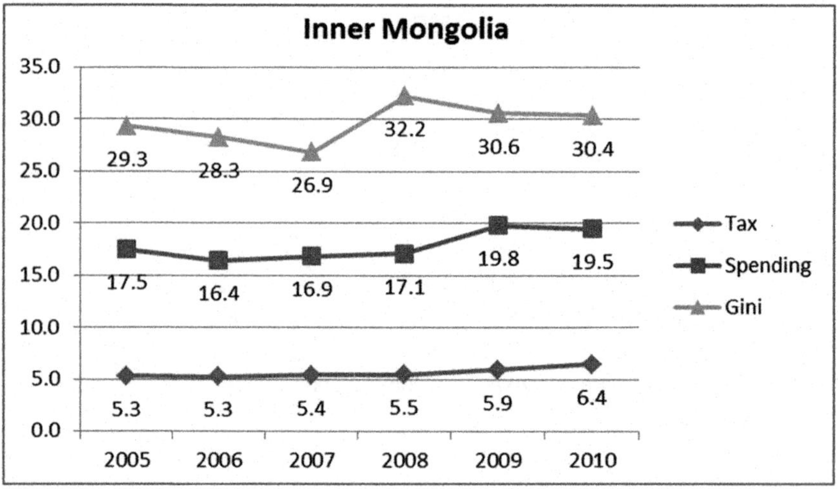
Inner Mongolia
35.0
30.0
25.0
20.0
15.0
10.0
5.0
0.0
29.3
28.3
26.9
32.2
30.6
30.4
17.5
16.4
16.9
17.1
19.8
19.5
5.3
5.3
5.4
5.5
5.9
6.4
2005
2006
2007
2008
2009
2010
Tax
Spending
Gini

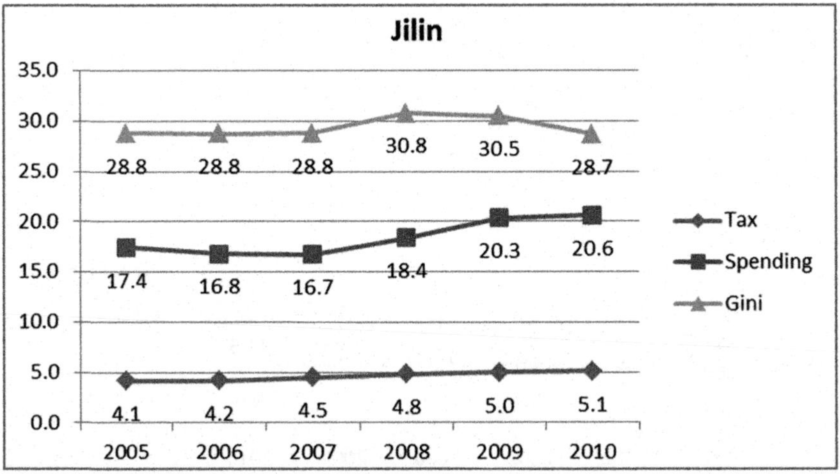
Jilin
35.0
30.0
25.0
20.0
15.0
10.0
5.0
0.0
28.8
28.8
28.8
30.8
30.5
28.7
17.4
16.8
16.7
18.4
20.3
20.6
4.1
4.2
4.5
4.8
5.0
5.1
2005
2006
2007
2008
2009
2010
Tax
Spending
Gini

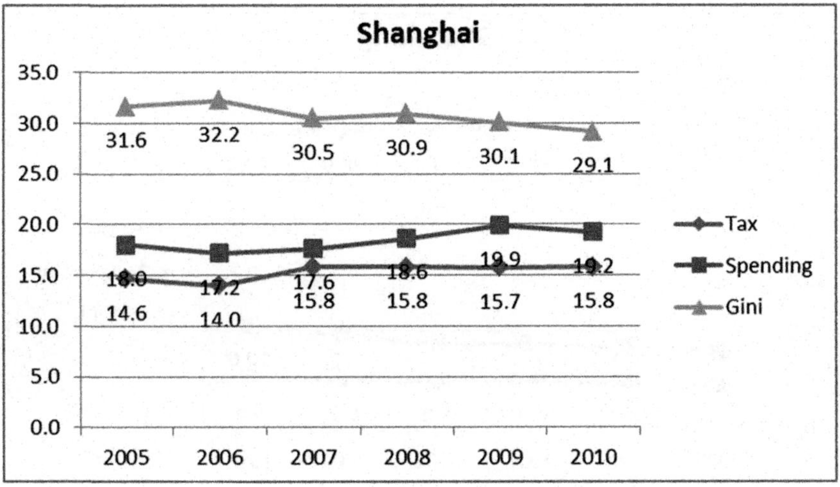
Shanghai
35.0
30.0
25.0
20.0
15.0
10.0
5.0
0.0
31.6
32.2
30.5
30.9
30.1
29.1
18.0
17.2
17.6
18.6
19.9
19.2
14.6
14.0
15.8
15.8
15.7
15.8
2005
2006
2007
2008
2009
2010
Tax
Spending
Gini

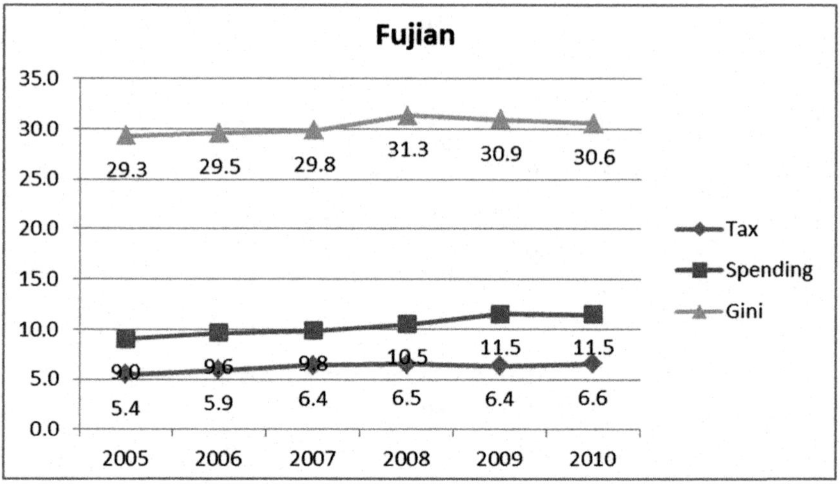
Fujian
35.0
30.0
25.0
20.0
15.0
10.0
5.0
0.0
29.3
29.5
29.8
31.3
30.9
30.6
9.0
9.6
9.8
10.5
11.5
11.5
5.4
5.9
6.4
6.5
6.4
6.6
2005
2006
2007
2008
2009
2010
Tax
Spending
Gini

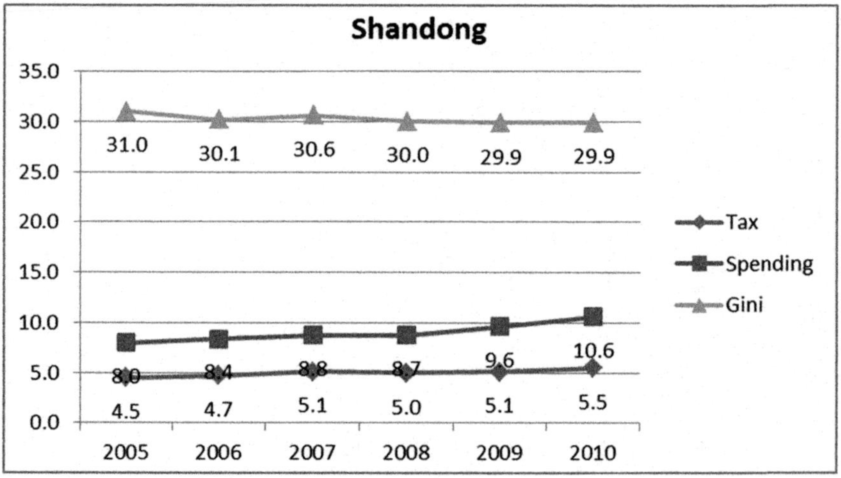
Shandong
35.0
30.0
25.0
20.0
15.0
10.0
5.0
0.0
31.0
30.1
30.6
30.0
29.9
29.9
8.0
8.4
8.8
8.7
9.6
10.6
4.5
4.7
5.1
5.0
5.1
5.5
2005
2006
2007
2008
2009
2010
Tax
Spending
Gini

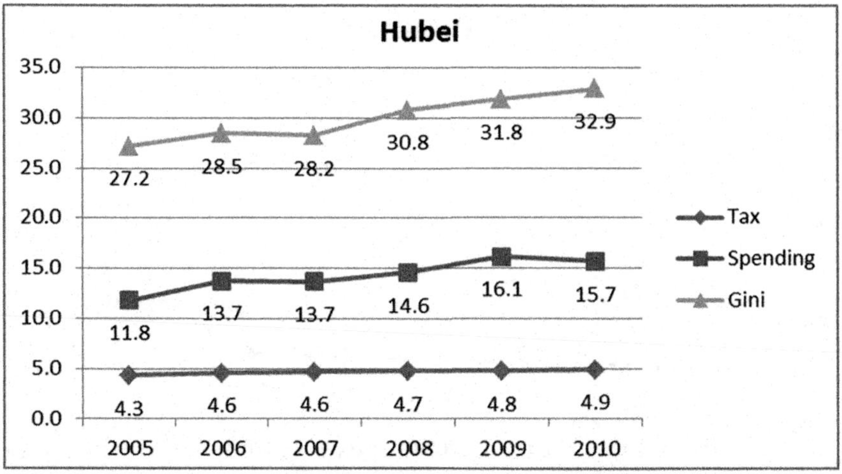
Hubei
35.0
30.0
25.0
20.0
15.0
10.0
5.0
0.0
27.2 28.5 28.2 30.8 31.8 32.9
11.8 13.7 13.7 14.6 16.1 15.7
4.3 4.6 4.6 4.7 4.8 4.9
2005 2006 2007 2008 2009 2010
Tax
Spending
Gini

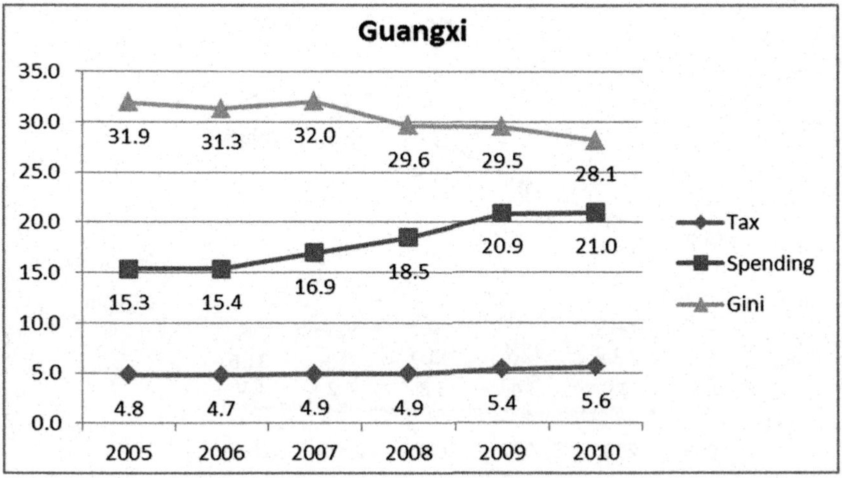
Guangxi
35.0
30.0
25.0
20.0
15.0
10.0
5.0
0.0
31.9 31.3 32.0 29.6 29.5 28.1
15.3 15.4 16.9 18.5 20.9 21.0
4.8 4.7 4.9 4.9 5.4 5.6
2005 2006 2007 2008 2009 2010
Tax
Spending
Gini

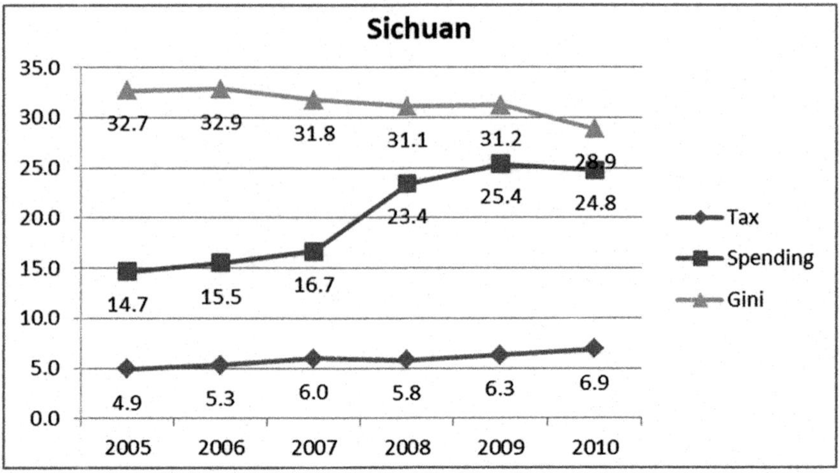
Sichuan
35.0
30.0
25.0
20.0
15.0
10.0
5.0
0.0
32.7
32.9
31.8
31.1
31.2
28.9
25.4
24.8
23.4
14.7
15.5
16.7
4.9
5.3
6.0
5.8
6.3
6.9
2005
2006
2007
2008
2009
2010
Tax
Spending
Gini

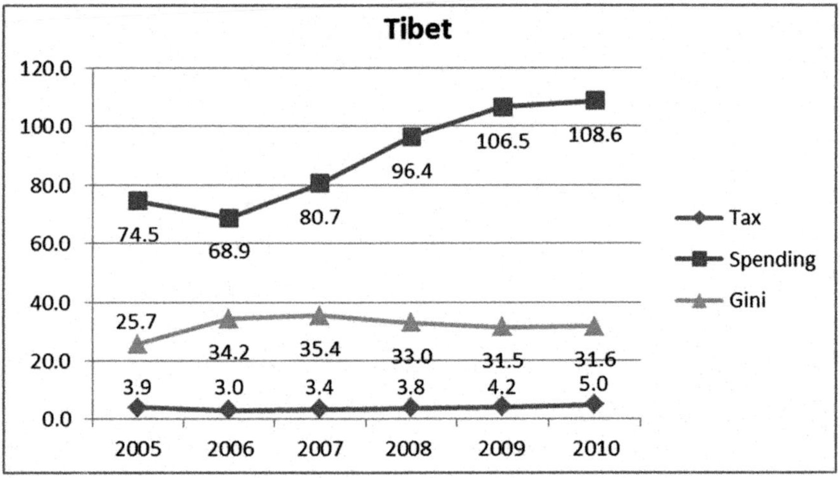
Tibet
120.0
100.0
80.0
60.0
40.0
20.0
0.0
106.5
108.6
96.4
80.7
74.5
68.9
25.7
34.2
35.4
33.0
31.5
31.6
3.9
3.0
3.4
3.8
4.2
5.0
2005
2006
2007
2008
2009
2010
Tax
Spending
Gini

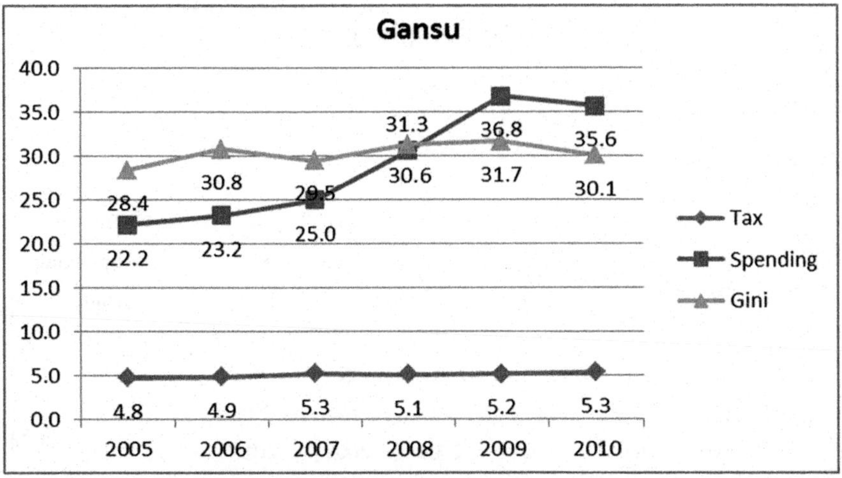
Gansu
40.0
35.0
30.0
25.0
20.0
15.0
10.0
5.0
0.0
31.3
36.8
35.6
30.8
30.6
31.7
30.1
28.4
29.5
22.2
23.2
25.0
4.8
4.9
5.3
5.1
5.2
5.3
2005
2006
2007
2008
2009
2010
Tax
Spending
Gini

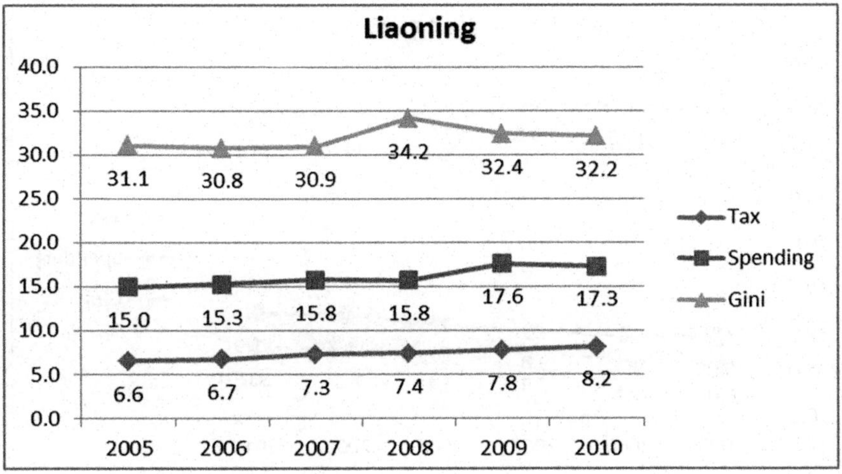
Liaoning
40.0
35.0
30.0
25.0
20.0
15.0
10.0
5.0
0.0
34.2
31.1
30.8
30.9
32.4
32.2
15.0
15.3
15.8
15.8
17.6
17.3
6.6
6.7
7.3
7.4
7.8
8.2
2005
2006
2007
2008
2009
2010
Tax
Spending
Gini

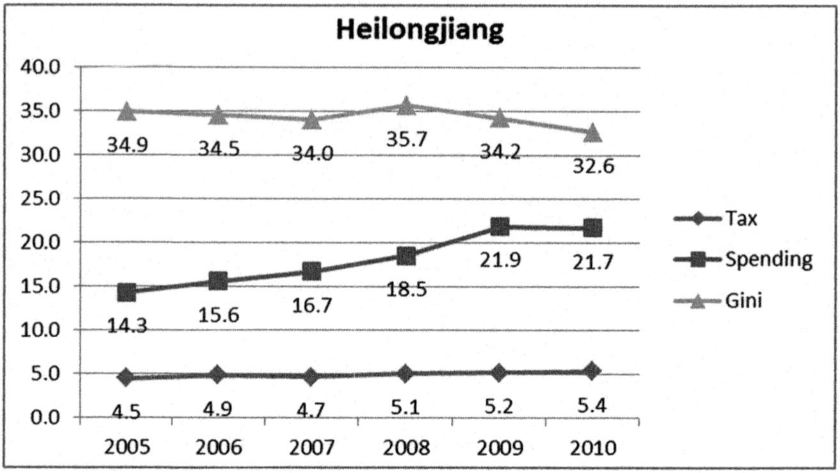
Heilongjiang
40.0
35.0
30.0
25.0
20.0
15.0
10.0
5.0
0.0
34.9
34.5
34.0
35.7
34.2
32.6
21.9
21.7
14.3
15.6
16.7
18.5
4.5
4.9
4.7
5.1
5.2
5.4
2005
2006
2007
2008
2009
2010
Tax
Spending
Gini

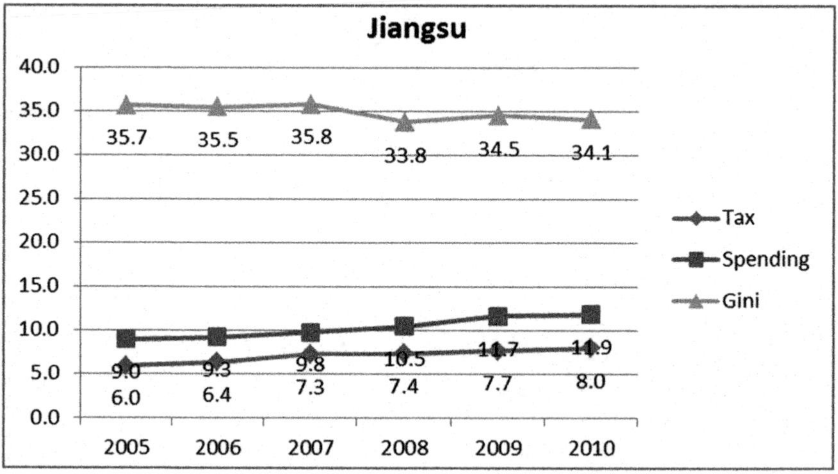
Jiangsu
40.0
35.0
30.0
25.0
20.0
15.0
10.0
5.0
0.0
35.7
35.5
35.8
33.8
34.5
34.1
9.0
9.3
9.8
10.5
11.7
11.9
6.0
6.4
7.3
7.4
7.7
8.0
2005
2006
2007
2008
2009
2010
Tax
Spending
Gini

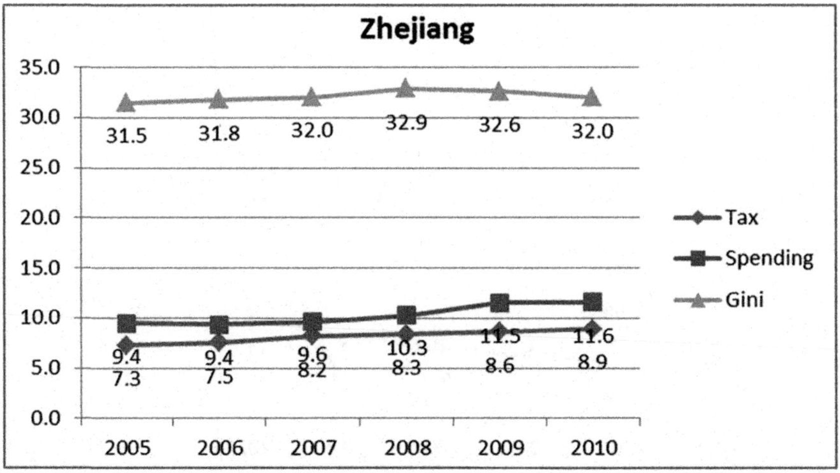
Zhejiang
35.0
30.0
25.0
20.0
15.0
10.0
5.0
0.0
31.5
31.8
32.0
32.9
32.6
32.0
9.4
9.4
9.6
10.3
11.5
11.6
7.3
7.5
8.2
8.3
8.6
8.9
2005
2006
2007
2008
2009
2010
Tax
Spending
Gini

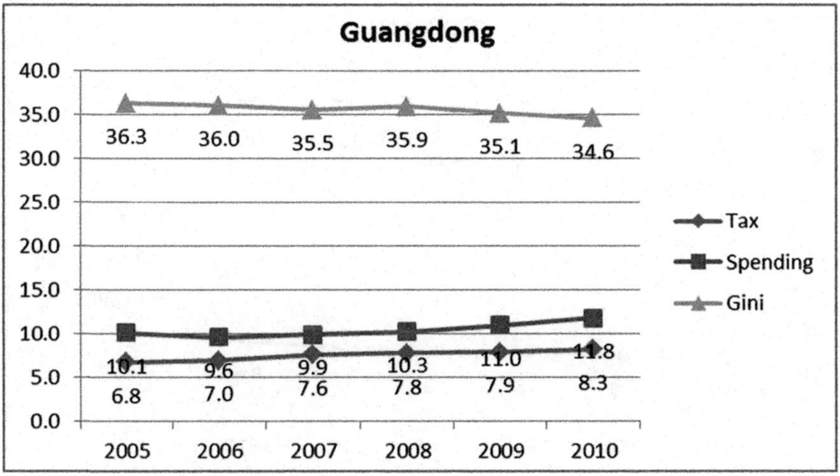
Guangdong
40.0
35.0
30.0
25.0
20.0
15.0
10.0
5.0
0.0
36.3
36.0
35.5
35.9
35.1
34.6
10.1
9.6
9.9
10.3
11.0
11.8
6.8
7.0
7.6
7.8
7.9
8.3
2005
2006
2007
2008
2009
2010
Tax
Spending
Gini

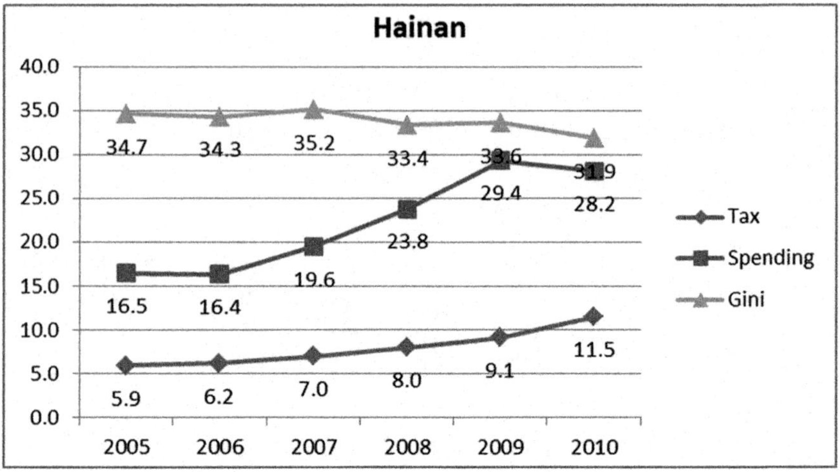
Hainan
40.0
35.0
30.0
25.0
20.0
15.0
10.0
5.0
0.0
34.7
34.3
35.2
33.4
33.6
31.9
29.4
28.2
23.8
19.6
16.5
16.4
11.5
9.1
8.0
7.0
6.2
5.9
2005
2006
2007
2008
2009
2010
Tax
Spending
Gini

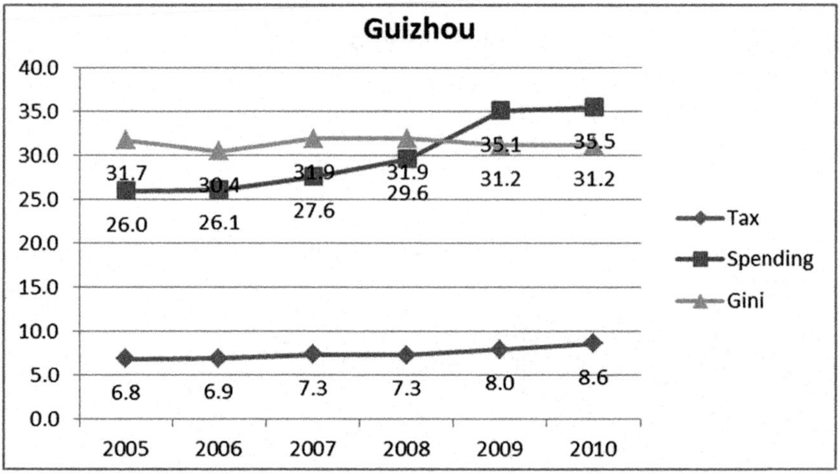
Guizhou
40.0
35.0
30.0
25.0
20.0
15.0
10.0
5.0
0.0
35.1
35.5
31.7
30.4
31.9
31.9
31.2
31.2
29.6
27.6
26.0
26.1
6.8
6.9
7.3
7.3
8.0
8.6
2005
2006
2007
2008
2009
2010
Tax
Spending
Gini

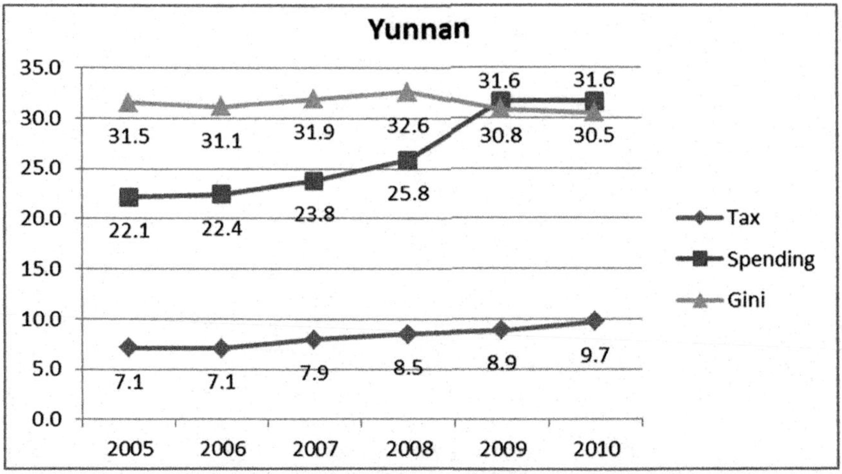
Yunnan
35.0
30.0
25.0
20.0
15.0
10.0
5.0
0.0
31.5 31.1 31.9 32.6 30.8 30.5
31.6 31.6
22.1 22.4 23.8 25.8
7.1 7.1 7.9 8.5 8.9 9.7
2005 2006 2007 2008 2009 2010
Tax
Spending
Gini

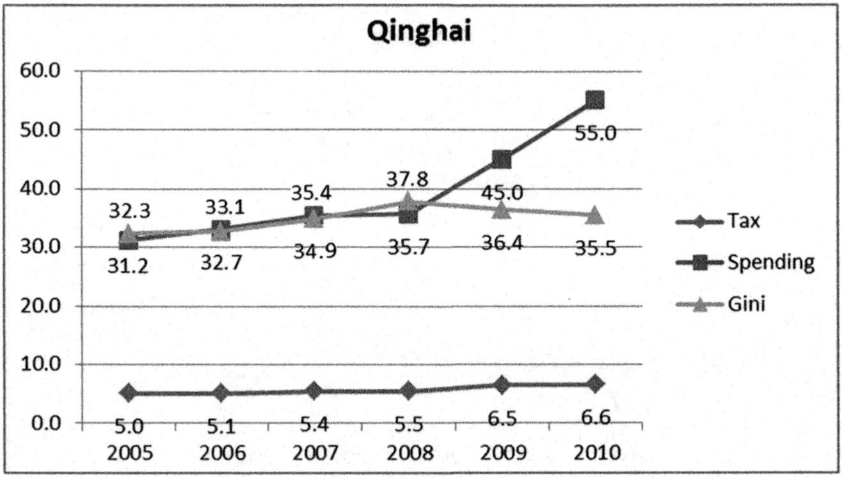
Qinghai
60.0
50.0
40.0
30.0
20.0
10.0
0.0
55.0
32.3 33.1 35.4 37.8 45.0
31.2 32.7 34.9 35.7 36.4 35.5
5.0 5.1 5.4 5.5 6.5 6.6
2005 2006 2007 2008 2009 2010
Tax
Spending
Gini

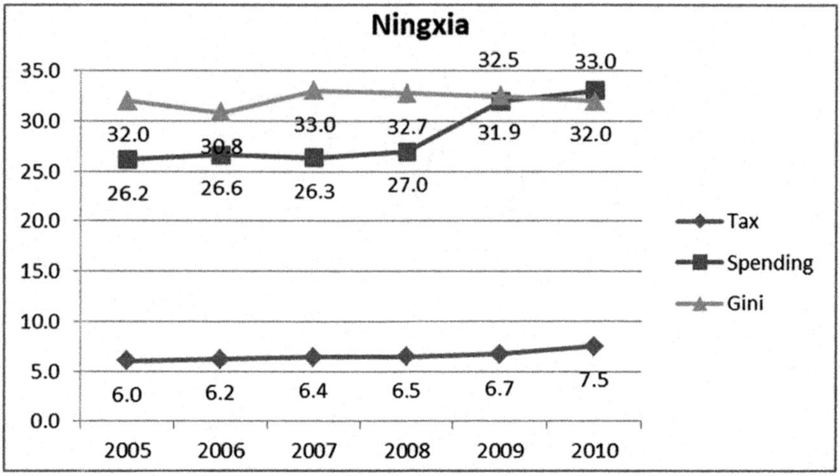

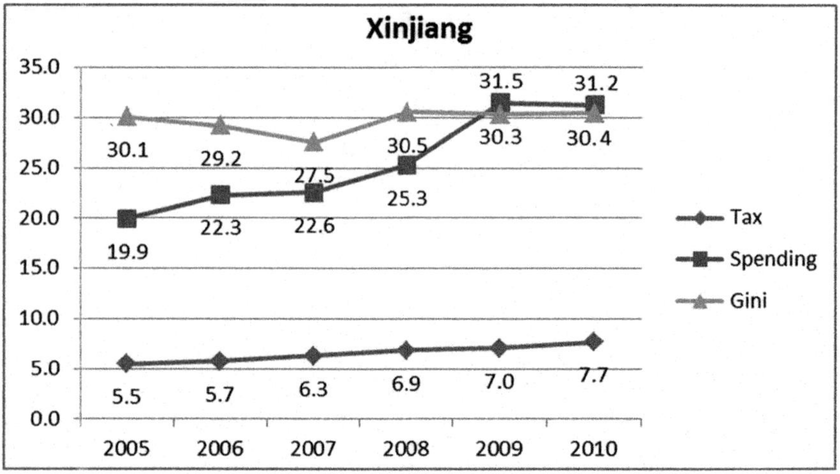

Appendix 2: Descriptions of Tax Categories[3]

VAT in China levies tax in selling goods or providing processing, repairing and replacement services, and on units and individuals for imported goods. Taxpayers are divided into general VAT taxpayers and small-scale VAT taxpayers. For general taxpayer, the basic tax rate is 17% and the low tax rate is 13%. For small-scale taxpayers, a simplified method is used for calculating the tax payment, yielding a rate of 3%.

Income tax consists of individual income tax and enterprise income tax. Individual income tax directs at taxable income of individuals of all kinds (including income from salaries of individuals and individual commercial production and operation). For the enterprise income tax, all enterprises in China and other income groups (not including sole individual proprietorship enterprises and partnership enterprises) are the taxpayers. Enterprises are classified into resident and non-resident enterprises. Resident enterprises shall pay enterprise income tax for their income from sources both inside and outside the territory of China. The amount of enterprise income tax paid by non-resident enterprises depends on whether they establish agencies and offices in China, and whether they have actual relationships with organizations or establishments within the territory of China. The taxable income for enterprise income tax is the total annual revenue of the enterprise, minus the tax-free income, the deduction and the amount of recovering the loss of the previous year; the tax rate shall be 25%.

Operation tax is taxed on the units and individuals who provide taxable services, transfer intangible assets and sell real estate. Taxable services include transportation, construction, finance, insurance and another seven items. The tax payment for operation tax is calculated in terms of the turnover, transfer or sales of taxable services or behaviors. In addition to the entertainment industry, which is taxed at 20%, the rate of other taxes shall be levied at the rate of 3% or 5%.

Notes

1. We cannot include Hunan province because we cannot find the corresponding Gini coefficient for that province from 2005 to 2010.
2. If the absolute value of the t-statistic of a variable is larger than 1.96, we can reject the null hypothesis that the coefficient of the corresponding variable equals zero at a 95% statistically significant level, and thus the variable is significantly different from zero.
3. Sources are from State Administration of Taxation.

References

Claus, I., Martinez-Vazquez, J. and Vulovic, V., (2013), "Coping with Rising Inequality in Asia: How Effective Are Fiscal Policies", *Asian Economic Papers*: 12(3).

de Mello and Tiongson, E., (2006), "Income Inequality and Redistributive Government Spending", *Public Finance Review*: 34(3), 282–305.

Hu, H. and Liu, Q. Z., (2009), "A study on redistribution effects of China's fiscal policy on income inequality between urban and rural inhabitants", *China Soft Science*: 9, 54–59.

Lee, J., (2013), "A provincial perspective on income inequality in urban China and the role of property and business income", *China Economic Review*: 26, 140–150.

Jia, J. X., Guo, Q. and Zhang, J., (2014), "Fiscal decentralization and local expenditure policy in China", *China Economic Review*: 28, 107–122.

Mi, Z. and Liu, Q. Z., (2014), "Income Inequality, Fiscal Redistribution, and Governmental Corruption: Evidence from Chinese Provincial Data", *The Journal of Developing Areas*: 48(4), 119–137.

Song, Y., (2013), "Rising Chinese regional income inequality: The role of fiscal decentralization", *China Economic Review*: 27, 294–309.

Wang, X. L., (2010), "China's Income Distribution: Present Situation, Tendency and Reform Thinking", *China Market*: 20, 8–19.

Weller, Christian E., (2007), "The Benefits of Progressive Taxation in Economic Development", *Review of Radical Political Economics:* 39(3), 368–376.

Zhu, Z. Q. and Wang, L. H., (2008), "The Evolution Characteristics and the Trends of Tax Structure in China since Reform and Opening up", *Journal of Shandong Institute of Business and Technology*: 22(5), 86–88.

CHAPTER 8

Does Economic Inequality Matter for Nationalism?

Rui Qian and Juann H. Hung

8.1 Introduction

China's rapid rise in its economic strength over the past three decades has boosted many Chinese people's pride of their countries. At the same time, however, the rapid rise of economic inequality (both income and wealth inequality) in China since the late 1990s is quite concerning to many Chinese and international observers alike. People are concerned about economic inequality not only because it is "unfair" for the rich to earn a disproportionately larger share of a country's income but also because economic inequality could have a negative impact on economic growth, political and social stability, education equality, and public health. Moreover, governments could also be concerned that a huge income disparity will lower citizens' allegiance due to dissatisfaction with the ability of their government and their country's income distribution system.[1]

Events such as the Arab Spring in 2010–2011 and Occupy Wall Street in 2011 are testimony to the potential effect of economic inequality on political and/or social instability.[2] Thus, it would not be surprising if states that place high priority on maintaining political/social stability but suffer

R. Qian • J. H. Hung (✉)
International Business School Suzhou, Xi'an Jiaotong-Liverpool University, Suzhou, China
e-mail: juann.hung@xjtlu.edu.cn

J. H. Hung, Y. Chen (eds.), *The State of China's State Capitalism*,
https://doi.org/10.1007/978-981-13-0983-0_8

a high degree of economic inequality resort to promoting nationalism through various propaganda, as a way to mitigate the destabilizing effect of economic inequality.

Against this backdrop, it is interesting to know in what way the rapid rise in China's economic inequality has affected Chinese people's nationalism (i.e., affection or sentiment toward their country)? Would the rise in income inequality overpower the substantial gain in China's economic wealth to result in a net decline in Chinese people's nationalism? Or could the positive effect of the government's promotion of nationalism, if any, have more than offset that net decline, so the rise in economic inequality actually led to an increase in nationalism in China?

This issue is of particular interest in the case of China because China's economic inequality has been on a rising trend until 2008 and stayed at an elevated level as of today. (Its Gini coefficient was 0.462 in 2015, significantly higher than the worrisome level of 0.4.) At the same time, the government has been stepping up its spending on maintaining domestic security, reflecting a stronger concern about potential social instability. However, the literature is relatively scant on the relationship between economic inequality and nationalism, with little to shed light on the case of China. Even though there is a sizable literature aiming at explaining why patriotic sentiment varies in degree across countries and over time, few studies have tried to detect the relationship between a country's economic inequality and the degree of nationalism among its citizens.

To help shed light on the relationship between economic inequality and nationalism in China, this chapter asks two research questions. First, what is the multi-country empirical evidence on the relationship between citizens' feelings of patriotism toward their country, controlling for other determinants of nationalism? Second, to what extent is the empirical finding applicable to the case of China? To address these two questions, we first review existing theories on the relationship between economic inequality and nationalism. We then estimate the partial effect of a country's economic inequality on nationalistic sentiments among its citizens, using a 20-country dataset from 1990 to 2014, to assess the validity of those theories. Finally, we examine recent developments in China's income inequality and the degree of Chinese people's national pride to assess the applicability of theories in the case of China.

The remainder of the chapter is organized as follows. Section 8.2 reviews two opposing strands of theories on the effect of economic inequality on nationalism. Section 8.3 conducts empirical research to test four of those theories. To do so, we measure nationalism and economic inequality of 20 different countries over a quarter of a century and conduct panel-regression analysis of those data. Section 8.4 reports and discusses the regression results. Section 8.5 reviews the evolution in China's income inequality and nationalism to comment on the applicability of theories in the case of China. Section 8.6 concludes.

8.2 Literature Review

It has been noted that the extent of nationalism differs between countries and varies over time within a nation (Dogan 1994). Several theories have been advanced to explain this variation in nationalistic sentiment across countries and over time. Those theories roughly fall into two categories, the first being those predicting a negative effect of economic inequality on nationalism, while the second predicts a positive effect.

Theories in the first category include the cohesion theory and the new-nations theory. The cohesion theory, proposed by Gilbert (1998), contends that when people's economic circumstances are similar, they are more likely to view themselves as part of a unified and independent nation. Conversely, "divisive disparities" will impede any development of patriotic sentiments among people. The cohesion theory indicates that greater economic inequality undermines the formation of national pride among citizens. The new-nations theory, advanced by Brass (1991), holds that a sharp economic inequality promotes the emergence of political entrepreneurs who seek to develop new national identities within the disadvantaged members of society. Hence, similar to the cohesion theory, the new-nations theory implies that a wider wealth gap is expected to decrease poor citizens' attachment to their country while increasing their recognition of these new national identities. This theory further maintains that such a nationalistic attachment indeed depends on the combination of people's own earnings and the extent of economic inequality. More specifically, the negative impact of inequality affects poor citizens more than it does for those who are affluent.

The psychological-benefits theory, proposed by Shayo (2009), also predicts that severe income inequality generates negative impacts on the formation of patriotic sentiments among citizens in a country. However, contrary to the new-nations theory, Shayo (2009) argued that lower-income individuals tend to cling more closely to nationalism, whereas richer ones with high social status do the opposite. Because the psychological benefits of nationalism tend to be inversely correlated with individuals' economic status within the society, a greater economic inequality heightens poor individuals' psychological need to cling to their identification with the nation, while it dampens such an emotion for richer ones.

Shayo's view suggests that there is room for the state to promote nationalism via propaganda, which could be strategically important for the state to maintain social/political stability, since the exacerbation of inequality could push people to demand redistribution via protests or even social revolution.[3] Moreover, as noted by Smith and Jarkko (1998), nearly all countries benefit from nationalism, which helps to strengthen the government's legitimacy and thus encourage their citizens' voluntary compliance. However, as Dahl (1971) puts it, the state's disregarding of severe economic inequality risks "widespread dissatisfaction and alienation", endangering the state's aim to continuously viable. Therefore, in countries with severe economic inequality the state also has a huge stake in promoting nationalism. Van Evera (1985) also contended that countries lacking the effective capacity to suppress massive opposition and that are reluctant to adopt redistribution policies will need to anesthetize their citizens with nationalism. In such cases, the state creates the nationalistic myth mainly to "persuade the public to accept the established social order".

The above views regarding the state's need to promote nationalism when faced with stiff economic inequality culminated in the proposal of the diversionary theory of nationalism, advanced by Solt (2011). This theory predicts that a severe economic inequality would induce states to implant more nationalism among their citizens, in order to divert their attention from the plight of their disadvantaged social status and preempt or mitigate potential social instability that could stem from the inequality.

In sum, the above theories suggest that empirically economic inequality may have a negative or positive effect on nationalism, in part depending on the degree of the government's intervention. What has been the empirical evidence?

Lan and Li (2015) conducted an empirical study to investigate how economic openness affects nationalism in China's different regions, using cross-sectional survey data collected from the *China Political Compass (CPoC)* and the *World Values Survey (WVS) database*. They then extended the analysis of regional nationalism to cross-country nationalism and found that increasing foreign trade will reduce domestic economic interests and thus weaken citizens' nationalistic sentiments.

Alesina et al. (2004) concluded that, controlling for a large set of personal characteristics as well as country and year dummies, individuals tend to report a lower level of happiness when economic inequality is great. This effect, however, is more applicable for Europeans than Americans statistically. In the United States, it is the rich rather than the poor who are bothered by income inequality and, interestingly, the happiness level of lower-income citizens is uncorrelated with inequality. The reason behind this curious phenomenon may be due to the fact that Europeans have been accustomed to lower social mobility than Americans.

Solt (2008) explored the nature of the relationship between the extent of economic inequality in a country and the political engagement of its citizens. Aiming to test several conflicting theories on how economic inequality affects democratic political engagement, the paper used data from the *World Values Survey (WVS)*, the *Eurobarometer*, and the *European Election Survey* to measure three different aspects of political engagement: political interest, political discussion, and electoral participation. These data worked as effective indicators of democratic political engagement and thus were included as dependent variables in the study, while the main independent variable is economic inequality, as reported by the *Luxembourg Income Study (LIS)*.[4] Furthermore, the author considered a large number of control variables, ranging from demographic characteristics to the country's political system, through three nested levels: individuals, country-years, and countries. The results suggest that a higher level of income inequality powerfully dampens citizens' interest in politics, the frequency of political discussion, and the participation in elections except for those who are affluent. This conclusion further explains that greater economic inequality yields greater political inequality, which may generate negative effects on the formation of nationalism.

Because of the limitations of existing inequality datasets, scholars interested in cross-national research on the causes and consequences of income inequality are forced to rely on other data.[5] As a result, Solt (2009) constructed a *Standardized World Income Inequality Database (SWIID)* to meet the needs of these researchers by maximizing the intertemporal and international comparability of income inequality data while maintaining the broadest possible coverage across countries and over time. It provides comparable Gini indices of gross and net income inequality for 153 countries from 1960 to the present, representing a balanced choice between comparability and coverage.

Despite the considerable theoretical literature on nationalism, economic inequality, and the opposing prediction of the diversionary theory versus that of the cohesion and new-nations theories, few empirical works have addressed the effects of economic inequality on nationalism directly. Neckerman and Torche (2007) commented that even though some progress has been achieved in recent years, the nationalism literature leaves many questions unanswered and the empirical research leaves ample room for future research on how economic inequality shapes political attitudes, such as nationalism.

8.3 Data and Research Methods

This section introduces data and research methods used for our empirical analysis.

8.3.1 Data Description

Our multinational panel dataset covers 20 economies from 1990 to 2014. (These 20 economies are Argentina, Australia, Brazil, Chile, China, Germany, India, Japan, Mexico, Nigeria, Peru, Poland, Russia, South Africa, South Korea, Spain, Sweden, Taiwan, Turkey, and the United States.) We selected these 20 economies from all countries with relatively complete data needed for this research by simple random sampling, aiming to ensure that their characteristics are independent of each other. This is to satisfy the second of the fixed-effects regression assumptions that the variables for one entity are distributed identically to, but independent of, the variables for another entity (Stock and Watson 2012).[6] The full dataset contains five waves (time periods), with each wave covering a five-year period. Specifically, the five waves are 1990–1994, 1995–1999, 2000–2004, 2005–2009, and 2010–2014. Breaking data by five-year time intervals like this aims to maintain consistency with our measurements of nationalism, which are compiled based on data from the *WVS* database (more on this later in the part of ***measuring nationalism and inequality***).

Measuring Nationalism The primary measure of individual citizens' feelings of patriotism toward their country is calculated using data from the *World Values Survey (WVS)*. WVS is a global research project carried out by worldwide social scientists since 1981, devoted to exploring how people's values and beliefs change over time and what impact they have on the politics and society in almost 100 countries. Unfortunately, the data in the wave of 1985–1989 are missing for all countries in the *WVS* database. Hence, our study only used data from 1990. Having examined all the survey questions related to how people value their country, we select answers to the six most relevant survey questions to generate our indicators of nationalism. These six questions are:

S1—*What level is your personal feeling of happiness in your country?* (Very happy, Quite happy, Not very happy, Not at all happy, No answer, Don't know)

S2—*Are you very confident that most people can be trusted or do you need to be very careful in dealing with people in your country?* (Most people can be trusted, Need to be very careful, No answer, Don't know)

S3—*How proud are you of your nationality?* (Very proud, Quite proud, Not very proud, Not at all proud, No answer, Don't know)

S4—*Of course, we all hope that there will not be another war, but if it were to come to that, would you be willing to fight for your country?* (Yes, No, No answer, Don't know)

S5—*How interested would you say you are in politics?* (Very interested, Somewhat interested, Not very interested, Not at all interested, No answer, Don't know)

S6—*How much confidence do you have in the armed force of your country?* (A great deal, Quite a lot, Not very much, Not at all, No answer, Don't know)

These survey questions, using either direct or indirect statements, asked respondents the degree of their patriotism in their respective nations from different dimensions, such as personal feelings, trust level between people, the sense of national pride and assertion of national unity, and more. We then recorded the percentage of positive answers to these questions in our panel dataset. For instance, when we recorded the data for the sixth survey question, we added the percentage of people who answered "A great deal" and "Quite a lot" together for each corresponding country and wave. More specifically, for Argentina in the period of 1990–1994, the percentage of people that answered "A great deal" and "Quite a lot" for their confidence in the armed force of their country was 9.3 and 19.1, respectively. Then the number in our record for Argentina in 1990–1994 of this survey question was 28.4 (=9.3 + 19.1), for which the unit was percentage. Responses to the remaining five survey questions are recorded in the same way. According to this, the more people that provide positive responses to these questions in a country over a particular sub-period, the larger the percentage will be recorded for that country in that sub-period, indicating a higher degree of citizens' nationalism in that country in that period.

The summary statistics of nationalism data are presented in Table 8.1. The number of observations of these six indicators is different and less than 100 (20 economies across 5 waves) due to missing data in some economies or time periods. Apart from that, the huge difference between the minimum and maximum percentage figures reflects that citizens' nationalism varies across economies over time. Table 8.2 shows the correlation coefficients of each pair of positive responses to six nationalistic statements. Although all of these six indicators can show people's patriotic emotions, they are not always positively related to each other.[7] Therefore, we construct the Nationalism Composite Index (NCI) for each economy in each sub-period by taking the arithmetic average of the six statements related to nationalism for that economy in that period. The NCI will be the dependent variable in the subsequent regression analyses.

Measuring Economic Inequality The *Standardized World Income Inequality Database (SWIID)*, constructed by Solt (2009), which maximizes the comparability of data on economic inequality for a wide range of countries and years, provides the source of inequality data required in this research. More specifically, we use the *SWIID* measure of the Gini Index of net income inequality as our indicator for economic inequality.

The Gini index, also known as the Gini coefficient or the Gini ratio, is the most commonly used measure of (income or wealth) inequality. A

Table 8.1 Summary statistics of nationalism data

Variable	*Obs.*	*Mean*	*Std. dev.*	*Min*	*Max*
S1—happy[a]	86	29.48953	12.79713	5.3	67.5
S2—mocatr	85	27.78824	14.66487	4.8	65.2
S3—profna	84	52.45357	20.80167	12	84
S4—fightfc	83	62.01928	19.49916	10.3	94.8
S5—npolitics	84	11.42738	6.098476	2.5	28.2
S6—coinarmf	85	59.70941	18.51713	21.9	96

Notes: [a]"happy" is the variable name used in the STATA when conducting regression analyses corresponding to the first survey question. It is the same for the other five abbreviated names

Table 8.2 Correlation matrix of positive responses to nationalistic statements

	S1	*S2*	*S3*	*S4*	*S5*	*S6*
S1	1					
S2	−0.15994	1				
S3	0.55098	−0.45163	1			
S4	0.07089	0.04816	0.24539	1		
S5	0.23327	0.39665	−0.03626	−0.01210	1	
S6	−0.02795	0.24885	0.07125	0.37885	0.30477	1

Source: World Values Survey

Gini index lies between 0 and 1. A Gini index of 0 indicates perfect equality (i.e., all net income is shared equally by all households), while a Gini index of 1 indicates perfect inequality (i.e., all net income goes into one single household). Since SWIID reports the Gini index by country by year, we use the average of each country's Gini indexes over the five years covered by each period as the Gini index of that country in the corresponding sub-dataset. Table 8.3 shows that, among the countries examined in this study, the Gini index varies from about 21 (e.g., Sweden in 1990–1994) to over 58 (e.g., South Africa in 2005–2009).

Measuring Control Variables A number of other variables are included as controls in order to avoid omitted variable bias.[8] The data source for all control variables is the Economist Intelligence Unit (EIU). The list of those control variables and the rationale for including them is as follows:

Real gross domestic product (GDP) per capita: Inglehart and Welzel (2005) argued that countries with higher levels of GDP per capita tend to be less nationalistic. However, richer countries could feel more confident about their country and their government, thereby increasing its citizens' nationalism.

Consumer Price Index (CPI): A degree of inflation, all else being equal, reduces people's purchasing power and undermines citizens' faith in their government's ability to manage the economy. Therefore, a high level of CPI could lower nationalism.

Foreign Trade to GDP ratio [= (export volume + import volume)/real GDP]: Lan and Li (2015) showed that an increase in foreign trade

Table 8.3 Summary statistics of panel dataset

Variable	*Obs.*	*Mean*	*Std. dev.*	*Min*	*Max*
NCI (avgnatlism)[a]	86	40.4769	8.193584	21.08	56.58
Income inequality	100	38.62872	9.286511	20.958	58.068
GDP per capita[b]	100	14610.95	14046.96	417.24	45331.78
Log (GDP per capita)[c]	100	8.992357	1.230861	6.033661	10.72176
CPI[d]	100	91.95031	44.33135	0.42	327.4036
Log (CPI)[e]	100	4.314135	0.9041156	−0.8675006	5.791193
Foreign trade/GDP	100	0.4180925	0.2423002	0.0971154	1.137017
Public expenditure/GDP	97	0.2728071	0.1433134	0.0672251	0.718347
Unemployment rate	87	8.559844	5.297634	1.5384	25.91

Notes: [a]"avgnatlism" is the NCI, which is calculated by the arithmetic average of positive responses to six nationalistic statements for a specific country or area in a certain wave

[b]The unit of GDP per capita is USD

[c]Log (GDP per capita) is the logarithmic form of GDP per capita

[d]The CPI index uses the year 2005 as base year

[e]Log (CPI) is the logarithmic form of CPI

Sources: World Values Survey, Standardized World Income Inequality Database and Economic Intelligence Unit

reduces domestic economic interests and thus weakens citizens' nationalistic sentiments.

Public expenditure to GDP ratio: Scott (2011) described that in the 1950s, the massive increase in the public expenditure on education, roads, energy and industries improved standards of living for Nigerians greatly, during which time modern Nigeria witnessed the golden era of hope and optimism. Hence, public expenditure to GDP ratio can be used as one of the control variables in order to avoid the problem of omitted variable bias.

The unemployment rate: People tend to feel less optimistic or even distrustful of their governments when they are unemployed for a sustained period of time. Therefore, the variable of unemployment rate is included as a control variable. The summary statistics of our panel dataset is presented in Table 8.3.

8.3.2 Research Method

Having constructed the panel dataset, we now proceed to conduct regression analysis to address our research questions. Altogether, we conduct seven regressions. The first two regressions are on the following simple univariate linear model, with and without correcting for clustered standard errors:

$$\mathrm{NCI}_{it} = \beta_0 + \beta_1 \text{ inequality}_{it} + u_{it}, \tag{8.1}$$

where u_{it} is the error term containing all the other factors besides the inequality that determine the value of the dependent variable, NCI_{it}, for a specific observation in certain time.

Note that in panel data, the regression error can be correlated over time within an entity. Although this correlation will not introduce bias into the estimator, it will affect the variance of the estimator and thus affect the standard errors. Hence, the standard errors for fixed-effects regressions in panel data should be reported as clustered standard errors, which are robust both to heteroskedasticity and to correlation over time within an entity (Stock and Watson 2012).

As mentioned before, regression with a univariate regression is most vulnerable to the problem of omitted variable bias. Consequently, we conduct two variations in the following multivariable regressions:

$$\begin{aligned}\mathrm{NCI}_{it} = \beta_0 + \beta_1 \text{inequality}_{it} + \beta_2 \text{ gdppc}_{it} + \beta_3 \text{ cpi}_{it} + \beta_4 \text{ftgdpr}_{it} \\ + \beta_5 \text{petgr}_{it} + \beta_6 \text{unem}_{it} + u_{it},\end{aligned} \tag{8.2}$$

where inequality, gdppc, cpi, ftgdpr, petgr, and unem are variable names of income inequality, GDP per capita, CPI, foreign trade to GDP ratio, public expenditure to GDP ratio and unemployment rate, respectively. Under this model, the coefficient on the regressor inequality_{it} is the partial effect of a change in this variable on the dependent variable, NCI_{it}, holding constant the other included regressors.

For control variables that can be observed and measured, multivariate regression is a powerful tool for controlling their effects on the dependent variable. However, not all control variables can be observed or measured. Stock and Watson (2012) demonstrated that multiple observations over time on the same entity can be used to control for unobserved omitted variables that vary across entities but are constant over time. The key insight is that if an omitted variable remains constant over time, then any change in the dependent variable over time cannot be caused by this omitted variable. This also works for those unobserved omitted variables that are the same across entities but differ over time. Hence, in order to gauge accurately the relationship between economic inequality and nationalism, it is appropriate to include both entity (country) and time (wave) effects. Otherwise, one of the least squares assumptions that the error term has conditional mean zero given the independent variable will be violated (Steenbergen and Jones 2002). Based on this consideration, we conduct the three variants of the following fixed-effect panel regression:

$$\begin{aligned} \mathrm{NCI}_{\mathrm{it}} = {} & \beta_0 + \beta_1\,\mathrm{inequality}_{\mathrm{it}} + \beta_2\,\mathrm{gdppc}_{\mathrm{it}} + \beta_3\mathrm{cpi}_{\mathrm{it}} + \beta_4\,\mathrm{ftgdpr}_{\mathrm{it}} \\ & + \beta_5\,\mathrm{petgr}_{\mathrm{it}} + \beta_6\,\mathrm{unem}_{\mathrm{it}} + \alpha\,Z_i + \lambda\,Z_{\mathrm{t}} + u_{\mathrm{it}}, \end{aligned} \tag{8.3}$$

where Z_i captures unobserved variables varying across countries or areas but constant over time, and Z_t represents those factors that remain the same across entities but change over time. In this model, $(\beta_0 + \alpha\, Z_i)$ can be regarded as entity-specific intercepts, in which case the above model has *n* intercepts, one for each entity (the same explanation for time-specific intercepts–$\beta_0 + \lambda\, Z_t$). Moreover, the *F*-test of time effects on the regression will be conducted to see whether they are jointly statistically significant. To summarize, in this combined country and wave fixed-effects regression model, omitted variable bias arising both from unobserved variables that are constant over time and/or that are constant across countries can effectively be eliminated.

8.4 Results and Analysis

Table 8.4 reports the pooled OLS regressions of the *NCI* on the measure of economic inequality (***inequality***) using data from 20 countries and areas over five waves (1990–1994, 1995–1999, 2000–2004, 2005–2009, and 2010–2014).[9] It is clear that we cannot find a significant correlation between NCI and economic inequality in any of the seven regressions presented in Table 8.5. Among the seven regressions reported, only column (5) has a coefficient estimate on inequality that is closer to being statistically significant, with a *t* statistic being equal to 1.62.

McCloskey (1985) and McCloskey and Ziliak (1996) pointed out that too much focus on statistical significance will result in the erroneous judgment of whether a variable is an important determinant of the dependent variable. We briefly summarize their discussion of statistical significance versus economic or practical significance as follows.

Table 8.4 Nationalism and economic inequality across 20 countries (areas) over 5 waves from 1990 to 2014, OLS estimates

Dependent variable: NCI (Nationalism Composite Index)							
Regressor	(1)	(2)	(3)	(4)	(5)	(6)	(7)
Inequality	−0.034	−0.034	−0.008	−0.025	0.360	−0.024	−0.025
	(0.142)	(0.136)	(0.142)	(0.106)	(0.222)	(0.174)	(0.167)
GDP per capita			−0.00005				
			(0.00014)				
Log (GDP per capita)				−2.983*	−11.265***	−2.896	−2.983*
				(1.663)	(3.114)	(1.891)	(1.620)
CPI			−0.015				
			(0.011)				
Log (CPI)				−0.114	0.014	−0.301	−0.114
				(0.388)	(0.397)	(0.984)	(0.651)
Foreign trade/GDP			−3.757	−2.423	−6.362*	−3.830	2.423
			(3.903)	(4.254)	(3.204)	(3.987)	(4.189)
Public expenditure/GDP			−1.627	−1.854	−0.027	−5.556	−1.854
			(7.922)	(7.000)	(6.099)	(7.994)	(7.225)
Unemployment rate			−0.222*	−0.193	−0.328*	−0.230	−0.193
			(0.133)	(0.146)	(0.164)	(0.166)	(0.202)
Constant	41.717***	41.717***	46.966***	72.319***	129.672***	72.263***	72.319***
	(5.769)	(6.402)	(7.004)	(15.004)	(20.331)	(19.992)	(16.497)
Entity effects?	No	No	No	No	Yes	No	No
Time effects?	No	No	No	No	No	Yes	No
Time effects = 0[a]						Yes (P=0.3718)	
Random effects?							Yes
Both fe and re are efficient[b]							Yes (P=0.2352)

(*continued*)

Table 8.4 (continued)

Dependent variable: NCI (Nationalism Composite Index)							
Clustered standard errors?	No	Yes	Yes	Yes	Yes	Yes	No
Adjusted R^2	0.0197	0.0197	0.0724	0.0986	0.0667	0.1253	0.0986
Observations	86	86	72	72	72	72	72

Notes: [a]The null hypothesis of F-test for the significance of time effects is that all the coefficients of time variables are jointly equal to zero and it cannot be rejected at the 5% level in column 6

[b]The null hypothesis of Hausman test for choice of random effects versus fixed effects is that both models yield consistent estimators. ***Significant at the 1% level; **Significant at the 5% level; *Significant at the 10% level. Robust standard errors are in parentheses, clustered at country level

Sources: World Values Survey, Standardized World Income Inequality Database and Economic Intelligence Unit

Table 8.5 Chinese response to survey on "how proud are you of your nationality?" (% of respondents)

	1990–1994	*1995–1999*	*2000–2004*	*2005–2009*	*2010–2014*
Proud	80.8	86.4	78	77.4	78.6
Very proud	42.5	39	24.7	22.4	22.2
Quite proud	38.3	47.4	53.3	55	56.4
Not proud	17.7	11.4	17.2	20.7	9.2
Not very proud	15.6	9.9	13.2	16.2	8.5
Not at all proud	2.1	1.5	4	4.5	0.7
Don't know or no answer	1.5	2.2	4.7	1.8	12.2
Number of respondents	1000	1500	1000	1991	2300

Source: World Values Survey

The two means of judging the significance of the estimates in the regression are t statistic and p-value. As p-value can be found from the t distribution, we focus on t statistic here for our discussion. Recall that the t statistic for testing the null hypothesis $\beta_i = 0$ is defined as dividing the estimate by its standard error: $t = \hat{\beta}_i / \text{se}(\hat{\beta}_i)$, a t statistic below the critical value indicates statistical insignificance, which can result from either small $\hat{\beta}_i$ or big se $(\hat{\beta}_i)$. Thus, the magnitude of the coefficient estimates related to the economic significance should be taken into consideration in addition to the size of the t statistic. Especially, when working with large samples, it is essential to interpret the magnitude of the coefficient. For example, consider a regression to estimate advertising investment on firm's profits. If the coefficient on the independent variable (advertising investment) is relatively small, say 0.00013, but it is statistically significant due to its smaller standard error (thus big t statistic), then there is no need for the firm to invest in advertisements though this variable is significant statistically. Because a one unit increase in advertising investment only leads to an increase in profits by 0.00013 unit, which has no practical meaning in reality. Moreover, when the sample size is small, a quantitatively significant parameter can be estimated as statistically insignificant because standard errors tend to be quite big relative to the coefficient estimates (thus small t statistic). In this case, the importance of one variable should not be ignored due to its statistical insignificance, as its coefficient may have economic significance and it may be important for explaining the dependent variable.

The preceding discussion sheds light on the explanation for the results in this research. It is true that the coefficients on income inequality and control variables are all statistically insignificant. However, that is more attributable to the large standard deviation of the coefficient (something that is not atypical in a relatively small sample size such as that used in our study), than a small coefficient estimate. With this in mind, the estimation results presented in column (5), with the coefficient on inequality being 0.36 and a standard deviation being 0.222, would appear to be the most acceptable among all regressions.

If we can base our analysis on column (5), we can infer that on average the extent of economic inequality in a country has a positive partial effect on citizens' nationalistic sentiments, with a one-percentage point increase in the inequality level leading to an increase in the degree of nationalism by 0.36 percentage points. This finding would suggest that the effect predicted by the diversionary theory of nationalism outweighs those predicted by the cohesion theory and the new-nations theory. In other words, the positive effect of heightened government promotion of nationalism more than offset inequality's negative effect on nationalism predicted by either the cohesion theory or the new-nations theory.

Does this make sense? On the one hand, this positive effect, which is predicted only by the diversionary theory, is only estimated by the entity fixed-effect panel regression would seem quite suspicious. This is because one would suppose whether a state intervenes to promote nationalism (as hypothesized by the diversionary theory) is a key distinct feature of each country. Thus, the effect of government intervention should have been purged from the coefficient estimate to a reasonable extent. On the other hand, it is interesting to note that the negative coefficient estimates on GDP per capita, both quantitatively and statistically significant, in column 5 do lend support to the diversionary theory. Without a heavy hand of the state, it is hard to make sense of this coefficient on GDP per capita (−11.27) either, since this negative coefficient means citizens of a poor country have much stronger nationalism (i.e., happier and more proud of their country) than a richer country. Of course, the hand of the state can take various forms such as active promotion of nationalism through propaganda (via media or the education system) and aggressive control of its citizens' freedom of speech.

On balance, we think a more reasonable interpretation of the results presented in Table 8.5 should be this: there is no strong evidence showing that income inequality has a significant effect on nationalism, either positive or negative. Indeed, this finding should not come as a surprise, in light of the opposing predictions of the diversionary theory versus that of the cohesion and new-nations theory. Most likely, what the state can do at best is to mitigate the negative effect predicted by the cohesion theory and the new-nations theory, not to overpower it. Indeed, this interpretation would accord better with China's experience, presented in the next section.

8.5 Recent Development in China's Income Inequality and Nationalism

Having experienced rapid economic growth for about three decades, China has become the second largest economy in the world. However, the impressive GDP growth rate also masked numerous problems, especially the high level of income inequality. Before China adopted its reform and open-up policies in late 1978, its income distribution pattern could be characterized as egalitarianism in all aspects, with the Gini coefficient for rural–urban inequality being only 0.16. According to the World Development Indicator (published by the World Bank), China's Gini coefficient then rose to 0.426 by 2000 and has since stayed above 0.42, considerably higher than the worrisome level of 0.4. Some researchers' estimates of Gini coefficients in China are even higher than those reported by the World Bank. For example, a survey conducted by Xiea and Zhou (2014) showed that estimates of China's Gini coefficient ranged between 0.563 and 0.515 in 2012 in three different studies.

Because culturally Chinese are mainly a people of collectivism, they tend to care more about their relative social standing than people with an individualistic cultural dimension (such as Americans). Consequently, a given rise in the degree of income inequality could have an even greater negative impact on the average happiness felt by Chinese than by American. Will this lowered degree of average happiness (induced by a higher income inequality) among Chinese lead to a decrease in their nationalism? Of course, nationalism is a multidimensional concept that is hard to measure since it can reflect citizens' sense of national identity in many respects. If we were to rely on results of one survey question, as provided by Table 8.5 below, it would appear the relationship between China's income inequality and nationalism over time is more consistent with that predicted by the cohesion theory and the new-nations theory than that predicted by the diversionary theory.

Table 8.5 shows clearly that from 1990 to 1998, a period of rapid economic growth with a Gini coefficient under 0.4, Chinese people's pride in their country rose substantially from 80.8% to 86.4%. However, that pride fell substantially afterwards as the Gini coefficient rose above 0.4, with its index staying below 79% from 1999 to 2014. Then, as the Gini index began to decline moderately after 2009, Chinese pride in their country also recovered somewhat (from 77.4% to 78.6%). This pattern would seem to lend support to the cohesion theory and the new-nations theory, both of which predict that a rise in income inequality has a negative effect on nationalism.

When we take a closer look, the movements in the percentage of "very proud" and "quite proud" are quite opposite to each other. From 1990 to 2004, a period that witnessed both rapid economic growth and sharp rise in income inequality, the percent share of Chinese respondents feeling "very proud" of their nationality declined steeply, while that of those feeling "quite proud" of their nationality rose steeply. One way to make sense of this pattern of opposite movements in these two sub-categories of national pride is to invoke the psychological-benefit theory of nationalism. That theory argues that psychological benefits of nationalism tend to be inversely correlated with individuals' economic status within the society. A greater economic inequality heightens poor individuals' psychological need to cling to their identification with the nation, while it dampens such an emotion for richer ones.

8.6 Conclusion

This chapter empirically investigates whether economic inequality influences nationalism. On balance, we find no strong evidence showing that income inequality has a significant effect on nationalism, either positive or negative. This may be because the negative effects predicted by the cohesion and new-nations theory are largely offset by the positive effect predicted by the diversionary theory.

When we examine the situation in China, we find that the relationship between China's income inequality and nationalism over time is more consistent with the cohesion theory, the new-nations theory, and the psychological-benefit theory. Both the cohesion theory and the new-nations theory predict that a rise in income inequality has a negative effect on nationalism, while the psychological-benefit theory argues that psychological benefits of nationalism tend to be inversely correlated with individuals' economic status within the society. In comparison, there is little evidence that the diversionary theory—which proposes that a rise in income inequality is positively correlated with nationalism due to the government's promotion—helps to explain the relationship between China's income inequality and nationalism. This suggests that either the Chinese government has not attempted to promote nationalism or its attempt has not been successful in promoting nationalism effectively to overpower the negative effect of income inequality on nationalism.

Appendix

Report of STATA Results, Six Nationalism Indicators and Economic Inequality across 20 Countries (areas) over 5 Waves from 1990 to 2014, OLS Estimates

Dependent Variable	happy	mocatr	profina	fightfc	inpolitics	coinarmf
Regressor	(1)	(2)	(3)	(4)	(5)	(6)
Inequality	−0.389	−0.204	0.653	0.547	0.326	1.074**
	(0.328)	(0.346)	(0.539)	(0.357)	(0.267)	(0.429)
Log (GDP per capita)	−5.774**	−1.889	−21.069**	−9.468**	−7.633*	−19.612***
	(2.671)	(5.811)	(8.278)	(4.503)	(4.001)	(6.094)
Log (CPI)	0.339	−0.724	2.588***	1.155	0.185	−1.366
	(0.443)	(1.163)	(0.542)	(0.919)	(0.515)	(1.101)
Foreign trade/GDP	19.956***	−4.195	15.090	−6.705	4.525	4.882
	(3.918)	(9.300)	(9.856)	(6.873)	(6.006)	(8.481)
Public expenditure/GDP	−18.116*	12.015	−19.929	−30.581**	−5.976	49.946**
	(10.203)	(15.500)	(11.921)	(12.987)	(6.122)	(18.563)
Unemployment rate	0.040	−0.479*	−0.668*	−0.017	−0.200	−0.613
	(0.301)	(0.253)	(0.373)	(0.222)	(0.140)	(0.473)
Constant	90.283***	59.413	211.945***	135.199***	69.209**	194.886***
	(21.953)	(45.533)	(54.951)	(30.759)	(25.696)	(45.191)
Entity fixed effects?	Yes	Yes	Yes	Yes	Yes	Yes
Clustered standard errors?	Yes	Yes	Yes	Yes	Yes	Yes
Adjusted R^2	0.0803	0.1606	0.0587	0.2059	0.0000	0.0075
Observations	72	71	70	70	70	71

Notes: ***Significant at the 1% level; **Significant at the 5% level; *Significant at the 10% level. Robust standard errors are in parentheses, clustered at country level

Sources: World Values Survey, Standardized World Income Inequality Database and Economic Intelligence Unit

Notes

1. Although there are subtle differences between nationalism and patriotism, they tend to be used interchangeably (Primoratz 2015). Apart from being a sense of pride in the nation's achievements, nationalism is a multidimensional concept that can reflect citizens' sense of national identity in many respects. Politically, it expresses the willingness of people to maintain self-governance or full sovereignty over their homeland, protecting it from alien invasions. Furthermore, it is oriented towards shared characteristics in a nation such as language, culture, religion, race, and a belief in a common ancestry, which can distinguish or differentiate the nation from other ethnic groups (Triandafyllidou 1998). Consequently, this national sentiment can penetrate into every aspect of social life and could be an important factor influencing the destiny of a country.
2. **The Arab Spring** refers to the democratic uprisings that arose independently and spread across the Arab world in 2011. The movement originated in Tunisia in December 2010 and quickly took hold in Egypt, Libya, Syria, Yemen, Bahrain, Saudi Arabia, and Jordan. The Arab Spring is generally attributed to dissatisfaction, particularly of youth and unions, with the rule of local governments and the wide gaps in income levels. The **Occupy Wall Street (OWS)** movement in 2011was a protest movement that began on September 17, 2011. The main issues raised by the movement were social and economic inequality, greed, and the perceived undue influence of corporations on government—particularly from the financial services sector. The OWS slogan, "We are the 99%", refers to income inequality and wealth distribution in the United States between the wealthiest 1% and the rest of the population.
3. For example, see Meltzer and Richard (1981).
4. The LIS data are derived from micro-economic data of national household income, which are carefully harmonized and standardized prior to being applied to computing income inequality statistics based on a uniform set of assumptions and definitions.
5. The LIS database has earned a good reputation as the best data available for cross-national comparisons of income inequality (Smeeding 2005). Unfortunately, they are at present available for only about 50 high- and middle-income countries over 30 years. Another influential project that compiles cross-national data sets on income inequality over the past few decades is the data set assembled by Deininger and Squire (1996) for the World Bank. They combined many earlier data sets, distributing unevenly for 138 countries and over the period from 1890 to 1996. However, as Deininger and Squire themselves pointed out after evaluating the quality of their observations, these data are rarely comparable across countries or

within a single country over time due to differences in income definitions (gross or net) and reference units (households or persons) of the underlying data.

6. If this assumption is violated, then regression estimators will be biased and inconsistent. For example, if these countries are all from developed economies in the world or they share the same geographical location, then their economic performance and cultural features may be similar to and dependent on each other, then the estimators of our regression will be biased and inconsistent.
7. The table of Stata results for the respective relationship between six nationalism indicators and income inequality is included in Appendix.
8. As Stock and Watson (2012) illustrated, if the omitted variable is correlated with the included regressors that partly determine the dependent variable, then the Ordinary Least Squares (OLS) estimator will be biased due to the violation of the first least squares assumption, which requires that the conditional distribution of error term given included regressors has a mean of zero.
9. The units of both dependent and independent variables are percentage, as reported in the previous text.

References

Alesina, A., Tella, R. D., & MacCulloch, R. (2004), "Inequality and happiness: are Europeans and Americans different?", *Journal of Public Economics*: 88 (2004), 2009–2042.

Brass, P. R. (1991), "Ethnicity and Nationalism: Theory and Comparison." New Delhi: Sage Publications.

Dahl, R. A. (1971), Polyarchy: Participation and Opposition. New Haven, CT: Yale University Press.

Deininger, K. and Squire, L. (1996), "A New Data Set Measuring Income Inequality", *The World Bank Economic Review*: 10(3), 565–591.

Dogan, M. (1994), "The Decline of Nationalisms within Western Europe", *Comparative Politics*: 26(3).

Gilbert, P. (1998), The Philosophy of Nationalism. Boulder, CO: Westview Press.

Inglehart, R. and Welzel, C. (2005), Modernization, Cultural Change and Democracy: The Human Development Sequence. Cambridge: Cambridge University Press.

Lan, X. and Li, B. G. (2015), "The Economics of Nationalism", *American Economic Journal:* 7(2), pp. 294–325.

McCloskey, D. (1985), "The loss function has been mislaid: The rhetoric of significance tests". *American Economic Review*, special issue: Papers and

Proceedings of the Ninety-Seventh Annual Meeting of the American Economic Association 75(2), 201–205.

McCloskey, D. and Ziliak, S. (1996), "The standard error of regressions", *Journal of Economic Literature*: 34(1), 97–114.

Meltzer, A. H. and Richard, S. F. (1981), "A Rational Theory of the Size of Government", *Journal of Political Economy*: 89(5), 914–927.

Neckerman, K. M. and Torche, F. (2007), "Inequality: Causes and Consequences", *Annual Review of Sociology:* 33, 335–357.

Primoratz, I. (2015), "Patriotism", *The Stanford Encyclopedia of Philosophy*, Available at: http://plato.stanford.edu/archives/spr2015/entries/patriotism/

Scott, C. (2011), The Rise of Nationalism in Nigeria, Available at: http://customessaypapers.com/free-essays/countries/essay-on-the-rise-of-nationalism-in-nigeria/#5

Shayo, M. (2009), "A Model of Social Identity with an Application to Political Economy: Nation, Class, and Redistribution", *American Political Science Review*: 103(2), 147–174.

Smeeding, T. M. (2005), "Public Policy, Economic Inequality, and Poverty: The United States in Comparative Perspective", *Social Science Quarterly*: 86(s1), 955–983.

Smith, T. W. and Jarkko, L. (1998), "National Pride: A Cross-national Analysis", National Opinion Research Center / University of Chicago, Available at: http://gss.norc.org/Documents/reports/cross-national-reports/CNR19%20National%20Pride%20-%20A%20cross-national%20analysis.pdf

Solt, F. (2011), "Diversionary Nationalism: Economic Inequality and the Formation of National Pride", *The Journal of Politics:* 73(3), 821–830.

Solt, F. (2009), "Standardizing the World Income Inequality Database", *Social Science Quarterly*: 90(2), 231–242.

Solt, F. (2008), "Economic Inequality and Democratic Political Engagement", *American Journal of Political Science:* 52(1), 48–60.

Steenbergen, M. R. and Jones, B. S. (2002), "Modelling Multilevel Data Structures", *American Journal of Political Science*: 46(1), 218–237.

Stock, J. H. and Watson, M. M. (2012), Introduction to Econometrics. 3rd ed. London: Pearson Education Limited.

Triandafyllidou, A. (1998), "National identity and the 'other"', *Ethnic and Racial Studies*: 21(4), 593–612.

Van Evera, S. (1985), "Why Cooperation Failed in 1914", *World Politics*: 38(1), 80–117.

Xie, Y. and Zhou, X. (2014), "Income Inequality in Today's China", *Proceedings of the National Academy of Sciences of the United States of America*: 111(19), 6928–6933.

CHAPTER 9

The Rise in China's Gender Income Inequality

Qi Sun and Juann H. Hung

9.1 Introduction

In the era of planned economy following the founding of the People's Republic of China in 1949, women's participation rate in China's labor force was higher than in most other countries at the time. Largely, that was because the new Chinese government regarded it important to promote women's labor force participation, gender equality, and the improvement in women's status.[1] During those years, the state controlled the work allocation of all workers, and men and women enjoyed relatively equal employment opportunities without a visible gap between men's and women's pay. After the economic reform began in the late 1978, however, the wage gap between men and women began to emerge as companies increasingly gained more autonomy in allocating work positions and wage payments in response to market forces or due to other considerations. The rise in the gender pay gap quickened after the early 1990s. In 1994, the ratio of female income to male income was 0.78, showing a male-female income gap of 22%. By 2004, that male-female income gap rose to 44%.

Q. Sun • J. H. Hung (✉)
International Business School Suzhou, Xi'an Jiaotong-Liverpool University, Suzhou, China
e-mail: juann.hung@xjtlu.edu.cn

J. H. Hung, Y. Chen (eds.), *The State of China's State Capitalism*,
https://doi.org/10.1007/978-981-13-0983-0_9

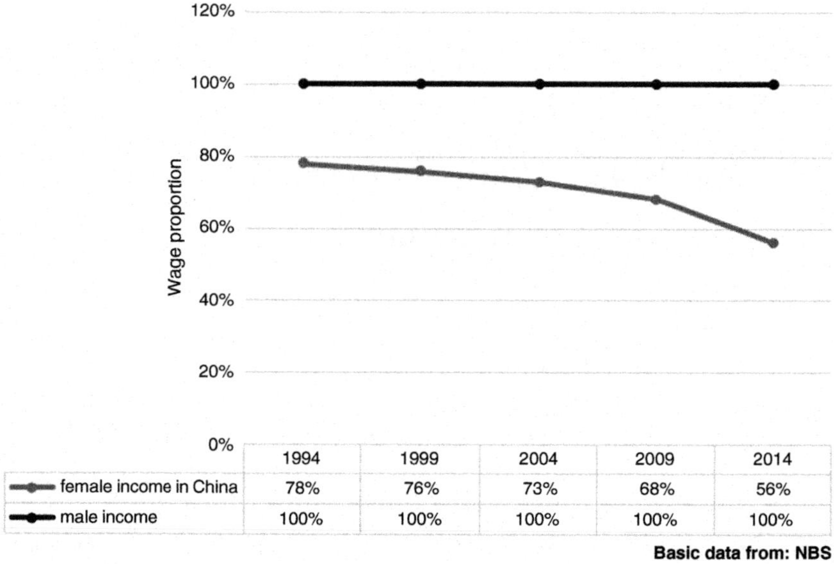

Fig. 9.1 Gender income gap in China, 1994–2014

In other words, between 1994 and 2004, China's gender income gap widened 22 percentage points (Fig. 9.1).

Gender income inequality has been a persistent phenomenon since the first Industrial Revolution.[2] However, that inequality has declined substantially in most advanced countries in the twentieth century, especially those in European countries. According to the Global Gender Gap Report (2011), China's female-male ratio of estimated earned income was 0.65, higher than the average among Asian countries (0.58) and at par with the average among European countries (Appendix 1). (See Appendix 2 for the female wage/male wage ratio of a longer list of countries.) In other words, as of 2011, China's gender income gap was 35%, significantly lower than the average 42% among Asian countries and at about the same level of that among European countries. However, only three years' later, China's gender income gap had risen to 44%.

The rising gender pay gap in China is somewhat puzzling in light of the fact that the gender gap in educational attainment among Chinese workers has narrowed significantly since the implementation of the market-oriented economic reform in 1978. In particular, urban women have generally gained equal access to education at all levels. According to An (2002), the share of female college students rose from 23.4% in 1989 to 50.8% by 2010. However, the narrowed gender gap in educational opportunity has not decreased the gender gap in income, even as income of both men and women increased. What has happened?

Economists have offered different theories to explain the male-female income inequity. For example, the Becker Discrimination Theory (Becker 1957) argued that employers who had the discriminatory preference would rather increase their productive cost than hire a group of female employees. Therefore, women workers have lower bargaining power and tended to accept a lower wage. Seguino (2002) maintained that there was fierce competition for women to obtain a lower paying job because the majority of them lacked high education and skills. Mincer and Polachek (1974) argued that, because females needed to shoulder the majority of family responsibility compared with the role of the male, they tend to have lower energy levels to finish the working task.

Has the rise in China's gender income disparity stemmed from a rise in discrimination against women? Or, was it a result of the change in economic structure, family structure, or something else? Unfortunately, so far the literature on this issue is still too young, and the findings too diverse, to provide a well-accepted answer to the question. Chi and Li (2014) argued that different occupational choices and the employment rate gap were the main factors that influenced the gender wage gap in China. The authors used the Heckman's selection-correction model to estimate the size of the gender wage gap. They found that the employment rate of young single females was higher than that of males, while this rate for old married women was dramatically lower than that of men. The authors thus claimed that family characteristics were the main determinant factor of women's employment decisions. Magnani and Zhu (2012) used the Oaxaca-Blinder decomposition method to analyze the cause of the gender pay gap among rural migrants working in Chinese cities. The authors found that male migrants could earn 30% more wages than female migrants on average, and that the discrimination effects contributed more to the gender wage gap than did the endowment (i.e., human capital) effects.

This research aims to shed light on the causes of the rising gender income gap in China. We apply the Oaxaca-Blinder decomposition method (Oaxaca 1973; Blinder 1973) to our survey data to estimate the extent to which that gap can be explained by the difference in human capital characteristics (such as years of education and years of experience), and the extent to which we need to find explanation somewhere else (such as discrimination or changes in economic structure).[3] To collect data for this research, we sent out a questionnaire to about 4000 workers with different educational backgrounds and age distribution (between 18 and 60 years old) in three types of occupations: bankers, engineers, and service providers.

Overall, the results based on our analysis of our survey data collected in 2015 indicate that the gender wage gap in that year was mainly due to different human capital characteristics, not discrimination or biases. We thus infer that a rising discrimination against females (either due to tradition or otherwise) is not the main cause of the rising gender income gap in China. It is more likely the rise in China's gender income inequality is related to China's growth pattern. China's rapid economic growth over the past 30 years has been driven by rapid export growth, privatization, and urbanization. We present evidence to propose that two of those three drivers of China's economic growth—namely, privatization and urbanization—have contributed to the rise in China's gender income gap.

9.2 Data and Methodology

9.2.1 Data

For this study, we designed a questionnaire to collect relevant data. We sent out about 4000 copies of the questionnaire and received over 2000 responses. To make sure we have roughly comparable numbers of male and female observations in each type of occupation and with a sufficiently diverse sample in terms of human capital characteristics, we ended up selecting responses from 277 males and 233 females for our China dataset based on the stratified sampling method. More specifically, we selected 275 respondents (130 males versus 145 females) who are in the banking profession, 135 respondents (100 males versus 35 females) from engineers, and 100 respondents (47 males versus 53 females) from service providers.

The summary statistics of Chinese male and female respondents in these three occupations are presented in Table 9.1. Overall, male respondents on average are older, with longer seniority and years of education. On average, their yearly income is about 20,000 yuan higher than that of female respondents. There is gender income disparity in all three occupations, although the male-female wage gap is the most severe in the engineer industry. At the same time, male respondents on average also had longer years of educa-

Table 9.1 Basic statistics of Chinese male and female workers (2015)

Overall	**Male mean (N = 277)**	**Female mean (n = 233)**	**Male-female gap**
Average annual wages (Yuan)	82,026	62,515	19,511
Average age	41.7	37.4	4
Average seniority	15.3	10.3	5
Years of education	15.1	14.0	1
Banking system	**Male mean (N = 130)**	**Female mean (n = 145)**	**Male-female gap**
Average annual wages (yuan)	87,553	80,017	7536
Years of education (year)	16	17	−1
Seniority (year)	15.4	14	1
Employment rate	0.35	0.54	0
Service	**Male mean (N = 47)**	**Female mean (n = 53)**	**Male-female gap**
Average annual wages (yuan)	50,514	41,357	9157
Years of education (year)	11	11.6	−1
Seniority (year)	4.7	2.7	2
Employment rate	0.58	0.46	0
Engineer	**Male mean (N = 100)**	**Female mean (n = 35)**	**Male-female gap**
Average annual wages (yuan)	108,012	66,171	41,841
Years of education (year)	18.2	13.4	5
Seniority (year)	25.8	14.3	12
Employment rate	0.87	0.13	1

tion and work experience. In both the banking industry and the service industry, female workers earned lower wages than did male workers, despite the former's slightly higher level of education than the latter.

9.2.2 *The Research Method*

The preceding data description shows that gender income disparities have not only existed in China, but also have widened in the past few years. To explore the reasons for the gender wage disparity, we use Oaxaca-Blinder decomposition method (Oaxaca 1973; Blinder 1973) as the main research method. We use the difference between log (male wage) and log (female wage) as our measure of gender wage gap.

The Oaxaca-Blinder decomposition method requires researchers to run two regressions of earnings for men and women, respectively, and then decompose the outcome variables into explained and unexplained parts. The explained component of the wage gap is attributable to the gap due to the difference in explanatory variables (such as different years of education and different years of experience) between male and female workers. If we include a sufficient number of explanatory variables, then we can infer that the unexplained variations are attributable to factors not included in the regression, such as discrimination.

For our study, the method requires that we first estimate Eq. (9.1) for male and female, respectively:

$$\ln Salary_i = \beta_{i0} + \beta_{i1}\, Seniority_i + \beta_{i2} Edu_i + \varepsilon_i, \tag{9.1}$$

where $E(\varepsilon_i) = 0$,

$\ln Salary_i$	is the log of salary for gender *i*, where *i* is either male or female.
Edu_i	is the years of education for gender i.
$Seniority_i$	is the years of experience, included as a control variable.

Let X_i be the vector of $[1, Seniority_i, Edu_i]'$, then after we obtain the vector of coefficient estimates, $\hat{\beta}_m$ and $\hat{\beta}_f$ from the regressions of Eq. (9.1), we can express the mean salary difference as the difference between the linear prediction of male salary and the female salary, which in turn can be decomposed into three components as in Eq. (9.2):

$$\begin{aligned} E(\ln Salary_m) - E(\ln Salary_f) = \hat{\beta}_m \left(E(X_m) - E(X_f)\right) + \left(\hat{\beta}_m - \hat{\beta}_f\right) \\ E(X_f) + \left(\hat{\beta}_m - \hat{\beta}_f\right)\left(E(X_m) - E(X_f)\right) \end{aligned} \tag{9.2}$$

The first component, $\hat{\beta}_m \left(E(X_m) - E(X_f)\right)$, is the explained difference or "the endowment effects", which measures the part of gender wage gap caused by the gender difference in endowments (i.e., characteristics) such as different productivities, skills, or the education level. The second component, $\left(\hat{\beta}_m - \hat{\beta}_f\right)E(X_f)$, is the "the coefficient effect", which measures the part of the unexplained wage gap due to factors such as gender discrimination or unequal social policy treatment between males and females.

The third component $\left(\hat{\beta}_m - \hat{\beta}_f\right)\left(E\left(X_m\right) - E\left(X_f\right)\right)$, is an interaction term, which measures the simultaneous effect of differences in endowments and coefficients.

9.3 Discussion of Estimation Results

Table 9.2 presents the result of applying the Oaxaca-Blinder decomposition method to study the causes of gender wage gap among three types of occupations: banking professional, engineers, and service providers.

The engineering profession shows the largest gender wage gap among the three occupations under study. The mean prediction of log (female wage) is lower than that of log (male wage) by 0.4948. The endowment effect, which reflects the mean increase in log (female wage) if females had the same characteristics as men, is both quantitatively and statistically significant, explaining about 84% (=0.4181/0.4948) of the average gender wage gap in the industry. The coefficient effect is "negative", though statistically insignificant, suggesting that there is some degree of "reverse discrimination"—that is, female engineers actually command a slight wage

Table 9.2 Estimated explanations for gender income gap in three Chinese occupations

	Banking professional		*Service provider*		*Engineer*	
Variables	*Coefficient*	*P-value*	*Coefficient*	*P-value*	*Coefficient*	*P-value*
log (Male wage)	11.3778	0.000	10.8348	0.000	11.5922	0.000
log (Female wage)	11.2886	0.000	10.6298	0.000	11.0975	0.000
Difference	0.0890	0.129	0.2050	0.000	0.4948	0.000
Endowments effect	0.0146	0.800	0.0969	0.117	0.4181	0.000
Education	−0.0573	0.000	−0.0200	0.171	0.0391	0.482
Seniority	0.0719	0.135	0.1169	0.019	0.3789	0.000
Coefficients effects	0.0123	0.513	0.1048	0.000	−0.3043	0.363
Education	−0.7882	0.003	0.2004	0.353	0.9322	0.000
Seniority	0.1391	0.001	0.0190	0.754	−0.2754	0.001
Constant	0.6613	0.003	−0.1146	0.473	−0.6872	0.000
Interactive effect	0.0622	0.002	0.0034	0.951	0.1072	0.000
Education	0.0491	0.007	−0.0106	0.415	0.3280	0.000
Seniority	0.0131	0.172	0.0140	0.754	−0.2208	0.001
Number of observations	N = 276		N = 100		N = 135	

premium over male engineers. This can make sense, considering female engineers are relatively scarcer than are male engineers.[4] Given the negative coefficient effect, we can safely infer that most of the interactive effect, which explains roughly 22% of the gender wage gap, reflects the difference between male and female engineers' human capital characteristics. Overall, we can conclude the gender wage gap in the engineering profession is not due to discrimination against female workers.

For service providers, the mean prediction of log (male wage) is 10.8348, and that for log (female wage) is 10.6298, yielding a modest mean wage gap of roughly 20%. The endowment effect is insignificant, as the positive seniority effect (due to female workers' slightly fewer years of work experience) is partially offset by the negative education effect (due to female workers' slightly higher education). The coefficient effect is both quantitatively and statistically significant, explaining about 50% of the mean difference between male and female wages among service workers.

Because most service workers (such as waiters, kitchen helpers, delivery workers, and security guards) do not require a high level of education, both male and female service workers tend to have up to high school education only. Thus, the gender wage gap for service workers is largely attributable to the coefficient effect, not the endowment effect. Moreover, since service workers tend to need to work long hours or work at night, companies will prefer to recruit and pay more to male workers who are perceived to be more energetic and enduring on the job. In this way, demand for female service workers is relatively lower than that for male workers, pressuring female workers to accept a lower wage than males for similar jobs even if they have a relatively higher level of education.

The banking profession shows the least degree of gender wage gap among the three occupations under study. The difference between mean prediction of log (male wage) and log (female wage) is only 0.089 (less than 10% of either the average wage of male or female bankers) and statistically insignificant. Indeed, neither the endowment effect nor the coefficient effect is statistically or quantitatively significant. The endowment effect is insignificant because the negative education effect (due to female workers' slightly higher education) is roughly offset by the positive seniority effect (due to female workers' slightly fewer years of work experience). The net coefficient effect is also insignificant, as the negative education effect—due to a higher reward on female education than the same level of male education—is roughly offset by other positive coefficient effects.

In sum, there is a very low degree of wage discrimination against female workers in both the banking and the engineering industry, despite the appearance of the large gender wage gap in the latter industry. There is evidence of wage discrimination against female service workers. However, that "discrimination" may have stemmed from employers' perception that males are more productive in some service jobs, or that female workers are subject to higher potential health or safety risks when working long hours or on night shifts than male workers.

9.4 Why Has China's Gender Income Inequality Been Rising Rapidly?

The above analysis suggests that much of the gender wage gap in China is attributable to the endowment effect, rather than discrimination against women. But that finding cannot answer why China's gender income gap has been rising since the early 1990s. The fact that rise in income gap took place in tandem with its rapid economic growth suggests that the cause of the rising gender income gap may be related to China's growth pattern. Theoretically, this is possible. But we will need to introduce the concept of occupational segregation between men and women before introducing those theories.

In part due to the traditional social division of labor and social norms, and in part due to different characteristics between genders, men and women tend be have different types of occupations and work in different sectors. For example, engineers, technicians, and senior managers are predominately men, whereas secretaries and nurses are mostly women. This is occupational segregation. In addition, men and women tend to work in different sectors too. For example, in China, male migrant workers are mostly in the construction sector, whereas female migrant workers are primarily concentrated in the hair salons, housekeeping, and other related services. One major reason for the gender wage gap in many countries is that female-intensive occupations and sectors pay less than male-intensive occupations.[5]

Thus, one possible cause of the rising gender wage gap in China is the much more rapid increase in demand for male workers than for female workers due to China's growth pattern. Since the early 1990s, China's rapid economic growth has relied on three drivers: privatization, urbanization, and export growth. Let us comment on the effect of these three drivers on China's gender income inequality in turn.

The Effect of Privatization

For the first 30 years following the founding of the People's Republic of China in 1949, China was a planned economy. During those years, families in China evolved from a patriarchal and male-dominated pattern in an agricultural society to a family pattern where the husband and wife shared more balanced decision-making power within the family (Ding 1999). Men and women enjoyed relatively equal employment opportunities without a visible gap between men's pay and women's pay. Although traditional gender stereotypes still applied, the social welfare policies and public services, provided through the work units, largely reduced urban women's dual burdens of work and family. After the implementation of the market-oriented economic reform, especially after the large-scale privatization of state-owned enterprises (SOEs) in the early 1990s, many work units began to phase out those public services. Consequently, the responsibilities of family care fell back on women's shoulders, especially for families who could not afford those services provided in the market place, constraining the types of jobs suitable to women with such family care responsibilities.

By the early 1990s, many of China's SOEs were required either to privatize, or to behave more like private companies, to stay competitive and to survive. As a result, many "redundant" employees were let go and the pay scale began to differentiate more according to the productivity of each employee. Since 1992, China's private companies have been rising in number and in size, thereby lowering the ratio of workers in the public sector and SOEs relative to those in the private sector (Fig. 9.2).

According to the Chinese Family Panel Studies (2011), men's average wages were higher than women's average wages in every sector in China. However, the gender gap in wage payment in the public sector and SOEs was smaller than that of the private sector or household businesses. This is a typical pattern in many countries largely because private companies' decisions are profit-driven, while the public sector and SOEs are more concerned with gender equality.

In China, most companies in the private sector require long working hours of their higher paid employees, effectively forcing women to take up lower paid positions in the company in exchange for more reasonable working hours. Given this difference between the workplaces of the public sector and the private sector, it is reasonable to infer that the expansion of the private sector relative to that of the public sector has contributed to the widening of the gender wage gap in China.

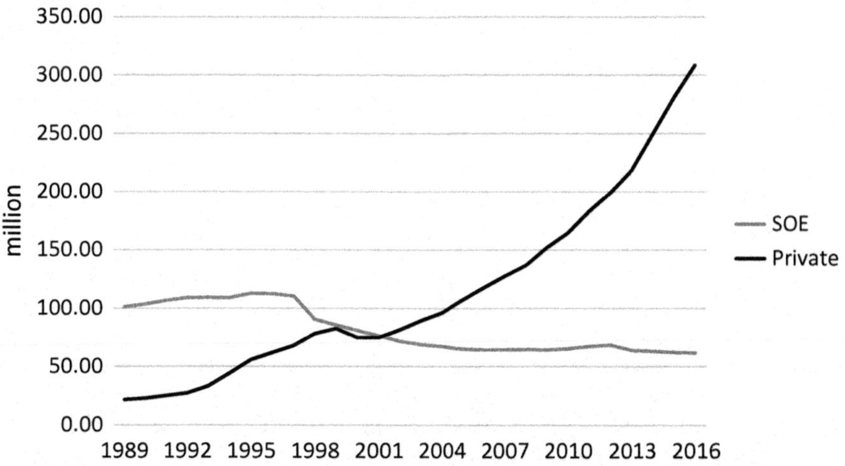

Fig. 9.2 Number of employees in SOE and private sector, 1989–2016. (Source: Ministry of Human Resources and Social Security)

The Effect of Urbanization

Urbanization in China started soon after the initiation of the reform and opening up policy. The pace then quickened after the early 1990s. In 1990, 26% of the total population lived in urban areas; that ratio more than doubled by 2014 at 54.8%. By the end of 2016, that ratio further rose to 57.4%.[6] The share of urban employees in total employees in China has been on a rapid upward trend as well, rising from 28.4% in 1980 to 54.7% in 2017 (Fig. 9.3).

China's rapid urbanization not only involves the rapid construction of glitzy skyscrapers as business buildings but also involves the massive construction of subways and residential buildings necessary to accommodate the huge influx of population. Indeed, massive construction activities have been going on in most major and even second-tier cities across China since the early 1990s (Fig. 9.4). It is no surprise that most migrant male workers from rural areas have found themselves employed in such construction jobs, which pay a lot more than what migrant female workers could earn in jobs such as household or restaurant/hotel helpers.

As argued by Clarke (2014), China has been an industry-oriented developing country with a great need for manual workers with physical strength and endurance. Because male workers typically have stronger

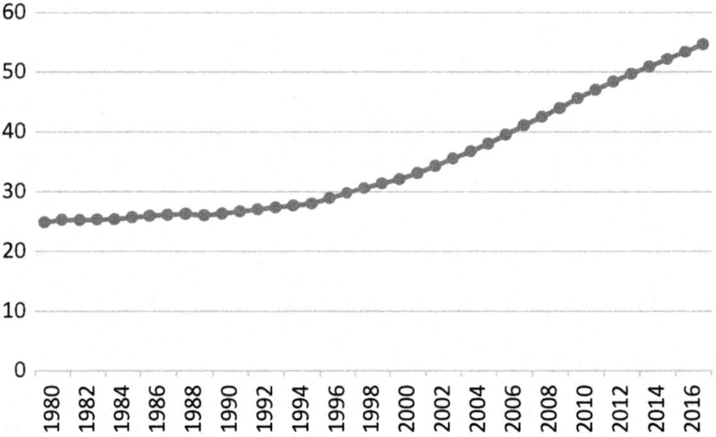

Fig. 9.3 Urban share of employment (%). (Source: Ministry of Human Resources and Social Security)

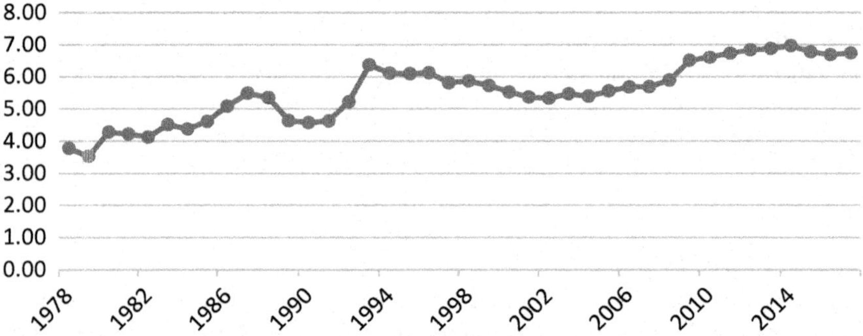

Fig. 9.4 GDP share of construction (%). (Data Source: National Bureau of Statistics)

physical strength and endurance than female workers, they tend to have more working opportunities. Indeed, among others, the rapid urbanization and expansion of China's transportation infrastructure have required hiring a large amount of physical labor. This greater demand for male workers is very likely to have contributed to the rise in the male-female income gap during those years of China's rapid economic growth.

9.5 Conclusion

In this chapter, we investigate why China's gender income inequality has been rising rapidly since the early 1990s by applying the Oaxaca-Blinder decomposition method on three Chinese occupations. To collect data for this research, we sent out a questionnaire to approximately 4000 workers with different educational backgrounds and age distribution (between 18 and 60 years old) in three types of occupation: bankers, engineers, and service providers.

Overall, we find that China's gender wage gap in the same occupation mainly reflects different human capital characteristics between males and females. Since our survey was conducted in 2015, we infer that a rising discrimination against females (either due to tradition or otherwise) is not the main cause of the rising gender income gap in China since the early 1990s. It is more likely that the rise in China's gender income inequality is partly attributable to China's growth pattern. The main drivers of China's rapid economic growth over the past 30 years have been export growth, privatization, and urbanization. This chapter presents evidence to argue that two of those three main drivers—namely, privatization and urbanization—have contributed to the rise in China's gender income gap.

Appendix

Appendix 1: The Female-to-Male Ratio of Estimated Earned Income in Asia and Europe, 2011

Asia		*Europe*	
Country	*Ratio*	*Country*	*Ratio*
Brunei Darussalam	0.97	Norway	1
Singapore	0.88	Luxembourg	1
Australia	0.82	Switzerland	0.89
Mongolia	0.8	Netherlands	0.83
New Zealand	0.7	Sweden	0.82
Vietnam	0.69	Denmark	0.81
Cambodia	0.66	Finland	0.74
China	0.65	Ireland	0.72
Thailand	0.63	United Kingdom	0.71
Philippines	0.6	Croatia	0.7
Maldives	0.57	Iceland	0.69

Asia		*Europe*	
Country	*Ratio*	*Country*	*Ratio*
Bangladesh	0.55	Germany	0.69
Japan	0.51	Romania	0.68
Malaysia	0.43	Belgium	0.67
Indonesia	0.42	Latvia	0.67
Korea, Rep.	0.41	Lithuania	0.67
Iran, Islamic Rep.	0.4	Moldova	0.67
Fiji	0.38	Bulgaria	0.66
Nepal	0.37	Russian Federation	0.65
Sri Lanka	0.36	France	0.65
India	0.31	Hungary	0.64
Average	0.58	Slovenia	0.62
		Estonia	0.62
		Ukraine	0.6
		Cyprus	0.58
		Spain	0.57
		Portugal	0.57
		Poland	0.57
		Slovak Republic	0.57
		Austria	0.56
		Italy	0.54
		Albania	0.54
		Macedonia, FYR	0.51
		Greece	0.5
		Armenia	0.5
		Czech Republic	0.48
		Malta	0.47
		Georgia	0.39
		Average	0.65

Data Source: The Global Gender Gap Report (2011)

Appendix 2: Ranking of Countries by Female-to-Male Earned Income Ratio

	Female-to-Male	
Country	*Ratio*	*Rank*
Luxembourg	1	1
Norway	1	1
Brunei Darussalam	0.97	3
Switzerland	0.89	4
United States	0.88	5

	Female-to-Male	
Country	*Ratio*	*Rank*
Singapore	0.88	6
Qatar	0.84	7
Netherlands	0.83	8
Sweden	0.82	9
Australia	0.82	10
Denmark	0.81	11
Mongolia	0.8	12
Burundi	0.8	13
Bolivia	0.77	14
Mozambique	0.76	15
Canada	0.75	16
Ghana	0.75	17
Finland	0.74	18
Lesotho	0.74	19
Malawi	0.73	20
Madagascar	0.73	21
Ireland	0.72	22
United Kingdom	0.71	23
Croatia	0.7	24
New Zealand	0.7	25
Iceland	0.69	26
Ethiopia	0.69	27
Germany	0.69	28
Vietnam	0.69	29
Romania	0.68	30
Lithuania	0.67	31
Belgium	0.67	32
Latvia	0.67	33
Tanzania	0.67	34
Moldova	0.67	35
Burkina Faso	0.67	36
Benin	0.66	37
Cambodia	0.66	38
Bulgaria	0.66	39
Kenya	0.66	40
Uganda	0.65	41
Russian Federation	0.65	42
China	**0.65**	**43**
Angola	0.65	44
France	0.65	45
Barbados	0.64	46
Israel	0.64	47
Hungary	0.64	48
Namibia	0.64	49

	Female-to-Male	
Country	*Ratio*	*Rank*
Gambia	0.64	50
Thailand	0.63	51
Estonia	0.62	52
Slovenia	0.62	53
Kuwait	0.61	54
Paraguay	0.61	55
Kazakhstan	0.61	56
Chad	0.61	57
Brazil	0.61	58
Ukraine	0.6	59
Philippines	0.6	60
Peru	0.59	61
Jamaica	0.58	62
Cyprus	0.58	63
Spain	0.57	64
Poland	0.57	65
Senegal	0.57	66
Slovak Republic	0.57	67
Maldives	0.57	68
Portugal	0.57	69
Tajikistan	0.57	70
Mauritania	0.56	71
Zambia	0.56	72
Austria	0.56	73
South Africa	0.56	74
Bahrain	0.56	75
Uruguay	0.56	76
United Arab Emirates	0.55	77
Costa Rica	0.55	78
Trinidad and Tobago	0.55	79
Bangladesh	0.55	80
Panama	0.55	81
Albania	0.54	82
Italy	0.54	83
Kyrgyz Republic	0.53	84
Azerbaijan	0.53	85
Argentina	0.52	86
Japan	0.51	87
Cameroon	0.51	88
Macedonia	0.51	89
Greece	0.5	90

Data Source: The Global Gender Gap Report (2011)

Notes

1. See United Nations (2000–2001).
2. The problem of gender discrimination in income existed since the Industrial Revolution began in England in the eighteenth century. Male employees occupied the advantages of physical capacity so that they could obtain the majority of working opportunities and earn more wages (Nyhus and Pons 2012).
3. See Oaxaca (1973) and Blinder (1973) for the Oaxaca-Blinder decomposition method.
4. Clark (2014) argued that, because working in the engineering industry contains some risks and dangers and also the working environment for engineering is relatively tough, a small number of female students will choose engineering as their major in universities and very few female students will continue to study further in this subject.
5. Reasons for segregation of occupations and sectors by gender have been attributable to both the supply side and the demand side in the literature. For example, on the supply side, under the traditional gender division of labor and social norms, women have to take up more responsibility of caring for the family. Therefore, many women take up jobs that are more flexible in working hours and/or less physically demanding despite being lower paid jobs. On the demand side, gender stereotypes or information asymmetry could lead to discrimination against women by employers.
6. See "China's permanent urbanization rate hits 57.4 per cent" by Wenyu Sun (July 13, 2017). *People's Daily.*

References

An, S. F. (2002), Study on the History and Status Quo of Higher Education of Chinese Women. Beijing: Higher Education Press.

Blinder, A. S. (1973), "Wage Discrimination: Reduced Form and Structural Estimates", *Journal of Human Resources*: 8(4), 436–455

Becker, G. S., (1957), Becker Discrimination Theory. Discrimination Economics. 1st ed. Chicago: The University of Chicago Press, 50–56.

Chi, W, and Li, B. (2014), "Trends in China's gender employment and pay gap: Estimating gender pay gaps with employment selection", *Journal of Comparative Economics*: 42(3), 708–725

Chinese Family Panel Studies. (2011), Published by the Institute of Social Science Survey (ISSS) of Peking University, China.

Clarke, N.R. (2014), "Of people, politics and profit: the political economy of Chinese industrial zone development", University of Oxford.

Ding, W. (1999), "Tremendous Changes in Chinese Families in the Fifty Years since the Foundation of People's Republic of China." *Study & Exploration:* 6(16).

The global gender gap report. (2011), published by the World Economic Forum.

Magnani, E., and Zhu, R. (2012), "Gender wage differentials among rural–urban migrants in China", *Regional Science and Urban Economics*: 42, Special issue on "Migration and Development", 779–793.

Mincer, J., and Polachek, S. (1974), "Family Investments in Human Capital: Earnings of Women", *Journal of Political Economy*: 2, S76.

Nyhus, E., and Pons, E. (2012), "Personality and the gender wage gap", *Applied Economics*: 44(1), 105–118.

Oaxaca, R. (1973), "Male-Female Wage Differentials in Urban Labor Markets". *International Economic Review*: 14(3), 693–709

Seguino, S. (2002), "Gender, Quality of Life, And Growth in Asia 1970-90", *The Pacific Review*: 15(2), 245–277.

United Nations. (2001), "The World's Women 2000: Trends and Statistics", *New York. Women in Action,* 61–62.

PART V

Foreign Direct Investment

CHAPTER 10

Inward FDI and Economic Growth: A Comparative Analysis of China Versus India

Ma Yingxi and Juann H. Hung

10.1 Introduction

In the era of globalization, foreign direct investments (FDI) have increasingly entered developing/emerging economies, such as China, India and Malaysia, likely in search of lower labor cost and access to larger markets and resources.[1] In 2014, the World Investment Report (WIR) reported that FDI flows into developing economies reached a new high of $778 billion, accounting for 54% of total global FDI inflows. Since capital stock and technology are vital determinants of economic growth that tend to be lacking in developing countries, such FDI inflows could potentially make a significant contribution to the host country's economic growth. Against this background, a large literature has emerged to study the impact of FDI on host countries' economic growth and development.

Despite the large number of studies, so far there is no consensus on the impact of FDI on host countries' economic development. Some papers

M. Yingxi • J. H. Hung (✉)
International Business School Suzhou, Xi'an Jiaotong-Liverpool University, Suzhou, China
e-mail: juann.hung@xjtlu.edu.cn

J. H. Hung, Y. Chen (eds.), *The State of China's State Capitalism*,
https://doi.org/10.1007/978-981-13-0983-0_10

found evidence supporting the view that FDI stimulates and increases economic growth in the host country. Those papers include Balasubramanyam et al. (1999), Bende-Nabende and Ford (1998), and Agrawal and Khan (2011). Some studies found that FDI was only weakly supportive of, or even negatively related to, economic growth in the host country. For example, Rodriguez-Clare (1996) and Haddad and Harrison (1993) are papers in this category. Still others, such as Borensztein et al. (1998) and Durham (2004), claimed that FDI's effect on growth differed depending on various economic/institutional conditions of the host country.

Nevertheless, the findings of research papers focusing on inward FDI's effects on China's growth are more consistent. Most of those studies found that inward FDI made a significant and positive impact on China's economic growth. Indeed, China's economic growth has been highly mirrored by the movement in its FDI inflows. Soon after China established several Special Economic Zones and launched preferential policies to promote inward FDI in 1980, FDI began to pour into China, especially after 1992. Meanwhile, China's average annual real GDP growth rate leaped to 9.7% during 1979–2000, from 5.4% during 1960–1978. An even greater magnitude of FDI entered China after its accession to the World Trade Organization (WTO) in 2000, and China's annual growth rate further accelerated to an average annual growth of 10.4% during 2000–2008.

What made FDI inflows more beneficial to China's growth than in most other developing countries? Could it be that China has managed its FDI inflows more smartly than did many other countries? This chapter aims to shed light on those two questions by comparing the cases of China and India. Given that there is already a large number of studies on the effect of inward FDI on economic growth, we decided to conduct an analytical review of the literature rather than implementing an original research. Moreover, we chose to focus on comparing FDI's estimated effect on growth in China versus that in India for three reasons. First, both countries have a large population and market size. Second, both countries were similar in the stage of economic development when they began to open up for inward FDI. Third, before they liberalized and opened up their economies, both countries depended largely on an inward, closed-door, development strategy.

Overall, our literature review indicates the following. FDI inflows have positively affected economic growth in both China and India, but that this positive impact was larger in China than in India. To gain insight into the difference between FDI's impacts on these two countries' growth rates, we then compared several factors that may have contributed to that difference; namely, the level of human capital, transportation and communication infrastructures, political environment and government policy and the status of financial market development.

Our analysis suggests that the key reasons for this difference are two-fold. First, China has better transportation and communication infrastructure, thereby improving business efficiency. Second, China's higher level of human capital means Chinese employees learn new technology and managerial know-how brought in by FDI more quickly, speeding up the spillover of technology, improving productivity rapidly in China.

10.2 Literature Review on Effect of FDI on Economic Growth

FDI has been recognized to have the potential of enhancing the host countries' economic growth by solving developing countries' problems with capital accumulation, and by transferring technology and management expertise to those countries.[2] Empirically, however, the evidence has been mixed. This section first reviews the general literature and then reviews the literature with a focus on estimating that effect in China and/or India.

Papers that have found a positive contribution of FDI to the host countries' economic growth include Balasubramanyam et al. (1999), Bende-Nabende and Ford (1998), Yao and Wei (2007) and Wei (2002). Balasubramanyam et al. (1999) found that FDI tended to be more successful in promoting economic growth of countries that are open to international trade than those less open to trade. Bende-Nabende and Ford (1998), based his research on Southeast Asia, proposed that FDI stimulated economic growth most effectively through human factors and knowledge or technological learning-by-doing effects. Yao and Wei (2007) found that FDI has pushed China's production frontier to a more advanced level, contributing to the nation's economic growth. Wei (2002) found that 90% of the difference in regional growth in China was due to different degrees of inward FDI in those regions.

However, some papers found that FDI was negatively related to economic development. Those papers include Rodriguez-Clare (1996) and Shaikh (2010). Rodriguez-Clare (1996) argued that FDI was weakly supportive or even negatively related with host countries' economies when multinational enterprises had no adequate connection with domestic companies. This is because in such cases, the managerial experiences as well as spillover effect have no proper way to influence domestic firms. Shaikh (2010) examined FDI's impact on different industrial sectors' performance and found that it had negative effects on the primary sectors.

Still other papers found that the effects of FDI on the economy differed across countries, depending on the economic and regulatory conditions of the host countries. These papers include Borensztein et al. (1998) and De Mello (1997). Borensztein et al. (1998) reported that the association between FDI and Organisation for Economic Co-operation and Development (OECD) countries' economic growth was positive because those countries met the condition of the minimum stock of human capital. They argued that the contribution of FDI could be enhanced by its active interaction with a higher level of human capital. Only when the host countries have a sufficiently high level of human capital are they able to capture the technological spillovers from more technologically advanced countries via FDI. Similarly, De Mello (1997) showed that FDI's impact on economic growth was manifold and diverse, depending on the host country's own economic condition and ability.

Likewise, Almsafir and Almfraji (2013), based on their survey of the literature, concluded that several factors have influenced the impact of FDI on economic growth:

- The level of human capital in the host country would positively affect the effectiveness of FDI on growth in industrial sectors, directly and indirectly with its interaction with labor.
- A well-structured financial market would reduce the investment risk and transaction cost, thereby improving FDI's efficiency.
- Too much dependence on foreign investment may drive out domestic enterprises and hurt host countries' domestic production. If the technological gap is too large between the home and host countries, FDI could induce a negative effect on the economic growth, especially in developing countries.
- A more open trade regime may increase the impact of market-orientation multinational enterprises on domestic economic development.

- A low-income country may absorb less benefit from FDI than a low-to-median-income country.
- Political environment is vital for a stable economy as well as investment condition.[3]

Some papers are more directly relevant to our inquiry of comparing FDI's effects on China and India. For example, Prime et al. (2012) conducted research to ascertain this issue by using an analytical framework based on Porter's four proposition diamond models. They found evidence to support the following arguments. First, China's substantial lead in FDI was in part attributable to its location and the timing of its economic reform. For instance, the Special Economic Zones established in Southern China in 1979 provided incentives and low-cost labor for multinational corporations from Taiwan and Hong Kong. It was convenient for them to build firms in China for geographical and cultural affinities' reasons. Once started, the agglomeration effects and supply chain-based economies of scale further enhanced China's attractiveness to FDI relative to that of India. Meanwhile, to encourage further FDI inflows, China heavily invested in improving its infrastructure, such as the transportation system, resulting in better infrastructure conditions in China than in India. On the human resources front, India had a relatively younger work force, while China had the advantage of a higher literacy rate. On the firm strategy front, corruption, which hinders foreign entries, was severe in both nations. Overall, India depended less on FDI as a main driver of its economic growth than did China. Nevertheless, the authors' focus was on why China attracted more FDI inflows than did India, providing little comparison of the effect of FDI on economic growth.

Tables 10.1, 10.2 and 10.3 summarize the results of our literature survey. Tables 10.1 and 10.2 present papers that find that FDI had a positive effect on economic growth. Table 10.3 presents papers with results showing that FDI had a negative, ambiguous, or null effect on economic growth. Altogether, there are 19 papers presented in these tables. Among them, 11 papers found that inward FDI had a positive effect on the host country's GDP growth. Six papers found weak or ambiguous evidence due to various domestic economy conditions. Two papers threw doubt on the merit of FDI inflows on growth, including one that found FDI had a negative effect on the host country's economic growth. However, the estimated effect of FDI on the Chinese economy was unanimously positive, while that on the Indian economy is more neutral.

10.3 Estimated Effect of FDI on Economic Growth in China and India

Among the papers listed in Tables 10.1 and 10.2, two papers offered estimates for the marginal effect of FDI growth on GDP growth in China, one paper offers that estimate for India, and two papers offer estimates for both China and India. Those five papers' point estimates of the marginal

Table 10.1 Summary of literature showing positive effect of FDI on economic growth

Paper	*Data*	*Empirical approach*	*Remark*	*FDI effects*
Wang (2009)	12 Asian Economies (India and China), 1987–1997	Endogenous growth model	Focus on heterogenous effects of different sector-level FDI; FDI in manufacturing sector has a significant and positive effect on economic growth	+
Ekanayake and Ledgerwood (2010)	Developing countries (including India and China), 1980–2007	Panel data; OLS regressions	Model was estimated for different time periods, different regions, different income levels. All show positive sign	+
Yao (2006)	China, 1978–2000	Pedroni's panel unit root test & Arellano dynamic panel data	Exports and FDI are important positive factors for China's economic success	+
Zhang (2010)	China, 1987–2008	Modified Vector Error Correct (VEC) model and granger causality test	FDI has a positive long-run effect on GDP, although FDI is not the main source of economic growth in the short run	+
Lombard and Lombard (2011)	China and India	Comparative analysis	FDI has a significant positive bearing on the Chinese economy and a considerably more moderate effect on that of India	+
Zhao (2013)	China, 1987–2008	Cobb-Douglas production function; panel cointegration test	FDI has played a more significant role than domestic investment in China's economic growth	+

Table 10.1 (continued)

Paper	*Data*	*Empirical approach*	*Remark*	*FDI effects*
Liu and Su (2012)	China, 1982–2010	Cointegration test and error correction model	There was no clear long-term equilibrium between FDI and GDP during 1983–2010, possibly due to changes in FDI policy. Chow test divided the sample into two periods, separated in 1994. The short-term effect of FDI on GDP was positive in both sub-periods	+
Mathiyazhagan and Sahoo (2003)	India, 1979–80; 2000–01, panel data	Johansen cointegration test	Positive relation between FDI and GDP	+
Chakraborty and Nunnenkamp (2006)	India, 1987–2000	Panel cointegration framework	FDI and economic growth in India are positively associated with each other; both the hypothesis of bi-directional links between FDI stocks and output is rejected in both short run and long run	+
Agrawal and Kahn (2011)	China and India, 1993–2009	Comparative analysis	The regression output shows that 1% increase in FDI would result in 0.07% increase in GDP of China, and 0.02% increase in GDP of India	+
Rodriguez-Clare Andres (1996)		Two-country model, mathematical analysis	Multinationals could hurt the developing economy if the linkage between home and host countries is not efficient	+

effect of FDI on economic growth of either or both countries are presented in Table 10.3, which suggests that the marginal effect of FDI on economic growth was larger in China than in India, with the average point estimate being 0.166% for China and 0.089% for India.

This section first takes a closer look at China and India in light of the regression results from these five papers. Then it offers further analysis to gain insight into what may have caused the effects of FDI on economic growth to be different between these two countries.

Table 10.2 Summary of literature showing weak, ambiguous or negative effect of FDI on economic growth

Paper	*Data*	*Empirical approach*	*Remark*	*FDI effects*
Shaikh (2010)	47 developing countries (India and China), 1981–1999	OLS regressions	Negative effect in the primary sector	–
Basu et al. (2003)	23 developing countries (India and China); 1978–1996	Two-way link between FDI and growth for a panel cointegration technique of Pedrioni	There is a long-run bi-directional causality between GDP growth and FDI for more open economies. For relatively closed economies, long-run causality appears uni-directional, only from GDP to FDI	Ambiguous (two-way causality)
Kasibhatla et al. (2008)	China, India, Mexico, United Kingdom and United States, 1970–2005	Cointegration methodology, ADF, KPSS and VEC model test	For low-medium-income country like China, the granger causality was bi-directional between FDI and GDP. For low-income country like India, there is only one-way causation form FDI to GDP	
Lai and Vanwyk (2012)	China and India	Standard econometric techniques	Uni-directional relationship between FDI and GDP for India; bi-directional relationship between FDI and GDP for China	

(*continued*)

Table 10.2 (continued)

Paper	*Data*	*Empirical approach*	*Remark*	*FDI effects*
Blomstrom et al. (1992)	78 developing countries, 1960–1989	Basic OLS tests	FDI has a positive effect on growth only for higher income developing countries, but not for lower income ones	Weak, null, or conditional
Borensztein et al. (1998)	69 developed and developing countries, 1970–1990	Regression estimations using SUR technique	Effect of FDI from OECD countries is positive on economic growth only for host countries with relatively high levels of human capital	
De Mello (1997)	32 developed and developing countries, 1970–1990	Stationarity tests	Weak evidence for FDI's positive effect on economic growth	
Bagli and Adhikary (2014)	India, 1980–1990; 1991–2010	Solow-swan growth model, ADF test and Phillips Perron test statistics	FDI's effect on India's economic growth is negative but statistically insignificant	

Papers on China Liu and Su (2012) and Zhang (2010) used similar model for their estimations. They firstly test the stationarity of variable ln(GDP) and ln(FDI). Their ADF test results show the variables are of order (1), but their cointegration test indicated there is a long-run relationship between the two variables. They then estimated a VEC model to confirm the short-run effects and conducted Granger Causality tests to identify the causality relationship between FDI and GDP.

The regression results of Liu and Su (2012) are as follows:

Year 1983–1994:

The estimated long-run relationship:

$$\ln GDP = \underset{(0.1375)}{7.5476} + \underset{(0.0260)}{0.4148}\ln FDI + u$$

Table 10.3 The impact of 1% FDI growth on GDP growth (different papers' results)

	Liu and Su (2012) (China)	*Zhang (2010) (China)*	*Chakraborty and Nunnenkamp (2006) (India)*	*Vanwyk and Lai (2012) (Both) (%)*	*Agrawal and Khan (2011) (Both) (%)*	*Average*[a] *(%)*
China	0.148% (1983–1994) 0.278% (1994–2010)	0.0936%	n.a.	0.233	0.07	0.166
India	n.a.	n.a.	Positive effect of FDI on growth in all sectors	0.159	0.02	0.089

[a]These average are not meant to provide more than a rough comparison

The estimated short-term ECM:

$$\Delta \ln GDP = \underset{(0.0523)}{0.1242} + \underset{(0.1066)}{0.1481} \Delta \ln FDI - \underset{(-1.2417)}{0.2908} et(-1) + \zeta$$

Year 1994–2010:

The estimated long-run relationship:

$$\ln GDP = \underset{(1.0888)}{7.4721} + \underset{(0.1298)}{2.3007} \ln FDI + \mu$$

The estimated short-term ECM:

$$\Delta \ln GDP = \underset{(0.0756)}{0.1080} + \underset{(0.0365)}{0.2785} \Delta \ln FDI - \underset{(-0.3439)}{0.0263} ET(-1) + \zeta$$

These results imply that the long-run positive relationship between FDI and GDP is positive in China. Between 1983 and 1994, a one percentage point increase in FDI growth rate led the GDP growth rate to rise by 0.148 percentage points. Between 1994 and 2010, that effect was even larger: a one percentage point increase in FDI growth rate led the GDP growth rate to rise by 0.278 percentage points.

In Zhang (2010), the estimated effect of FDI on China's economic growth is also positive, but smaller. The coefficient on ΔlnFDI is only 0.0936%, compared to 0.1481 (1983–1994) or 0.2785 (1994–2010) estimated in Liu and Su (2012). That difference could be due to different time phases among other factors. For instance, the sample period in Zhang (2010) is 1987–2008, while Liu and Su (2012) used the Chow test to break their period into 1983–1994 and 1994–2010 sub-periods.

Paper on India Chakraborty and Nunnenkamp (2006) tested panel cointegration of different sectors in India, from 1987 to 2000. Their dynamic error correction model took the following form:

$$\Delta \mathrm{FDI}_{\mathrm{it}} = \alpha_{1\mathrm{i}} + \eta_{1\mathrm{i}}\varepsilon_{\mathrm{it}-1} + \Sigma k\beta_{1\mathrm{ik}}\Delta \mathrm{FDI}_{\mathrm{i,t-k}} + \Sigma k\beta_{2\mathrm{ik}}\Delta \mathrm{Y}_{\mathrm{i,t-k}} + \mu_{1\mathrm{it}} \quad (10.1)$$

$$\Delta Y_{\mathrm{it}} = \alpha_{2\mathrm{i}} + \eta_{2\mathrm{i}}\varepsilon_{\mathrm{it}-1} + \Sigma k\gamma_{1\mathrm{ik}}\Delta Y_{\mathrm{i,t-k}} + \Sigma k\gamma_{2\mathrm{ik}}\Delta \mathrm{FDI}_{\mathrm{i,t-k}} + \mu_{2\mathrm{it}} \quad (10.2)$$

The authors found that FDI stocks and Y (sector output) are both nonstationary variables and that those two variables are co-integrated; that is, FDI and Y have a stable long-run relationship. They found that an increase in FDI has a positive effect on output growth in all tested sectors. But their causality tests could not find significant bi-direction causality between FDI and Y either in the long or the short run.

Papers on Both China and India Vanwyk and Lai (2012) assessed FDI's impact on economic growth in both China and India by estimating the following Error Correction Model:

$$\Delta \log(\mathrm{FDI})\mathrm{t} = \alpha + \Sigma\mathrm{i}\beta\mathrm{i}\Delta \log(\mathrm{FDI})\mathrm{t} - \mathrm{i} + \Sigma\mathrm{i}\theta\mathrm{i}\Delta \log(\mathrm{GDP})\mathrm{t} - \mathrm{i} + \lambda\mu t - 1 + \mathrm{Wt} \quad (10.3)$$

$$\Delta \log(\mathrm{GDP})\mathrm{t} = \alpha + \Sigma\mathrm{i}\gamma\mathrm{i}\Delta \log(\mathrm{GDP})\mathrm{t} - \mathrm{i} + \Sigma\mathrm{i}\xi\mathrm{i}\Delta \log(\mathrm{FDI})\mathrm{t} - \mathrm{i} + \rho\psi t - 1 + \mathrm{Wt} \quad (10.4)$$

Their estimation results suggested that the impact of a one percentage point increase in FDI growth led to a 0.159 percentage point increase in India's economic growth and a 0.233 percentage point increase in China's growth.

Agrawal and Khan (2011) assessed FDI's impact on growth in both China and India by estimating the multivariate-regression derived from growth accounting, instead of an Error Correction Model:

$$Y = \beta 0 + \beta 1K + \beta 2L + \beta 3FDI + \beta 4H + \varepsilon \qquad (10.5)$$

Where Y = GDP (in current international US dollars in millions), K= Gross capital formation (as % of GDP), L=labor force, FDI=foreign direct investment (as % of GDP), H=human capital (proxied by Human Development Index).

The estimation results showed that the coefficient on FDI is significant at 10% level of significance for China and India, with high adjusted R^2 (0.99 in China and 0.98 in India). The coefficient on FDI in China's equation is 0.07, implying that a 1% increase in FDI would result in 0.07% growth in GDP in China. By comparison, the coefficient of FDI in India's equation implies that a 1% increase in FDI would result in a 0.02% increase in GDP in India. The paper's estimation results thus suggest that the effect of FDI on economic growth is considerably higher in China than in India.

On balance, our literature survey shows (1) the impact of FDI on economic growth was mixed among a diverse group of developing/emerging countries; (2) the impact of FDI on growth in China and India was mainly positive, with it being larger in China than in India; (3) in China, FDI both led and was driven by GDP growth. In India, there is only a uni-directional effect, running from FDI to GDP growth.

10.4 Why Was the Effect of FDI on Growth Greater in China Than in India?

In this section, we undertake further analysis to gain insight into why the effect of FDI on growth is greater in China than in India. We do so by examining the extent to which these two countries are different in four types of economic or institutional conditions: human capital, infrastructure, political environment and government policy, and financial market development.

10.4.1 Human Capital

De Mello (1997) argued that FDI could increase economic growth in host countries in two ways, by transferring technology and knowledge through labor training, and by spreading better management practices. In other words, the extent to which FDI could help promote economic growth in the host country critically depends on the degree to which a host country's labor force is able to absorb those transfers of technology and practices. Theoretically, workers with higher education tend to learn new knowledge and complex techniques more efficiently. Therefore, it is reasonable to expect that FDI's impact on economic growth is higher in host countries with a higher literacy rate (i.e., the proportion of people who can read among those aged 15 and above) and average education level of its population, both of which are components of human capital in a country.

The literacy rate in China has been consistently better than that in India (Table 10.4). For instance, the literacy rate was around 91% in China in 2000, but only 61% in India in 2001. A decade later, China's literacy rate rose to 95% while India's literacy rate only rose to 69.3%.

For education level, Table 10.5 shows that, on average, the school enrolment ratio in China during 1980–2015 was also higher than that in India. China's average secondary school enrolment ratio from 1980 to 2015 was 57%, considerably higher than that in India (49%). China's average tertiary school enrolment ratio over the same period was 12.3%, moderately higher than that in India (11.2%).

The above analysis would seem to suggest that, during the period in which studies have found that FDI's contribution to economic growth was greater in China than in India, China had a moderate amount of advantage over India in terms of the literacy rate and average education ratios. However, one should also note that India had two relative advan-

Table 10.4 Literacy rate, adult total (% of people ages 15 and above)

China		*India*	
1982	65.51	40.76	1981
1990	77.79	48.22	1991
2000	90.92	61.01	2001
2010	95.12	69.30	2011

Source: The World Bank—World Development Indicators (1981–2011)

Table 10.5 School enrolment ratio (% gross) from 1980 to 2015

India					*China*			
	Mean	*Std. dev.*	*Max.*	*Min.*	*Mean*	*Std. dev.*	*Max.*	*Min.*
Secondary	49.13	12.82	74.28	28.95	57.13	21.22	96.24	30.13
Tertiary	11.16	6.87	26.87	4.96	12.34	11.39	43.39	1.16

Source: World Development Indicator

tages. First, given the fact that English is one of the official languages widely used by Indian people, Indian workers have an advantage over Chinese workers in their relative ease of working for multinational companies. Second, according to the study by Prime et al. (2012), India had more skilled workers among its work force than did China, especially in IT service sectors. (They found that the percentage of unskilled workers in China was 89%, compared to 36% in India.) Therefore, on balance, we do not have unambiguous evidence to support the view that the difference in human capital condition was a major cause of the gap between FDI's impacts on growth in China and India.

10.4.2 *Infrastructure*

Borensztein et al. (1998) suggested that, in addition to a higher level of education, better conditions of infrastructure—such as the information network, communication technology and the transportation system—are crucial to attract inward FDI and to benefit more fully from FDI. This view makes sense since local infrastructure condition is one of major factors that affect business investment strategy. Few would dispute that a supportive infrastructure helps to attract more FDI and enhances the impact of foreign investment on gross production. For instance, a better transportation condition makes it easier to ship material/goods between ports to local factories, as well as to distribute products across different regions. Likewise, well-structured telecommunication services improve communications not only between subsidiaries and headquarters, but also between foreign enterprises and domestic firms and government.

We can see from Table 10.6 that China had sustained an advantage in transportation infrastructure compared to India, especially in air transport and shipping connectivity, between 2006 and 2010. That advantage has further enlarged since then, indicating that China's local infrastructure

Table 10.6 Transportation infrastructure in China and India

		Road, total network (km)	*Railways lines, total route (km)*	*Air transport, registered carrier departures*	*Air transport, freight (million)*	*Shipping connectivity index*
2006	China	3,456,999	63,412	1,542,564	7692.2	113.1
	India	3,316,452	63,332	453,921	842.6	42.9
	China/India ratio	1.04	1.00	3.40	9.13	2.64
2010	China	4,008,229	66,239	2,377,789	17,193.9	143.6
	India	3,323,557	63,974	623,197	1631.0	41.4
	China/India ratio	1.21	1.04	3.82	10.54	3.47

Source: World Bank data

had been growing faster than India's. On the shipping connectivity front, India even slipped somewhat from 2006 to 2010. It implies that, for India, its inland water transportation is still a problem, which might affect its ability for inland or even international trade with its business partners.

China also sustained an advantage in communication infrastructure compared to India between 2001 and 2013. During that period, both countries significantly improved their communication system and services. In both countries, Internet, telephone and mobile cellular, convenient communication technology spread to a wider user base. By 2013, 88.71% of citizens in China had their own mobile phones, compared to 70.78% in India (Table 10.7). Both countries made a large leap in communication infrastructure, and India's rapid catchup indeed reduced the gap between the two countries' communication infrastructure. However, China retained its advantage in communication infrastructure relative to India as of 2013. This very likely reflects China's strategy of signing more FDI programs that helped to build part of its infrastructure, in addition to its massive government spending on physical infrastructure.

In sum, the available data suggest that China has sustained a competitive advantage in both transportation and communication infrastructure in recent decades. Indeed, Ramzan et al. (2013) also arrived at a similar conclusion that China is in a better position in infrastructure as compared to India. Thus, it would be reasonable to infer that China's advantage in

Table 10.7 Communication infrastructure in China and India

		Mobile cellular subscriptions (per 100 people)	*Telephone line (per 100 people)*	*Fixed broadband Internet subscribers (per 100 people)*	*Secure Internet severs (per 1 million people)*	*Internet user (per 100 people)*
2001	China	11.24	14.00	0.03	0.14	2.64
	India	0.62	3.64	0	0.12	0.66
	China/India ratio	18.13	3.85	NA	1.17	4.00
2013	China	88.71	19.27	13.68	3.87	45.8
	India	70.78	2.32	1.16	3.90	15.1
	China/India ratio	1.25	8.31	11.79	0.99	3.03

Source: World Bank data

infrastructure is a key cause of its ability to attract more sizeable FDI inflows as well as its ability to reap more benefits from those FDI inflows than India.

10.4.3 Political Environment and Government Policy

Findings in the literature suggest that a more stable political environment makes a host country more attractive to FDI because it provides a more convincing assurance to forward-looking multinational enterprises that existing government policies would be sustained. Moreover, government policies that reduce the risk of doing business in the host country—such as openness to international trade, enforcement of property rights, maintaining a transparent and just legal system, and responsible fiscal policies and so on—are important factors in making the country more attractive to foreign investment.[4]

In this section, we use indices reported by the Global Competitiveness Report to compare the political environment and policy situation in China and India, aiming to determine whether this factor may help explain the difference in the FDI's impacts on growth in these two countries. More specifically, we will do so by finding out whether we can connect large changes in FDI with the adoption of government policies aimed to attract inward FDI.

Before 1978, there was nearly zero foreign investment allowed into China. Then, Deng Xiaoping put forward the economic reform and open up policy in late 1978 and established four Special Economic Zones (SEZs)—namely, Shenzhen, Xiamen, Zhuhai and Shantou—to attract FDI. In 1984, China further opened 14 coastal cities to overseas investment. Meanwhile, China's government announced several preferential policies—such as, lower tariff, preferential tax treatments and less principle control—to attract multinational corporations to invest in these SEZs. With these policy initiatives, China gained the first-move advantage to absorb FDI during 1980s (Fig. 10.1).

FDI into China surged from 1992 to 1993, following the pronouncement of a further "opening" policy of the Chinese economy. After that, both FDI and GDP witnessed a faster growth rate. (The decline of the FDI/GDP ratio after 1993 simply reflects an even higher growth in GDP than in FDI, as indicated in Fig. 10.2.) After China's accession to the WTO, FDI into China further surged.

In comparison, FDI did not begin to flow into India until 1992, lagging behind China for nearly a decade. In part, this is because the Indian government's distrust of FDI had resulted in policies intended to hinder the rise of FDI. It was not until 1984 that India's government began to open up by establishing four Export-Procession Zones—namely, Chennai, Cochin, Falta and Noida. As India's economic reform continued, growth in both FDI inflows and GDP also accelerated in India. For instance, after the economic openness policy freed the caps on foreign inflow capitals and reduced several strict regulations, inward FDI nearly quadrupled, from an

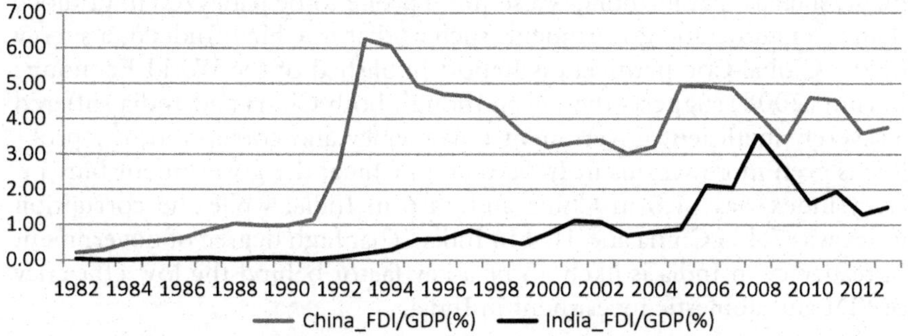

Fig. 10.1 FDI/GDP ratio in China and India (1980–2013)

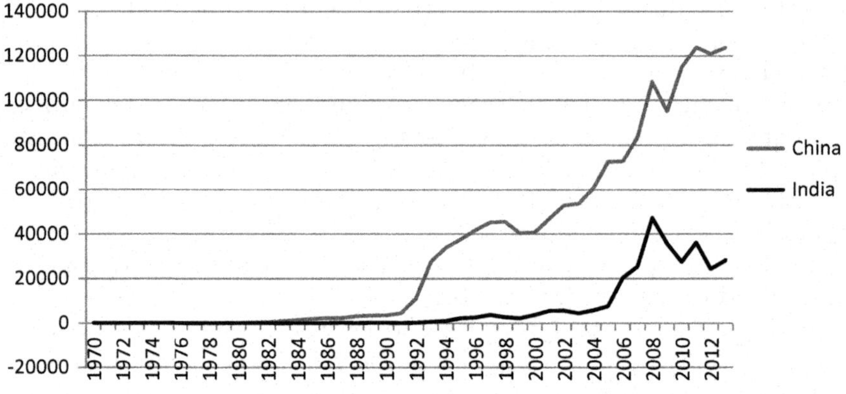

Fig. 10.2 FDI inflows in China and India (million of USD)

average 124 million net inflows in 1982–1990 to more than 460 million on average in 1991–1994. After India joined WTO in 1995, five years prior to China, its FDI inflows gained further growth momentum.

Nevertheless, perhaps in part because China's one-party rule made its government more decisive and powerful in implementing pro-growth policies, including preferential tax treatments to foreign-owned enterprises, China remained a more attractive destination for FDI than India. In turn, those FDI inflows helped China to gain access to modern technology and increased its economic growth. Many observers, for example, Prime et al. (2012), have argued that India's democratic political structure, with its judicial system in the British common law tradition and an independent press, is better than China's. However, a democratic government, such as that in India, is also more prone to be paralyzed in gridlock than is an autocratic government, such as that in China. Indeed, a survey by the Global Competitiveness Report published of the World Economic Forum (2008) suggests that, even though both China and India suffered a severely inefficient government bureaucracy and corruption, the problem is even more serious in India than in China: the government bureaucracy index was 11.5 in China and 14.6 in India, while the corruption index was 7.4 in China and 10.1 in India. That high degree of government bureaucracy in India is likely to be a key factor behind the low efficiency of FDI and domestic investment in India.

10.4.4 Financial Market Development

The financial market and financial institutions are channels through which resources, either domestic or from abroad, find their most productive uses. Thus, a sound and well-functioning financial system is critical to productivity and economy growth. We will compare the status of financial market development in China and India by using the Global Competitiveness Report by the World Economic Forum and other related research papers.

According to the World Economic Forum's Global Competitiveness Report, China's financial market development lagged behind that of India for years until 2014–2015. (See the Appendix for the Global Competitiveness Indicators, including financial market development, of China versus India, provided in the Global Competitiveness Report in 2008–2009, 2010–2011 and 2014–2015.) China's financial market was found to be less developed than that in India for the following reasons. First, access to loans is difficult for a large number of small and medium enterprises (SMEs) in China due to restrictive and complicated assessment in local banking sectors. Second, India has British-based auditing and accounting standards, while China's auditing and reporting standards still need to be strengthened and standardized to an international system. This helped India to attract more FDI originating in OECD countries, while a large share of China's inward FDI is from regions with cultural or geographical proximity, such as Taiwan and Hong Kong. It is worthwhile to note that China has improved its financial market development rather quickly over the past decade. For example, its financial market sophistication ranking improved from 109th to 54th from 2008 to 2014, quite a leap forward over a six-year period.

10.5 Conclusion

Most empirical studies have found diverse results regarding FDI's effect on economic growth, and that many economists agreed that FDI's effect on growth differed depending on various economic and institutional conditions of the host country. However, we find that there is less controversy on the finding that FDI has made a positive contribution to China's economic growth. We thus tried to identify what the key reasons for China's "success" are by comparing the effect of FDI on economic growth in China and in India.

We found that China had attracted more sizeable FDI inflow than India, even though India's workers have the advantage of being able to communicate in English. Our analysis indicates the reason for China's higher degree of attractiveness for FDI lies in (1) its more aggressive policy promotion, including preferential tax treatment for foreign-owned enterprises; (2) its better human capital condition; and (3) its more developed transportation and communication infrastructure. China's more aggressive policy promotion, in turn, reflected its one-party rule political system, which avoids government gridlock that is more common in a democratic system such as in India.

Our survey also highlights that, by most papers' estimates, the marginal effect of FDI on real GDP was larger in China than in India. Our analysis suggests that the key reasons for this difference are twofold. First, China has better transportation and communication infrastructure, thereby improving business efficiency. Second, China's higher level of human capital means Chinese employees learn new technology and managerial know-how brought in by FDI more quickly, speeding up the spillover of technology, improving productivity rapidly in China.

Appendix

Appendix 1: Global Competitiveness Index in 2008–2009

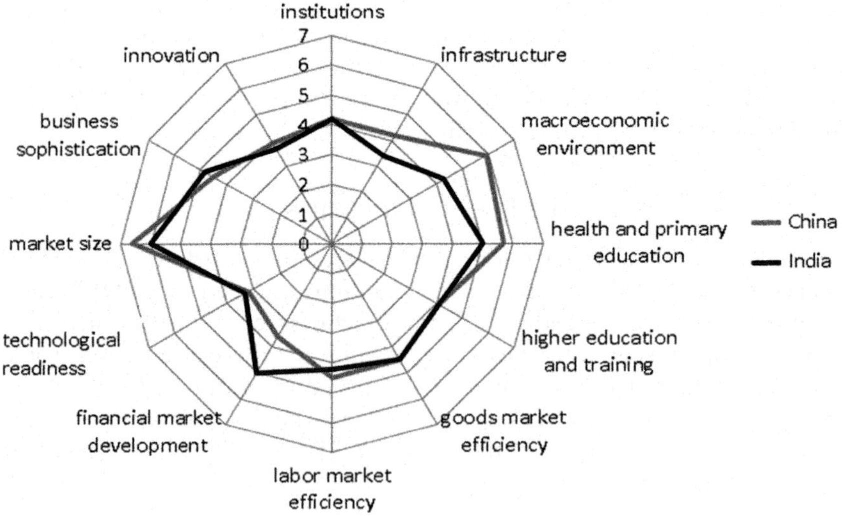

Appendix 2: Global Competitiveness Index in 2010–2011

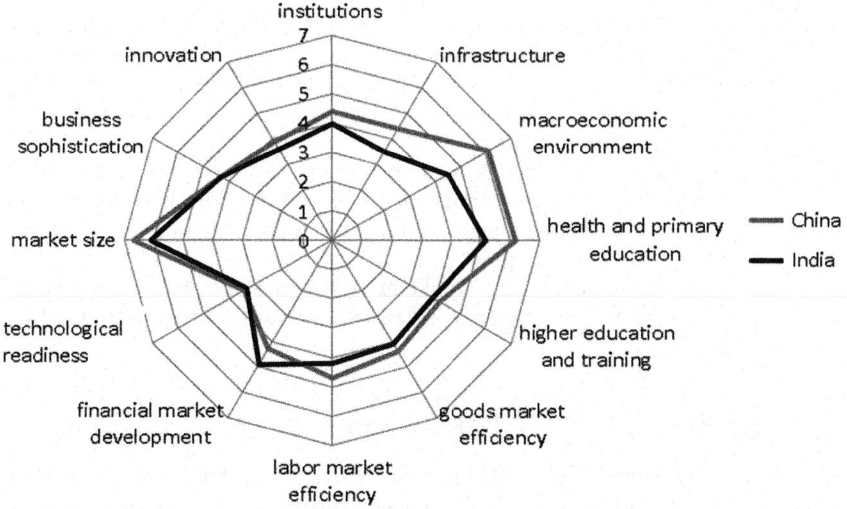

Appendix 3: Global Competitiveness Index in 2014–2015

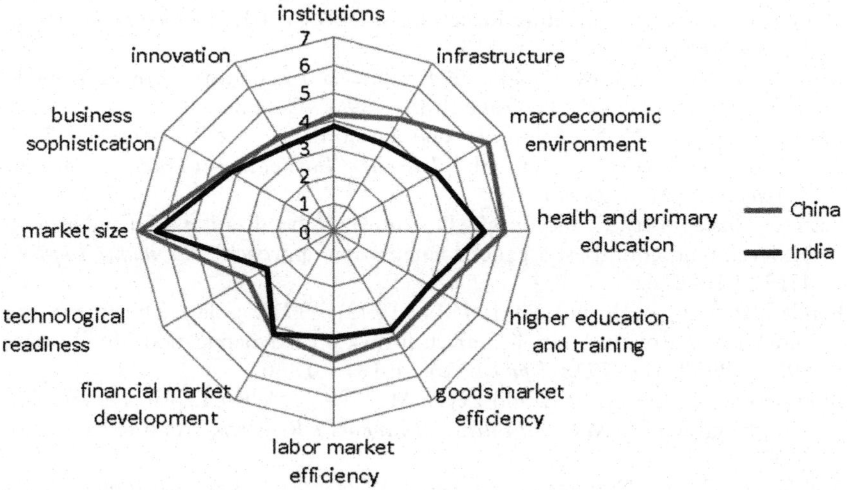

Notes

1. Typically, FDI refers to investment in a (host) country by a multinational firm, which has a home base in another country. Thus, FDI typically involves transferring of assets, such as capital stock, technology, and management know-how and human capital to the host country. See UNCTAD (2015).
2. For example, see Wang (2009).
3. This last point is consistent with the observation by Forte and Moura (2013): host countries' governments are responsible for obtaining positive effects of FDI on their countries' economic growth by improving their legal system and market conditions.
4. For example, Jadhav (2012) found empirical results showing that in BRICS economies, trade openness, rule of law and accountability were vital determinants of FDI.

References

Agrawal, G. and Khan, M. A. (2011), "Impact of FDI on GDP: A Comparative Study of China and India", *International Journal of Business and Management*: 6(10), 71–79.

Almsafir, M. K. and Almfraji, M. A. (2013), "Foreign Direct Investment and Economic Growth Literature Review from 1994 to 2012", *Procedia Social and Behavioral Sciences:* 129, 206–213.

Bagli, S. and Adhikary, M. (2014), "FDI inflow and Economic Growth in India: An Empirical Analysis", *Economic Affairs*: 59(1), 23–33.

Balasubramanyam, V. N., Salisu, M. and Sapsford, D. (1999), "Foreign direct investment as an engine of growth", *Journal of International Trade & Economic Development*: 8(1), 27–40.

Basu, P., Chakraborty, C. and Reagle, D. (2003), "Liberalization, FDI and growth in developing countries: a panel cointegration approach", *Economic Inquiry*: 41(3), 510–516.

Bende-Nabende, A. J. and Ford, J. L. (1998), "FDI, policy adjustment and endogenous growth: Multiplier effects from a small dynamic model for Taiwan, 1959–1995", *World Development*: 26(7), 1315–1330.

Blomstrom, M., Lipsey, R. E. and Zejan, M. (1992), "What Explains developing country growth?", *National Bureau of Economic Research*, Working Paper No. 4132.

Borensztein, E., De Gregorio, J. and Lee, J. W. (1998), "How does foreign direct investment affect economic growth?", *Journal of International Economics:* 45 (1), 115–135.

Chakraborty, C. and Nunnenkamp, P. (2006), "Economic Reforms, Foreign Direct Investment and its Economic Effects in India", Available at: https://

www.ifw-members.ifw-kiel.de/publications/economic-reforms-foreign-direct-investment-and-its-economic-effects-in-india-1/kap1272.pdf

De Mello Jr, L. R. (1997), "Foreign direct investment in developing countries and growth: A selective survey", *Journal of Development Studies*: 34(1), 1–34.

Durham, J. B. (2004), "Absorptive capacity and the effects of foreign direct investment and equity foreign portfolio investment on economic growth", *European Economic Review*: 48(2), 285–306.

Ekanayake, E. M. and Ledgerwood, J. R. (2010), "How Does Foreign Direct Investment Affect Growth in Developing Countries? An Empirical Investigation", *The International Journal of Business and Finance Research*: 4(3), 43–53.

Haddad, M., and Harrison, A. (1993), "Are there positive spillovers from direct foreign investment? evidence from panel data for morocco", *Journal of Development Economics:* 42(1), 51–74.

Forte, R. and Moura, R. U. I. (2013), "The Effects of Foreign Investment on The Host Country's Economic Growth: Theory and Empirical Evidence", *Singapore Economic Review:* 58(3), 1–20.

Kasibhatla, K. M., Stewart, D. B. and Khojasteh, M. (2008), "The Role of FDI in High Medium, Low Medium and Low Income Countries during 1970-2005: Empirical Tests and Evidence", *Journal of Business & Economics Studies*: 14(2), 60–72.

Liu, Y. O. and Su, H. L. (2012), "The Relationship between Foreign Direct Investment and Economic Growth", *On Economic Problems*, 8, 105–108.

Lombard, M. and Lombard, A. (2011), "A Comparative Analysis of the Effects of Foreign Direct Investment on China's and India's Economic Development in Recent Years", *Economic Papers*: 30(4), 522–529.

Lal, A. K, and Vanwyk, J. (2012), "FDI and economic growth in China & India–case of two giants", *Indian Journal of Economics and Business*: 3, 529.

Mathiyazhagan, M.K. and Sahoo, D. (2003), "Economic Growth in India: Does Foreign Direct Investment Inflow Matter?", *The Singapore Economic Review:* 48(2), 151–171.

Prime, P. B., Subrahmanyam, V. and Lin, C. M. (2012), "Competitiveness in India and China: the FDI puzzle", *Asia Pacific Business Review*: 18(3), 303–333.

Ramzan, M., Imran, M. and Zafar, I. (2013), "Foreign Direct Investment and Economic Growth: Comparative Position of Chinese and Indian Economies", *Journal of Business Studies Quarterly*: 4(3), 1034–2152.

Rodriguez-Clare, A. (1996), "Multinationals, linkages and economic development", *American Economic Review*: 86(4), 852–873.

Shaikh, F. M. (2010), "Causality Relationship Between Foreign Direct Investment, Trade and Economic Growth in Pakistan", *International Business Research*, 1, 11–18. Harvard Business School.

UNCTAD. (2015), United Nations Conference on Trade and Development statistics: foreign direct investment flows and stock data package, Available at: http://unctadstat.unctad.org/wds/ReportFolders/reportFolders.aspx?sRF_ActivePath=p,5&sRF_Expanded=,p,5

Vanwyk, J. and Lai, A. K. (2012), "FDI and Economic Growth in China & India – Case of Two Giants", *Indian Journal of Economics & Business,* 11(2), 529–541.

Wang, M. (2009), "Manufacturing FDI and Economic Growth: Evidence from Asian Economies", *Applied Economics:* 41(8), 991–1002.

Wei, H. (2002), "Effects of foreign direct investment on regional economic growth in China", *Economic Research Journal:* 4, 19–26.

World Economic Forum. (2008), "The Global Competitiveness Report 2008–2009", Available at: http://www.weforum.org/reports/globalcompetitiveness-report-2008-2009

World Economic Forum. (2010), "The Global Competitiveness Report 2010–2011", Available at: http://www.weforum.org/news/globalcompetitiveness-report-2010-2011-news-release-0

World Economic Forum. (2014), "The Global Competitiveness Report 2014–2015", Available at: http://www.weforum.org/reports/globalcompetitiveness-report-2014-2015

World Trade Organization. (2014), The World Trade Report – Trade and development: recent trends and the role of the WTO, Available at: https://www.wto.org/english/res_e/publications_e/wtr14_e.htm

Yao, S. and Wei, K. (2007), "Economic growth in the presence of FDI: the perspective of newly industrializing economies", *Journal of Comparative Economics:* 35(1), 211–234.

Yao, S. J. (2006), "On Economic Growth, FDI and exports in China", *Applied Economics:* 38, 339–351

Zhang, X. L. (2010), "ZHONGGUO LIYONG FDI DE JINGJI XIAOYING JI DUI JINGJI ANQUAN YINGXIANG DE PINGJIA", Economic Science Press.

Zhao, S. Y. (2013), "Privatization, FDI inflow and economic growth: evidence from China's provinces, 1978-2008", *Applied Economics:* 45(15), 2127–2139.

CHAPTER 11

The Role of the Exchange Rate in China's Outward Foreign Direct Investment

Xinyun Ding and Nimesh Salike

11.1 Introduction

China has been one of the prime home destinations for foreign direct investment (FDI) over the past few decades. Starting in 2005/2006, China began to be earnest in making outward FDI as well, with its aggregate outward FDI reaching over USD 180 billion by 2016, which was over 12.6% of global outward FDI flows. That outward FDI was a mere USD 5.5 billion in 2004, started to pick up in 2005 and grew rapidly after 2010, with an annual average growth rate of 19% during 2010–2016 (Fig. 11.1).

Moreover, the structure of Chinese outward FDI has changed over the period, becoming more and more complex and diversified (*The Economist* 2014). China is prepared to become a net capital exporter (*Financial Times* 2014) and continues to accelerate the outward investment. It is evident from Fig. 11.2 that the margin between Chinese outward FDI and inward FDI over gross domestic product (GDP) has narrowed over the years, and inward FDI was surpassed by inward FDI in 2016.

X. Ding • N. Salike (✉)
International Business School Suzhou, Xi'an Jiaotong-Liverpool University, Suzhou, China
e-mail: Nimesh.Salike@xjtlu.edu.cn

J. H. Hung, Y. Chen (eds.), *The State of China's State Capitalism*,
https://doi.org/10.1007/978-981-13-0983-0_11

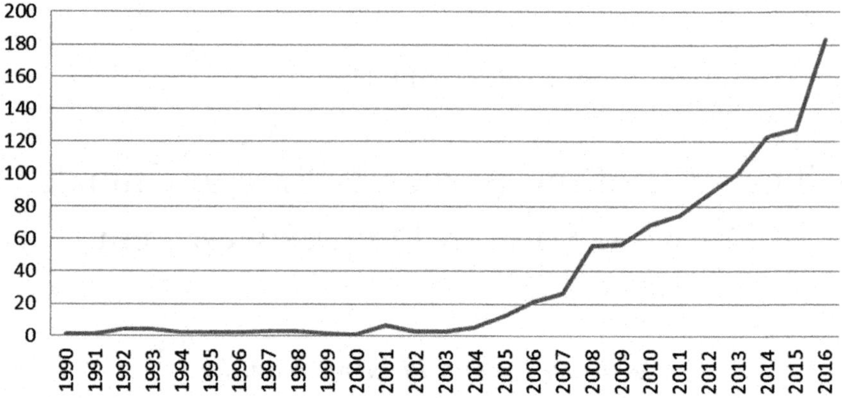

Fig. 11.1 Chinese outward FDI flow, 1990–2016 (billion USD). (Source: UNCTAD, Division on Investment and Enterprise)

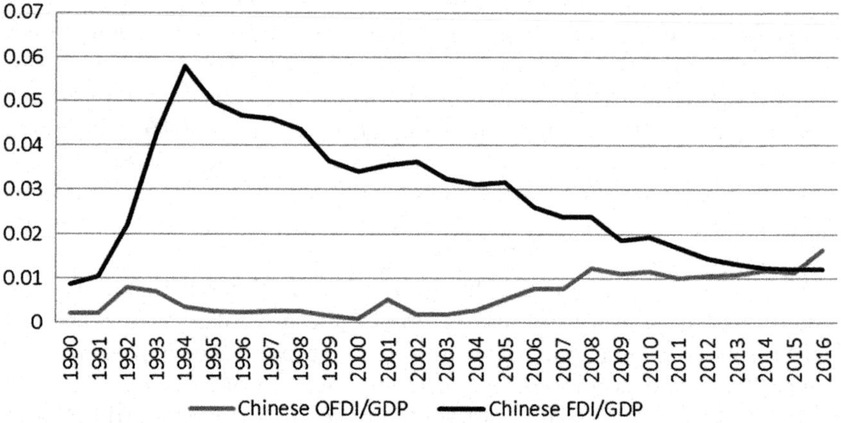

Fig. 11.2 Ratio of Chinese outward FDI and inward FDI over GDP (1990–2016). (Source: UNCTAD, Division on Investment and Enterprise)

The upsurge in Chinese outward FDI has attracted much attention among researchers on what motivates Chinese multinational corporations to invest abroad. Since the Chinese outward FDI is a relatively new phenomenon, there are limited studies that looked into the determinants of these FDIs. Some literature investigated the issues like host economies' policy risk, natural resources and market size (Buckley et al. 2007; Cheung and Qian 2009; Zhang and Daly 2011; Kolstad and Wiig 2012). Sector-specific studies have also been carried out (like Amighini and Franco 2013). There is ample research on Western and Japanese experiences, which may provide good insights on the issues. The motivation for FDI could be divided into four categories: resource seeking, market seeking, efficiency seeking and strategic asset seeking (Dunning 1998). Likewise, one important variable that affects the decision on foreign investment is the exchange rate of the host economy.

The status of exchange rate fluctuation and exchange rate volatility has been increasingly important in international business and the trade pattern of countries. Taking the essential benefits that FDI brings to both home and host countries and the close relationship between exchange rate volatility and relative policy formulation, exchange rate fluctuation and exchange rate volatility are supposed to affect the choices of FDI and their impacts cannot be ignored (Kiyota and Urata 2004). Furthermore, Lin et al. (2010) found that exchange rate fluctuation and exchange rate volatility can alter a firm's investment attitudes and signals the economic uncertainty that may increase investment risks in global business and trade. These studies were based on the experiences of the United States, Japan and European countries. Nevertheless, there is not a study that specifically deals with exchange rate issues vis-à-vis Chinese outward FDI to our knowledge. China practices a 'managed floating exchange rate' regime since 2005 until when Chinese renminbi (RMB) was pegged with USD. RMB began to appreciate, in general, over time from then onwards, although both the fluctuation and volatility of RMB exchange are somehow small compared to other major currencies. For example, the RMB appreciated 34% against USD on nominal basis and 42% on real basis from 2005 to 2013 (Morrison and Labonte 2013).

This chapter explores the impact of host economies' exchange rate and volatility on Chinese outward FDI. The contribution of this chapter lies in the aspects of exchange rate, where we investigate if the appreciation or depreciation of host economy currency affects the decisions of Chinese firms in locating their investment abroad. In addition to looking into the levels of exchange rate, the chapter further investigates the influence of exchange rate volatility of the host economies. Further, we also analyze if there is a specific preference over developed or developing economies for Chinese multinationals.

Our results from a gravity model-based panel regression, using data of 21 host economies from 2004 to 2013, indicate that the host country's exchange rate level is not a significant determinant of Chinese outward

FDI while its exchange rate volatility is. A rise of 1% volatility in the exchange rate of the host economy could deter as much as 16.6% of Chinese outward FDI. Regarding other variables, we found that market-seeking motivation and economic openness are important determinants. We also found the evidence that Chinese outward FDI has preference toward developed economies over developing ones as its outward FDI host economy.

11.2 Existing Literature and Methodology

11.2.1 Brief Review of FDI Studies

It is widely accepted that there are three mainstream viewpoints about the relationship between traditional variables and Chinese outward FDI: host country's market size, policy on FDI and natural resources.

Buckley et al. (2007) used a gravity model on panel data covering 49 countries from the period 1984–2001. Using different estimation techniques—random effects (RE) generalized least squares (GLS) and pooled ordinary least squares (POLS)—they found that Chinese outward FDI is attracted to countries with large-size markets, high levels of political risk and culture and geographic proximity. Cheung and Qian (2009) modified the traditional gravity model to improve the goodness of fit by introducing lagged variables and interaction variables with dummies, and illustrated that a larger GDP, higher availability of natural resources and lower levels of wages are the main determinants for Chinese outward FDI.

Kolstad and Wiig (2012) found that Chinese outward FDI is market-oriented and there is an interactive effect of poor institutions and large natural resources. They used POLS on Chinese outward FDI data from 2003 to 2006. Their results also revealed that Chinese outward FDI is attracted to large markets in developed economies, and to the combination of natural resources and policies in developing economies. In addition to these, Wei et al. (2014) looked into a firm's decision on whether to serve the foreign country by exporting or by direct investment. They showed that a firm's choice would alter depending upon the importance of global trade experience and barriers to bilateral trade.

In general, much existing theoretical and empirical literature has found evidence that market size is a significant determinant of Chinese outward FDI. In addition, an increasing number of studies provide evidence that there are other determinants, such as host countries' economic openness and availability of natural resources, which influence Chinese outward FDI. However, there are still limitations on evaluating the impact of exchange rate and its volatility on Chinese outward FDI, although such similar studies have been carried out for other countries.

There are a number of studies providing strong evidence to highlight that depreciation of a host country currency is able to facilitate outward FDI flows. Stressing the example of Japanese investment in Asia and utilizing the panel data from 1987 to 2008, Takagi and Shi (2011) explained that an appreciation of host country currency discourages Japanese outward FDI flows. They conducted the panel regression with the dummy variable, financial crisis and adopted the GLS to test their model equation. Moreover, they also identified that the Asian financial crisis did not seriously affect Japanese outward FDI. This result is in line with Kahouli and Maktouf (2015) where they studied the impact on regional trade agreements.

On the impact of exchange rate volatility on outward FDI flows, the existing literature provides strong evidence to support the hypothesis that exchange rate volatility deters FDI flows. Kiyota and Urata (2004) investigated the impacts of exchange rate volatility by using the data from 1990 to 2000 and found that exchange rate volatility is a deterrent for Japanese outward FDI flows to several countries. Furthermore, Kiyota and Urata (2008) used firm level data of Japanese multinational corporations for 1995, 1998 and 2001 to explore the significance of maintaining a stable exchange rate environment in global business and trade in terms of the impacts of exchange rate volatility. Manop et al. (2009), for instance, analyzed the data from 1990 to 2002 in the United States where both fixed and RE models were considered and tested, respectively, and found that exchange rate volatility signals the uncertainty of a country's economy, which has a negative effect on FDI flows. This is consistent with MacDermott's (2008) findings.

One of the much-used methodologies in the field of trade and investment to access the impact of specific variables is the gravity model. The gravity model has been used primarily in the trade theories and has been highly successful explaining the trading behavior between economies, based on the size of respective trading partners and the distance between them.[1] Its use in FDI theories gained prominence in the past decade where a similar argument (like in trade theories) has been provided that countries with a large economic size and with closer geographic proximity would be interested in investing abroad. Several studies have also found that the gravity model has been relatively successful in explaining the FDI pattern.

11.3 Research Model

To examine the impact of exchange rate fluctuation and exchange rate volatility on Chinese outward FDI in developed and developing economies, we used Chinese outward FDI as a dependent variable in the augmented gravity model. The data is panel in nature that ranges from 2004 to 2013. The start year of 2004 is taken considering the remarkable increase in Chinese outward FDI from that year onwards (see Fig. 11.1).

The basic gravity model uses economic size of respective economies, measured by GDP, and geographical distance between them. The augmented model also includes other variables that are key determinants as supported by literature. Further, we included our main variables of interest, exchange rate fluctuation and exchange rate volatility in the model. The resulting equation is as follows:

$$\begin{aligned} \boldsymbol{lnOFDI}_{cit} &= \beta_0 + \beta_1 \boldsymbol{ERG}_{it} + \beta_2 \boldsymbol{Vol}_{it} + \beta_3 \boldsymbol{lnGDP}_{it} + \beta_4 \boldsymbol{lnGDP}_{ct} \\ &+ \beta_5 \boldsymbol{lnGDPPC}_{it} + \beta_6 \boldsymbol{lnGDPG}_{it} + \beta_7 \boldsymbol{lnDis}_{cit} + \beta_8 \boldsymbol{lnEnergy}_{it} \\ &+ \beta_9 \boldsymbol{Openness}_{it} + \beta_{10} \boldsymbol{lnMobile\ phone}_{it} \\ &+ \beta_{11} \boldsymbol{lnInternet\ users}_{it} + \beta_{12} \boldsymbol{lnRoad\ density}_{it} + \mu_i + \varepsilon_{it} \ldots\ldots, \end{aligned} \tag{11.1}$$

where i denotes a host economy ($i = 1, \ldots, 21$); subscript c denotes China, t stands for a year. β_j ($j = 0, \ldots, 12$) represents the estimated coefficients. ε_{it} is an error term and μ_i is an unobserved fixed effect. Both μ_i and ε_{it} are followed by an independent and identical distribution with mean equals to 0 and variance equals to σ_μ. All variables are in the logarithmic form, except Openness which is already scaled by GDP and our variables of interest.

Following Cheung and Qian (2009), independent variables were lagged with one period, accounting for the impact of time series on economies. Lagged effect, under this circumstance, refers to the phenomenon that economic adjustments yield outcomes after an interval period of time instead of an immediate realization. This is a common macroeconomic phenomenon as illustrated by Elsayir (2013). Therefore, Eq. (11.1) is modified as follows:

$$\begin{aligned} \boldsymbol{lnOFDI}_{cit} &= \beta_0 + \beta_1 \boldsymbol{ERG}_{i,t-1} + \beta_2 \boldsymbol{Vol}_{i,t-1} + \beta_3 \boldsymbol{lnGDP}_{i,t-1} \\ &+ \beta_4 \boldsymbol{lnGDP}_{c,t-1} + \beta_5 \boldsymbol{lnGDPPC}_{i,t-1} + \beta_6 \boldsymbol{lnGDPG}_{i,t-1} \\ &+ \beta_7 \boldsymbol{lnDis}_{cit} + \beta_8 \boldsymbol{lnEnergy}_{i,t-1} + \beta_9 \boldsymbol{Openness}_{i,t-1} \\ &+ \beta_{10} \boldsymbol{lnMobile\ phone}_{i,t-1} + \beta_{11} \boldsymbol{lnInternet\ users}_{i,t-1} \\ &+ \beta_{12} \boldsymbol{lnRoad\ density}_{i,t-1} + \mu_i + \varepsilon_{it-1} \ldots\ldots, \end{aligned} \tag{11.2}$$

Detailed explanation about data and sources is provided in Table 11.1 as follows.

The host economy's exchange rate growth and exchange rate volatility are our main variables of interests. We measure the fluctuation in exchange rate by the change in exchange rate over the period. Further, exchange rate volatility is calculated by using the monthly nominal exchange rate. The monthly nominal exchange rate of host economies is generated from the CEIC database. GDP, GDP per capita and GDP growth rate are considered to be essential factors affecting Chinese outward FDI, especially for market-oriented FDI. In addition, GDP can be widely recognized as a proxy of market size and GDP per capita is commonly used as a measure of market opportunities and GDP growth rate is usually used as an indicator of potential future market growth. We expect the market-related variables to be positively related with Chinese outward FDI.

In the gravity model, bilateral distance is an important factor. The weighted bilateral distance is considered, which includes the weighted distance regarding the share of a certain city among the overall economy's population and the sensitivity of the bilateral trade flows. These data are taken from CEPII database. It is noteworthy that there are no acceptable statistics of the weighted bilateral distance between Macao and China. Based on a similar geographic position to Hong Kong, the weighted bilateral distance of Hong Kong is used for Macao to make a complete panel data set.

Existing academic research suggests that natural resources seeking type of investments plays a crucial role in explaining the motivation behind Chinese outward FDI (Ramasamy et al. 2012). In this case, energy production is related to forms of primary energy such as petroleum, natural gas, solid fuels and primary electricity. Takagi and Shi (2011) and Wei et al. (2014) found that economy openness is a determining variable for FDI. The relative export and import data is taken from the International Monetary Fund to calculate the openness level or respective host economy. Three variables mobile phone users, Internet users (per 100 people) and road density are used as proxies for infrastructure level. The related data is obtained from the World Bank Development Indicators. In general, the infrastructure variables are expected to be positively related with Chinese outward FDI.

Moreover, the host economy's wage is also an important factor that affects FDI (Cheung and Qian 2009). However, we did not include it in the model due to the collinearity relationship between wage and GDP per capita. In effect, GDP per capita could be a proxy for wage.[2]

Table 11.1 Summary of variables

Variables	*Description*	*Variable code*	*Data source*
OFDI (dependent variable)	Chinese outward foreign direct investment to host economy *i*	$lnOFDI_i$	Chinese Statistical Yearbook
Exchange rate growth	The nominal exchange rate growth in host economy *i*	ERG_i	CEIC
Exchange rate volatility	The nominal exchange rate volatility in host economy *i*	Vol_i	CEIC
GDP *i*	GDP of host economy *i*	$lnGDP_i$	World Bank Development Indicators
GDP *c*	GDP of China	$lnGDP_C$	World Bank Development Indicators
GDP per capita	GDP per capita of host economy *i*	$lnGDPPC_i$	World Bank Development Indicators
Growth rate of GDP	GDP growth rate of host economy *i*	$lnGDPG_i$	World Bank Development Indicators
Bilateral distance	The bilateral distance between China and host economy *i*	$lnDis_i$	www.cepii.com
Energy production	A proxy of natural resources of host economy *i*	$lnEnergy_i$	World Bank Development Indicators
Openness	The economic openness of host economy *i*	$Openness_i$	International Monetary Fund
Mobile phone users	The number of mobile phone subscriptions in host economy *i*	$lnMobile\ phone_i$	World Bank Development Indicators
Internet users	The number of Internet users per 100 people in host economy *i*	$lnInternet_i$	World Bank Development Indicators
Road density	The road density of host economy *i*	$lnRoad\ density_i$	World Bank Development Indicators

We considered the '*i*' economies from across the world, limiting to the availability of data in the China Statistical Yearbook. Table 11.2 lists 21 host economies where Chinese outward FDI occurred during 2004–2013.[3]

11.4 Results and Discussion

11.4.1 The Exchange Rate

We conducted the econometric estimation based on Eq. (11.2). First of all, to illustrate the underlying implications of all other control variables, we conducted OLS as a benchmark estimation. Before carrying out the estimations, we conducted the collinearity check, normally present in multiple regression models.[4] When the correlation among the variables is high, it becomes hard to identify the individual impact of each of the variables that may lead to unreliable regression estimates, in particular resulting in increased standard errors and misleading signs and magnitude of the coefficients. The presence of multicollinearity would threaten the analysis of coefficient estimates, which results in the increase of the *p*-value of a certain estimate coefficient and decrease the R^2 value of the whole estimated regression equation. In particular, two groups of variables are

Table 11.2 List of host economies by continent

Continent					
Asia	*Africa*	*Europe*	*South America*	*North America*	*Oceania*
Hong Kong	Algeria	United Kingdom	Mexico	Canada	Australia
Indonesia	Sudan	Germany		United States	New Zealand
Japan	Nigeria	France			
Macao	South Africa	Russia			
Singapore					
Republic of Korea					
Thailand					
Vietnam					

Among these host economies, eight are classified as developing economies: Indonesia, Thailand, Vietnam, Algeria, Sudan, Nigeria, South Africa and Mexico

And the other 13 are classified as developed economies: Hong Kong, Japan, Macao, Singapore, Republic of Korea, United Kingdom, Germany, France, Canada, United States, Australia, New Zealand and Russia

Note: This grouping is based on the World Bank classification, 'Country and Lending Groups' where it defines developed economies as high income and developing economies as low and middle income, calculated by the World Bank Atlas method in 2015 found to have high correlations: Internet and GDPPC (0.922), and Openness and Energy (−0.919). To avoid the problem of multicollinearity as noted above and to improve the goodness of fit of the estimated model regression, we set three specifications to examine the Eq. (11.2) step-by-step. Table 11.3 reports these three specification regression results respectively.

Our main variables of interests, exchange rate growth ($ERG_{i,\,t-1}$) and exchange rate volatility ($Vol_{i,\,t-1}$), are included in all specifications. The initial impression is that growth rate in exchange rate does not have an impact on Chinese outward FDI, whereas volatility tends to have a negative significant effect. The results also show that the independent variable *Openness* is positive and significant at the 1% level although economy *i*'s GDP is positive but not significant. This implies that *Openness* is an important determinant for Chinese outward FDI.

We found that other independent variable, GDP per capita ($lnGDPPC_{i,\,t-1}$), GDP growth rate ($lnGDPG_{i,\,t-1}$), mobile phone users ($lnMobile\ phone_{i,\,t-1}$), Internet users ($lnInternet\ users_{i,\,t-1}$) and energy production ($lnEnergy_{i,\,t-1}$) have lesser effects on Chinese outward FDI.

In order to look into the effect of gravity variables in particular, next, we considered the different specifications by including traditional gravity variables and the significant variable *Openness* along with our variable of interest, as shown in Table 11.4. From specification 4, it is obvious that these observed data fit the traditional gravity model well and these estimate coefficients are significant. Additionally, as expected, the coefficients of $lnGDP$ and $lnGDP_C$ are found to be positive, meaning that these two factors have positive effects on Chinese outward FDI. This is consistent with other studies, Buckley et al. (2007), Cheung and Qian (2009) and Kolstad and Wiig (2012) in that Chinese outward FDI is a market-oriented investment. On the contrary, bilateral distance has a reverse effect on Chinese outward FDI, taking the negative sign of *lnDis*. It suggests that a 10% rise in the bilateral distance will lead to 6.6% drop in Chinese outward FDI, holding other variables constant.

In specification 5, we added our variable of interest–exchange rate growth and exchange rate volatility. GDP in host economy *i*, Chinese GDP and bilateral distance are consistent with the previous conclusions. All variables are significant at the 5% level, except the independent variable exchange rate growth. In line with our expectation, the exchange rate volatility discourages Chinese outward FDI as evidenced by the negative coefficient. This implies that a 1% rise in exchange rate volatility at time

Table 11.3 OLS results including all control variables (dependent variable: *lnOFDI*)

Variables	*Spec 1*	*Spec 2*	*Spec 3*
$lnGDP_{i,t-1}$	0.69	0.11	0.12
	(0.2981)	(0.3885)	(0.6699)
$lnGDP_{c,t-1}$	2.35***	1.96***	2.13***
	(0.3534)	(0.3669)	(0.3966)
$lnGDPPC_{i,t-1}$		0.59	0.66
		(0.2653)	(0.5079)
$lnGDPG_{i,t-1}$	0.14	0.19	0.64
	(0.2606)	(0.2579)	(0.3160)
$lnDis_{cit}$	−0.68**	−0.62***	−0.46
	(0.2374)	(0.2228)	(0.3379)
$lnEnergy_{i,t-1}$			−0.39
			(0.2585)
$Openness_{i,t-1}$	1.18***	1.14***	
	(0.1652)	(0.1643)	
$lnMobile\ phone_{i,t-1}$	−0.33	0.23	0.38
	(0.3134)	(0.3863)	(0.4126)
$lnInternet\ users_{i,t-1}$	0.078		
	(0.2613)		
$lnRoad\ density_{i,t-1}$	−0.46**	−0.54***	−0.58***
	(0.1614)	(0.1555)	(0.2345)
$ERG_{i,t-1}$	3.43	3.70	4.66
	(2.4039)	(2.4244)	(2.9801)
$Vol_{i,t-1}$	−30.46**	−29.54**	−37.24**
	(15.6603)	(15.0890)	(18.7614)
Constant	−64.66	−52.73	−57.51
No. of observations	103	104	97
R^2	0.5794	0.5829	0.5490

Note: *, ** and *** denote statistical significance at 10%, 5% and 1% respectively

Numbers in parentheses indicate robust standard error

$t-1$ will cause a drop in Chinese outward FDI of 20.5% at time t, holding other independent variables constant.

Specification 6 in Table 11.4 includes all underlying working variables. The results strengthen the discussion that Chinese outward FDI is driven by market-seeking motivation, consistent with the previous literature. Chinese investors are able to pay much attention to the potential market size of the host economy. In addition, *Openness* is positive and highly significant at the 1% level, revealing that the degree of openness of business and trade in the host economy has a vital effect on Chinese

Table 11.4 OLS results including variables of interests (dependent variable: *lnOFDI*)

Variables	*Spec 4*	*Spec 5*	*Spec 6*
$lnGDP_{i,t-1}$	0.19**	0.18**	0.29***
	(0.0730)	(0.0687)	(0.0615)
$lnGDP_{c,t-1}$	1.75***	1.81***	1.74***
	(0.2490)	(0.2583)	(0.2230)
$lnDis_{cit}$	−0.66***	−0.54***	−0.15
	(0.2019)	(0.1881)	(0.1362)
$Openness_{i,t-1}$			1.08***
			(0.1562)
$ERG_{i,t-1}$		1.29	1.33
		(1.4821)	(1.4278)
$Vol_{i,t-1}$		−20.05***	−13.98**
		(6.2956)	(5.3826)
Constant	−40.3687	−42.50	−47.91
No. of observations	180	180	180
R^2	0.2824	0.3187	0.4758

Note: *, ** and *** denote statistical significance at 10%, 5% and 1% respectively

Numbers in parentheses indicate robust standard error

outward FDI. As Takagi and Shi (2011) and Wei et al. (2014) illustrated, economic openness is highly related to the trade barriers, which are concerned with outward FDI. If the international trade of a host economy is relatively open and free, meaning the global business and trade barriers are fewer and there is supporting government policy, it will attract an increasing amount of FDI flows to the host economy. In short, economic openness plays a considerable role in prompting Chinese outward FDI flows to the host economy. Similar to the previous discussion, the exchange rate volatility of host economy i is negative and significant at the 5% level, in line with the findings of existing studies. Kiyota and Urata (2004, 2008), MacDermott (2008) and Manop et al. (2009) argued that exchange rate volatility is detrimental to outward FDI since it implies economic uncertainty. In other words, the increase in the exchange rate volatility could induce more and more investment risks. It suggests that a 1% rise in exchange rate volatility of the host economy i at $t - 1$ will lead to almost a 14% drop in Chinese outward FDI at time t keeping other variables constant, indicating the enormously lagged and adverse impact on Chinese outward FDI. The exchange rate volatility's effect is magnified since its coefficient is almost 10 times higher than other independent variables.

However, exchange rate growth still is found to be not significant. The underlying cause influencing Chinese outward FDI is that to compare with the exchange rate itself, exchange rate volatility is a more concerned issue in international business and trade (Wali and Manzur 2013), which explains the little influence of exchange rate growth on Chinese outward FDI in this case.

Given that the data is panel in nature, there is a possibility of bias and inconsistency in the OLS results. Therefore, we conducted further analysis by employing fixed and REs estimation in Eq. (11.2). Hausman test is applied to test the appropriability between these models (Bole and Rebec 2013). Table 11.5 shows the results.

Specification 7 in Table 11.5 shows the fixed effects regression results and specification 8 shows the REs results. The results of the Hausman Test indicate that the REs model is more appropriate in this case. The results indicate that exchange rate volatility has a significant negative effect. It suggests that a 1% rise in exchange rate volatility at time $t - 1$ will cause a 14.6% decline in Chinese outward FDI at time t, addressing the importance of exchange rate volatility in this case. Clearly, a sharp fluctuation of

Table 11.5 Panel regression (dependent variable: *lnOFDI*)

Variables	*Spec 7*	*Spec 8*
$lnGDP_{i, t-1}$	−1.15**	0.12
	(0.4894)	(0.17)
$lnGDP_{c, t-1}$	2.58***	1.95***
	(0.2843)	(0.178)
$lnDis_{cit}$	Omitted	−0.13
		(0.35)
$Openness_{i, t-1}$	−0.39	0.87**
	(0.7530)	(0.33)
$ERG_{i, t-1}$	−0.21	0.71
	(1.2044)	(1.18)
$Vol_{i, t-1}$	−12.23**	−14.62***
	(4.8283)	(4.75)
Constant	−33.30	−49.28
No. of observations	180	180
Fixed effect model	Yes	
Random effect model		Yes
Hausman test (HT) (Prob>chi^2)		0.3798

Note: *, ** and *** denote statistical significance at 10%, 5% and 1% respectively

Numbers in parentheses indicate robust standard error

exchange rate volatility will lead to the exacerbation of Chinese outward FDI flows to the host economy. Corresponding with the crucial status of exchange rate volatility raised by Wali and Manzur (2013), the impact of past exchange rate shocks has been paid close attention by Chinese investors. This also explains that China prefers those economies with a stable economy (Amighini and Franco 2013).

11.4.2 Country Dummies

Next, we investigate whether Chinese outward FDI has a specific preference between developed and developing economies. To do this, we introduced the dummy variable representing the level of development of economies in our original model. The dummy variable, *Country dummy*, can be interpreted as 0 = *developing country* and 1 = *developed country*. We use similar specifications as that of Table 11.3, where different sets of variables are used for different specifications in order to avoid the problem of multicollinearity (Table 11.6).

Our variable of interest in this particular context, *Country dummy*, is highly significant in all three specifications. This indicates that Chinese outward FDI tends to prefer developed economies over developing economies as the destination for their investments. Depending upon the specifications, the magnitude varied between 2 and 3. These results give evidence that the nature of the host economy has influence over the decision of Chinese multinationals. The investments being made in the developed economies are, in particular, mergers and acquisitions seeking better technology.

In regard to other independent variables, the results do not vary much from our earlier conclusions that both GDP and openness of host economy continue to be significant, while exchange rate volatility discourages Chinese outward FDI.

11.5 Conclusion

China has been one of the favorite inward FDI destinations for decades. It continues to attract investments from around the world. Nevertheless, the rise of China as the source of FDI, in particular starting from 2005, has been an important shift in this investment environment. As more Chinese companies become engaged in investing abroad, a topic of interest has been what factors influence Chinese investment decisions. Although there

Table 11.6 Results for country dummy

Variables	*Spec 9*	*Spec 10*	*Spec 11*
$lnGDP_{i,t-1}$	0.30	0.18	1.07
	(0.3079)	(0.3823)	(0.6016)
$lnGDP_{c,t-1}$	2.57***	2.32***	2.58***
	(0.3429)	(0.3782)	(0.4080)
$lnGDPPC_{i,t-1}$		−0.21	−1.15
		(0.3848)	(0.5861)
$lnGDPG_{i,t-1}$	−0.06	0.10	0.41
	(0.2485)	(0.2480)	(0.3120)
$lnDis_{cit}$	−0.48**	−0.38	0.21
	(0.2189)	(0.2252)	(0.3068)
$lnEnergy_{i,t-1}$			−0.81***
			(0.2215)
$Openness_{i,t-1}$	1.22***	1.15***	
	(0.1612)	(0.1669)	
$lnMobile\ phone_{i,t-1}$	0.05	0.13	0.03
	(0.3273)	(0.3904)	(0.4035)
$lnInternet\ users_{i,t-1}$	−0.77***		
	(0.2676)		
$lnRoad\ density_{i,t-1}$	−0.40**	−0.45***	−0.75***
	(0.1623)	(0.1630)	(0.2101)
$ERG_{i,t-1}$	4.10	4.40	3.27
	(2.3508)	(2.4456)	(2.8634)
$Vol_{i,t-1}$	−29.07**	−30.14**	−26.45
	(14.2534)	(14.2594)	(17.2335)
$Country\ dummy_{it}$	2.68***	2.18***	3.15***
	(0.5635)	(0.7769)	(0.8210)
Constant	−67.34	−59.31	−75.48
No. of observations	103	104	97
R^2	0.6379	0.6156	0.5993

Note: *, ** and *** denote statistical significance at 10%, 5% and 1% respectively

Numbers in parentheses indicate robust standard error

are some papers that look into the determinants of Chinese outward FDI in general, this chapter in particular looked into the impact of exchange rate fluctuation and exchange rate volatility on the decisions made by Chinese multinationals when making investments abroad. Exchange rate consideration has been one of the important determinants for such decisions. China is practicing 'managed float' exchange rate regime starting in 2005. Although Chinese RMB does not fluctuate like other major currencies, this system has allowed RMB to fluctuate within the managed bandwidth and resulted in appreciation of RMB vis-à-vis USD over the years. Moreover, the chapter also analyzes the preference of Chinese outward FDI for developed markets rather than developing markets.

A panel dataset is established covering Chinese outward FDI in 21 host economies for the period 2004–2013. An augmented gravity model is adopted to analyze the underlying effects of different variables on Chinese outward FDI. OLS is used as a benchmark specification, whereas fixed and REs models are applied to cater to the potential bias and inconsistency in the empirical model.

We found that Chinese outward FDI is typically market-oriented where a large market size of host economy attracts more Chinese investments, consistent with most existing empirical studies. Furthermore, economic openness cannot be neglected as it is able to facilitate Chinese outward FDI when the international trade barriers are reduced. Focusing on the exchange rate fluctuation and exchange rate volatility, a depreciated host economy currency will drive and promote current Chinese outward FDI, while exchange rate volatility has a seriously negative impact on current Chinese outward FDI. We did not find strong evidence that fluctuation in the exchange rate has significant influence over Chinese outward FDI; however, we found strong evidence that exchange rate volatility would deter Chinese outward FDI significantly. With regard to the preference for developed or developing economies, we found that Chinese outward FDI has a tendency of preference toward the developed economies.

In China, outward FDI is also influenced by government decisions since some of the major and large firms are owned by the government. There have been strong encouragements from the government to enhance China's innovative capability by leveraging foreign resources. Chinese firms may benefit from innovation centers and sources of new technology from collaborations with firms in advanced countries. Therefore, the Chinese government has, to a great extent, played a crucial role in shaping the structure of China's outward investment (Deng 2007). In this regard, the government needs to take into consideration the exchange rate effect, in particular, the volatility. China has been, time and again, accused of artificially keeping the value of RMB low for trade benefits. However, from the perspective of the investment, the stronger RMB does exert benefits for Chinese firms. Therefore, the Chinese central bank, People's Bank of China, has a challenging task to keep the proper balance of the RMB exchange rate.

Appendix

Appendix 1: A Brief on Gravity Model

The traditional gravity model equation could be written as follows:

$$Q_{ijk} = \alpha_k X_i^{\beta k} X_j^{\gamma k} Y_j^{\delta} Y_j^{\epsilon} d_{ij}^{\mu} U_{ijk} \dots\dots\dots\dots \quad (11.3)$$

Where Q_{ijk} is the volume of trade of commodity k from country i to j; X_i and X_j are incomes in country i and j, respectively; Y_i and Y_j are population in country i and j, respectively; and d_{ij} is the bilateral distance between these countries i and j and $E(U_{ijk}) = 0$, which means the error term U_{ijk} is followed by a lognormal distribution (Anderson 1979). In addition, Bergstrand (1985) specified that the log linear equation is able to explain the economic flows from origin country i to destination country j based on the traditional gravity model. The use of the gravity model in trade-related studies has been increasingly recognized (Deardorff 1995; Evenett and Keller 2002). In the case of FDI, Buckley et al. (2007) and Cheung and Qian (2009) used the classical gravity model as their benchmark model in their research studies to investigate the underlying determinants of FDI.

As discussed above, it is appropriate to convert the traditional gravity model Eq. (11.3) into the following logarithm form:

$$\ln Q_{ijk} = \alpha + \beta lnx_i + \gamma lnx_j + \delta lny_i + \epsilon lny_j + \mu lnd_{ij} + \varepsilon_{ijk} \dots\dots \quad (11.4)$$

Where the respective coefficients of the variables are represented by β, γ, δ, ϵ and μ. ε_{ijk} is the error term.

Appendix 2: Detailed Description of Variables

The dependent and independent variables are explained as follows:

- $\ln OFDI_{cit}$ is the natural logarithm of outward FDI flow from China to recipient economy i in year t, expressed in current USD (10,000 USD).
- ERG_{it} is the growth in exchange rate of economy i in year t. It is noteworthy that the China practices managed float exchange rate

system (Zhang and Daly 2011). Therefore, host economies' exchange rate fluctuations are calculated by the average of the monthly nominal exchange rate of each host economy against the USD (Takagi and Shi 2011). In this case, the calculation of exchange rate growth is done as follows:

$$\text{Exchange Rate Growth}_t = \frac{\text{Exchange Rate}_t}{\text{Exchange Rate}_{t-1}} - 1.$$

We expect the estimated coefficient of exchange rate growth to be positive; aligning with the theory that Chinese outward FDI flow would rise if the depreciation of host currency occurs. As noted, exchange rates are generated from the distributional properties of the monthly nominal average exchange rate although these variables are annual series in the model.

- Vol_{it} is the exchange rate volatility of host economy i in year t, calculated by the standard deviation of monthly exchange rate (Takagi and Shi 2011). The formula for calculation of volatility is as follows:

$$\text{Volatility} = \sqrt{\frac{1}{n}\sum_{i=1}^{n} \text{v}\ln ER_{t+i}{}^2}$$

which takes the following form in our case:

$$\text{Volatility} = \sqrt{\frac{1}{11}\sum_{i=1}^{10} \left(\ln ER_{t+1} - \ln ER_t\right)^2}.$$

As found in the literature, we expect exchange rate volatility to have a negative effect on FDI.

- $\ln GDP_{it}$ is the natural logarithm of gross domestic product of host economy i in year t, measured in current USD.
- $\ln GDP_{ct}$ is the natural logarithm of gross domestic product of China in year t, measured in current USD.

- $\ln GDPPC_{it}$ is the natural logarithm of gross domestic products per capita of host economy i in year t, measured in current USD.
- $\ln GDPG_{it}$ is the natural logarithm of gross domestic product annual growth rate of host economy i in year t.
- $\ln Dis_{cit}$ is the natural logarithm of the bilateral distance between China and the host economy i. As explained by theory, the distance is expected to have an adverse effect on Chinese outward FDI, because the further the bilateral distance is, the amount of cost associated with management and transports may increase, thus discouraging Chinese outward FDI flows.
- $\ln Energy_{it}$ is the natural logarithm of energy production measured by kiloton. It is the proxy for natural resources seeking investment. We expect this variable to be positive.
- $Openness_{it}$ is the degree of openness of host economy i in year t, which is the ratio of sum value of export and import to GDP.

$$\text{Openness}_{it} = \frac{\text{Export}_{it} + \text{Import}_{it}}{\text{GDP}_{it}}.$$

Theoretically, host openness is positively correlated with Chinese outward FDI.

- $\ln Mobile\ phone_{it}$ is the natural logarithm of the number of mobile phone users of host economy i in year t, belonging to infrastructure aspect and an indicator for technology communication infrastructure.
- $\ln Internet\ users_{it}$ is the natural logarithm of the number of Internet users (per 100 people) of host economy i in year t, belonging to infrastructure aspect and an indicator for technology information infrastructure.
- $\ln Road\ density_{it}$ is the natural logarithm of road density, measured by kilometers of road per square kilometers of land area. It is also one of infrastructure indicators and in particular the transportation aspect.

Appendix 3: Correlation Matrix

	lnOFDI	*lnGDPi*	*lnGDPc*	*lnGDPG*	*lnGDPPC*	*lnEnergy*	*lnMobile*	*lnInternet*	*lnRoad*	*lnDistance*	*lnOpenness*	*ERG*	*Volatility*
lnOFDI	1.0000												
lnGDPi	−0.0027	1.0000											
lnGDPc	0.4588	0.1144	1.0000										
lnGDPG	0.1435	−0.4538	−0.2023	1.0000									
lnGDPPC	0.2292	0.4982	0.1919	−0.4665	1.0000								
lnEnergy	−0.3699	0.5728	0.0134	−0.2680	−0.2147	1.0000							
lnMobile	0.0054	0.7838	0.1791	−0.1839	−0.0585	0.7031	1.0000						
lnInternet	0.2444	0.4081	0.2316	−0.4318	0.9220	−0.2649	−0.0743	1.0000					
lnRoad	0.1631	0.1080	−0.0482	−0.0250	0.4951	−0.5880	−0.1929	0.5239	1.0000				
lnDistance	−0.3758	0.2497	0.0584	−0.3555	0.0628	0.5766	0.1436	−0.1159	−0.3366	1.0000			
lnOpenness	0.4921	−0.5231	0.0035	0.3910	0.1191	−0.9190	−0.5670	0.1569	0.5193	−0.5295	1.0000		
ERG	0.0637	−0.0189	−0.0079	0.0065	−0.2550	0.0138	0.1370	−0.2412	−0.0336	−0.0973	0.0262	1.0000	
Volatility	−0.2027	0.0846	0.2734	−0.3587	0.1293	0.2397	0.0240	0.1153	−0.1897	0.2346	−0.3564	0.1212	1.0000

Note: All variables except ***lnOFDI*** and ***lnDis*** are generated as first-order lagged variables

Notes

1. Refer to Appendix 1 for brief on gravity model.
2. Refer to Appendix 2 for a detailed description of the variables.
3. The number of economies with the data information in the China Statistical Yearbook is 26. However, it should be noted that the Cayman Islands, Virgin Islands (E), Bahamas, Madagascar and Guinea are disregarded in this study, leaving only 21 economies in the sample. There are two main reasons for this. Firstly, Chinese OFI in these economies is not significant in absolute value; their proportion on overall Chinese outward FDI is lower than 0.05%. Secondly, they are omitted owing to the tax haven or tax benefit nature of these economies. Sutherland and Matthews (2009) argued that the motivation for Chinese multinational corporations is to invest capital in these Caribbean tax havens such as the Cayman Islands and Virgin Islands (E) is not only a round-tripping of capital, but also a capital augmentation. Therefore, inclusion of these economies could produce a biased estimation.
4. Refer to Appendix 3 for correlation matrix.

References

Amighini, A. A., and Franco, C. (2013), "A sector perspective on Chinese outward FDI: The automotive case", *China Economic Review*: 27, 148–161.

Anderson, J. (1979), "A theoretical foundation for the gravity equation", *The American Economic Review*: 69(1), 106–116.

Bergstrand, J. H. (1985), "The gravity equation in international trade: some microeconomic foundations and empirical evidence", *The Review of Economics and Statistics*: 67(3), 474–481.

Bole, V. and Rebec, P. (2013), "Bootstrapping the Hausman test in panel data models", *Communications in Statistics-Simulation and Computation*: 42, 650–670.

Buckley, P. J., Clegg, L. J., Cross, A. R., Liu, X., Voss, H., and Zheng, P. (2007), "The determinants of Chinese outward foreign direct investment", *Journal of International Business Studies*: 38, 499–518.

Cheung, Y. W., and Qian, X. W. (2009), "The empirics of China's outward direct investment", *Pacific Economic Review*: 14(3), 312–341.

Deardorff, A. V. (1995), "Determinants of bilateral trade: Does gravity work in a neoclassical world?", NBER Working Paper No. 5377, Cambridge.

Deng, P. (2007), "Investing for strategic resources and its rationale: The case of outward FDI from Chinese companies", *Business Horizons*: 50, 71–81.

Dunning, J. H. (1998), "Location and the multinational enterprise: A neglected factor?", *Journal of International Business Studies*: 29(1), 45–66.

The Economist. (2014), China's outward investment: the second wave. Available at: http://www.economist.com/news/business/21588369-what-make-chinese-firms-latest-foreign-purchases-second-wave

Elsayir, H. A. (2013), "Using PC regression for multicollinear model with lagged variable", *Journal of Statistical and Econometric Methods*: 2(1), 33–41.

Evenett, S. J., and Keller, W. (2002), "On theories explaining the success of the gravity equation", *Journal of Political Economy*: 110(2), 281–316.

Financial Times. (2014), China's outbound investment set to eclipse inbound for first time. Available at: http://www.ft.com/intl/cms/s/0/28f6b8d4-59cd-11e4-9787-00144feab7de.html?siteedition=intl#axzz3K2lqy9Mo

Kahouli, B. and Maktouf, S. (2015), "The determinants of FDI and the impact of the economic crisis on the implementation of RTAs: A static and dynamic gravity model", *International Business Review*: 24, 3, 518–529.

Kiyota, K. and Urata, S. (2004), "Exchange rate, exchange rate volatility and foreign direct investment", *The World Economy*: 27, 1501–1536.

Kiyota, K. and Urata, S. (2008), "Exchange rate volatility and MNC's production and distribution networks: the case of Japanese manufacturing MNCs", *Singapore Economic Review*: 53(3), 523–538.

Kolstad, I., and Wiig, A. (2012), "What determines Chinese outward FDI?", *Journal of World Business*: 47, 26–34.

Lin, C. C., Chen, K. M. and Rau, H. H. (2010), "Exchange rate volatility and the timing of foreign direct investment: market-seeking versus export-substituting", *Review of Development Economics*: 14(3), 466–486.

MacDermott, R. (2008), "Linking exchange rates to foreign direct investment", *The International Trade Journal:* 22(1), 3–16.

Manop, U., Oliver, M. and Holger, G. (2009), "Exchange rates and outward foreign direct investment: US FDI in emerging economies", *Review of Development Economics*: 13(4), 754–764.

Morrison, W. M. and Labonte, M. (2013), "China's Currency Policy: An Analysis of the Economic Issues", RS21625, Congressional Research Service, CRS Report for Congress, Available at: www.crs.gov

Ramasamy, B., Yeung, M. and Laforet, S. (2012), "China's outward foreign direct investment: location choice and firm ownership", *Journal of World Business*: 47, 17–25.

Sutherland, D and Matthews, B. (2009), "'Round tripping' or 'Capital augmenting' OFDI? Chinese outward investment and the Caribbean tax havens", Paper prepared for Leverhulme Centre for Research on Globalisation and Economic Policy (GEP). University of Nottingham.

Takagi, S. J. and Shi, Z. Y. (2011), "Exchange rate movements and foreign direct investment (FDI): Japanese investment in Asia, 1987–2008", *Japan and the World Economy*: 23, 265–272.

Wali, M. and Manzur, M. (2013), "Exchange rate volatility before and after the float", *The World Economy*: 36, 8, 1091–1097.

Wei, Y. Q., Zheng, N., Liu, X. H. and Lu, J. Y. (2014), "Expanding to outward foreign direct investment or not? A multi-dimensional analysis of entry mode transformation of Chinese private exporting firms", *International Business Review*: 23, 356–370.

Zhang, X. X. and Daly, K. (2011), "The determinants of China's outward foreign direct investment", *Emerging Markets Review*: 12, 389–398.

PART VI

Corporate Finance

CHAPTER 12

Corporate Marginal Tax Rate Estimation: Evidence Based on China's Listed Companies

Jin Nong and Yang Chen

12.1 Introduction

To understand the tax effect on corporation financial decision making, financial economists usually use corporate marginal tax rate as the main proxy. As defined by Graham (1996a and 1996b), the marginal tax rate is the present value of current and expected future taxes paid on an additional dollar of income earned today. In other words, it measures the marginal effect of the current tax rate on one extra dollar earned. There are several reasons to explain why researchers have great interest in this particular tax proxy. First, the corporate marginal tax rate is an important instrument when considering the company's capital structure, debt policy, and tax strategy (Graham 2000). It is likewise a measurement of investment behavior which is a determinant of the capital location decision (Devereux and Griffith 2003). More importantly, it reflects the differences in the tax burden of companies among various industries, periods, and scales (Wang 2003), giving the policymakers a reference tool on designing and improving their national tax scheme. However, obtaining the accurate corporate marginal tax rate is not straightforward. What makes the estimation

J. Nong • Y. Chen (✉)
International Business School Suzhou, Xi'an Jiaotong-Liverpool University, Suzhou, China
e-mail: yang.chen@xjtlu.edu.cn

J. H. Hung, Y. Chen (eds.), *The State of China's State Capitalism*,
https://doi.org/10.1007/978-981-13-0983-0_12

difficult is the dynamic effect of net operating loss (NOL). A NOL is a loss taken in a period where a company incurs more expense than revenue. When there is a NOL, the company can apply this tax relief in two ways: it can either apply the NOL to its past tax payments and receive a tax refund which is tax carry backward; or it can defer the NOL to its future taxable income to reduce the tax payments in later periods, in other words, tax carry forward. Since the tax carry forward or tax carry backward has a crucial intertemporal effect on a company's taxable income, the process of calculating marginal tax rate should be well-designed and the effect of changes in tax liabilities should be carefully considered.

The Chinese economy is currently undergoing a massive transformation, within which the tax reform with an intention to reduce enterprises' financial burden plays an important role in promoting production efficiency. This phenomenon has been termed as "tax competition" and has been studied widely by Ramb (2007), Devereux et al. (2002), and Devereux et al. (2008). Since 2000, China's authority has published a series of tax regulations to simplify China's tax regime (Shi 2015). In 2002, the State Council banned unauthorized corporate tax rebate from the local government. In 2007, the top statutory corporate tax rate was lowered from 33% to 25%, and the dual tax rate system in which foreign firms had a lower tax rate (30%) than domestic ones (33%) was abandoned (An 2012). From 2007 onwards, to increase the domestic companies' competitiveness, both foreign and domestic enterprises complied with the same reduced corporate tax rate (25%) thereafter. The previous studies on China's corporate marginal tax rate were more concerned about capital structure and debt policy, though few explore the effects of tax reform on the marginal tax rate. Thus, in this chapter, we are interested to answer two main questions: (1) what are the distribution and trend of China's listed companies' corporate marginal tax rate before and after the tax reform; and (2) how the marginal tax rate varies across ownership and industry?

Many researchers sought to improve the process of the marginal tax rate estimation. Shevlin (1990) was the first who examined the marginal tax rate estimation and illustrated the impact of different tax proxies on the measurement of the marginal tax rate of a firm. Based on Shevlin's paper, Graham (1996a, b) developed a simulated tax proxy based on the mean and standard deviation of change in observed taxable income for a firm which incorporated the dynamic effect of NOL. This is widely known as the Random Walk (RW) model and has been adopted in many tax studies. However, there are certain potential problems in Graham's method. For example, when it comes to extremely negative or positive taxable income, the RW model might not be able to revise the forecasted future taxable income back to its "normal" level. As a result, the forecasted taxable income might be biased upward or downward which is not consistent with the actual future taxable income.

To solve these problems and provide a more reliable method to forecast future taxable income, Blouin et al. (2008) explored a non-parametric method. Unlike the RW model whose forecasted taxable income relied on the actual income in the last period, Blouin et al. (2008)'s method followed Barber and Lyon (1996), claiming that it was reasonable to assume that future expected profitability was similar to the mean performance of firms with similar profitability. Hence, they matched firms to subsample bins based on two characteristics of the firm: size and profitability. In other words, if a company was large and earned high profit at current period, it was very likely that it would grow at a rate that was quite similar to other companies which were both large and profitable. The empirical results proved their method effectively avoided the limitations of the RW model as the distribution of the forecasted future income generated by the non-parametric method matched the actual taxable income. We thus follow Blouin et al. (2008)'s method to estimate corporate marginal tax rate for listed firms in China.

In the next section, we review the relevant literature. In Sect. 12.3, we explain our empirical strategy to estimate corporate marginal tax rate. In the results section, we analyze how corporate marginal tax rate differs by industry and by firm ownership. We then conclude in the last section.

12.2 Literature Review

There are two methods to estimate marginal tax rates—the static and the dynamic method. The main difference lies in how NOL are treated in the estimation. The static method uses taxable income and NOL as indicator variables to estimate marginal tax rates. Thomas (1988), Scholes et al. (1990), Graham (1996a, b), and Plesko (2003) used this approach. In their work, the marginal tax rate could be equal to the statutory rate with positive taxable income without NOL, or equal to half of the statutory rate if a company has either negative taxable income or a NOL carry forward, and equal to zero in other cases (Shevlin 1990; Graham 1996a, b; Plesko 2003). The principle of using such a uniform statutory method is that marginal tax rate can be mapped into evenly spaced incremental four segments between zero and the statutory rate (Plesko 2003; Graham and Mills 2008).

However, the tax code allowed losses in period t to be used as a tax shield to offset taxable income in both previous and future periods and this led to an intertemporal dynamic effect on taxable income which was captured by Shevlin (1990). The estimation used company's financial statements to infer taxable income and simulated a series of future taxable incomes assuming that taxable income followed a RW with drift. The state-of-the-art method developed by Graham's (1996a, b) came from the idea of Shevlin (1990). The main model identified that the firm i's taxable income followed a RW with drift process (Graham and Kim 2009):

$$TI_{t+1} = \mu_i + TI_t + \varepsilon_{t+1},\ \varepsilon_{t+1} \sim i.i.d.N\left(0, \sigma i\right), \tag{12.1}$$

where TI_{t+1} was the taxable income of firm i in time t, and μ_i and ε_{t+1} were company-specific estimates of the mean and standard deviation of changes in taxable income. The simulation was designed to construct a series of taxable incomes over the sample period. The change of taxable income was assumed to have a stationery average trend. This easy-to-implement method has been adopted by many researchers for years, and the superiority of the RW simulation approach has been documented in existing studies (e.g., Graham 1996a, b; Pattenden 2002; Plesko 2003; Graham and Mills 2008).

Nevertheless, Graham's (1996a, b) RW model has several potential drawbacks that might cause biases, leading to inaccuracy of the estimation. First, the mean reversion may not be present in the RW model. The condition in which taxable income is extremely high or low has not been incorporated (Blouin et al. 2008). Thus, it is expected that the level of future taxable income in the RW simulation will be too high for firms with large positive shocks to income and too low for firms with large negative shocks to its income. Second, the drift parameter (μ_i) is estimated by historical data, so profitable (loss) firms often have positive (zero) drift estimates. This might lead to upward (downward) biases in future expected taxable income. Therefore, Graham and Kim (2009) claimed that the desirable method to estimate marginal tax rate should incorporate mean reversion, firm's information under different economic conditions, and scaled income rather than dollar-level income.

In order to capture the mean reversion effect and avoid the problems of introducing new parameters into the autoregressive process, Blouin et al. (2008) developed a simulation procedure called "non-parametric" bin model to forecast future taxable income. Departing from the original autoregressive form, it forecasted taxable income by estimating the probability in scaled income using return on asset (ROA) and firm-size using total assets based on the empirical distribution of changes for firms with similar scaled income and size (Graham and Kim 2009). This method effectively reduced biases generated from abnormal level of past performance. To test the validity of their method, they simulated the distribution of future taxable income and examined how much proportion of the actual taxable income fell in the 90% range between the 5th and 95th percentiles of the simulated distribution. The bin's result showed that the actual taxable income fell in the effective range 87% of the time while in RW distribution, actual taxable income fell into the range 63% of the time (Blouin et al. 2008). That is to say, the bin method effectively improved the accuracy of marginal tax rate estimations.

The simulated marginal tax rates can be applied widely. For example, Graham (1996a, b) provided evidence that tax rebate on debt could add to firms' value. There was also evidence suggesting that the higher the tax burden of the firm, the higher leverage it would adopt. In terms of tax shield effect, Graham (2005) claimed that non-debt tax shield was likely to have a significant impact on those modestly profitable firms. Padovano and Galli (2002) documented that marginal tax rate served as a better macro variable in studying the link between tax and economic growth compared with the average tax rate. Sinha and Bansal (2012) used Monte Carlo to simulate marginal tax rate of Indian companies to develop algorithms based on Graham (1996a, b)'s method. Their algorithms were helpful in facilitating our understanding on how and why the Graham method differs from Blouin's method. The simulated marginal tax rate may be used to analyze the corporation investment decisions as well. Ramb (2007) applied the RW model to investigate the relationship between the investment behavior of firms and marginal tax rates of Germany. The results indicated that the long-run elasticity of the marginal tax rate to investment activity was between 0.1 and 0.2. Using Portuguese data, Bartholdy and Mateus (2011) analyzed the influence of marginal tax rates on the capital structure decision of private bank-financed firms. They found that the marginal tax rate had an important impact on smaller private firms' capital structure due to asymmetric information.

In China, researchers estimate corporate marginal tax rate primarily to discuss companies' debt versus equity financing issues. Gu (2005) discussed the influence of employees' stock option incentive system on the corporate marginal tax rate, and debt scheme. Chan et al. (2013) pointed out that non-state-owned firms tended to use a more aggressive tax strategy than state-owned firms. However, a few papers analyzed the tax reform effect on the change of marginal tax rate. We will fill the gap by introducing the policy effect and also compare the marginal tax rate distribution across industry and ownership.

12.3 Methodology

Through comparison of the RW model and the non-parametric bin method, we find that using the latter approach can obtain more reliable and more accurate results. We thus adopt the bin method to compute 1041 China's listed companies' marginal tax rate during the period of 2004–2014. In the later sub-section, we introduce the details of the bin method and its implementation process. We also adjust the bin method in accordance with China's tax regime, where the changes in statutory tax rate and preferential policies to different types of firms are carefully considered. After computing the marginal tax rate, we compare the marginal tax rate before and after 2007 to identify the impact of tax reform.

12.3.1 The Bin Method

The initial idea of the bin method came from a matching method of predicting expected future performance for a given firm, which was originally developed by Barber and Lyon (1996). Their research indicated when measuring the firm's future performance the best way is to match the firm to the firms with similar past performance in the full sample. Blouin et al. (2008) claimed that it seemed reasonable to think those firms with similar performance and size tended to have similar distribution of their future performance as well. Given this assumption, Blouin et al. (2008) pointed out the future taxable income in $t + 1$ (TI_{t+1}) could be the product of company *i*'s expected total assets in year t (TAt) and the expected taxable return on those assets in year $t + 1$ (ROA_{t+1}). Hence, they estimated both TA_t and ROA_{t+1} to predict the taxable income in t + 1 (TI_{t+1}). To implement the bin method, there are several steps to follow:

1. Bins' allocation:

The first step is to allocate the firm into its particular "bin", which is characterized by size and profitability. Separate all the firms in the sample at time t – 1 into 6 income groups. Two are loss groups and four are profitable groups. The first ranking variable we use to group the firm is year t – 1's return on assets where $ROA_{t-1} = TI_{t-1}/TA_{t-2}$. Within each income group, use the second ranking variable asset size at the beginning of time t – 1 (TA_{t-2}) to divide firms into 5 bins. At the end of this stage, there are totally 30 bins with equal observations. After grouping, we collect data of the current year's ROA_t and calculate the total asset growth AG_t (TA_t/TA_{t-1}) to ensure that the bins could have similar distribution in terms of future performance and size (Blouin et al. 2009).

2. Matching:

The second step is to simulate future taxable income (TI_{t+n}). Since we have already formed the bins every year in the first step, we can easily match the firm to its most recent cross-section bins. Based on firm's current year ROA and beginning-of-year total asset (i.e., ROA_t and TA_{t-1}), we match firm *i* at time t into its performance-size bin. After matching the firm to its particular bin, we randomly select a firm *f* from this specific bin and use firm *f*'s ROA_t (i.e., TI_t/TA_{t-1}) and asset growth $AG_{t-1}(TA_{t-1}/TA_{t-2})$ as the forecasts of firm *i*'s ROA_{t+1} and asset growth AG_t (TA_t/TA_{t-1}). After that, multiply TA_{t-1} to the forecasted one-year-ahead asset growth (AG_t) to have TA_t. Similarly, TI_{t+1} is obtained by multiplying the beginning total assets TA_t to forecasted ROA_{t+1}. To forecast TI_{t+2}, just re-match the firm *i* into its performance-size bin based on its forecasted ROA_{t+1} and forecasted TA_t then repeat the procedure. The relationship of these accounting variables is summarized as:

$$ROA_{i,t+1,predicted} = ROA_{f,t} = TI_{f,t} / TA_{f,t-1} \quad (12.2)$$

$$TA_{i,t,predicted} = TA_{i,t-1,actual} \times AG_{f,t-1} \quad (12.3)$$

$$TI_{i,t+1} = ROA_{i,t+1,predicted} \times TA_{i,t,predicted}. \quad (12.4)$$

Calculate Marginal Tax Rate

The third step is to calculate the marginal tax rate taking the change of China's tax code into consideration. Note that firm *i*'s marginal tax rate at t = 0 is defined as the present value of taxes paid on an extra yuan gained in the same period. We first compute tax liabilities (TL_t), then add 1 RMB to taxable income at t = 0 to re-compute each period's tax liabilities (ETL_t). The present value of the tax liabilities (TL_t) for each series is discounted at the benchmark loan rate. Finally, we divide the incremental tax liabilities ($\Delta TL_t = TL_t - ETL_t$) by the discount rate r in each year to get $MTR_t = \Delta TL_t + \frac{\Delta TL_{t+1}}{(1+r)} + \frac{\Delta TL_{t+2}}{(1+r)^2} + \ldots + \frac{\Delta TL_{t+5}}{(1+r)^5}$. If the firm earns a positive income this year, its tax liabilities equal to TL_t (TL_t= taxable income× tax rate); whereas if the firm earns a negative income this year, TL_t is zero and the net operating loss can be carried forward to offset the next period's tax liabilities.

The final step is to repeat this simulation procedure 50 times and average across these estimations to obtain each firm's expected marginal tax rate. Note that only if the distribution of ROA and asset size is stationary over time, the bin method could yield a reasonable result in which the distribution of the simulated data approximately matches the distribution of the actual data (Blouin et al. 2008). To ensure the distribution of current period performance and size is stationary over the simulation horizon, we need to hold the original 30 bins constant throughout the whole process of estimation.

12.3.2 Model Adjustment

Because China's tax environment is quite different from that of the United States, two particular rules need to be carefully considered in this model. First, under the US tax rules, the NOL can be carried back to claim a tax refund or carried forward to offset the future income for up to 20 years. According to China's tax regulations, tax carry backward is not allowed and the loss can only be carried forward to maximum of 5 years. Thus, the number of years required to be included in the computation is at most 5 years ($t + 1, t + 2 \ldots t + 5$). In addition, tax reform happened during the sample period so it is necessary to assign the correct statutory tax rate to each accounting period. Precisely, before 2007, we use 33% top statutory tax rate for domestic enterprises and 30% for foreign enterprises; after

Table 12.1 A brief summary of tax reform in China's corporate statutory tax rate

Before 2007	Domestic enterprises (DEs): 33% Foreign enterprises (FIEs): 30%
After 2007	Both kinds of enterprises enjoy the same rate: 25%

2007, we use 25% for both kinds of enterprises. Note that some economic regions and innovation companies might enjoy a preferential rate, so the tax rate will be even less than 25% (Huang and Song 2006), for which their tax rates should be more carefully matched. Table 12.1 illustrates the changes in the statutory tax rate in 2007 tax reform.

12.4 Data Description and Choice of Variables

Before we actually start the simulation process, we need to obtain the taxable income at the current period. However, the taxable income and NOL are not disclosed to the public in China. Hence, the taxable income used in this research has to be the mimic taxable income, which is derived from financial statements. As suggested in Graham (1996a, b), the taxable income is defined as the pre-tax accounting book income adjusted for deferred tax.

1. Taxable Income (TI) = Pre-tax Income – (Deferred Tax Expense/ Statutory Tax Rate)
2. Deferred Tax Expense (DTE) = Δ Deferred Tax Liabilities – Δ Deferred Tax Assets

In Eq. (12.1), the mimic taxable income is equal to the pre-tax income minus the ratio of deferred tax expense over statutory tax rate. Pre-tax income is the total profit recorded in the income sheet. In Eq. (12.2), deferred tax expense represents the changes in deferred tax liabilities and changes in deferred tax assets. The purpose of this adjustment is to eliminate the effects of using different accounting methods.

With the information for taxable income, we can derive the ROA. Following Blouin et al. (2008)'s bin method, ROA_t is defined as

$$ROA_t = TI_t / TA_{t-1} \tag{12.5}$$

12.4.1 Data Selection

There are five variables collected from CSMAR. They are the pre-tax income, deferred tax liabilities, deferred tax asset, and total asset. Table 12.2 lists the sources of suggested variables. Table 12.3 shows the descriptive statistics of the suggested variables for later analysis.

Table 12.2 Variable definitions

Variable name	*CSMAR variable name*	*CSMAR data code*
Pre-tax income	*Total profit from income statement*	CSMAR data B001000000
Deferred tax liabilities	*Deferred tax liabilities in balance sheet*	CSMAR data A002208000
Deferred tax asset	*Deferred tax asset in balance sheet*	CSMAR data A001222000
Total asset	*Total asset in balance sheet*	CSMAR data A001000000

Table 12.3 Summary statistics of key variables

Variable	*Obs*	*Mean*	*Std. dev.*	*Min*	*Max*
Deferred tax assets	11,451	10,400,000	126,000,000	−1,920,000,000	4,850,000,000
Deferred tax liabilities	11,451	5,788,640	98,400,000	−1,560,000,000	3,890,000,000
Deferred tax expenses	11,451	−4,419,874	142,000,000	−4,590,000,000	1,920,000,000
Pre-tax income	11,451	359,000,000	1,900,000,000	−14,000,000,000	62,000,000,000
Taxable income	11,451	376,000,000	2,200,000,000	−14,100,000,000	68,800,000,000
Total asset	11,451	10,400,000,000	98,700,000,000	0	4,200,000,000,000

Notes: Results are based on authors' calculations

12.4.2 Sample Selection

Following Blouin et al.'s instructions, we need to exclude banks and insurance companies since concepts of leverage for these financial institutions are different. One reason is that their debt-to-equity ratios are usually

Table 12.4 Sample classification by industry

Industry	*No. of companies*	*Proportion*
A. Agriculture/fishing/forestry	14	0.01
B. Mining	34	0.03
C. Manufacturing	557	0.54
D. Utilities/energy	64	0.06
E. Architectural services/construction	19	0.02
F. Wholesale/retail	128	0.12
G. Transportation/logistic/distribution	50	0.05
H. Accommodation/ restaurant and food services	10	0.01
I. Telecom operators/service providers	17	0.02
J. Real estate	118	0.11
K. Leasing and business services	14	0.01
L. Cultural sports and entertainment	15	0.01
M. Education	1	0.00
Total	1041	1.00

Table 12.5 Sample classification by ownership

Types of company	*[1] SOEs*	*[2] Non-SOEs*	*[3] FIEs*	*Total*
No. of companies	669	334	38	1041

Notes:

[1] State-owned enterprises, state-run enterprises, and institutional organization

[2] Non-SOEs: including private enterprises and collectively owned enterprises

[3] Foreign enterprises and joint ventures

quite high. Besides, data required for computing future taxable income (e.g., deferred taxes) is frequently missing for these firms. Therefore, only firms with complete data from 2004 to 2014 (11 years) from the CSMAR Database are used. We have a full sample with a size of 11,451 observations, that is, a total of 1041 firms in the sample period.

Recall that one aim of this research is to discuss the relationship between corporate marginal tax rates and companies' characteristics (ownership, industry). Hence, we also collect company-level information such as stock code, ownership, industry, and registered capital. For consistency, they are matched into the full sample using data collected from Wind Financial Database for further analysis.

According to China's industry classification standards published by the National Bureau of Statistics of the People's Republic of China (GB/T 4754-2011), companies in the sample can be divided into 13 industries. Table 12.4 shows the industry code and the number of companies in each industry. As illustrated in the table, more than half of listed companies are in the manufacturing industry.

In terms of types of business, we classify companies into three different kinds of ownership: state-owned or state-controlled enterprises (SOEs), foreign enterprises (FIEs), other domestic enterprises (non-SOEs), and foreign-invested enterprises (FIEs). Table 12.5 shows the number of firms in each type of business. SOEs form the majority in the sample (669), non-SOEs comprise 1/3 of the proportion, while the FIEs are the least (38).

12.5 Main Results

The marginal tax rate analysis begins with the descriptive statistics of the annual marginal tax rate estimations and is followed by industrial and ownership analyses and comparisons. We provide estimations to enable comparisons across periods, industries, and ownership. In particular, we focus on the deviations of the mean to see how marginal tax rate changes before and after the 2007 tax reform.

Table 12.6 lists descriptive statistics for all the annual marginal tax rates from 2004 to 2014 which includes the mean, median, standard deviation, skewness, and kurtosis. The minimum and maximum are ignored because

Table 12.6 Descriptive statistics of the annual Marginal Tax Rates (MTRs)

Year	*Observations*	*Mean*	*Std. dev.*	*Skewness*	*Kurtosis*
2004	1041	0.27	0.10	−1.34	3.38
2005	1041	0.24	0.11	−0.84	2.19
2006	1041	0.25	0.10	−0.88	2.27
2007	1041	0.19	0.08	−0.83	2.17
2008	1041	0.19	0.08	−0.93	2.35
2009	1041	0.20	0.07	−1.38	3.72
2010	1041	0.20	0.08	−1.13	2.77
2011	1041	0.20	0.08	−1.31	3.20
2012	1041	0.20	0.08	−1.24	3.00
2013	1041	0.20	0.08	−1.24	2.96
2014	1041	0.19	0.09	−1.02	2.37
Average	–	0.21	0.09	−1.1	2.76

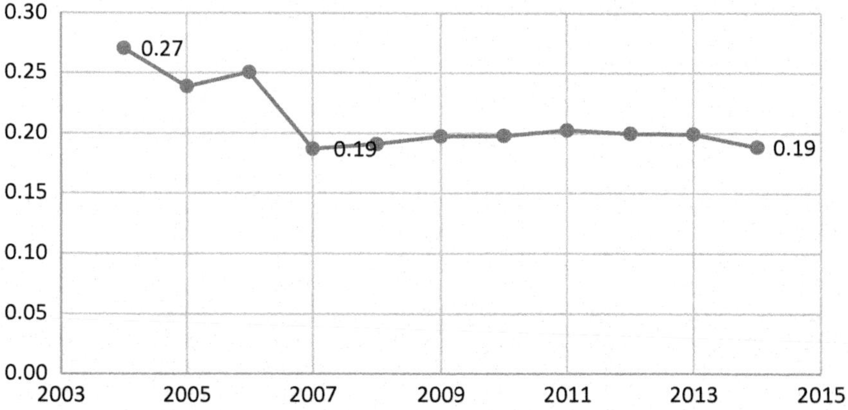

Fig. 12.1 Trend of annual mean of MTRs

they are 0 and 0.33 for all the estimations. The average marginal tax rate drops from 0.27 in 2004 to 0.19 in 2014, with a rate of decline by 29.6%. Moreover, the average annual marginal tax rate also decreases from 0.25 in Period 1 (2004–2006) to 0.20 in Period 2 (2007–2014). The standard deviation of the annual marginal tax rate is relatively small (0.09), which means on average they do not deviate much from 0.21 every year. The average skewness and kurtosis suggest the spread of values are clustering around the mean, which in turn suggests the mean of the annual marginal tax rate can be used to represent one year's marginal tax rate.

Figure 12.1 demonstrates the changing tendency of the mean marginal tax rate from 2004 to 2014. The vertical axis represents the annual marginal tax rate, while the horizontal axis represents the year. Before 2007, the changes in marginal tax rate are relatively large, which drop from 0.25 to 0.19. After 2007, the fluctuations of the marginal tax rate become smaller. From the starting point to the end of the sample period, the mean of marginal tax rate decreases by 0.08.

Table 12.7 presents the proportion of companies in each range of marginal tax rate. The majority of marginal tax rates are in the range of the highest annual statutory tax rate, that is, 30–33% before 2007 and 25% after 2007. Other ranges share a quite similar proportion, usually less than 15% of the entire sample.

Figure 12.2 provides the visualized distribution. As shown in the figure, the proportion of highest statutory tax rate range (33–33% before

Table 12.7 The distribution of annual MTRs in each range

Year	*Relative frequency (%)*						
	0–5%	*5–10%*	*10–15%*	*15–20%*	*20–25%*	*25–30%*	*30–33%*
2004	4.46	5.00	7.20	8.60	4.70	4.60	65.43
2005	4.00	5.00	7.20	10	4.10	4.60	65.03
2006	5.63	7.69	10.30	10.1	6.00	4.23	56.10
2007	9.40	11.53	11.72	8.26	2.02	57.00	N/A
2008	8.74	10.76	11.24	7.68	2.40	59.17	N/A
2009	6.72	6.72	7.88	11.62	37.66	29.39	N/A
2010	7.11	9.89	9.70	7.49	2.31	63.50	N/A
2011	7.49	8.45	8.45	5.38	1.44	68.78	N/A
2012	8.36	8.74	8.74	5.28	1.06	67.82	N/A
2013	9.61	7.88	9.99	2.59	0.86	69.07	N/A
2014	14.22	8.17	8.45	2.98	0.58	65.61	N/A

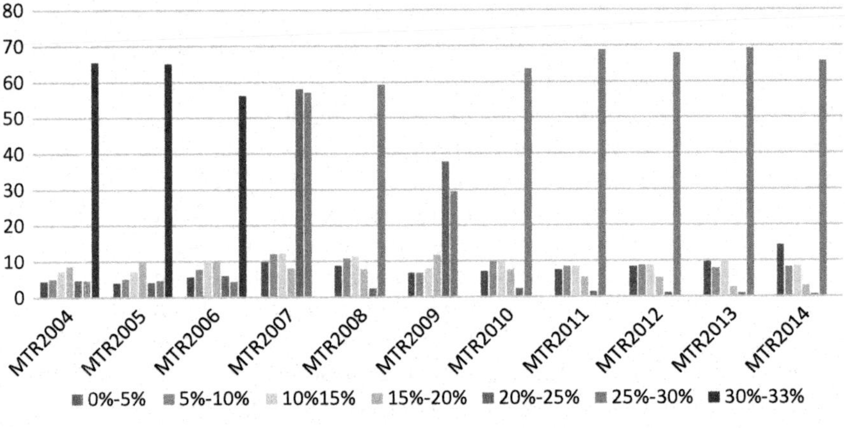

Fig. 12.2 Frequency table for annual MTRs (%)

2007, 25–30% after 2007) is significantly greater than others. Note that starting from 2007 the income tax rate is reduced from 0.33/0.3 to 0.25, thus, the information of the last column in Table 12.7 after 2007 is not applicable.

We now compare the weighted mean of marginal tax rates across three different ownership to show the changes in marginal tax rates.

In Table 12.8, the weighted mean of marginal tax rate for three kinds of ownership are all above 0.2 throughout the sample periods, where non-

Table 12.8 The weighted MTRs by ownership

Types of business	*[1] SOEs*	*[2] Others*	*[3] FIEs*
2004	0.27	0.29	0.21
2005	0.23	0.26	0.22
2006	0.24	0.27	0.23
2007	0.19	0.20	0.18
2008	0.19	0.20	0.16
2009	0.20	0.21	0.19
2010	0.19	0.21	0.18
2011	0.20	0.22	0.19
2012	0.20	0.22	0.21
2013	0.21	0.22	0.20
2014	0.21	0.19	0.21
Std. dev.	0.03	0.03	0.02
Average	0.21	0.23	0.20
Mean before 2007	0.25	0.27	0.22
Mean after 2007	0.20	0.21	0.19
△ in mean	−0.05	−0.06	−0.03

Notes:

[1] The mean is weighted by the registered capital

[2] △ in mean: changes in the weighted mean before and after 2007

SOEs has the highest marginal tax (0.23), followed by SOEs (0.21) and FIEs (0.20). In addition, the mean for each ownership before 2007 is much higher than the mean after 2007. Looking at the changes in mean, the table suggests although non-SOEs has the highest marginal tax rate in both periods, it enjoys the greatest tax reductions (6%) than other two kinds of business.

As shown in the Fig. 12.3, we found that the trend of the weighted mean of these three different kinds of ownership is quite similar as all three show a declining trend. The movements of SOEs and non-SOEs are relatively small. This is especially so after 2007 when the changes in marginal tax rate for both are smaller and both look like constant lines slightly above 0.20. However, the line for FIEs shows a different trend. It starts with the lowest rate of marginal tax in 2004 but ends up at the same level with the other two kinds of ownership in 2014. Unlike SOEs and non-SOEs, which the lowest point of marginal tax rate was achieved in 2007, the lowest point of FIE's marginal tax rate was achieved one year after 2007. One possible reason to explain this difference is the 2008 financial crisis. However, surprisingly, just after 2008, FIEs' marginal tax rate starts to increase again until 2014.

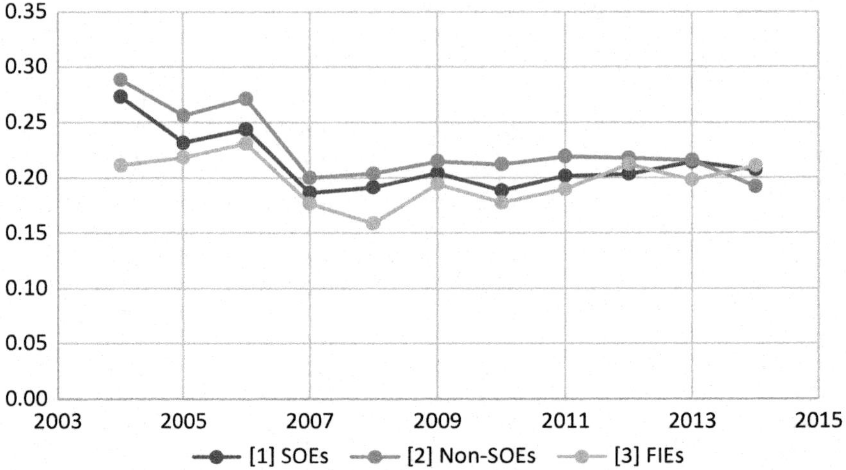

Fig. 12.3 The trend of weighted mean for each kind of ownership

Table 12.9 presents a similar image as Table 12.6. Again, most marginal tax rates are clustering around the range of its highest annual statutory tax rate, which is 30%–33% before 2007 and 25% after 2007. This is especially so for SOEs. Then non-SOEs' average MTRs come in the second place followed by the FIEs. The distribution of other ranges is usually less than 20% of the entire sample. After 2007 the authority has reduced the income tax rate from 0.33/0.3 to 0.25 for all three kinds of ownership, thus, the last range of frequency is not available (N/A).

We now focus on the movements of the annual weighted mean of marginal tax rate for all industries. Note that there is only 1 company in the Education industry (M). Thus, the weighted mean of the education industry is the same as its ordinary arithmetic mean, which suggests that this number could be biased, and it might not be able to be representative of the entire educational industry. Therefore, in the later analysis, we exclude this particular industry and try to give a more general explanation for the overall results.

Architectural Services/Construction and Cultural sports and entertainment share the highest weighted average marginal tax rate (0.24) while Mining has the lowest (0.15) throughout the entire sample period. Before 2007, the top 3 industries with the highest weighted average marginal tax

Table 12.9 The distribution of companies' annual MTRs in each range by ownership

Year	*Ownership*	*Relative frequency (%)*						
		0–5%	*5–10%*	*10–15%*	*15–20%*	*20–25%*	*25–30%*	*30–33%*
2004	[1]	4.33	4.33	5.83	7.77	4.78	2.69	71.75
	[2]	6.90	5.75	10.34	11.21	4.02	1.72	60.06
	[3]	5.26	2.63	7.89	10.53	2.63	5.26	65.79
2005	[1]	8.07	7.32	9.42	7.92	3.29	0.90	65.62
	[2]	11.49	10.92	10.63	10.92	4.02	12.07	39.94
	[3]	7.89	7.89	10.53	13.16	5.26	0.00	52.63
2006	[1]	5.23	7.32	9.42	9.87	6.28	2.54	60.00
	[2]	6.90	9.77	12.36	14.37	5.46	2.30	48.85
	[3]	2.63	7.89	13.16	15.79	5.26	2.63	50.00
2007	[1]	8.52	11.21	11.06	9.57	1.79	57.85	N/A
	[2]	11.08	15.57	14.97	11.68	2.69	44.01	N/A
	[3]	13.16	10.53	23.68	2.63	2.63	47.37	N/A
2008	[1]	9.42	8.82	11.06	6.88	2.69	61.14	N/A
	[2]	11.68	12.87	11.98	11.38	2.10	50.00	N/A
	[3]	10.53	10.53	23.68	7.89	5.26	42.11	N/A
2009	[1]	6.43	6.88	7.77	10.91	35.43	32.59	N/A
	[2]	6.89	5.69	11.38	15.87	38.92	20.66	N/A
	[3]	7.89	7.89	15.79	15.79	21.05	31.58	N/A
2010	[1]	7.92	8.37	8.52	7.77	1.79	65.62	N/A
	[2]	12.28	11.98	11.68	8.98	1.80	53.29	N/A
	[3]	2.63	13.16	18.42	13.16	2.63	50.00	N/A
2011	[1]	7.62	8.07	8.67	5.23	1.64	68.76	N/A
	[2]	8.68	10.48	13.17	6.29	2.40	58.98	N/A
	[3]	2.63	10.53	10.53	10.53	2.63	63.16	N/A
2012	[1]	8.67	8.52	7.47	5.08	1.35	68.91	N/A
	[2]	8.68	10.48	11.68	4.79	2.10	62.28	N/A
	[3]	0.00	7.89	10.53	7.89	2.63	71.05	N/A
2013	[1]	10.16	7.32	8.67	2.09	0.60	71.15	N/A
	[2]	9.88	10.18	11.08	2.99	0.60	65.27	N/A
	[3]	5.26	2.63	10.53	7.89	2.63	71.05	N/A
2014	[1]	14.05	8.37	8.07	2.39	0.60	66.52	N/A
	[2]	13.77	10.48	10.18	3.89	0.30	61.38	N/A
	[3]	5.26	10.53	2.63	2.63	0.00	78.95	N/A

Notes:

[1] State-own enterprises, state-run enterprises, and institutional organization

[2] Non-SOEs: including private enterprises and collectively run enterprises

[3] Foreign invest enterprises and joint venture

rate were Architectural Services/Construction, Transportation/Logistic/Distribution and Cultural Sports and Entertainment. However, after 2007, Cultural Sports and Entertainment came in top. The reason why the marginal tax rate of Architectural Services/Construction and Cultural Sports and Entertainment became so high might be because of its relatively small sample size. Comparing the weighted mean before and after 2007, we found that all industries enjoy a tax reduction by more than 3%. In particular, Transportation/Logistic/Distribution, Accommodation/Restaurant & Food Services and Telecom Operators/Service Providers decreased by 8% while the Utilities/Energy was the least affected decreasing only by 3%. Note that the marginal tax rate in the real estate industry also decreased at a comparatively high rate and after 2007, its average marginal tax rate is just 0.20. This lower marginal tax rate might partly explain why investment on real estate is so popular in China. From Fig. 12.4, we show that there is an overall downward trend of in the marginal tax rate. Although the overall declining trend is similar across industries, each industry has unique movement characteristics after the tax reform (Table 12.10).

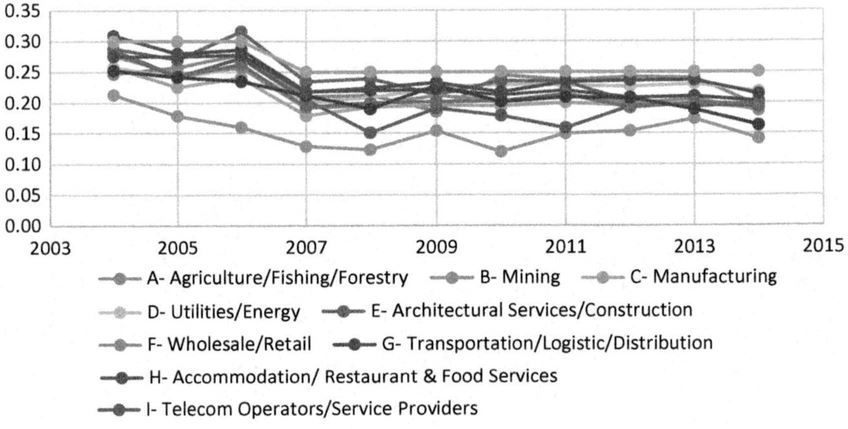

Fig. 12.4 Trend of weighted mean of MTRs by industry

Table 12.10 Weighted mean in terms of registration capital

Year	*A. Agriculture/ fishing/ forestry*	*B. Mining*	*C. Manufacturing*	*D. Utilities/ energy*	*E. Architectural Services/ construction*	*F. Wholesale/ retail*	*G. Transportation/ logistic/ distribution*	*H. Accommodation/ restaurant & food service*	*I. Telecom operators/ service providers*	*J. Real estate*	*K. Leasing and business services*	*L. Cultural sports and entertainment*	*M. Education*
2004	0.25	0.21	0.26	0.26	0.29	0.28	0.31	0.28	0.28	0.29	0.25	0.28	0.30
2005	0.26	0.18	0.23	0.24	0.27	0.25	0.28	0.24	0.24	0.24	0.24	0.27	0.30
2006	0.28	0.16	0.24	0.26	0.32	0.26	0.29	0.27	0.27	0.26	0.23	0.28	0.30
2007	0.21	0.13	0.18	0.20	0.23	0.19	0.22	0.20	0.20	0.19	0.21	0.22	0.25
2008	0.21	0.12	0.19	0.21	0.24	0.20	0.22	0.15	0.15	0.20	0.19	0.22	0.25
2009	0.18	0.15	0.20	0.23	0.21	0.21	0.22	0.19	0.19	0.20	0.23	0.23	0.25
2010	0.24	0.12	0.19	0.23	0.24	0.20	0.21	0.18	0.18	0.20	0.20	0.22	0.25
2011	0.24	0.15	0.20	0.23	0.23	0.21	0.22	0.16	0.16	0.21	0.21	0.23	0.25
2012	0.24	0.15	0.19	0.23	0.20	0.20	0.21	0.19	0.19	0.19	0.21	0.24	0.25
2013	0.24	0.17	0.20	0.23	0.19	0.21	0.21	0.20	0.20	0.20	0.19	0.24	0.25
2014	0.19	0.14	0.19	0.22	0.20	0.19	0.20	0.19	0.19	0.20	0.16	0.21	0.25
Std. dev.	0.03	0.03	0.02	0.02	0.04	0.03	0.04	0.04	0.04	0.03	0.03	0.02	0.02
Average	0.23	0.15	0.21	0.23	0.24	0.22	0.23	0.21	0.21	0.22	0.21	0.24	0.26
Mean before 2007	0.26	0.18	0.24	0.25	0.29	0.26	0.29	0.27	0.27	0.26	0.24	0.28	0.30
Mean after 2007	0.22	0.14	0.19	0.22	0.22	0.20	0.21	0.18	0.18	0.20	0.20	0.23	0.25
△ in mean	−0.04	−0.04	−0.05	−0.03	−0.07	−0.06	−0.08	−0.08	−0.08	−0.06	−0.04	−0.05	−0.05

Notes:

1. The mean is weighted by the registry capital

2. △ in mean: changes in the weighted mean before and after 2007

12.6 Conclusion

The marginal tax rate is an important measurement for firm's capital structure, debt policy, and so on. Therefore, obtaining accurate corporate marginal tax rates is very useful for tax studies. Rather than using the traditional method to obtain the marginal tax rate, we apply Blouin et al. (2008)'s bin method to obtain a more reliable result for corporate marginal tax rate from 2004 to 2014. Furthermore, the sample period covers the tax reform in 2007; hence, the comparison of the before-and-after 2007's marginal tax rate could be used to measure the effect of this new tax policy.

Besides providing an index for the China's listed companies' corporate marginal tax rate, we also discuss the corporate marginal tax rate in terms of both ownership and industry. We find that the overall annual marginal tax rate has declined throughout the whole sample period. Comparing the tax reduction effect, it also suggests that the annual marginal tax rate decreased by about 1/3 from period 1 (2004–2006) to period 2 (2007–2014). One particular feature of the spread of the marginal tax rate is that many of them cluster around its current year statutory tax rate. The movements of FIE's marginal tax rate are quite different from SOEs and non-SOEs. It starts with the lowest marginal tax rate among all ownerships in 2004 but ends up with a relatively higher rate in 2014. Moreover, the lowest FIE's marginal tax rate is achieved in 2008 instead of 2007, one year after the tax reform. Regarding the industrial marginal tax rate, we find that Architectural Services/Construction and Cultural Sports and Entertainment have the highest weighted average marginal tax rate (0.24), while Mining has the lowest (0.15). Within the sample, Transportation/Logistic/Distribution is most affected by the tax reduction and its marginal tax rate declines by over 8%.

References

An, Z. (2012), "Taxation and capital structure: Empirical evidence from a quasi-experiment in China", *Journal of Corporate Finance*: 18(4), 683–689.

Barber, B. and Lyon, J. (1996), "Detecting abnormal operating performance: The empirical power and specification of test statistics", *Journal of Financial Economics*: 41(3), 359–399.

Bartholdy, J. and Mateus, C. (2011), "Debt and taxes for private firms", *International Review of Financial Analysis*: 20(3), 177–189.

Blouin, J., Core, J. and Guay, W. (2008), "Improved estimates of marginal tax rates: Why they are needed, approach, and implications", Memo.

Blouin, J., Hail, L. and Yetman, M. H. (2009), "Capital gains taxes, pricing spreads, and arbitrage: Evidence from cross-listed firms in the US", *The Accounting Review*: 84(5), 1321–1361.

Chan, K., Mo, P. and Zhou, A. (2013), "Government ownership, corporate governance and tax aggressiveness: Evidence from China", *Accounting & Finance*: 53(4), 1029–1051.

Devereux, M. and Griffith, R. (2003), "The impact of corporate taxation on the location of capital: A Review", *Economic Analysis and Policy*: 33(2), 275–292.

Devereux, M., Griffith, R. and Klemm, A. (2002), "Corporate income tax reforms and international tax competition", *Economic Policy*: 17(35), 449–495.

Devereux, M., Lockwood, B. and Redoano, M. (2008), "Do countries compete over corporate tax rates?" *Journal of Public Economics*: 92(5–6), 1210–1235.

Graham, J. (1996a), "Debt and the marginal tax rate", *Journal of Financial Economics*: 41(1), 41–73.

Graham, J. (1996b), "Proxies for the corporate marginal tax rate", *Journal of Financial Economics*: 42(2), 187–221.

Graham, J. (2005), "A Review of taxes and corporate finance", *FNT in Finance*: 1(7), 573–691.

Graham, J. (2000), "How big are the tax benefits of debt?", *The Journal of Finance*: 55(5), 1901–1941.

Graham, J. R. and Mills, L. F. (2008), "Using tax return data to simulate corporate marginal tax rates", *Journal of Accounting and Economics*: 46(2–3), 366–388.

Graham, J. R. and Kim, H. (2009), "The effects of the length of the tax-loss carryback period on tax receipts and corporate marginal tax rates (No. w15177)", *National Bureau of Economic Research*.

Gu, S. (2005). Effects of stock option marginal tax rate system on corporate and debt policy. Group Economics Research, 6.

Huang, G. and Song, F. (2006), "The determinants of capital structure: Evidence from China", *China Economic Review*: 17(1), 14–36.

Pattenden, K. (2002), "Estimating and evaluating proxies for the marginal tax rate", *Australian Journal of Management*: 27(2), 187–202.

Padovano, F. and Galli, E. (2002), "Comparing the growth effects of marginal vs. average tax rates and progressivity", *European Journal of Political Economy*, 18(3), 529–544.

Plesko, G. (2003), "An evaluation of alternative measures of corporate tax rates", *Journal of Accounting and Economics*: 35(2), 201–226.

Ramb, F. (2007), "Corporate marginal tax rate, tax loss carryforwards and investment functions-empirical analysis using a large German panel data set", *SSRN Electronic Journal*.

Scholes, M., Wilson, G. and Wolfson, M. (1990), "Tax planning, regulatory capital planning, and financial reporting strategy for commercial banks", *Review of Financial Studies*: 3(4), 625–650.

Shevlin, T. (1990), "Estimating corporate marginal tax rates with asymmetric tax treatment of gains and losses", *Journal of the American Taxation Association:* 11(2).

Shi, J. (2015). Renmin Chinese law review. Cheltenham: Edward Elgar Pub. Ltd.

Sinha, P. and Bansal, V. (2012), "Algorithm for calculating corporate marginal tax rate using Monte Carlo simulation", MPRA Paper.

Thomas, J. (1988), "Corporate taxes and defined benefit pension plans", *Journal of Accounting and Economics*: 10(3), 199–237.

Wang, Y. (2003), "Study on the income tax burden of listing Corporation", *Management World*: 3(1) (in Chinese).

CHAPTER 13

The Optimal Model for Operating Cash Flow in Chinese Industries

Xiaoyang Tan and Lingyan Zuo

13.1 Introduction

Cash flow is the lifeblood of a firm. Whether a firm can predict and generate adequate cash in a timely fashion to cover daily operating expenses hugely affects its ability to create value, or even its survival. Prediction of cash flow and forecast of earnings are important tasks relevant in diverse decision-making scenarios. Bowen et al. (1986) argued that forecasts of cash flow and earnings are key to financial distress prediction, corporate risk management, stock valuation and business analysis. Standard-setting bodies have emphasized the rationale for accounting accruals to predict cash flows. Specifically, according to International Accounting Standards, the objective of financial statements is to provide useful information in the form of financial position, comprehensive income and cash flow to a wide range of stakeholders to make and evaluate business decisions regarding the entity (IAS1 1997). It clearly underscores the need to delineate the predictability of cash flow expectation models (Lorek and Willinger 1996).

However, the statement of cash flow provides only historical cash flow information, not complete information of future cash flows or the

X. Tan • L. Zuo (✉)
International Business School Suzhou, Xi'an Jiaotong-Liverpool University, Suzhou, China
e-mail: lingyang.zuo@xjtlu.edu.cn

J. H. Hung, Y. Chen (eds.), *The State of China's State Capitalism*,
https://doi.org/10.1007/978-981-13-0983-0_13

management story behind the book value. For example, a substantial cash balance at the year-end might not be a good signal of working capital management since the free cash flow could be reinvested back in to the business to generate profits. If managers only focus on the current cash inflow, at the cost of ignoring investment opportunities, it would be too shortsighted for the long-term success of their business. Therefore, it is necessary for a business to predict future cash flows and justify the philosophy of cash flow management.

The study intends to investigate the relationship between accruals and cash flow prediction in a list of Chinese industries, drawing upon existing models explored in studies of US and UK industries. Evidence from both US and UK studies supports the hypothesis that accruals contain significant explanatory power for future cash flows, over and above that contained in current cash flow data (e.g. Barth et al. 2001; Al-Attar and Hussain 2004). However, there is no consensus regarding the forecast superiority of using models of aggregated accruals (e.g. Bowen et al. 1986; Ali and Pope 1995; Clubb 1995) versus models of disaggregating accruals into components of earnings (e.g. Barth et al. 2001; Al-Attar and Hussain 2004). In addition, since net cash inflow within each industry exhibits a strong pattern of seasonality, this study also introduces seasonal time-series regressions for predictions of net cash inflow in some industries in China.

The remainder of this study is organized as follows. Section 13.2 relates the study to prior research and presents a literature review. Section 13.3 outlines the objective and methodology of the study. Section 13.4 presents the analysis and results. Section 13.5 summarizes the research outputs, limitations and further developments.

13.2 Literature Review

Most prior UK and US studies on the usefulness of accounting data for explaining future cash flows have examined price levels, returns, or cumulative abnormal returns (e.g. Bowen et al. 1986; Ali and Pope 1995; Clubb 1995; Charitou and Clubb 1999; Garrod et al. 2000). In such studies, it is necessary to assume that prices reflect information about future cash flows in an efficient manner. However, papers by Barth et al. (2001) and Al-Attar and Hussain (2004) propose decomposing earnings into cash flows plus individual reported accruals items (changes in accounts payable, accounts receivable and inventories, and depreciation). These papers report that such a disaggregation of earnings provides significant additional explanatory power for future cash flows, over and above current cash flows and total accruals. The reason behind was that in the previous study by Lipe (1986) and Dechow (1994), comparing with disaggregate accruals, aggregate ones would mask information useful to prediction. Mooi (2007) later found that long-term accruals such as depreciation and amortization could exert significant predictive impact over future cash flows. This evidence was inconsistent with previous suggestions in the financial press that depreciation and amortization did not predict future firm performance in the case study of MacDonald (1999), calling into question analysts' recent focus on "cash earnings," which excluded these accruals (Andrew et al. 2013). Additionally, Subramanyam (1996) decomposed accounting earnings into cash flows, normal and abnormal accruals, to examine the explanatory power of these components with regard to future cash flows using ordinary least squares (OLS) regression analysis. Evidence to support the utility of abnormal accruals comes from Xie (2001) who found that abnormal (discretionary) accruals have value-relevance in the market place.

In addition, many prior studies that addressed how accounting accruals helped predict future cash flows used small samples without considering long time-series requirements. For example, Lorek and Willinger (1996) improved upon earlier time-series models by developing a multivariate time-series model, which includes a list of independent variables such as cash flow of the last accounting period, disaggregated accruals and earnings.

This study is also related to research comparing the predictability of earnings and cash flow and treating share prices as proxies for expected future economic benefits. For example, Beaver and Dukes (1972) and Dechow (1994) found that returns were highly in line with aggregate earnings rather than with cash flow. Several other studies including Rayburn (1986), Wilson (1986) and Pfeiffer et al. (1998) documented that aggregate earnings and cash flow were incrementally informative for returns. Some prior research also found that components of earnings, including accruals and accrual components, had different pricing multiples, as predicted by differences in the components (e.g. Lipe 1986; Barth et al. 1990).

13.3 Methodology

In the literature, models of cash flows have been evaluated by using UK and US market data. Since different accounting rules and principles applied to different markets, it is meaningful to evaluate which of those models would have superior cash flow forecasts using financial data of Chinese listed firms. Thus, this study intends to investigate whether the breakdown of cash flow and analysis of major components of accruals could significantly increase the predictability relative to operating cash flows, and if so, to what extent the improvement will be. Then, this study would apply time-series analysis based on data from different industrial firms and predict future operating cash flows in each industry for the next two years. However, due to the large samples in each industry, the study would select a typical firm from each different industry for cash flow forecasting.

There are mainly three steps in the study. The first step intends to evaluate the optimal model for future cash flow forecast. Following Ali and Pope (1995) and many similar studies that have revealed that aggregated accruals would improve the predictability of cash flow, we develop cash flow model I presented below:

$$OCF_{i,t+1} = \lambda_0 + \lambda_{11} OCF_{i,t} + \lambda_{12} ACC_{i,t} + \pi_{i,t}, \quad \text{(Model I)}$$

where OCF= operating cash flows, ACC= aggregated accruals, defined as the differences between earnings and cash flow; λ_0 to λ_n= model parameters, to be estimated using OLS regression; $\pi_{i,t}$ = random error term following usual OLS assumptions.

The estimation of abnormal accruals follows the approach used in studies by Peasnell et al. (2000, 2001), denoted PPY hereinafter. They used a cross-sectional version of the modified Jones (1991) model and focused on working capital accruals rather than total operating accruals. Their rationale for this focus is that systematic earnings management via the depreciation accrual is likely to have limited potential (see Beneish 1999). Following Jones (1991) and many similar studies, we deflate all variables by lagged total assets:

$$WC_{j,s,t} = \alpha_{0,s,t} + \alpha_{1,s,t} \cdot \left(\Delta REV_{j,s,t} - \Delta REC_{j,s,t} \right) + \tau_{j,s,t}, \qquad (13.1)$$

where $WC_{j,s,t}$ = working capital accruals for firm *j* (in sector *s* and year *t*) = the change in non-cash current assets minus the change in current liabilities; $\Delta REV_{j,s,t}$ = the change in revenues from year *t–1* to *t*; Δ sector *s* and year *t*; $\tau_{j,s,t}$ = the residual error (denote abnormal accruals estimate AA).

Then, cash flow model II represents the modified version of Subramanyam's model (1996), assuming which disaggregated accruals into normal and abnormal accruals and is estimated using OLS:

$$OCF_{i,t+1} = \lambda_0 + \lambda_{21} OCF_{i,t} + \lambda_{22} AA_{i,t} + \lambda_{23} NA_{i,t} + \pi_{i,t}, \quad (\text{Model II})$$

where OCF= operating cash flows, AA = abnormal accruals (for which defined by Eq. 13.1 above); NA = normal accruals, defined as total accruals less abnormal accruals; λ_0 to λ_n= model parameters, to be estimated using OLS regression; $\pi_{i,\ t}$ = random error term following usual OLS assumptions.

Lastly, Barth et al. (2001) and Al-Attar and Hussain (2004) proposed decomposing earnings into cash flows plus individual reported accruals items,

$REC_{j,s,t}$ = the change in receivables from year *t–1* to *t*; $\alpha_{0,s,t}$ and $\alpha_{1,s,t}$ are the model parameters estimated for

$$\begin{aligned} ACC_{i,t} + \alpha_1 &= \alpha_0 AR_{i,t} + \alpha_2 INV_{i,t} + \alpha_3 AP_{i,t} \\ &\quad + \alpha_4 Depr_{i,t} + \alpha_5 OTHER_{i,t} + \varepsilon_{i,t}. \end{aligned} \tag{13.2}$$

Therefore, our cash flow model III takes the following form, consisting of full disaggregated accruals:

$$\begin{aligned} OCF_{i,t+1} &= \lambda_0 + \lambda_{31} OCF_{i,t} + \lambda_{32} AR_{i,t} + \lambda_{33} INV_{i,t} + \lambda_{34} AP_{i,t} \\ &\quad + \lambda_{35} DEP_{i,t} + \lambda_{36} OTHER_{i,t} + \pi_{i,t}, \quad (\text{Model III}) \end{aligned}$$

where

OCF = operating cash flows;
AR = change in accounts receivable;
INV = change in inventory;
AP = change in accounts payable;
DEP = depreciation on tangible assets;

OTHER = represents other accruals {reported earnings – [OCF + AR + INV – AP – DEP]};
γ_0 to γ_n = model parameters, to be estimated using OLS regression;
$u_{i,t+1}$ = the regression model residual.

We use Kappa statistics to test whether there is multicollinearity effect among independent variables and whether instrumental variables shall be introduced to reduce that effect. For each model, there will also be a residual plot indicating whether the model is suitable. If the residuals have the pattern of linear distribution alongside the horizontal line, the model is adequate to fit the data.

In the second step, this study would apply Moran's I statistics to justify whether in each year, selected firms in different industries could represent the condition in the whole industry. According to Moran's Theory (Ren 2014), spatial autocorrelation is an assessment of the correlation of one variable in reference to spatial location of the variable, that is, it is the correlation of a variable with itself over space. If the observations $x_1, x_2 \ldots\ldots x_n$ of a geo-referenced variable X display interdependence over space, the data are said to be spatially auto-correlated. By the same token, it is reasonable to assume that each different geological space represents various industries in this research. In order to rationally imply the whole story of specific industry using a representative firm in that industry, we should make sure that within each industry, there is spatial autocorrelation and outside different industries; there are no correlations with each other. Moran's I helps to solve this problem.

Moran's I is calculated as follows:

$$\text{Moran I} = \frac{\sum_{i=1}^{n}\sum_{j=1}^{n} w_{ij}\left(x_i - \overline{x}\right)}{\sum_{i=1}^{n}\left(x_i - \overline{x}\right)^2} \tag{13.3}$$

where w_{ij} is the standardized weight matrix. Moran's I is within range of $-1 \leq I \leq 1$ for standardized weight matrix. x_i is the ith observation in industry i, $\overline{x}$ is the average of total observation in industry i.

In the third step, seasonal time series will be used to forecast operating cash flows in the near future. Kim and Kross (2005) ran the model to predict cash flow using cross-sectional data each year. However, in this research, industry-specified time-series data are used in time-series analysis and future cash flow prediction. The model that this study uses for prediction or forecasting is invariably estimated from historical values of the time series. The logic behind the time series is that the researcher uses historical values to estimate the dynamic properties of time series, that is, the dependence between current and past values, and then uses these estimated dynamics to forecast the future. In the study, for instance, the net operating cash flow and operating cash inflow each year form the data set of time-series models. In the second step, applying the theory of spatial autocorrelation and Moran's I statistic, the researchers find that the operating cash flow has a similar pattern within each industry. It is consistent with common sense that in each industry, the cash flow pattern will exhibit similar patterns given that the risk exposure to a particular industry is within justifiable range.

If the operating cash flow exhibits a periodic behavior, seasonal time-series models are used. Normally, the patterns of cash flow are often affected seasonally per industry. It is evident that some industries are sensitive to weather effects. Examples usually include industries such as agriculture, farming and fishery. Some industries are sensitive to cyclical financial effects. Manufacturing industries normally boom during prosperous years. In the study, the researchers collect the data of operating cash inflow from different industries, investigate the relationship between present cash inflow and past cash inflow and provide a reasonable prediction based on seasonal time-series prediction. Since the data set contains quarterly cash inflow, the famous "airline model" for quarterly time series is used:

$$(1-\mathrm{B})(1-\mathrm{B}^4)\mathrm{r}_t = (1-\theta_1\mathrm{B})(1-\theta_4\mathrm{B}^4)\mathrm{a}_t \tag{13.4}$$

The fitted model is examined carefully to check for possible model inadequacy. If the model is adequate, the residual series should behave as a white noise. Ljung-Box statistics are used to test whether the models are adequate or not. The null hypothesis is that there is not an autocorrelation effect in the residuals, while the alternative states there still exists an autocorrelation effect in the residuals. If the test statistic is rejected at a certain significance level, then the model is not adequate and has to be refined.

The data are collected from financial statements of listed firms in China from 2005 to 2014, excluding firms in the finance sector to be consistent with previous studies; the components of financial sector's financial statements are different from those of the non-finance sector. Key variables include the following: change in revenues, change of working capital accruals, change in accounts payable, change in inventory, change in accounts receivable. Depreciation on tangible assets is extracted from the statement of financial position, the statement of comprehensive income and the statement of cash flow with respect to each firm. The cash flows' data are extracted from companies' statements of cash flow and the period is selected from 31 March 2006 (for fiscal year ending 2005) to 31 March 2015 (for fiscal year ending 2014). There are two reasons for selection of this period. First, many listed companies were not listed until 2003; therefore, it is not easy to find true and fair representations of cash flows before 2003. Second, for statistical reasons, cash flow prediction will become less accurate as lags become longer so the degree of freedom becomes smaller. Therefore, we think ten years of cash flow data are adequate for time-series analysis in this case.

Annual firm-year observations are used for empirical testing, as cash flow forecasts are provided on a semi-annual basis. Panel A of Table 13.1 presents the sample selection procedure. The initial sample consists of 31,981 firm-year observations obtained from the China Stock Market & Accounting Research Database (CSMAR) and categorized into 18 different industries according to the China Securities Regulatory Commission (CSRC). The intersection of the two databases leaves 26,158 observations with 90 invalid blank data and 714 financial sector data deducted. Panel B of Table 13.1 lists the number of valid observations in each industry according to CSMAR and CSRC and it also calculates the percentages of observations from each specific industry.

13.4 Results

Table 13.2 reports descriptive statistics of variables in different partitions. Panel A of Table 13.2 reports the descriptive statistics for the full sample. The full sample consists of 12 different industries with time spans from 2005 to 2014. Both the mean and the median of change in inventory and receivables are negative, suggesting that on average, the inventory and receivables component of accruals are increasing during the sample period. Evidently, the means and medians of the variables also exhibit large differences, which suggests the distribution of the data is skewed. In the sample, for instance, means and standard deviations for depreciation of assets are 3.94 and 35.70, respectively. Many other key variables also have high standard deviations, indicating potential outliers may be present. In empirical tests, therefore, robust regressions are used to minimize the effect of outliers.

Table 13.1 Sample selection and distribution

Panel A: Sample selection

	Sample selection and distribution	*No. of firm-year observations*
Initial sample:	China Stock Market & Accounting Research Database (CSMAR)	31,981
Less:	Missing observations when categorized with China Securities Regulatory Commission (CSRC)	(5019)
Equals:		26,962
Less:	Lost observations when valid data for variables are collected	(90)
	Observations from financial sector	(714)
Total		26,158

Panel B: Sample distribution

Different industries	*Number of valid observations*	*Percentage*
Agriculture, forestry and fishery	1140	4.36
Mineral mining	1096	4.19
Manufacturing	13,898	53.13
Electricity, heat and gas supply	1570	6.00
Architecture	820	3.13
Whole and retail sales	2544	9.73
Transportation	1584	6.06
Real estate	2210	8.45
Business services	244	0.93
Natural resources	240	0.92
Entertainment	285	1.09
Others	527	2.01
General	26,158	100.00

Panel B and Panel C of present the descriptive statistics of variables based on different reference levels. Panel B presents data based on different industries. Evidently, Panel B of Table 13.1 shows that the manufacturing industry accounts for most observations. To be more representative, Panel B of Table 13.2 therefore summarizes the data from the manufacturing industry. Panel C presents data based on year 2014. It is reasonable to assume that the most recent data contain much more information and would therefore help regression analysis strongly.

Panel D of Table 13.2 reports means and medians and tests of comparison for variables of interest between the full sample and industrial-specific

Table 13.2 Descriptive statistics

Variables	*Mean*	*Std. dev*	*5%*	*25%*	*Median*	*75%*	*95%*
Panel A: Full sample (CNY ×10^8)							
ACC	−144.00	1590.00	−62.20	−6.16	−1.49	−0.12	3.41
EARN	−121.00	1460.00	−39.80	−3.52	−0.44	0.95	12.80
OCF_{t+1}	21.80	229.00	−4.65	−0.14	0.57	2.79	30.30
OCF	21.70	228.00	−4.63	−0.13	0.58	2.81	30.20
WC	−140.00	1580.00	−46.30	−4.41	−0.82	0.21	5.15
ΔREV	−55.60	697.00	−29.00	−2.03	−0.15	1.08	13.00
ΔREC/AR	−65.20	771.00	−17.10	−1.72	−0.33	0.12	2.57
AP	72.30	820.00	−4.14	−0.37	0.18	1.54	20.10
INV	−2.59	19.30	−9.73	−1.01	−0.15	0.06	1.65
DEP	3.94	35.70	0.02	0.13	0.39	1.15	9.31
OTHER	0.32	2.05	0.00	0.01	0.03	0.11	1.07
Panel B: Sample by manufacturing industry (CNY ×10^8)							
ACC	−6.06	25.50	−27.00	−4.76	−1.37	−0.15	2.94
EARN	−3.21	22.80	−19.70	−3.27	−0.65	0.53	7.37
OCF_{t+1}	2.85	14.40	−2.68	−0.13	0.50	2.12	12.70
OCF	2.83	14.30	−2.68	−0.13	0.50	2.12	12.70
WC	−4.36	23.10	−22.10	−3.54	−0.82	0.15	4.47
ΔREV	−1.35	16.00	−11.90	−1.83	−0.26	0.69	7.07
ΔREC/AR	−1.86	9.60	−8.90	−1.62	−0.39	0.06	2.09
AP	1.36	12.00	−3.56	−0.36	0.16	1.16	9.30
INV	−1.13	6.74	−5.97	−0.96	−0.20	0.08	1.65
DEP	1.58	5.92	0.04	0.17	0.42	1.09	5.24
OTHER	0.13	0.56	0.00	0.01	0.03	0.09	0.48
Panel C: Sample by time as of 31 December 2014 (CNY ×10^8)							
ACC	−152	1580	−28,100	−26,800	−2.17	0.02	7.11
EARN	−129	1440	−83.00	−8.49	−1.13	1.35	17.00
OCF_{t+1}	21.30	232	−13.60	−0.98	0.26	3.16	28.00
OCF	20.00	229	−14.70	−0.99	0.28	3.16	25.30
WC	−147.00	1570	−82.20	−8.92	−1.37	0.44	8.37
ΔREV	−61.70	669	−68.80	−5.83	−0.58	1.31	15.80
ΔREC/AR	−67.10	778	−21.10	−2.26	−0.31	0.36	5.56
AP	74.30	806	−6.41	−0.60	0.29	3.23	34.50
INV	−6.04	31.10	−28.20	−2.87	−0.33	0.08	3.00
DEP	4.06	43.60	0.01	0.06	0.22	0.81	8.99
OTHER	0.43	3.05	0.00	0.01	0.03	0.11	1.28

Notes: Variables Definitions:
where *ACC* = aggregated accruals; *EARN* = reported earnings; *OCF* = operating cash flows; *WC* = working capital accruals; *ΔREV* = the change in revenues; *ΔREC/AR* = change in accounts receivable; *AP* = change in accounts payable; *INV* = change in inventory; *DEP* = depreciation on tangible assets; *OTHER* = represents other accruals {reported earnings − [*OCF* + *AR* + *INV* − *AP* − *DEP*]}

(*continued*)

Table 13.2 (continued)

Panel D: Comparisons between time interval with and without industry specified

Variables	*Mean*			*Median*		
	With	*Without*	*t-statistics*	*With*	*Without*	*Wilcoxon Z*
ACC	−6.06	−144.00	−14.0693***	−1.37	−1.49	−5.586***
EARN	−3.21	−121.00	−12.9809***	−0.65	−0.44	6.186***
OCF_{t+1}	2.85	21.80	13.3255***	0.50	0.57	5.724***
OCF	2.83	21.70	13.3510***	0.50	0.58	5.973***
WC	−4.36	−140.00	−13.8649***	−0.82	−0.82	−2.994*
ΔREV	−1.35	−55.60	−12.5734***	−0.26	−0.15	5.192***
ΔREC/AR	−1.86	−65.20	−13.2595***	−0.39	−0.33	2.600*
AP	1.36	72.30	13.9735***	0.16	0.18	4.818***
INV	−1.13	−2.59	−11.0332***	−0.20	−0.15	0.601
DEP	1.58	3.94	10.4130***	0.42	0.39	−4.881***
OTHER	0.13	0.32	14.6266***	0.03	0.03	3.752**

Notes: Here two-sample t test with unequal variances; two-sample Wilcoxon rank-sum (Mann-Whitney) test; and *, **, *** Significant at 0.10, 0.05 and 0.01 levels, respectively

subsample. Student t-test is used to test the difference in means and the Wilcoxon rank-sum test indicates the differences in medians across two subsamples. Both the two-sample t test with unequal variances and the Wilcoxon rank-sum (Mann-Whitney) test suggest significant differences.

Table 13.3 reports both the Pearson and Spearman correlation coefficients for the variables. The Pearson correlation is more efficient to describe data that are assumed to be continuously, linearly and normally distributed, while Spearman is more efficient for data that are excluded from the above assumptions. The Pearson correlation between operating cash flow and earnings ($\rho = 0.4833$) suggests a relatively strong positive relationship. In addition, the Spearman correlation between total accruals and operating cash flow is −0.2521, while the Pearson correlation for these two is −0.5957. Both statistics indicate negative relationships. However, since the absolute value of the two correlations are significantly different, it is reasonable to decompose the accruals and investigate correlations between different components of the accruals and operating cash flow, respectively. For instance, Pearson correlation between depreciation and operating cash flow is lower than that of Spearman, with 0.4282 and 0.5178, respectively. In the meantime, the Pearson correlation between payables and operating cash flow is higher, which are 0.6535 and 0.2728, respectively. Many other variables in between also present

Table 13.3 Pearson (Spearman) correlations below (above) the diagonal of matrix

Variables	*ACC*	*EAR*	REV	OCF_{t+1}	*OCF*	*DEP*	*OTHERS*	*INV*	*AR*	*AP*	*WC*
ACC	1.0000	0.6298	0.5051	−0.3521	−0.0462	−0.4722	−0.3804	0.5040	0.6516	−0.7473	0.9311
EARN	0.9906	1.0000	0.9069	0.3420	0.0879	−0.0188	−0.0497	0.4685	0.5919	−0.5092	0.7317
ΔREV	0.9808	0.9957	1.0000	0.4220	0.1078	0.0822	0.0346	0.5613	0.3646	−0.4527	0.6167
OCF_{t+1}	−0.4957	0.4833	0.4494	1.0000	0.1501	0.5178	0.3556	0.0518	−0.0085	0.2728	−0.1164
OCF	−0.1754	−0.1671	−0.1654	0.1382	1.0000	0.1721	0.1168	0.0315	−0.0165	−0.0007	0.0057
DEP	−0.1723	−0.0964	−0.0445	0.4282	0.0563	1.0000	0.6296	−0.1639	−0.2853	0.1672	−0.2754
OTHERS	−0.3013	−0.2329	−0.1919	0.4757	0.1263	0.8221	1.0000	−0.1575	−0.2472	0.1470	−0.2477
INV	0.0264	0.0064	0.0125	−0.0925	−0.0150	−0.3339	−0.2234	1.0000	0.1172	−0.3447	0.5197
AR	0.9924	0.9965	0.9851	−0.5092	−0.1672	−0.1424	−0.2685	0.0009	1.0000	−0.4305	0.6676
AP	−0.9933	−0.9754	−0.9691	0.6535	0.1765	0.1466	0.2876	−0.0112	−0.9739	1.0000	−0.8112
WC	0.9997	0.9920	0.9833	−0.5885	−0.1743	−0.1495	−0.2826	0.0185	0.9928	−0.9937	1.0000

different correlations and those correlations are sometimes significantly different from the two statistics. Therefore, to generate a relatively perfect model to measure operating cash flow, both aggregated and disaggregated accruals and earnings are separately used in the panel data regression presented later in this section.

Table 13.4 summarizes the results of tests on the accrual model proposed by Subramanyam (1996) and Barth et al. (2001), who showed that the accruals of a firm could be decomposed and explained by independent variables including change in revenues, change in receivables, change in inventory and depreciation from the firm. To test the scope of model application and to know how significantly each variable could explain accruals, the researcher uses panel data that consist of a total of 26,158 firm-year observations over the years 2005–2014. All observations are categorized into 12 main industries according to CSRC. Coefficient estimates are based on Maximum Likelihood Estimation (MLE) using R package (plm) for panel data regression. The coefficients in the model are listed by each different industry. The standard errors are in parentheses. The last two columns of Table 13.4 present the adjusted R-squared and Kappa statistics for model checking.

However, examination of the summary data for the abnormal accruals regression equations displays some notable variations in the adjusted R-squared values across sectors (Panel A). This is worth noting because the regression residuals provide the estimates for abnormal accruals, and regressions with low R-squared values may tend to have a greater number of large residuals due to the inferior model-fit. With regard to the regression coefficients pooled across all sector-years, it can see from panel A that the average regression slope for the $\Delta REV - \Delta REC$ term is positive, mirroring the results reported in studies by Jones (1991) and Jeter and Shivakumar (1999).

On panel B for disaggregated accruals, it is evident that for all industries except Mineral Mining, change in accounts payable is significant at 1% statistical level to explain accruals. Change in depreciation, however, has less explanatory power in industries such as Transportation, Mineral Mining and Business Services. Change in inventory is useful to explain the accruals for industries including Agriculture, Forestry and Fishery, Manufacturing, Architecture, Whole and Retail Sales and Real Estate where inventories are quite important for daily operations. Adjusted R-squared has the largest value in Real Estate and the smallest in Mineral Mining. However, Kappa statistic of 308.18 in Real Estate suggests that multicollinearity problem exists for this model regression. The accrual

Table 13.4 Abnormal accrual model

Panel A: $WC_{j,s,t} = \alpha_{0,s,t} + \alpha_{1,s,t} \cdot (\Delta REV_{j,s,t} - \Delta REC_{j,s,t}) + \tau_{j,s,t}$

Industry	λ_0	λ_{11}	λ_{12}	*Adjusted* R^2	*Kappa*
Agriculture, forestry and fishery	−0.005	−0.025	−0.014	0.229	133.49
Mineral mining	−0.004	−0.078	0.0129	0.504	88.27
Manufacturing	−0.001	−0.044	−0.027*	0.308	7.82
Electricity, heat and gas supply	0.003	0.092*	−0.693***	0.547	52.96
Architecture	0.015	−0.055	−0.007	0.149	151.81
Whole and retail sales	−0.021*	0.031*	−0.486***	0.419	26.28
Transportation	−0.0012	−0.008	−0.006	0.325	2.77
Real estate	0.0075	0.021	−0.004	0.294	108.21
Business services	−0.0088	0.066	−0.018	0.078	23.07
Natural resources	−0.0078	0.043	−0.423***	0.442	75.43
Entertainment	0.0090	0.021	−0.566***	0.351	84.58
Others	0.2551***	0.378***	−0.245***	0.432	109.22

Notes: *, **, *** Significant at 0.10, 0.05 and 0.01 levels, respectively

Panel B: $ACC_{i,t} = \alpha_0 + \alpha_1 AR_{i,t} + \alpha_2 INV_{i,t} + \alpha_3 AP_{i,t} + \alpha_4 Depr_{i,t} + \alpha_5 OTHER_{i,t} + \varepsilon_{i,t}$

Industry	λ_0	λ_{21}	λ_{22}	λ_{23}	*Adjusted* R^2	*Kappa*
Agriculture, forestry and fishery	−0.009	0.720**	−0.428***	1.558***	0.653	6.45
Mineral mining	−0.001	0.056	−0.810***	0.289***	0.804	30.08
Manufacturing	−0.002	0.831**	−0.574***	0.896***	0.608	11.21
Electricity, heat and gas supply	0.004*	1.052***	−0.680***	0.932***	0.849	17.68
Architecture	0.008	1.042***	−0.744***	0.993***	0.632	20.83
Whole and retail sales	−0.02*	0.761	−0.477***	0.378**	0.724	22.46
Transportation	−0.001	1.058***	−0.556***	0.983***	0.828	5.94
Real estate	0.007	0.042	−0.594***	2.976***	0.703	108.23
Business services	0.032	0.026*	−0.323***	3.2222**	0.305	24.52
Natural resources	−0.009	0.212	−0.723***	0.895**	0.638	24.71
Entertainment	0.003	0.892***	−0.452***	2.7124***	0.516	9.79
Others	0.254***	0.446**	−0.243***	0.210	0.487	16.41

Notes: *, **, *** Significant at 0.10, 0.05 and 0.01 levels, respectively model in this case should be refined, otherwise, it should be dropped. In general, accruals models proposed by Subramanyam (1996) and Barth et al. (2001) could adequately cover many industries. The model is most powerful to explain accruals in Whole and Retail Sales and least powerful to explain that in Mineral Mining. Almost all change in accounts receivable, accounts payable and inventory are jointly significant to explain accruals at 1% level. Depreciation and other accruals have less power to explain accruals in some industries as listed in Table 13.4.

Figure 13.1 is the residual plot for the accruals model in Whole and Retail Sales. Though the adjusted R-squared suggests the model is most powerful to explain accruals in Whole and Retail Sales, it by no means produces a perfect residuals plot.

The model might be good in certain magnitudes of accruals ranging from 150 to 400. However, the model does not generate good residuals for accruals with either small or large magnitudes. The findings suggest that in order to have more accurate description of accruals, more data from different industries need to be collected and to determine relative optimal model for accruals in different industries, respectively.

Table 13.5 summarizes the regression results of three cash flow models. Panel A is for cash flow model I and includes variables of previous operating

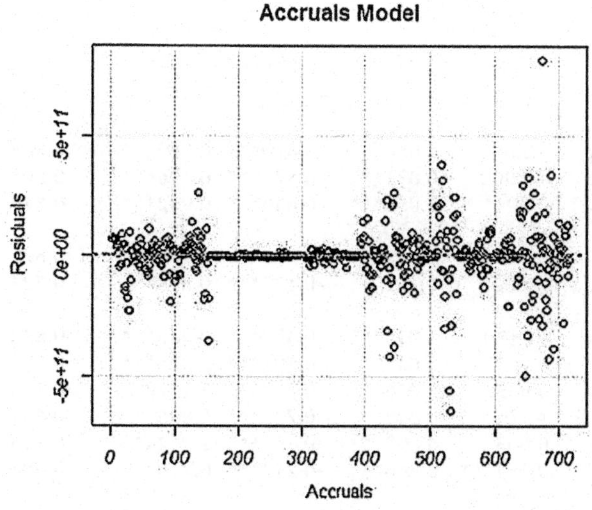

Fig. 13.1 Residual plot of whole and retail sales

Table 13.5 Cash flow regression model results

Panel A: Cash Flow Model I $OCF_{i,t+1} = \lambda_0 + \lambda_{11} OCF_{i,t} + \lambda_{12} ACC_{i,t} + \pi_{i,t}$

Industry	λ_0	λ_{11}	λ_{12}	*Adjusted* R^2	*Kappa*
Agriculture, forestry and fishery	−0.005	−0.025	−0.014	0.229	133.49
Mineral mining	−0.004	−0.078	0.0129	0.504	88.27
Manufacturing	−0.001	−0.044	−0.027*	0.308	7.82
Electricity, heat and gas supply	0.003	0.092*	−0.693***	0.547	52.96
Architecture	0.015	−0.055	−0.007	0.149	151.81
Whole and retail sales	−0.021*	0.031*	−0.486***	0.419	26.28
Transportation	−0.0012	−0.008	−0.006	0.325	2.77
Real estate	0.0075	0.021	−0.004	0.294	108.21
Business services	−0.0088	0.066	−0.018	0.078	23.07
Natural resources	−0.0078	0.043	−0.423***	0.442	75.43
Entertainment	0.0090	0.021	−0.566***	0.351	84.58
Others	0.2551***	0.378***	−0.245***	0.432	109.22

Notes: Variables Definitions:
$OCF_{i,t+1}$=operating cash flow=Total net operating cash flow in year t+1 for industry i;
$OCF_{i,t-1}$=operating cash flow of previous period=Total net operating cash flow in year t for industry i;
$ACC_{i,t}$=aggregated accruals=differences between earnings and cash flow in Year t for Industry i.
And *, **, *** Significant at 0.10, 0.05 and 0.01 levels, respectively

Panel B: Cash Flow Model II $OCF_{i,t+1} = \lambda_0 + \lambda_{21} OCF_{i,t} + \lambda_{22} AA_{i,t} + \lambda_{23} NA_{i,t} + \pi_{i,t}$

Industry	λ_0	λ_{21}	λ_{22}	λ_{23}	*Adjusted* R^2	*Kappa*
Agriculture, forestry and fishery	−0.009	0.720**	−0.428***	1.558***	0.653	6.45
Mineral mining	−0.001	0.056	−0.810***	0.289***	0.804	30.08
Manufacturing	−0.002	0.831**	−0.574***	0.896***	0.608	11.21
Electricity, heat and gas supply	0.004*	1.052***	−0.680***	0.932***	0.849	17.68
Architecture	0.008	1.042***	−0.744***	0.993***	0.632	20.83
Whole and retail sales	−0.02*	0.761	−0.477***	0.378**	0.724	22.46
Transportation	−0.001	1.058***	−0.556***	0.983***	0.828	5.94
Real estate	0.007	0.042	−0.594***	2.976***	0.703	108.23
Business services	0.032	0.026*	−0.323***	3.2222**	0.305	24.52
Natural resources	−0.009	0.212	−0.723***	0.895**	0.638	24.71
Entertainment	0.003	0.892***	−0.452***	2.7124***	0.516	9.79
Others	0.254***	0.446**	−0.243***	0.210	0.487	16.41

Notes: Variables Definitions:
OCF = operating cash flow; *AA* = abnormal accruals (for which defined by Eq. 13.1 in the main text); *NA* = normal accruals, defined as total accruals less abnormal accruals
And *, **, *** Significant at 0.10, 0.05 and 0.01 levels, respectively

(*continued*)

Table 13.5 (continued)

Panel C: Cash Flow Model III $OCF_{i,t+1} = \lambda_0 + \lambda_{31}OCF_{i,t} + \lambda_{32}AR_{i,t} + \lambda_{33}INV_{i,t} + \lambda_{34}AP_{i,t} + \lambda_{35}DEP_{i,t} + \lambda_{36}OTHER_{i,t} + \pi_{i,t}$

Industry	λ_0	λ_{31}	λ_{32}	λ_{33}	λ_{34}	λ_{35}	λ_{36}	*Adjusted* R^2	*Kappa*
Agriculture, forestry and fishery	−0.005	0.820***	0.707***	0.413***	−0.433 ***	0.728***	−0.336	0.646	24.80
Mineral mining	−0.004	−0.014	0.722***	0.609***	−1.134***	1.05***	−6.459***	0.355	11.91
Manufacturing	−0.001	4.639***	0.853***	0.297**	−0.3780***	0.831***	0.285**	0.502	65.43
Electricity, heat and gas supply	0.003	2.494***	1.118***	0.789***	−0.941***	1.053***	1.305***	0.508	42.66
Architecture	0.015	0.245	1.04***	0.693***	−0.114**	1.040***	−11.564***	0.608	54.99
Whole and retail sales	−0.021*	3.872*	0.735***	0.486***	−0.185***	0.053	2.337***	0.706	17.76
Transportation	−0.001	0.896*	1.144***	0.012	−0.433***	5.248*	1.221***	0.732	42.52
Real estate	−0.016	5.483*	1.582***	0.761***	−0.454***	0.704***	6.313***	0.802	51.6
Business services	0.007	−2.19	0.705***	0.206**	−0.064	0.007	−0.761	0.299	112.36
Natural resources	−0.008	10.952***	0.611***	0.023	−0.602***	0.012	3.076*	0.533	18.42
Entertainment	−0.007	2.292*	1.271***	0.759***	−0.404***	0.024*	−0.715	0.449	11.73
Others	0.009	0.007	1.044***	0.560***	−0.073***	0.446***	0.675**	0.492	34.03

Notes: Variables Definitions:
OCF = operating cash flow; *AR* = change in accounts receivable; *INV* = change in inventory; *AP* = change in accounts payable; *DEP* = depreciation on tangible assets; *OTHER*=represents other accruals {reported earnings–[*OCF*+*AR*+*INV*–*AP*–*DEP*]}
And *, **, *** Significant at 0.10, 0.05 and 0.01 levels, respectively

cash flows and aggregated accruals. It shows that current cash flows variable $OCF_{i,t}$ is not significant for all. Table 13.3 correlation matrix also suggests there is weak correlation between one-year-ahead and current cash flows, with 0.1382 or 0.1501, respectively. (Whether current cash flows have power to explain and predict cash flow will be discussed later in seasonal time series regression.) There are some notable variations in the adjusted R-squared values across sectors. The Electricity, Heat and Gas Supply industry enjoys the highest adjusted R-squared and have acceptable Kappa statistic. According to Panel A, in the Electricity, Heat and Gas Supply industry, approximately 55% movements from independent variables are jointly significant to predict operating cash flows.

Thus, the model is built as: $OCF_{i,\ t+1} = 0.003 + 0.092OCF_{i,\ t} + 0.693ACC_{i,\ t} + \pi_{i,\ t.}$

Figure 13.2 is the residual plot of the above equation measuring the operating cash flow in Electricity, Heat and Gas Supply. The dotted points represent the difference between actual value and predicted value from cash flow model I. The red line is horizontal level.

It is obvious that many dotted points lie along the horizontal level, implying that the model is adequate enough to fit operating cash flows. However, there are also some points staying away from the zero line. Possible explanation of these points could be the large outliers, missing

Fig. 13.2 Residual plot of electricity, heat and gas supply

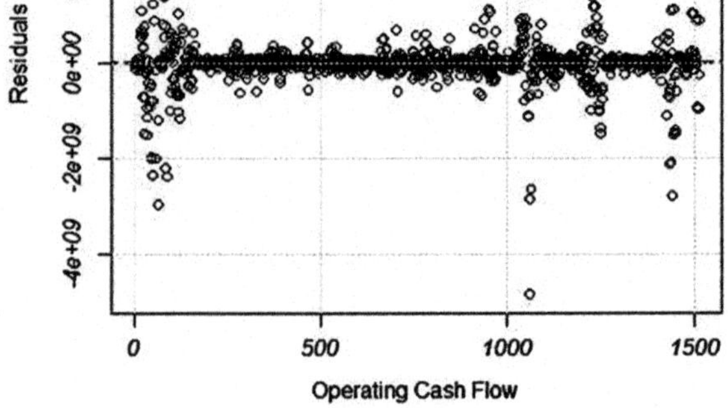

values or unknown errors. In general, the model is adequate to fit the data given high adjusted R-squared and good residuals.

Panel B reports cash flow model II to predict operating cash flows. Compared to model I, aggregated accruals have been replaced by abnormal accruals and normal accruals that contain extra information from working capital accruals, such as change in account receivables and change in revenues. Satisfactorily, the adjusted R-squared has become larger for all industries and kappa statistics have become relative smaller. For example, in model I, $ACC_{i,\,t}$ cannot significantly explain all industries. However, in model II, $AA_{i,\,t}$ explains all industries at 1% significance level, and $NA_{i,\,t}$ also exhibit a significant association at 5% level for most sectors except Others.

In model I, adjusted R-squared has the smallest value of 0.078 in the Business Services Sector, indicating independent variables have only 7.8% movement in line with movements in operating cash flows. In model II, adjusted R-squared becomes 0.305. This improvement indicates that model II is much more suitable to analyze the cash flow situation in the Business Services Sector. Many other industries also exhibit similar patterns. For example, Architecture improves from 0.149 to 0.632, Natural Resources improves from 0.442 to 0.638 and Real Estate improves from 0.294 to 0.703. Apart from adjusted R-squared, residual plots of the model are also suggestive of model adequacy.

Figure 13.3 demonstrates the residuals plot in Business Services using cash flow models I and II. It is obvious that in model I, dots are randomly distributed above or below the horizontal line while the majority of dots are distributed alongside the horizontal line in model II. The findings are consistent with the previous analysis stating that in general, model II is much better than model I to explain data from different industries.

Panel C summarizes the regression results for cash flow model III to analyze and predict operating cash flows, and model III uses the disaggregated components of accruals replacing aggregate accruals. The results are compared with those from Panel A where aggregated accruals model I is applied. Statistically, in model III, adjusted R-squared has become larger for all industries excluding Mineral Mining and Electricity, Heat and Gas Supply. Kappa statistics are all smaller than 100, implying there are no multicollinearity problems.

Also, Panel C shows that disaggregated components of accruals, within different industries, change in accounts receivable are significant at 1% level; changes in inventory are significant at 5% level to predict cash flow

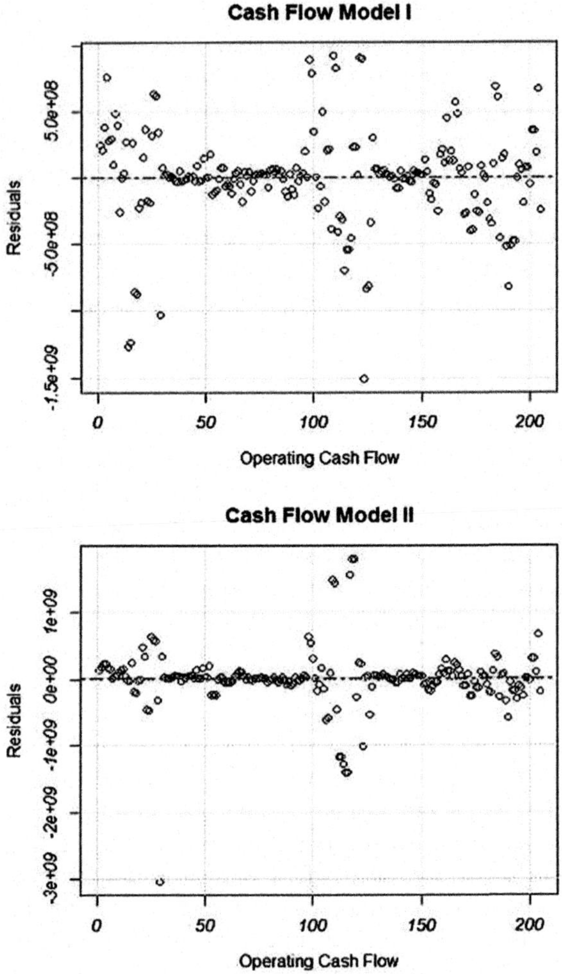

Fig. 13.3 Residual plot of business services in cash flow Model I and cash flow Model II

except Transportation and Natural Resources where inventories do not account for most of their business operations. In a similar manner, changes in accounts payable are significant in all industries except for business services with a coefficient of 0.06. The figure implies that whenever there is a one unit increase in accounts payable, only a 0.06 unit increase will happen in operating cash flows. Depreciation and other accruals are significant at 5% level for most sectors, generally, for about two thirds of all industry sectors.

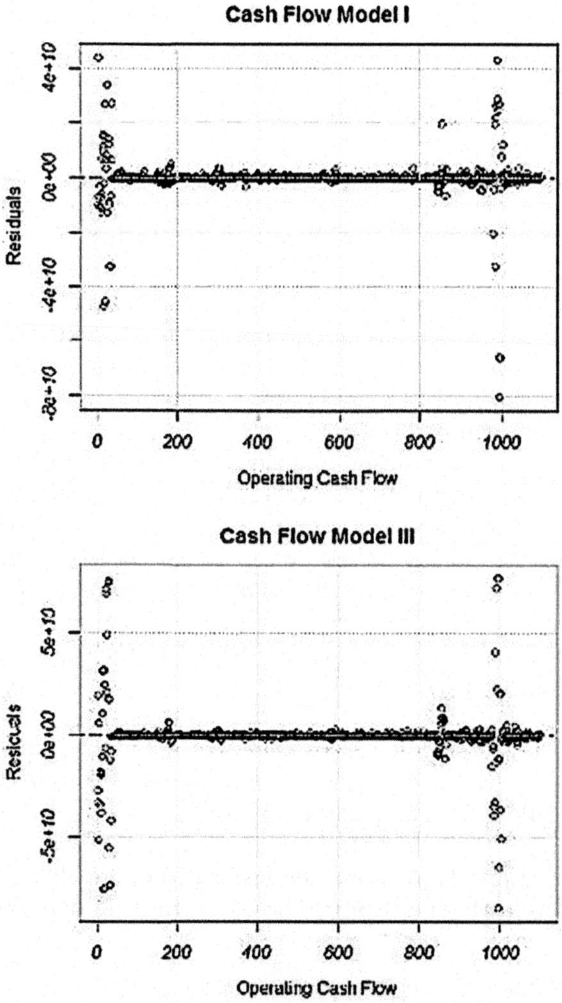

Fig. 13.4 Residual plot of mineral mining in cash flow Model I and cash flow Model III

Figure 13.4 shows the residuals plots are as follows. Both plots indicate the models are good fits for operating cash flows ranging from 0 to 1000. However, large outliers still exist for both models as well. Since model III produces lower kappa values of 11.91 compared with 88.27 in model I, model III is slightly better.

Looking at the three different models, results are slightly different for one or two individual sectors. In general, model III is better than model I in terms of both adjusted R-squared and kappa statistics. However, for most industry sectors, model III is not as good as model II. Namely, disaggregated accruals have more explanatory power than aggregated accruals for operating cash flows. Additionally, it does not mean a large portion of future cash flows can be explained when accruals items are broken down into individual components (AP, INV, AR, DEP, OTHER). It is possible that the explanatory power from the disaggregation of accruals is extracted from the information content of abnormal accruals identified by Subramanyam (1996). Essentially, model II examines the explanatory power of abnormal accruals for future cash flows once the explanatory power of current cash flows and individual accruals items has been stripped out.

It is not realistic to analyze every individual firm from different industries. Sometimes, researchers will choose a particular firm of interest within each industry as a representative for analysis that can be applied to the whole industry. However, this methodology needs to be validated by the Moran spatial autocorrelation test. Significance of Moran's I can be assessed under either normal approximation or randomization. This study uses a standardized weight matrix for the significance test of Moran's I for normal approximation.

Null hypothesis: No spatial autocorrelation (Spatial Randomness)
Alternative hypothesis: Spatial autocorrelation (Spatial Dependence) or Positive spatial autocorrelation.

Table 13.6 shows the test statistics are all significant at 5% confidence level, which is 1.644. Therefore, the null hypothesis is rejected, implying

Table 13.6 Results for Moran's I spatial autocorrelation test

Year	*2005*	*2006*	*2007*	*2008*	*2009*
Moran's I	0.1263	0.1447	0.1453	0.1878	0.9525
Test statistic	3.0983	3.5208	3.5355	4.5121	22.1042
Year	2010	2011	2012	2013	2014
Moran's I	0.2700	0.2280	0.1857	0.1835	0.1562
Test statistic	6.4037	5.4374	4.4640	4.4146	3.7854

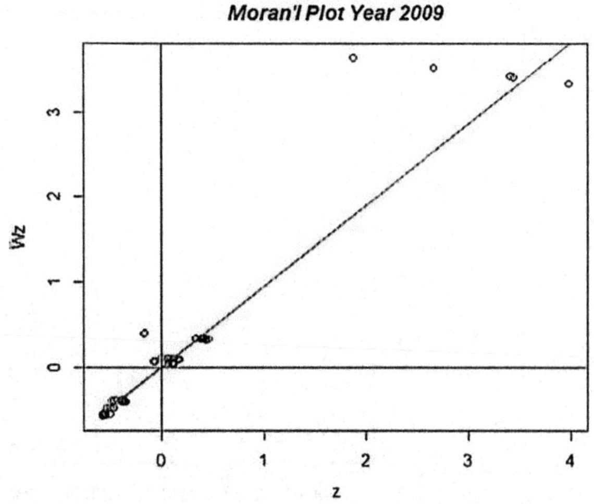

Fig. 13.5 Moran' I scatter plot for different industries in year 2009

that there is spatial autocorrelation. In this sense, it is reasonable to use an individual firm to reflect the whole industry.

And Fig. 13.5 is the Moran's Scatter Plot. In this diagram, it clearly shows that most dots lie alongside the red line. *z* consists of 12 operating cash flows from each typical firm within different industries. *Wz* consists of 12 industrial weighted average cash flows excluding the cash flows from typical firms. The typical firm for each industry is the firm that has the largest proportion of operating cash flows in the whole industry. The slope of this line is positive, indicating that there is a positive correlation between the cash flow from the typical firm and that from the industrial average. Therefore, it is reasonable to infer the whole industry through a representative firm. For the limited main text, Moran's scatter plots in other years from 2005 to 2014 are omitted here. Satisfactorily, within this time scale, the positive correlation exists between *z* and *Wz* every year, and so the philosophy still holds. The later section uses this methodology to use a firm's cash flow to simulate the pattern of whole industrial operating cash flows.

Some financial time series such as quarterly cash flows of a company exhibit certain cyclical or periodic behavior. Such a time series is called a seasonal time series. Figure 13.6 shows the time plot of quarterly cash

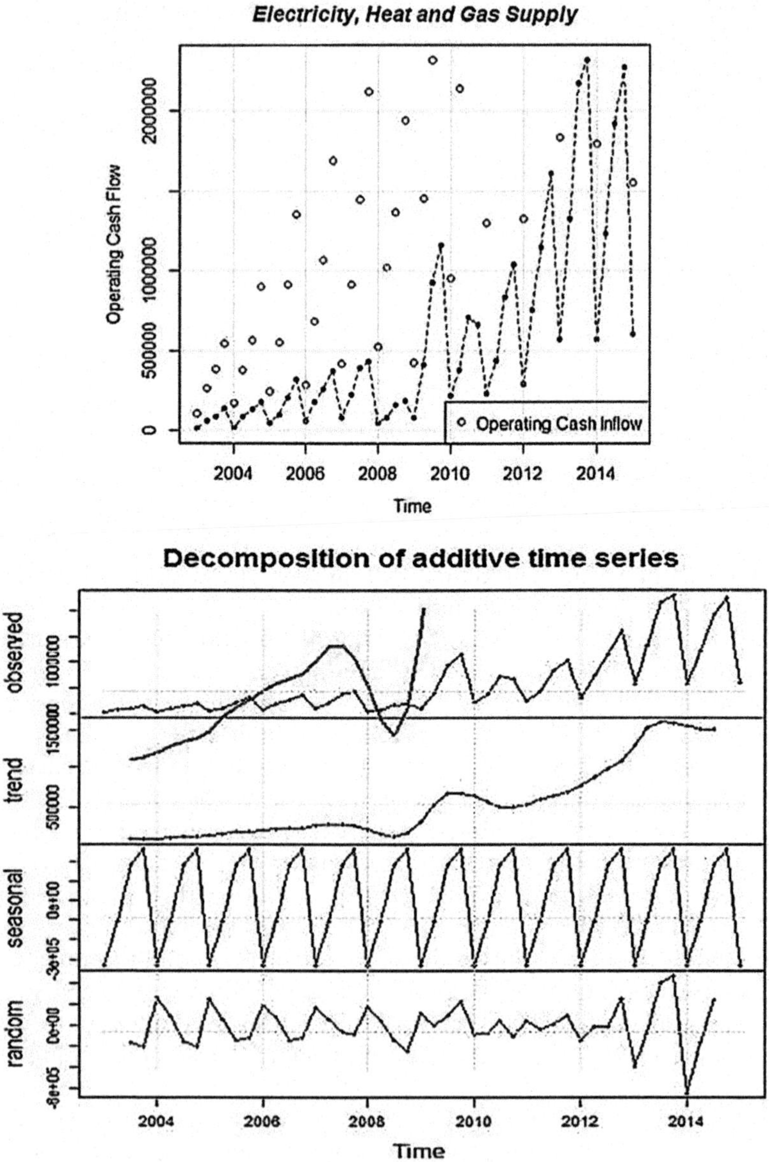

Fig. 13.6 Time and decomposition plots of quarterly operating cash inflow and net flow of electricity, heat and gas supply

flows from the first quarter of 2003 to the first quarter of 2015. The data obtained possess some noticeable features. In particular, the cash flows grow exponentially during the sample period and show a pattern of strong seasonality. The cyclical pattern repeats and enlarges itself every four years. In this sense, the seasonality has a periodicity of four. The graph on the left shows the pattern of both cash net flow and cash inflow. A good cash management will help narrow the gap in between. Interestingly, the patterns for these two cash flows exhibit seasonality effects. Therefore, it is useful to analyze both to further investigate operating cash flows changes.

The plot on the right of Fig. 13.6 decomposes operating cash flows into four different parts. Part A (upper one) is the observed values, part B is the simulated trend from part A, part C is the seasonality component and part D is the random component of observed values. Part D clearly shows the dots distributed randomly alongside the horizontal line 0, meaning that the cash flow has strong seasonality effects. Furthermore, the variability of cash flows increases over time as demonstrated in part D. We also draw plots of both cash inflow and net flow from different industries and find that most of the industries exhibit seasonal patterns. Therefore, in this session, time series with seasonality effects have been introduced for a cash flow forecast.

In some model applications, seasonality is the noise of the model and the model will have seasonal adjustment. After the adjustment, the model will become a seasonally adjusted time series that is then used to make inferences. In other applications such as forecasting, which as a major objective of financial time-series analysis, seasonality is as important as other characteristics of the data and must be handled accordingly. The researcher in the study focuses on the latter to discuss some econometric models that are useful in modeling and forecasting seasonal time series. Figure 13.7 shows the time plot of cash flows from both regular differencing and seasonal differencing. The left panel shows the pattern of autocorrelation function of original data. From the graph, it is easy to find within the first eight lags that Auto Correlation Functions (ACFs) are significant. A traditional method to handle such strong serial correlations is to consider the first differenced series of operating cash flows. The upper right panel is a sample ACF of regular differencing. It shows that the ACF is strong when the lag is a multiple of periodicity four. This is a well-documented behavior of a seasonal time series. Then the researcher

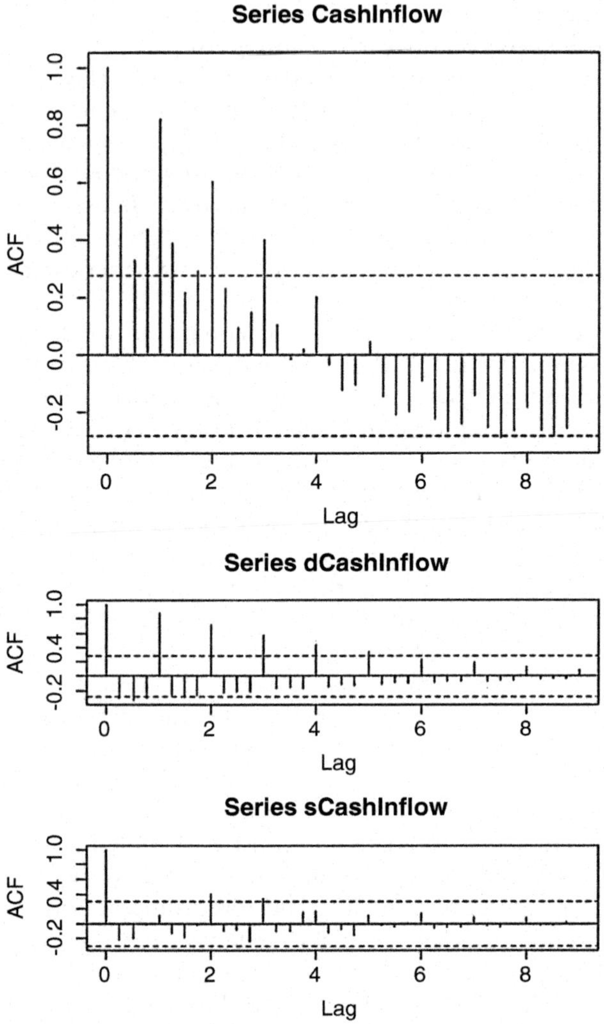

Fig. 13.7 Sample ACF of quarterly operating cash inflow, first differenced series and seasonally differenced series

uses seasonal differencing and generates another sample ACF. At this time, serial correlations have been greatly reduced as shown in the lower right panel. Most ACFs are within their two standard error limits, indicating that they are not significant.

Following the procedure of Box et al. (2008), the researcher takes differences for a sample ACF.

$$\Delta_4(\Delta x_t) = (1 - B^4)\Delta x_t = \Delta x_t - \Delta x_{t-4} = x_t - x_{t-1} - x_{t-4} + x_{t-5}.$$

The upper figure shows the ACF plot of regular differencing, that is, $\Delta x_t = x_t - x_{t-1}$, and the lower figure shows the seasonal ACF plot, which has a marginal positive correlation at lag 2 and 4. In this example, the researcher applies the famous airline model (Young 2015) to both operating cash flows and operating cash inflows.

Table 13.7 summarizes the results of a seasonal model for different industries based on the exact-likelihood method. For example, in the Agriculture, Forestry and Fishery industry, the fitted model for operating cash inflow is $(1 - B)(1 - B^4)r_t = (1 - 0.3888B)(1 + 0.7708B^4)a_t$, where standard errors of the two moving average parameters are 0.1916 and 0.1998, respectively. The Ljung-Box statistics of the residuals show 5.4128 with a p-value of 0.862. Therefore, the model appears to be adequate.

By the same token, the seasonal time-series model for other industries could also be derived from Table 13.7. Interestingly, the researcher finds that industries including Agriculture, Forestry and Fishery, Manufacturing, Architecture, Whole and Retail Sales and Business Services have most significant seasonal effects in terms of both cash inflow model and net cash flow model.

For example, the cash inflow model for the Manufacturing industry is $(1 - B)(1 - B^4)r_t = (1 + 0.2913B)(1 + 0.3977B^4)a_t$ and the net cash flow model within the same industry is $(1 - B)(1 - B^4)r_t = (1 + 0.3266B)(1 + 0.8029B^4)a_t$. The coefficients are all significant at 5% level. These two models contain the information that using cash inflow to model the whole industry's net cash flow will generate similar results. The results also suggest that companies within the manufacturing industry should be well prepared before entering into cash generating season. Seasonal patterns of cash flow will help manage business operations, thereby creating more value if the company can make the best of this philosophy.

Figure 13.8 presents two Ljung-Box Test results to justify whether the seasonal time-series model is adequate to fit data and is proper to forecast future operating cash flows. The two plots are similar in terms of ACF of residuals. Both residuals plots show no serial autocorrelations, indicating

Table 13.7 Results of seasonal model for different industries using exact-likelihood method $(1-B)(1-B^4)r_t = (1-\theta_1 B)(1-\theta_4 B^4)a_t$

Industry	*Operating cash inflow*				*Operating cash flow*			
	θ_1	θ_4	*Log likelihood*	*AIC*	θ_1	θ_4	*Log likelihood*	*AIC*
Agriculture, forestry and fishery	−0.3888	−0.7708	−372.46	750.93	−0.4389	−0.9999	−334.9	675.8
Mineral mining	0.0907	0.1044	−656.81	1319.6	0.0376	−0.321	−525.67	1057.34
Manufacturing	−0.2913	−0.3977	−320.53	647.05	−0.3266	−0.8029	−295.87	597.73
Electricity, heat and gas supply	−0.3852	0.0129	−633.62	1273.2	0.0211	−0.262	−608.72	1223.44
Architecture	−0.8447	0.324	−412.77	831.54	−1	−0.5723	−394.53	795.06
Whole and retail sales	−0.2974	−1	−545.81	1097.6	0.0772	−0.7637	−508.67	1023.34
Transportation	−0.1434	0.1465	−651	1308	−0.4849	−0.283	−594.73	1195.47
Real estate	0.0332	0.2047	−424.41	854.82	0.4078	−1	−412.95	831.91
Business services	−0.8431	0.7436	−554.14	1114.3	−0.2992	0.1114	−528.42	1062.85
Natural resources	0.4242	0.2642	−156.16	318.32	−0.5747	−0.9995	−149.12	304.23
Entertainment	−0.3915	−0.2699	−481	968.01	−0.613	−0.6614	−352.45	710.9
Others	−0.1868	−0.0918	−534.61	1075.2	0.12	−1	−515.21	1036.42

Notes: Log Likelihood: the larger the log likelihood is, the smaller the AIC will be. The best model is the model with the minimum AIC and largest log likelihood. Akaike Information Criterion (AIC) (Akaike 1973) is defined as $AIC = -\frac{2}{T} \times \ln(likelihood) + \frac{2}{T} \times (number\ of\ parameters)$, AIC measures the goodness of fit of the model that the model is white noise. The two lower plots are p-values for the Ljung-Box statistics. Similarly, for lags smaller than six, both models have p-values higher than 0.4, which means the null hypothesis that without serial correlation among residuals has to been accepted. However, for larger lags, the cash inflow model becomes inferior, while the net cash flow model is still superior to simulate the pattern of cash flows. Therefore, it is reasonable to predict future cash flows based on these two models, respectively, from the second quarter of 2015 to 2017. Table 13.8 has summarized prediction results of operating cash inflow and operating net cash flow starting from 30 June 2015 to 31 March 2017. The results could be compared with actual data collected in the future to measure whether the model is accurate or needs to be refined.

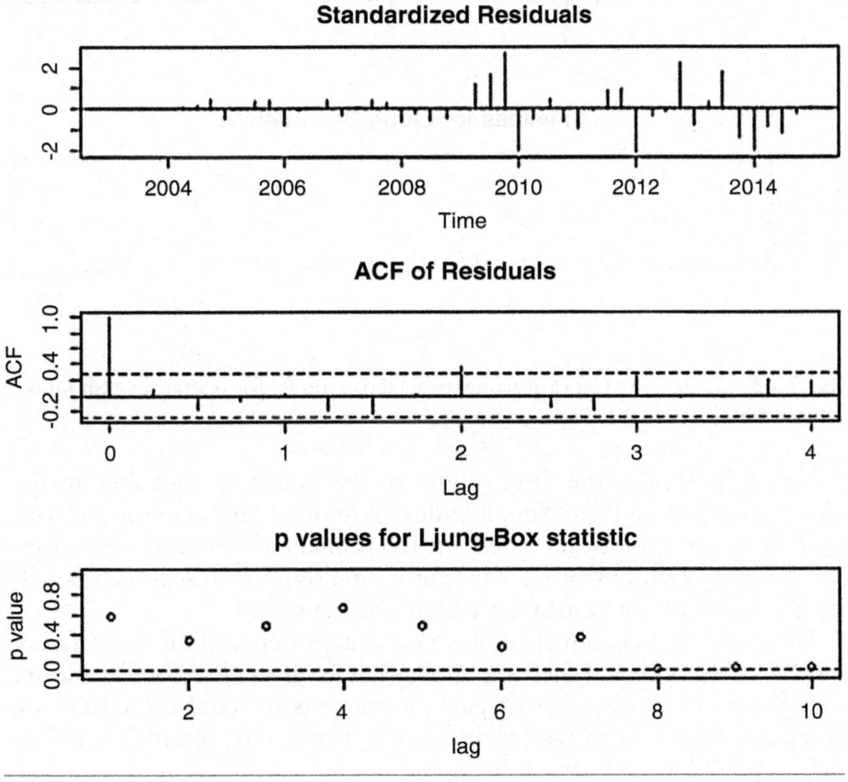

(*continued*)

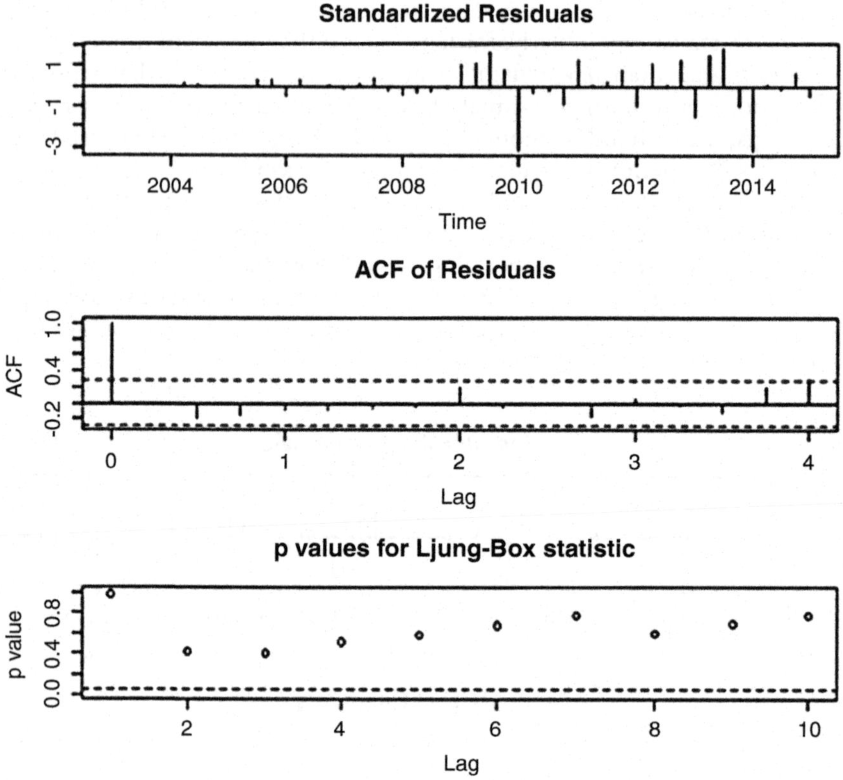

Fig. 13.8 Ljung-box test of seasonal time-series model for operating cash inflow and net flow

Figure 13.9 plots the fitted values of the operating cash flow in the Electricity, Heat and Gas Supply industry (dashed line). Compared with the original data points, the fitted line has simulated the trend of the original operating cash flow well. Therefore, time series with seasonal models are good enough for companies within this industry.

However, the diagram also shows some gaps between the fitted values and the actual values. When the model has been used to forecast future operating cash flows, it has to pass several tests to see if the results are significant or not. Such tests include white noise tests, sensitivity analysis and even the Monte-Carlo simulation.

Table 13.8 Prediction results of two-year-ahead operating cash inflow and operating net cash flow

Industry	*30/06/2015*	*30/09/2015*	*31/12/2015*	*31/03/2016*	*30/06/2016*	*30/09/2016*	*31/12/2016*	*31/03/2017*
Panel A: Prediction of operating cash inflow starting from 30 June 2015 to 31 March 2017								
Agriculture, forestry and fishery	4745.898	4715.087	17039.717	2042.611	4506.798	4475.988	16800.617	1803.512
Mineral mining	134,347,656	220,625,512	302,911,693	42,726,405	118,949,492	205,227,348	287,513,529	27,328,241
Manufacturing	3,378,638	4,925,421	6,288,514	1,991,594	3,788,193	5,334,976	6,698,069	2,401,149
Electricity, heat and gas supply	3,315,832	5,235,245	6,829,503	1,288,354	3,050,638	4,970,051	6,564,308	1,023,159
Architecture	51,939,562	61,644,030	82,942,549	27,435,725	58,465,171	68,169,640	89,468,159	33,961,335
Whole and retail sales	346521.4	511347.4	667553.4	180629.5	354777.2	519603.2	675809.2	188885.3
Transportation	5,028,650	8,004,062	10,656,978	2,294,175	5,046,514	8,021,927	10,674,842	2,312,039
Real estate	5,828,662	8,640,108	12,432,060	3,312,134	6,207,837	9,019,282	12,811,235	3,691,309
Business services	488,311	1220371.2	844732.6	365418.4	626575.5	1358635.7	982997.1	503682.9
Natural resources	73602.5313	552.7106	−11048.53	4255.3365	34319.4249	−38730.396	−50331.636	−35027.77
Entertainment	17264.955	44395.594	73959.814	−10669.482	1423.543	28554.183	58118.402	−26510.893

(*continued*)

Table 13.8 (continued)

Industry	*30/06/2015*	*30/09/2015*	*31/12/2015*	*31/03/2016*	*30/06/2016*	*30/09/2016*	*31/12/2016*	*31/03/2017*
Others	258032.2	369522.9	504,587	179564.9	276695.5	388186.2	523250.3	198228.1
Panel B: Prediction of operating net cash inflow starting from 30 June 2015 to 31 March 2017								
Agriculture, forestry and fishery	8546.12	8660.894	17826.988	6000.697	7459.674	7416.288	19309.103	4877.217
Mineral mining	2963560.1	7467840.3	14449080.3	−267365.9	4134099.7	8964228.2	13,974,131	189008.8
Manufacturing	168626.368	6675.595	271467.625	185965.752	222904.63	60953.857	325745.886	240244.013
Electricity, heat and gas supply	1264193.7	1964194.4	2,276,247	645436.8	1,302,891	2002891.7	2314944.3	684134.1
Architecture	−3024720.7	−3744398.7	372923.49	−4292820.6	−3360384.7	−4080062.7	37259.47	−4628484.6
Whole and retail sales	22702.068	17649.315	4976.93	6610.522	23755.747	18702.995	6030.61	7664.202
Transportation	532517.2	1002001.7	1230607.3	265750.8	556495.7	1025980.2	1254585.8	289729.3
Real estate	−654462.5	−727808.4	−849702.8	−753459.6	−724,945	−798,291	−920185.3	−823942.1
Business services	241694.5	323189.8	491862.2	167933.3	262028.6	343,524	512196.4	188267.4
Natural resources	2021.388	1973.435	7647.646	1497.731	1913.348	1865.396	7539.606	1389.691
Entertainment	14957.091	25778.704	38400.946	3708.926	16930.369	27751.982	40374.224	5682.203
Others	−16104.87	−23979.318	−9291.067	−18634.178	−17482.129	−25356.578	−10668.327	−20011.437

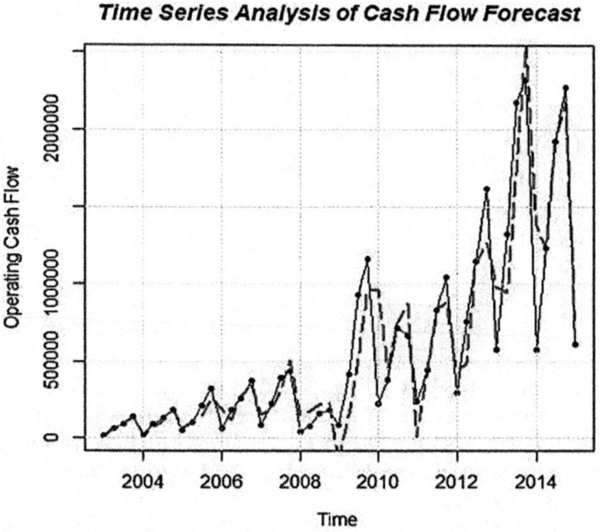

Fig. 13.9 Fitted vs actual model of operating cash flow for electricity, heat and gas supply

In general, using an appropriate way to forecast operating cash flows will help the company manage cash flows, achieve long-term lasting financial freedom of cash and unlock the cash flows that have been improperly used in the business.

13.5 Conclusion

This chapter examines three models by panel regressions to find out which best explains operating cash flows in China's industries. Its key findings are as follows. First, cash flow model II, which disaggregates accruals into normal and abnormal accruals, has the best explanatory power for cash flows in different industries. Second, there is a relationship between abnormal accruals and one-year-ahead operating cash flows, similar to that found by Bernard (1989) and Dechow and Dichev (2002). Third, there is a positive association between individual accrual items and future cash flow levels, which goes beyond the finding of Subramanyam (1996). Fourth, the comparison between model II and model III indicates that abnormal accruals provide insights into the portion of future cash flows that is not explained by the inclusion of the current year's earnings components (cash flows and individual accruals items) as independent variables. Finally, the seasonal time-series model fits all industries' data well in general, but the model's ability in predicting cash flows varies across different industries, working much better for industries subject to seasonality (such as Agriculture, Forestry and Fishery) than those that are not.

References

Akaike, H. (1973), "Information theory and an extension of the maximum likelihood principle", *Proceedings of the Second International Symposium on Information Theory*: 267–281.

Al-Attar, A. and Hussain, S. (2004), "Corporate data and future cash flows", *Journal of Business Finance and Accounting*: 31(7&8), 861–903.

Ali, A. and Pope, F. P. (1995), "The incremental information content of earnings, funds flow and cash flow: the UK evidence", *Journal of Business Finance and Accounting*: 22, 19–34.

Andrew, C., Chen, S. P., and Tong, Y. H. (2013), "Are analysts' cash flow forecasts naïve extensions of their own earnings forecasts", *Contemporary Accounting Research*: 30(2), 438–465.

Barth, M. E., Beaver, W. H., and Wolfson, M. A. (1990), "Components of earnings and the structure of bank share prices", *Financial Analysts Journal*: 46(1), 53–60.

Barth, M.E., Cram, D. P., and Nelson, K. K. (2001), "Accruals and the Prediction of Future Cash Flows", *The Accounting Review*: 76(1), 27–58.

Beaver, W. H. and Dukes, R. E. (1972), "Interperiod tax allocation, earnings expectations, and the behavior of security prices", *The Accounting Review*: 47(2), 320–332.

Beneish, M. (1999), "A discussion of 'Are accruals during initial public offerings opportunistic'", *Review of Accounting Studies:* 3, 209–221.

Bernard, V.L. (1989), "Capital market research during the 1980s: a critical review", The State of Accounting Research as We Enter the 1990s, Urbana-Champaign: University of Illinois.

Bowen, R., Burgstahler, D., and Daley, L. (1986), "Evidence on the relationships between earnings and various measures of cash flow", *The Accounting Review*: 61(10), 713–725.

Box, J. E. P., Jenkins, G. M., Reinsel, G. C. and Ljung, G. M. (2008), Time Series Analysis: Forecasting and Control. 4th Ed. New Jersey: John Wiley and Sons Inc.

Clubb, C. D. B. (1995), "An empirical study of the information content of accounting earnings, funds flow and cash flows in the UK", *Journal of Business Finance and Accounting*: 22, 35–51.

Charitou, A. and Clubb, C. (1999), "Earnings, cash flows and security returns over long return intervals: analysis and UK evidence", *Journal of Business Finance and Accounting*: 26, 283–312.

Dechow, P. M. (1994), "Accounting earnings and cash flows as measures of firm performance: The role of accounting accruals", *Journal of Accounting and Economics*: 18(1), 3–42.

Dechow, P. and Dichev, L. (2002), "The quality of accruals and earnings: the role of accrual estimation errors", *Accounting Review*: 77 (supplement), 35–59.

Garrod, N., Giner, B. and Larran, M. (2000), "The value relevance of earnings, cash flow and accruals: the impact of disaggregation and contingencies", Working paper, University of Glasgow.

International Accounting Standards Board. (1997), International Accounting Standard (IAS) 1: Presentation of Financial Statements.

Jeter, D.C. and Shivakumar, L. (1999), "Cross-sectional estimation of abnormal accruals using quarterly and annual data: effectiveness in detecting event-specific earnings management", *Accounting & Business Research:* 29(4), 299–319.

Jones, J. (1991), "Earnings management during import relief investigations", *Journal of Accounting Research:* 29, 193–228.

Kim, M. and Kross, W. (2005), "The ability of earnings to predict future operating cash flows has been increasing—not decreasing", *Journal of Accounting Research*: 43(5), 753–780.

Lipe, R. (1986), "The information contained in the components of earnings", *Journal of Accounting Research*: 24(1), 37–68.

Lorek, K.S., Willinger, G.L. (1996), "A multivariate time-series prediction model for cash-flow data", *The Accounting Review*: 71(1), 81–101.

MacDonald, E. (1999), "Analysis increasingly favor using cash flow over reported earnings in stock valuations", *The Wall Street Journal:* April (1), C2.

Mooi, T.L. (2007), "Predicting future cash flows: does cash flow have incremental information over accrual earnings", *Malaysian Accounting Review:* 6(2), 63–80.

Peasnell, K., Pope, P. and Young, S. (2000), "Accrual management to meet earnings targets: UK evidence pre- and post-Cadbury", *British Accounting Review:* 32(4), 415–445.

Peasnell, K., Pope, P. and Young, S. (2001), "Board monitoring & earnings management: do outside directors influence abnormal accruals", Working paper (2001/016), University of Lancaster.

Pfeiffer, R. J., Elgers, P. T., Lo, M. H., and Rees, L. L. (1998), "Additional evidence on the incremental information content of cash flows and accruals: The impact of errors in measuring market expectations", *The Accounting Review:* 73(1), 373–385.

Rayburn, J. (1986), 'The association of operating cash flow and accruals with security returns", *Journal of Accounting Research:* 24(1), 112–133.

Ren, T. X. (2014), "Moran's I test of spatial panel data model—based on bootstrap method", *Economic Modelling:* 41, 9–14.

Subramanyam, K. R. (1996), "The pricing of discretionary accruals", *Journal of Accounting and Economics:* 22, 249–281.

Wilson, G. P. (1986), "The relative information content of accruals and cash flows: Combined evidence at the earnings announcement and annual report release date", *Journal of Accounting Research:* 24(1), 165–200.

Young, P. C. (2015), "Refined instrumental variable estimation: Maximum likelihood optimization of a unified Box–Jenkins model" *Automatic:* 52, 35–46.

Xie, H. (2001), "The mispricing of abnormal accruals", *Accounting Review:* 76, 357–373.

Index[1]

[1] Note: Page numbers followed by 'n' refer to notes.

J. H. Hung, Y. Chen (eds.), *The State of China's State Capitalism*,
https://doi.org/10.1007/978-981-13-0983-0

Printed by Printforce, the Netherlands